Technological Know-How, Organizational Capabilities, and Strategic Management

Business Strategy and Enterprise Development
in Competitive Environments

Technological Know-How, Organizational Capabilities, and Strategic Management

Business Strategy and Enterprise Development
in Competitive Environments

DAVID J TEECE
University of California, Berkeley, USA

 **World Scientific**

NEW JERSEY · LONDON · SINGAPORE · BEIJING · SHANGHAI · HONG KONG · TAIPEI · CHENNAI

Published by

World Scientific Publishing Co. Pte. Ltd.

5 Toh Tuck Link, Singapore 596224

USA office: 27 Warren Street, Suite 401-402, Hackensack, NJ 07601

UK office: 57 Shelton Street, Covent Garden, London WC2H 9HE

Library of Congress Cataloging-in-Publication Data
Teece, David J.
    Technological know-how, organizational capabilities, and strategic management :
business strategy and enterprise development in competitive environments / by David J. Teece.
        p. cm.
    Includes bibliographical references.
        ISBN-13 978-981-256-850-2
        ISBN-10 981-256-850-6
    1. Strategic planning. 2. Business enterprises--Technological innovations.
    3. Technological innovations--Management. 4. Industrial organization.
        HD30.28.T413 2007
        658.4'012--dc22
                                            2006049151

British Library Cataloguing-in-Publication Data
A catalogue record for this book is available from the British Library.

Printed in Singapore by World Scientific Printers

Contents

Introduction

This volume contains a selection of articles that I have written over the last two decades which analyze business issues associated with technological innovation. Each article constitutes a separate chapter. Tshe reader will hopefully find that each chapter is written to address very practical management and policy issues, in a way that is explicitly linked to research in the social sciences. Put differently, I have endeavored to keep inquiry both scholarly and practical at the same time. This approach runs the risk of pleasing neither scholars nor practitioners. Hopefully, however, there is a constituency of executives of an intellectual persuasion who will find this book helpful, along with scholars interested in understanding management issues surrounding technological innovation, technology transfer and licensing.

Part I contains a series of papers that develop the conceptual foundations necessary for the analysis of strategic management in a world characterized by rapid technological change.

The first chapter, written for the *California Management Review*, discusses the importance of knowledge as a source of competitive advantage. The transformation of developed economies from raw-material processing and manufacturing activities to the development, application and transfer of new knowledge requires that firms not only combine factor inputs, but that they generate new knowledge and become excellent at storing knowledge, drawing from it, and combining knowledge inside the firm with know-how obtained externally. The evolution of competitive markets for final products as well as many inputs leaves the creation, augmentation and orchestration of intangible assets as a primary (if not in the primary) basis for competitive differentiation in many sectors. Competitive environments in new technology-based industries also require business enterprises to develop the ability to sense as well as seize new opportunities, and to reconfigure and protect knowledge assets so as to achieve sustainable competitive advantage.

Chapter 2 contains my *Strategic Management Journal* article co-authored with Gary Pisano and Amy Shuen that develops the "dynamic capabilities" approach to strategic management. This paper has had considerable impact on the study of strategic management and was recently identified by *Science Watch* magazine (December 2005) as the most cited article in economics, business and finance for the decade 1995–2005. The "dynamic capabilities" approach derives from the resource-based or "firm competence" theory of the firm; but while the resource-based theory focuses on those capabilities which form the basis for competitive advantage in a static environment, dynamic capabilities emphasize those traits which enable the firm to sustain its competitive advantage over time in response to change. This chapter explains the significance of processes, positions and paths, and defines some of the key terminology used in strategic management analysis today.

Chapter 3, written in conjunction with J. Lamar Pierce and Christopher S. Boerner for a conference in memory of Richard Cyert, highlights the major influence that Cyert and March's *Behavioral Theory of the Firm* (1963) had on the "firm competence" and "dynamic capabilities" approaches to strategic management. Both theories build on the foundational concept of "standard operating procedures", introduced by Cyert and March and called "routines" by Nelson and Winter (1982). Moreover, Cyert and March's focus on the heterogeneity of firm characteristics is consistent with the development of the "firm competence" or resource-based theory of the firm. Cyert and March's portrayal of the firm as an inherently rigid entity in a dynamic environment is a starting point for the "dynamic capabilities" theory, which seeks to explain the differential ability of firms to change with their environment. The dynamic capabilities approach recognizes certain rigidities but does not see them as completely beyond management ability to modify.

Chapter 4 in this volume, written with Mie Augier, discusses the important contribution that Edith Penrose's work on *The Theory of the Growth of the Firm* (1959) made to the resource-based and "dynamic capabilities" theories of the firm. Penrose's main contribution was defining the firm as an administrative framework for utilization of the firm's "pool" of resources — a concept that substantially underpins the resource-based view of the firm. Penrose also recognized the fungibility of certain resources and the explicit role managers and entrepreneurs play in marshalling resources behind productive opportunities. Until the emergence of the "resources" and "dynamic capabilities" literatures, Penrose's most recognized insight was the argument that the ability of firms to grow depends on the unused capacities of management. This insight, along with her concept of fungible resources, influenced my 1982 article on the multiproduct firm. However, the usefulness of Penrose's theory for strategic management is limited in that she does not address how firms develop competitive advantage. She also sometimes underplays the importance of knowledge assets. Nevertheless, Penrose's insights remain good starting points for developing a theory of the firm and understanding the role of the manager. She highlights many important issues "swept under the rug" by others.

In Chapter 5, I attempt to elucidate the role of entrepreneurs and managers in a market economy, an issue left undeveloped by mainstream economic theory as well as by Cyert and March, and by Penrose. I analyze the essential role that managers play in orchestrating the deployment of assets in "thin" (illiquid) markets where the price mechanism does not work well. Because of "thin" markets, management plays a role in deciding to build assets rather than buy them, and in redeploying assets inside the firm (rather than selling them). The manager's role in orchestrating the deployment of assets is particularly important when the property rights associated with assets have "fuzzy boundaries" (as with intangibles), suffer from appropriability concerns, and are highly co-specialized. This role is magnified further in "n-sided" markets (where demand for a product is driven by multiple, interdependent groups situated in separate but complementary markets) and in rapidly changing environments. Since managers play such an important role in these situations, understanding the role managers can play in creating value is a critical component of the "dynamic capabilities" approach to strategic management.

The chapters in Part II develop these foundational concepts in the context of intellectual capital, technology transfer and organizational learning.

Chapter 6, also written with Mie Augier, develops the notion of intellectual capital, the development, ownership and use of which is key to business performance in the economic system. The important role that intellectual — or knowledge — capital plays in the modern economy is increasingly being realized. However, although the early (classical) economists recognized the importance of innovation, the inherent limitations of neoclassical theorizing mean that mainstream economic theory has not been particularly insightful with respect to the causes and nature of technological progress and learning. This article surveys the valuable insights that have been generated by a few economists and social scientists who have investigated the phenomena of organizational learning and technological change more deeply. It also discusses the key features of intellectual capital that differentiate it from other forms of capital, and some of the issues involved in measuring intellectual capital.

Chapter 7 in this volume was written for a special issue of the *Journal of Technology Transfer* in memory of my distinguished thesis advisor, Edwin Mansfield. This paper highlights the influence that Edwin Mansfield had on my initial research into technology transfer and on understanding the role of the multinational corporation. Mansfield rejected the static analysis of mainstream economic theory, and favored an interdisciplinary approach to understanding the role of technology and technological change. As a consequence, he was attuned to the costs of technology transfer, and encouraged me to empirically investigate what was then a virgin area of research. This work in turn laid the foundations for understanding the role of the multinational firm. When combined with Mansfield's work on spillovers and the high social rates of return to innovation, my work and Mansfield's strongly supports the thesis that the multinational firm is an instrument of economic development, rather than a tool for the extraction of monopoly rents and the amplification of poverty.

Chapter 8, an article I wrote with Gary Pisano in 1989, investigates the role that collaborative arrangements play in firm strategy for exploiting new technology in a dynamic technological environment. When technology is changing rapidly, the competitive advantage of an incumbent firm is continuously under threat. The firm faces important strategic decisions in choosing where to source new technology, and (if it sources that technology externally) what organizational mode it should adopt for commercializing that technology. The article discusses how the "location" of the invention, the ease of appropriability, and the "transaction costs" of writing and executing contractual relationships affect the technology sourcing strategies and the choice of organizational mode for external procurement. It also illustrates them in the context of the telecommunications equipment industry. These decisions are important strategic choices made by managers and entrepreneurs. The ability to match correctly the strategy to the environment — key elements of a firm's business model — is a key element of the dynamic capabilities of the firm.

Chapter 9 of this volume extends the research of firm capabilities to economic development and highlights the role of the firm as a central agent of economic development. While the differences in institutional context mean that much of the mainstream economic analysis of industrial organization and regulation is irrelevant for newly industrialized economies, firms in developing economies face very similar problems to those in advanced industrial countries in trying to leverage existing assets into new and/or related business. Hence, the insights gained from research on the basic processes of organizational learning and advancement can more plausibly be extended to the developing-country context. Moreover, firms in newly industrialized economies can take advantage of the institutional context of developed countries (particularly, the open intermediate product markets and international market for know-how) to access the complementary assets and technology developed elsewhere.

Chapter 10 was originally written with Christopher S. Boerner and Jeffrey T. Macher for the *Handbook of Organizational Learning and Knowledge*. It reviews the research in economics that speaks to the critical phenomena of organizational learning. The ability of mainstream economic theory to inform organizational learning is limited by the highly stylized set of assumptions about the behavior of managerial and economic decision-makers. Insights into organizational learning have been generated by modifying some of the behavioral, institutional and equilibrium assumptions of the neoclassical economic model. Even more significant insights into learning have come from scholars analyzing the economics of innovation and the theory of the firm. They have relaxed many of the strict assumptions used by many economic theorists.

Scholars of innovation, for whom the processes by which firms acquire new knowledge is a central concern, have identified the different learning processes that apply to internal sources of knowledge, and recognized that the unique trajectories of incremental and cumulative technological innovation are a consequence of the existing pool of knowledge capital and specific learning processes. Meanwhile, economic researchers studying the theory of the firm, who seek to understand how firms adapt to changing circumstances, have elucidated the limitations and possibilities for learning associated with different forms of organization, the crucial dimensions along which firms vary in their ability to acquire and exploit knowledge, and the processes and mechanisms that firms employ to create new knowledge. The insights from these two strands of literature form the basis for the "dynamic capabilities" approach to strategic management.

Chapter 11, written with Ikujiro Nonaka, presents some suggested directions for research in knowledge management that evolved out of the U.C. Berkeley Forum on Knowledge and the Firm. This advice is still very pertinent today. In this chapter, we urge that research in this area be conducted in a transdisciplinary fashion — that is, integrating the existing approaches from different disciplines and creating a new, multifaceted view of human behavior. A key proposition of the knowledge management literature is that firm-level competitive advantage in open economies follows from creating, protecting and using difficult-to-replicate knowledge assets. However, establishing this proposition quantitatively is quite challenging methodologically because in order to do so, one needs to establish measures for intangible assets as well as dynamic capabilities. Therefore, careful efforts to quantify the value of intangible assets and to understand how they feed into profitability are highly desirable.

Part III contains three articles that apply the concepts developed in Parts I and II to address several key strategic issues faced by firms in innovative industries.

Chapter 12, originally published in 1988, outlines a framework for analyzing how an innovator captures value from its innovation. The chapter introduces three concepts — the appropriability regime, the notion of complementary assets, and the dominant design paradigm — that are useful in determining the optimal strategy of a firm commercializing a new technology, and understanding why imitators sometimes can capture more value from innovation than its inventor. The key insight is that in weaker appropriability regimes, the control of complementary assets becomes critical to enterprise profitability once the market settles on a dominant design.

Chapter 13, written with Peter C. Grindley for the *California Management Review*, discusses intellectual property (IP) management and licensing strategies in the context of the history of the semiconductor and electronics industries. The evolution of licensing practices within these industries highlights how optimal strategies change with the increasing importance of intellectual capital. Although royalty-free cross-licensing initially evolved as a response to regulatory and judicial constraints in the early days of the industry, amplified by the consent decrees signed as a solution to AT&T and IBM's antitrust problems, this strategy became inappropriate as the regulatory environment changed, global competition sharpened, and the value of intellectual capital increased. In recent years, IP owners have begun to enforce their intellectual property rights more aggressively. This article highlights the importance of intellectual property and intellectual capital in the current environment. It also provides lessons for managing intellectual capital.

The final chapter, a recent paper co-authored with Deepak Somaya, builds on the discussion of IP management of semiconductors and electronics in Chapter 13 and the organizational modes discussed in Chapter 12 to describe how entrepreneurs can effectuate and capture value from innovation in multi-invention contexts. The chapter also introduces the various patent strategies available to entrepreneurs to support their choice of organizational mode, and discusses which business models and patent strategies are most appropriate in different situations.

In addition to the co-authors already identified, there are numerous colleagues, students and friends who have helped with preparing this monograph. They include: Mie Augier, Sebastien Belanger, Frances Darnley, Doug Kidder,

Patricia Lonergan, Patricia Murphy, Edward F. Sherry, Anita Stephens and Simon Wakeman. I am deeply thankful for their assistance.

David J. Teece
Thomas W. Tusher Chair in Global Business
Director, Institute of Management, Innovation and Organization
Haas School of Business
University of California, Berkeley
Berkeley, CA 94720-1930
USA

References

Cyert, R. M. and March, J. G. (1963). *A Behavioral Theory of the Firm*. Englewood Cliffs, NJ: Prentice-Hall.

Nelson, R. and Winter, S. (1982). *An Evolutionary Theory of Economic Change*. Cambridge, MA: Belknap Press of Harvard University Press.

Penrose, E. T. (1959). *The Theory of the Growth of the Firm*. New York: John Wiley.

Part I

FOUNDATIONS

Capturing Value from Knowledge Assets:

THE NEW ECONOMY, MARKETS FOR KNOW-HOW, AND INTANGIBLE ASSETS

David J. Teece

Management is always confronting new challenges. Sometimes these are simply yesterday's challenges presented anew in a slightly different context. But from time to time, new challenges emerge that have no close precedent. Managing intellectual capital in the information age is possibly one such challenge, as advanced industrial economies have entered a new epoch. Many sectors are animated by new economics, where the payoff to managing knowledge astutely has been dramatically amplified, in part because of the phenomena of increasing returns, in part because of new information technology, and in part because of the changing role of intellectual property. Moreover, the context in which knowledge assets are created and exploited is today truly global.

Knowledge and Competitive Advantage

It has long been recognized that "economic prosperity rests upon knowledge and it useful application."[1] Indeed, "the increase in the stock of useful knowledge and the extension of its application are the essence of modern economic growth."[2] Enlightened economic historians have long emphasized the role of technology and organization in economic development.

Accordingly, one must inquire about the present cacophony on knowledge management. At least two classes of explanations appear to be valid. One class is simply that policy and strategy analysts have worn intellectual blinders, so that what has been obvious to some—namely, that knowledge and its applications are at the very roots of modern economic growth and prosperity—has not been transparent to all. Competing theories that stressed the role of the capital stock and natural resources would appear to have received unwarranted extended play in textbooks and policy pronouncements. Meanwhile, the study of innovation and knowledge transfer has been, until quite recently, relegated to a backwater in mainstream economics as well as in the other social sciences.

However, a small cadre of dedicated economists have long emphasized the role of technological innovation, often with few accolades.[3] Now the mainstream economic theorists[4] and mainstream business have begun to recognize the importance of this literature. Moreover, the ideas have become established and disseminated to a wider audience through the efforts of insightful protagonists like Ikujiro Nonaka and Hirotaka Takeuchi.[5]

The second class of factors relates to structural changes that have occurred in the economies of advanced developed countries. These have modified the nature of what is strategic and have served to highlight the importance of knowledge and its management.

Liberalization of Markets

Since the Kennedy round of trade negotiations in the 1960s, markets for goods and services have become increasingly liberalized. Tariff and non-tariff barriers have been lowered. While the world is far from being properly characterized as having adopted free trade, significant progress has been made. Final goods, intermediate goods, and factors of production flow globally with far more freedom than in earlier times. Restrictions on knowledge transfers by both importers and exporters have also been relaxed.

Accordingly, firms cannot so rapidly earn supra-competitive returns by locating behind trade barriers. Transportation costs have also fallen, and information about market opportunities often diffuses instantaneously. Together, these developments have reduced the shelter previously afforded to privileged positions in domestic markets. Competition has been sharpened.

Expansion of What's Tradable

Markets have not only liberalized, but also have been created for many types of "intermediate" products where markets hitherto didn't exist. This has been most amplified in securities markets where swaps and swaptions, index futures, program trading, butterfly spreads, puttable bonds, eurobonds, collateralized mortgage bonds, zero-coupon bonds, portfolio insurance, and synthetic cash are now commonplace.[6] This sudden burst of financial innovation began but 20 years ago, propelled by the move to floating exchange rates and the need to protect transactions from uncertainty. It has been aided by developments in computer and information technology, which have enabled the design of new financial products and the execution of complex transactions. Also contributing has been the desire to circumvent taxation and regulation.

In addition, firms have shown greater affection for outsourcing as suppliers take advantage of the growth in the number of potential suppliers at home and abroad. In the petroleum industry, for instance, markets exist not only for many grades of crude oil and refined products, but also for a range of intermediate products (e.g., MTB) which were rarely traded, if at all, a mere decade ago. Moreover, certain forms of intellectual property are "exchanged" (cross-licensed) or sold with far greater frequency than was hitherto experienced.[7]

Whenever a market exists that is open to all qualified comers, including newcomers, then competitive advantage for firms cannot flow from participation in that market.[8] Except in rare instances where one or a few firms can "corner the market," having a market-based exchange relationship cannot yield competitive advantage because it can be so easily replicated by others, who can simply enter the same (efficient) market and secure access to the same inputs or dispose of the same outputs. In short, efficient markets are a great leveler.

Strengthening of Intellectual Property Regimes

Intellectual property is an aspect of property rights which augments the importance of know-how assets. Knowledge assets are often inherently difficult to copy; moreover, like physical assets, some knowledge assets enjoy protection against theft under the Intellectual property laws of individual nation states. In advanced nations, these laws typically embrace patents, trademarks, trade secrets, and copyright.

Intellectual property systems have been strengthened since the 1980s, both in the U.S. and abroad. Moreover, intellectual property is not just important in the new industries—such as microelectronics and biotechnology—it remains important in pharmaceuticals and chemicals and is receiving renewed interest in more mature industries such as petroleum and steel.

The growth of information technology has also amplified the importance of intellectual property and has injected intellectual property into new contexts. For example, it is not uncommon to discover the foundations of corporate success for wholesalers and retailers buried in copyrighted software and in information technology supporting order entry and logistics.

The Growing Importance of Increasing Returns

Contemporary textbook understandings of how markets operate and how firms compete has been derived from the work of economists such as Marshall and Chamberlain. These views assume diminishing returns and assign industry participants identical production functions (implying the use of identical technologies by all competitors) where marginal costs increase. Industry equilibrium with numerous participants arise because marginal-cost curves slope upwards, thereby exhausting scale advantages at the level of the firm, making room for multiple industry participants. This theory was useful for understanding 18th century English farms and 19th century Scottish factories and even some 20th century American manufacturers. However, major deficiencies in this view of the world have been apparent for some time—it is a caricature of the firm.

6   *D. J. Teece*

Moreover, knowledge is certainly not shared ubiquitously and passed around at zero cost.[9]

In this century, developed economies have undergone a transformation from largely raw material processing and manufacturing activities to the processing of information and the development, application, and transfer of new knowledge. As a consequence, diminishing returns activities have been replaced by activities characterized by increasing returns. The phenomena of increasing returns is usually paramount in knowledge-based industries. With increasing returns, that which is ahead tends to stay ahead. Mechanisms of positive feedback reinforce the winners and challenge the losers. Whatever the reason one gets ahead—acumen, chance, clever strategy—increasing returns amplify the advantage. With increasing returns, the market at least for a while tilts in favor of the provider that gets out in front. Such a firm need not be the pioneer and need not have the best product.

The increasing returns phenomena is itself driven by several factors. Consider, first, standards and network externalities. To establish networks and interoperability, compatibility standards are usually critical. If such standards are proprietary, ownership of a dominant standard can yield significant "rents." The more a protocol gains acceptance, the greater the consumer benefits (network externalities), and the better the chance the standard has of becoming dominant.

Second, consider customer lock-in. Customer learning and customer investment in high-technology products amplify switching costs. This pushes competition "forward" in the sense that providers will compete especially hard for the original sale, knowing that sales of follow-along equipment and other services will be easier. While such "lock-in" is rarely long lived, it need not be momentary.

Third, consider large up-front costs. Once a high-tech industry is established, large up-front research, development, and design engineering costs are typical. This is most amplified with software products where the first copy costs hundred of millions, and the original cost of the second copy is zero, or very nearly so.

Fourth, consider producer learning. In certain cases, producers become more efficient as experience is gained. If the underlying knowledge base is tacit, so that it resists transfer to other producers, competitors with less experience are at a comparative disadvantage. Producer learning is important where complex processors and complex assembly is involved.

The economics of increasing returns suggest different corporate strategies. In winner-take-all or winner-take-the-lion's-share contexts, there is heightened payoff associated with getting the timing right (one can be too early or too late) and with organizing sufficient resources once opportunity opens up. Very often, competition is like a high-stakes game of musical chairs. Being well positioned when standards gel is essential. The associated styles of competition are, as Brian Arthur points out, much like casino gambling.[10] Strategy involves choosing what games to play, as well as playing with skill. Multimedia, web services, voice recognition, mobile (software) agents, and electronic commerce are all technological/market plays where the rules are not set, the identity of the players poorly appreciated, and the payoffs matrix murky at best. Rewards go to those good at sensing and seizing opportunities.

Seizing opportunities frequently involves identifying and combining the relevant complementary assets needed to support the business. Superior technology alone is rarely enough upon which to build competitive advantage. The winners are the entrepreneurs with the cognitive and managerial skills to discern the shape of the play, and then act upon it. Recognizing strategic errors and adjusting accordingly is a critical part of becoming and remaining successful.

In this environment, there is little payoff to penny pinching, and high payoff to rapidly sensing and then seizing opportunities. This is what is referred to here and elsewhere[11] as dynamic capabilities. Dynamic capabilities are most likely to be resident in firms that are highly entrepreneurial, with flat hierarchies, a clear vision, high-powered incentives, and high autonomy (to ensure responsiveness). The firm must be able to effectively navigate quick turns, as Microsoft did once Gates recognized the importance of the internet. Cost minimization and static optimization provide only minor advantages. Plans are often made and junked with alacrity. Companies must constantly transform and retransform. A "mission critical" orientation is essential.

Decoupling of Information Flows from the Flow of Goods and Services

New information technology and the adoption of standards is greatly assisting connectivity. Once every person and every business is connected electronically through networks, information can flow more readily. The traditional nexus between the economics of goods and services and the economics of information can be broken, and information can be unbundled.

The traditional trade-off between reach (connectivity) and richness (customization, bandwidth) is also being transformed, or at least modified. An insurance salesman is no longer needed to sell term life policies. Sufficient information can be collected by mail or on an internet to enable customers to engage in comparative shopping, and for underwriters to do sufficient assessment of policy holders. As a result, traditional distribution channels are no longer needed for simple life or auto insurance products.

Historically, the transfer/communication of rich information has required proximity and specialized channels to customers, suppliers, and distributors. New developments are undermining traditional value chains and business models. In some cases, more "virtual" structures are viable, or shortly will be viable, especially in certain sectors like financial services. New information technology is facilitating specialization. Bargaining power will be reduced by an erosion in the ability to control information, and customer switching costs will decline, changing industry economics.

The new information technology is also dramatically assisting in the sharing of information. Learning and experience can be much more readily captured and shared. Knowledge learned in the organization can be catalogued and transferred to other applications within and across organizations and geographies. Rich exchange can take place inside the organization, obviating some of the need for formal structures.

Ramifications of New Information and Communications Technologies

Linked information and communications systems in production, distribution, logistics, accounting, marketing, and new product development have the potential to bring together previously fragmented flows of data, thereby permitting the real time monitoring of markets, products, and competitors. The requisite data can then be fed to multifunctional teams working on new product development. Networked computers using rapid communications systems thus enable major advances in corporate and intercorporate monitoring and control systems. Within organizations, computer networks can strengthen links between strategic and operations management, while also assisting linkages externally to discrete and geographically dispersed providers of complementary services.

Network computing, supported by an advanced communications infrastructure, can thus facilitate collaborative entrepreneuralism by stripping out barriers to communication. It challenges existing organization boundaries, divisions, and hierarchies and permits formal organization to be more specialized and responsive. Interorganizationally, networked organizations have blurred and shifting boundaries, and they function in conjunction with other organizations. The networked organization may be highly "virtual," integrating a temporary network of suppliers and customers that emerge around specific opportunities in fast-changing markets. Recurrent reorganization becomes the norm, not the exception.

Service firms, such as lawyers, accountants, management consultants, and information technology consultants—pose interesting issues. If knowledge and experience remain personal and are not somehow shared (either by transfer to other organization members or by being embedded in product) then the firm can at best expect to achieve constant return to scale. Larger organizations will have no advantage over boutiques and will possibly suffer bureaucratic burdens that will sap productivity.

Formalization, the sharing of personal knowledge, and the development of structural approaches as a mechanism to transfer learning throughout the firm may on the other hand sap creativity and impede learning. Ideally, one would like to develop approaches or models which have a common essential logic, but which enable customization of particular features. This is but one of the many challenges to service firms in the new economy where knowledge sharing itself can often be the basis of competitive advantage.

Product Architecture and Technology "Fusion"

With complexity becoming increasingly common, new products are rarely stand-alone items. Rather, they are components of broader systems or architectures. Innovation at the architectural level is more demanding and takes place with less frequency than at the component level, but it has greater impact.

The development of system-level integration [SLI] of ASICs—so-called systems on a chip—illustrates the point. New manufacturing processes and improved design tools have fostered SLI. Because million-gate ASICs are now possible, they can support entire systems on a single piece of silicon. If Dataquest is right, and if industry will be able to place 40 million gates on a single chip by 2000, it will be technically possible to place multiple systems on a single chip.[12]

SLI ASICs have already been designed into high-volume applications such as set-top boxes, multimedia, and wireless telephony. Dataquest estimates that SLI ASICs will pass $15 billion in revenues by the year 2000. However, what is even more significant is the ability of SLI ASICs to fuel further growth of consumer electronics through dramatic reductions in size and power usage, enhanced differentiation and functionally, quicker product development, and still lower cost. This is what the technology can deliver.

Whether the technology does in fact yield its potential depends, however, on certain organizational and managerial changes. Design reuse is of paramount importance when designing high-complexity ASICs or SLI devices. System designers must design on the block level and be able to reuse and alter intellectual property in a number of subsequent designs. As Dataquest notes, "design methodology, design reuse, and intellectual property will play vital roles in determining the winners among both suppliers and users."[13]

The organization of firms and industries and the architecture of products are interrelated. Since, the relevant intellectual property needed to effectuate SLI is almost never owned by a single firm but is widely distributed throughout the industry, new arrangements are needed to support rapid diffusion and expansion of SLI architecture. Indeed, harnessing the full potential of the technology necessarily involves cooperation amongst industry participants, many of whom might also be competitors.

A related development is the increase in convergence or integration of previously disparate technologies. One thinks not just of the convergence of computers and communications, but of mechanical industries and electronics ("mechatronics")[14] or of "robochemistry," the science of applying computerization to drug molecule research, which according to some accounts is leading to "a new age in medicine."[15] This by no means occurs automatically and requires internal structures that are flexible and permeable.

Implications

These developments suggest a different dynamic to competition and competitive advantage. The expansion of markets illustrates the point. Since markets are a great leveler, competitive advantage at the level of the firm can flow only from the ownership and successful deployment of non-tradable assets. If the asset or its services are traded or tradable in a market or markets, the assets in question can be accessed by all; so the domains in which competitive advantage can be built narrows as markets expand. Not even human resources can provide the basis for competitive advantage if the skills at issue can be accessed by all in an open labor market.

One class of assets that is especially difficult, although not impossible, to trade involves knowledge assets and, more generally, competences. The market for know-how is riddled with imperfections and "unassisted markets are seriously faulted as institutional devices for facilitating trading in many levels of technological and managerial know-how."[16] Hence, the development of many types of new markets has made know-how increasingly salient as a differentiator, and therefore as a source of the competitive advantage of firms. This can be expected to remain so until know-how becomes more commodity like; and this may happen soon for some components of intellectual property.

The strengthening of intellectual property is an important counterforce to the growing ease of imitation. As the diffusion of knowledge and information accelerates, intellectual property becomes more salient. While intellectual property can be traded, and can sometimes be invented around, it can no longer be infringed with impunity and without penalty.

Increasing returns frequently sharpens the payoff to strategic behavior and amplifies the importance of timing and responsiveness. Meanwhile, the decoupling of information flows from the flow of goods and services is transforming traditional value analysis, and it is suggesting the benefits of more virtual structures and obviating some of the need for hierarchy. Simultaneously, the march of technologies such as integrated circuits is transforming the linkage between intellectual property and products. Technological innovation is requiring the unbundling of the two and the formation of more robust markets for intellectual property. It is in this new environment that a critical dimension of knowledge management has emerged: capturing value from innovative activity.

Capturing Value from Knowledge and Competence

The proper structures, incentives, and management can help firms generate innovation and build knowledge assets. The focus here is not, however, on the creation of knowledge assets, but on their deployment and use.[17] While knowledge assets are grounded in the experience and expertise of individuals, firms provide the physical, social, and resource allocation structure so that knowledge can be shaped into competences. How these competences and knowledge assets are configured and deployed will dramatically shape competitive outcomes and the commercial success of the enterprise. Indeed, the competitive advantage of firms in today's economy stems not from market position, but from difficult to replicate knowledge assets and the manner in which they are deployed. The deployment dimension—involving as it does both entrepreneurial and strategic elements—is where dynamic capabilities are especially important.

It is always useful to distinguish between the creation of new knowledge and its commercialization. The creation of new knowledge through autonomous (specialized) innovation is a critical function. It can be the domain of the individual, or of the research laboratory, or of autonomous business units. It need not require complex organization. Indeed, one can argue that such knowledge creation is increasingly well suited to smaller organizational units.

However, the commercialization of new technology is increasingly the domain of complex organization. The new challenges require new organizational forms and the development and astute exercise of dynamic capabilities. They also require an understanding of the nature of knowledge and competence as strategic assets. The nature of knowledge and the manner in which it can or cannot be bought and sold is critical to the strategic nature of knowledge and competence.

The Nature of Knowledge

Knowledge can be thought of in many ways. In a business context, the following taxonomies are useful.

Codified/Tacit[18]

Tacit knowledge is that which is difficult to articulate in a way that is meaningful and complete. The fact that we know more than we can tell speaks to the tacit dimension. Stand-alone codified knowledge—such as blueprints, formulas, or computer code—need not convey much meaning.

There appears to be a simple but powerful relationship between codification of knowledge and the costs of its transfer. Simply stated, the more a given item of knowledge or experience has been codified, the more economically it can be transferred. This is a purely technical property that depends on the ready availability of channels of communication suitable for the transmission of well-codified information—for example, printing, radio, telegraph, and data networks. Whether information so transferred will be considered meaningful by those who receive it will depend on whether they are familiar with the code selected as well as the different contexts in which it is used.[19]

Uncodified or tacit knowledge, on the other hand, is slow and costly to transmit. Ambiguities abound and can be overcome only when communications take place in face-to-face situations. Errors of interpretation can be corrected by a prompt use of personal feedback. Consider the apprenticeship system as an example. First, a master craftsman can cope with only a limited number of pupils at a time. Second, his teaching has to be dispensed mostly through examples rather than by precept—he cannot easily put the intangible elements of his skill into words. Third, the examples he offers will be initially confusing and ambiguous for his pupils so that learning has to take place through extensive and time-consuming repetition, and mystery will occur gradually on the basis of "feel." Finally, the pupil's eventual mastery of a craft or skill will remain idiosyncratic and will never be a carbon copy of the master's. It is the scope provided for the development of a personal style that defines a craft as something that goes beyond the routine and hence programmable application of a skill.

The transmission of codified knowledge, on the other hand, does not necessarily require face-to-face contact and can often be carried out largely by impersonal means, such as when one computer "talks" to another, or when a technical manual is passed from one individual to another. Messages are better structured and less ambiguous if they can be transferred in codified form.

Observable/Non-Observable in Use

Much technology is (publicly) observable once sold. A new CT scanner, laser printer, or microprocessor is available for conceptual imitation and reverse engineering once it has been introduced into the market. New products are typically of this kind. Process technology, however, is often different. While in some cases the "signature" of a process may be embedded in a product and is therefore ascertainable through reverse engineering, this is generally not the case. While clues about a manufacturing process may sometimes be gleaned by closely observing the product, much about process technology can be protected if the owners of process technology are diligent in protecting their trade secrets in the factory. Thus, process technology is inherently more protectable than product technology, the patent system put to one side.

Positive/Negative Knowledge

Innovation involves considerable uncertainty. Research efforts frequently go down what turns out to be a blind alley. It is well recognized that a discovery (positive knowledge) can focus research on promising areas of inquiry, thereby avoiding blind alleys. However, it is frequently forgotten that knowledge of failures ("this approach doesn't work") is also valuable as it can help steer resource allocation into more promising avenues. For this reason, firms often find it necessary to keep their failures as well as their successes secret, even holding aside issues of embarrassment.

Autonomous/Systematic Knowledge

Autonomous knowledge is that which yields value without major modifications of systems in which it might be embedded. Fuel injection, the self-starter, and power steering were innovations that did not require major modifications to the automobile, although the latter did enable manufactures to put more weight on the front axle and to more readily fit cars with radial tires. Systematic innovation, on the other hand, requires modification to other sub-systems. For instance, the tungsten filament light bulb would not have found such wide application without the development of a system for generating and distributing electricity.

Intellectual Property Regime

There are many other dimensions along which knowledge could be defined or along which innovations could be classified.[20] However, the only other key dimension to be identified here is whether or not the knowledge in question enjoys protection under the intellectual property laws.

Patents, trade secrets, trademarks provide protection for different mediums in different ways. The strongest form of intellectual property is the patent. A valid patent provides rights for exclusive use by the owner, although depending on the scope of the patent it may be possible to invent around it, albeit at some cost. Trade secrets do not provide rights of exclusion over any knowledge domain, they do protect covered secrets in perpetuity. Trade secrets can well enhance the value of a patent position. Different knowledge mediums qualify for different types of intellectual property protection. The degree that intellectual property keeps imitators at bay may depend also on other external factors, such as regulations, which may block or limit the scope for invent-around alternatives.

Replicability, Imitability, and Appropriability[21]

Replication involves transferring or redeploying competences from one concrete economic setting to another. Since productive knowledge is typically embodied, this cannot be accomplished by simply transmitting information. Only in those instances where all relevant knowledge is fully codified and understood can replication be collapsed into a simple problem of information transfer. Too often, the contextual dependence of original performance is poorly appreciated, so unless firms have replicated their systems of productive knowledge on many prior occasions, the act of replication is likely to be difficult.[22] Indeed, replication and transfer are often impossible absent the transfer of people, though this can be minimized if investments are made to convert tacit knowledge to codified knowledge. Often, however, this is simply not possible.

In short, knowledge assets are normally rather difficult to replicate. Even understanding what all the relevant routines are that support a particular competence may not be transparent. Indeed, Lippman and Rumelt have argued that some sources of competitive advantage are so complex that the firm itself, let alone its competitors, does not understand them.[23] As Nelson and Winter[24] and Teece[25] have explained, many organizational routines are quite tacit in nature. Imitation can also be hindered by the fact that few routines are stand-alone. Imitating a part of what a competitor does may not enhance performance at all. Understanding the overall logic of organization and superior performance is often critical to successful imitation.

Some routines and competences seem to be attributable to local or regional forces that shape a firm's capabilities. Porter, for example, shows that differences in local product markets, local factor markets, and institutions play an important role in shaping competitive capabilities.[26] Replication in a different geographical context may thus be rather difficult. However, differences also exist within populations of firms from the same country. Various studies of the automobile industry, for example, show that not all Japanese automobile companies are top performers in terms of quality, productivity, or product development.[27] The role of firm-specific history is a critical factor in such firm-level (as opposed to regional- or national-level) differences.[28]

At least two types of strategic value flow from replication. One is simply the ability to support geographic and product line expansion. To the extent that the capabilities in question are relevant to customer needs elsewhere, replication can confer value. Another is that the ability to replicate indicates that the firm has the foundations in place for learning and improvement. Understanding processes, both in production and in management, is the key to process improvement, so that an organization cannot improve that which it does not understand. Deep process understanding is often required to accomplish codification and replication. Indeed, if knowledge is highly tacit, it indicates that underlying structures are not well understood, which limits learning because scientific and engineering principles cannot be as systematically applied. Instead, learning is confined to proceeding through trial-and-error, and the leverage that might otherwise come from the application of modern science is denied.

Imitation is simply replication performed by a competitor. If self-replication is difficult, imitation is likely to be even harder. In competitive markets, it is the ease of imitation that determines the sustainability of competitive advantage. Easy imitation implies the rapid dissipation of rents.

Factors that make replication difficult also make imitation difficult. Thus, the more tacit the firm's productive knowledge, the harder it is to replicate by the firm itself or its competitors. When the tacit component is high, imitation may well be impossible, absent the hiring away of key individuals and the transfer of key organizational processes.

Intellectual property rights impede imitation of certain capabilities in advanced industrial countries and present a formidable imitation barrier in certain particular contexts. Several other factors, in addition to the patent system, cause there to be a difference between replication costs and imitation costs. The observability of the technology or the organization is one such important factor. As mentioned earlier, vistas into product technology can be obtained through strategies such as reverse engineering, this is not the case for process technology, as a firm need not expose its process technology to the outside in order to benefit from it. Firms with product technology, on the other hand, confront the unfortunate circumstances that they must expose what they have got in order to profit from the technology. Secrets are thus more protectable if there is no need to expose them in contexts where competitors can learn about them.

The term "appropriability regimes" describes the ease of imitation. Appropriability is a function both of the ease of replication and the efficacy of intellectual property rights as a barrier to imitation. Appropriability is strong when a

technology is both inherently difficult to replicate and the intellectual property system provides legal barriers to imitation. When it is
inherently easy to replicate and intellectual
property protection is either unavailable or
ineffectual, then appropriability is weak. Intermediate conditions also exist (see Figure 1).

Appropriability and Markets for Know-How and Competence

Assets can be the source of competitive
advantage only if they are supported by a
regime of strong appropriability or are non-
tradable or "sticky." As discussed earlier, once
an asset is readily tradable in a competitive
market it can no longer be a source of firm-
level competitive advantage. Financial assets
today are of that kind.

FIGURE 1. Appropriability Regimes
for Knowledge Assets

		Inherent Replicability	
		Easy	Hard
Intellectual Property Rights	Loose	Weak	Moderate
	Tight	Moderate	Strong

The main classes of assets that are not
tradable today are locational assets, knowledge assets, and competences.[29]
Were a perfect market for know-how to someday emerge, knowledge would no
longer be the source of competitive advantage. This is unlikely to happen any-
time soon, but understanding the limits on the market for know-how is important to understanding how firms can capture value from knowledge assets.

Like the market for pollution rights, or the market for art, buying and
selling know-how and intellectual property has special challenges. These complicate exchange, and may limit in some fundamental sense the level of sophistication to which the market can ever evolve. They also explain why the market
today is rather primitive.

By way of foundation, it is well recognized that markets work well when:

- there are informed buyers and sellers aware of trading opportunities,
- the objective performance properties or subjective utility of products can
  be readily ascertained,
- there are large numbers of buyers and sellers, and
- contracts can be written, executed, and enforced at low cost.

Thus the market for (standard) commodities like wheat, coal, stocks,
bonds, and sports utility vehicles works well because these properties are largely
satisfied.

However, know-how and intellectual property are "products" of an
entirely different kind. These products have properties which complicate purchase and sale (see Figure 2). These include:

FIGURE 2. Inherent Tradeability of Different Assets

Characteristics	Know-How/IP	Physical Commodities
1. Recognition of trading opportunities	Inherent difficulty	Posting frequent
2. Disclosure of attributes	Relatively difficult	Relatively easy
3. Property Rights	Limited [patents, trade secrets, copyright, etc.]	Broad
4. Item of Sale	License	Measurable units
5. Variety	Heterogeneous	Homogeneous
6. Unit of consumption	Often Unclear	Weight, volume, etc.
Inherent tradeability	Low	High

- *Recognition of Trading Opportunities*—Parties typically don't know who owns what, and who might be interested in trading. This is less so for patents since they are published. But software (particularly source code) protected by copyright and trade secrets is frequently a matter of great secrecy. There are obvious reasons why even knowledge about the existence of such intellectual property is held very close. Accordingly, out of ignorance, software is often "reinvented" despite the fact that potentially advantageous trades could be consummated.

- *Disclosure of Performance Features*—Buyers must be well informed as to the availability of intellectual property but sellers may be reluctant to negotiate because their intellectual property rights are problematic. Sellers might be reluctant to negotiate because of fear that disclosure, even if pursuant to a nondisclosure agreement, might inadvertently lead intellectual property rights to be jeopardized.

- *Uncertain Legal Rights*—When property rights are uncertain, and confidence in nondisclosure agreements or the law of confidences less than complete, beneficial transactions may be eschewed because of perceived risks. In addition to the disclosure issues identified above, sellers may be uncertain about factors such as the enforceability of use restrictions and sublicensing rights or simply about the ability to measure and collect royalties.

- *Item of Sale*—The "item of sale" may be know-how, or intellectual property rights, complete or partial. When intellectual property is bought and sold, what is transacted is simply a bundle of rights. While rights are frequently bought and sold [e.g., view rights, pollution rights, airspace rights, mineral rights, rights to use the electromagnetic spectrum, queuing rights], such rights are not a pure commodity. Moreover, ownership requires special policing powers for value preservation. Physical barriers to theft (e.g., locks and keys) don't suffice to protect owners; confidence in contracting and the legal system is necessary to support value.

- *Variety*—While there may be multiple transactions for a given piece of intellectual property (e.g., identical nonexclusive patent license), intellectual property is itself highly variegated. This complicates exchange by making valuation difficult and by rendering markets thin. Thin markets are likely to be less robust than thick markets. Moreover, both buyers and sellers are likely to wish to customize transactions. To the extent to which this occurs, transaction costs increase, and the difficulties of setting up an exchange increase.

- *Unit of Consumption*—Intellectual property is rarely sold lock, stock, and barrel. Hence, metering arrangements of some kind must be devised. These are by no means readily identifiable, particularly for software. Is it a component and if so, should the royalty be a function of the value of the component or the system in which it is embedded. Clearly, the value is a function of other intellectual property located alongside the intellectual property at issue. Questions of the royalty/sales base are by no means straightforward.

Some Sectoral Differences in the Market for Know-How

The inherent difficulties just identified vary according to the type of know-how/intellectual property at issue. It is instructive to compare chemicals and pharmaceuticals with electronics. Indeed, even a cursory examination would suggest that in chemicals and pharmaceuticals, the inherent difficulties associated with licensing are less than in other sectors, like electronics. Figure 3 summarizes some of these difficulties.

There are a number of reasons why the market for know-how generally works better for chemicals and pharmaceuticals. In chemicals and pharmaceuticals, patents work especially well and are ubiquitous. A survey of the efficiency of patents conducted by researchers at Yale University showed high scores for patent effectiveness in this sector.[30] Patents are in one sense the strongest form of intellectual property because they grant the ability to exclude, whereas copyright and trade secrets do not prevent firms that make independent but duplicative discoveries from practicing their inventions/innovations. Accordingly, problems of recognition and disclosure disappear when patents are at issue. Also regulation often bolsters intellectual property since "me too" misappropriators may sometimes face additional hurdles (in the U.S., FDA approval) before being able to launch a product in the market.

3

FIGURE 3. Some Sectoral Differences in the Market for Know-How

Challenge	Chemical/Pharmaceuticals	Electronics
Recognition	Manageable	Extremely complex, often impossible
Disclosure	Handled by NDA, patents common	More difficult
Interface issues	Compatability generally not an issue	Compatability generally critical
Royalty stacking, royalty base dilemmas	Infrequent	Frequent
Value context dependent	Strongly so	Very strongly so
Patent strength	Generally high	Sometimes limited
Development cycle	Often long	Generally short
Know-How Market Works:	Generally Well	Often Poorly

Compatibility/interface issues are also less severe in this sector than in some others. While technologies often must work together in chemicals and pharmaceuticals, the close coupling of the kind that characterizes electronics is usually not an absolute prerequisite. Also, the number of individual items of external intellectual property that must be brought together to design a new product is often rather limited. Indeed, the items used may all come from inside the firm, although alliances and licenses are increasingly common. Because there are less complementarities necessary to make a particular product, intellectual property is often less context dependent, and the same royalty rate is appropriate in a multitude of contexts e.g., the float glass process was licensed for the same amount (i.e., 6% of sales) to multiple jurisdictions around the world. Finally, the product life cycle is defined not in months, but often in decades. Hence, requirements for speedy execution of transactions are less severe, and the opportunity to amortize set-up costs over enormous volumes of business is often possible.

The situation in the electronics industry is different. For software, patent protection is uncommon. Hence, if purchasers receive components in source code, they can read and modify programs, thereby possibly skirting intellectual property protection. Put differently, source code can be more readily converted to new programs that don't leave fingerprints. Object code, on the other hand, must first be reverse engineered into a reasonable approximation of source code before it can be advantageously modified. Thus, disseminating software components (in source code) for external use creates misappropriation hazards. While encryption creates barriers to reverse engineering (decryption), it does not compensate for weak intellectual property. The problem of disclosure (necessary to inform buyers about what they are being offered) has clear hazards in this sector. Furthermore, interface issues are critical, as integration is paramount. Because multiple sources of intellectual property must be combined for systems on silicon, intellectual property rights must be amalgamated.[31]

The market for know-how in electronics thus creates considerable challenges and is unlikely, therefore, to be completely efficient. Accordingly, new innovations (such as system-level integration in silicon) involve new organizational challenges, orders of magnitude greater than previously encountered, and perhaps orders of magnitude greater than the technological challenges. Royalty stacking situations—where intellectual property owners fail in their pricing proposals to take into account the need for the buyer to combine other intellectual property to create value—are likely to be frequent, at least until a new business model is firmly established. Also, the tremendous premium on speed and time to market puts enormous pressure to accomplish intellectual property transactions quickly. This is impossible if intellectual property agreements are customized. However, there is at present almost no standardization in intellectual property agreements, so the market can readily become bogged down by transactional complexity.

Because of these difficulties, there is at present little if any market for software components. Estimates of the annual aggregate costs in the U.S. for "reinvention" are put at between $2 and $100 billion. These estimates, if correct, speak to the value of a properly functioning market for software intellectual property. Absent such a market, certain new product architectures (e.g., systems on Silicon) may just not happen, or may not realize but a fraction of their potential.

What was just described for know-how assets also applies to competences, which can be thought of as clusters of know-how assets. Competences include discrete business-level organizational processes fundamental to running the business (e.g., order entry, customer service, product design, quality control). But they also include generalized organizational skills such as "miniaturization," "tight tolerance engineering," and "micromotors."

Competences are tangible, and can be quite durable. They are typically supported by routines, not dependent on a single individual, and generally reside inside the business functions. Like know-how assets, they cannot be readily bought and sold, absent a transaction for the entire business.

Profiting from innovation is more readily assured when high-performance business processes and/or world-class competences support a product or process offering. This is because the asset/competences cannot be traded, and the forces of imitation are muted. Not only are such assets/competences inherently difficult to imitate because they are likely to be built on a high tacit component, but there may be opaqueness to the underlying processes and uncertainty, even within the firm, as to the organizational foundations of the competence.

Complementary Assets

The asset structure of the firm is perhaps the most relevant aspect of its positioning when the commercialization of knowledge in tangible products and processes is at issue. Such (upstream) positioning may be more important than the downstream positioning in the product markets for yesterday's product. In many cases there may be a high correlation between a firm's upstream position in an asset and its downstream market position.

Complementary assets matter because knowledge assets are typically an intermediate good and need to be packaged into products or services to yield value. There are notable exceptions, of course. Software is a classic exception as it does not need to be manufactured, and with the internet, distribution becomes instantaneous and almost costless.

However, when the services of complementary assets are required, they can play an important role in the competitive advantage equation. For instance, the design for a new automobile is of little value absent access to manufacturing and distribution facilities on competitive terms.

The effort to embed knowledge in products and to bring the new product to market must confront the whole question of access to complementary assets. If already owned by the knowledge owner, there is no issue. If not, then one must build, or buy if one can. Because the market for complementary assets is itself riddled with imperfections, competitive advantage can be gained or lost on how expertly the strategy for gaining access is executed.

Circumstances of such co-specialization can benefit the asset owner, as demand for the innovation will increase demand for the co-specialized asset. If difficult to replicate or work around, the complementary asset may itself become the "choke point" in the value chain, enabling it to earn supernormal rents. Thus, ownership of difficult to replicate complementary assets can represent a second line of defense against imitators and an important source of competitive advantage.

Dynamic Capabilities

In many sectors in today's global market, competitive advantage also requires dynamic capabilities. (See Figure 4.) This is the ability to sense and then to seize new opportunities, and to reconfigure and protect knowledge assets, competencies, and complementary assets and technologies to achieve sustainable competitive advantage.

It is relatively easy to define dynamic capabilities, quite another to explain how they are built. Part of the answer lies with the environmental and

FIGURE 4. Capturing Value from Knowledge Assets

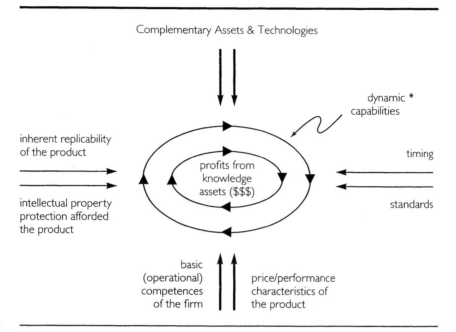

Complementary Assets & Technologies

dynamic *
capabilities

inherent replicability
of the product

timing

profits from
knowledge
assets ($$$)

intellectual property
protection afforded
the product

standards

basic
(operational)
competences
of the firm

price/performance
characteristics of
the product

*Dynamic Capabilities are the capacity to sense opportunities, and to reconfigure knowledge assets, competencies, and complementary assets and technologies to achieve sustainable competitive advantage.

technological sensing apparatus that the firm has established, and part lies with the choice of organizational form, and part lies with the ability to strategize.

External Sensing

In order for an organization to exhibit dynamic capabilities, it must sense the opportunity and the need for change, properly calibrate responsive actions and investments, and move to implement a new regime with skill and efficiency. During "sensemaking," the organization receives and interprets messages about new markets, new technologies, and competitive threats. This information is necessarily evaluated in the light of the individuals' and the organization's experience and knowledge. In formulating an action plan, the organization is necessarily guided to some extent by rules and routines, which structure inquiries and responses.

Sensemaking, or interpretation, is a critical function. Well performed, it can enable the organization to connect with its environment and invest its resources wisely, thereby generating superior returns. The fundamental challenge to sensemaking is bounded rationality; one cannot learn all there is to learn about a situation or an opportunity, and action must proceed based on hunches and informed guesses about the true state of the world. In essence, business organizations and their management must interpret the world about them. Interpretative activity is basically a form of theorizing about market and firm behavior.

Sensemaking can be assisted by sensemaking tools, like scenario planning, as well as the insights of brilliant outsiders—like a Peter Druker or Gordon Moore. Scenario planning can help managers develop mental maps of possible complex future realities. Such mental maps assist in the interpretation of new data and information from the market and help chart courses of action. Shell Oil is well known for its effective use of scenario planning, and its investment in this activity is widely recognized inside and outside the company to have enabled planners and managers to have extended conversations resulting in shared visions of possible futures. The object of the exercise has never been to predict the future, but to understand the fundamental drivers of change and to quickly chart action plans once key uncertainties are resolved.

When the organization has figured out what is going on, and calibrated the opportunity, it must choose among available action plans. These are not infinite in number, but may be restricted to one or two or maybe a handful of viable alternatives that are satisfactory. Actions are likely to be similar to those used in the past. Organizational routines—distinct ways of doing things—come into play. Actions and decision routines are part of the organization's procedural memory. Procedures and policies enable internal competition to be fair, objective, and legitimate. Organizational rationality can exist, despite individuals' bounded rationality, if rules, routines, and procedures guide individual decision making.

The openness of markets, stronger intellectual property protection, increasing returns, the unbundling of artifacts and information, and the possibilities for "integration" using new information technology are necessarily a part of the sensemaking milieu.

Information receipt and interpretation is by no means restricted in its importance to the understanding of business, market, and technological trends. There is also the need to identify relevant external technology and bring it into the firm. An organization's absorptive capacity with respect to external technology is a function of "the technical and managerial competence of the transferee."[32] Absorptive capacity is greatest when what is to be learned is related to what is already known.[33] As Mowery has explained, a firm is far better equipped to absorb the output of external R&D if one is performing some amount of R&D internally.[34] In short, internal and external R&D are complements, not substitutes.

Organizational Action

Once an opportunity is sensed, it must then be seized. This is where the organization's ability to quickly contract up the requisite external resources and direct the relevant internal resources comes into play. Schumpeter referred to the importance of effectuating "new combinations." This is precisely what management must do. It increasingly involves forming alliances to access the requisite complementary technologies and complementary assets. The alliance structure is favored because markets simply don't exist for much of what must be accessed, and the alliance is a (hybrid) way to do so that shares risks and rewards but achieves a coalignment of strategy.

However, it also requires an organizational structure where decision making is immediate and action is swift. This typically implies high-powered incentives and decision making that is anything but bureaucratic. Smaller entrepreneurial companies appear to excel in many such environments, although dynamic capabilities are certainly not restricted to small companies. Larger enterprises can also deliver much of what is required if they are tuned to changes in their external environments, and if they have adopted decision-making processes that both enable and require quick response.

Implications for the Theory of the Firm

The firm is a repository for knowledge—the knowledge being embedded in business routines and processes. Distinctive processes undergird firm-specific assets and competences (defined as integrated clusters of firm-specific assets). The firm's knowledge base includes its technological competences as well as its knowledge of customer needs and supplier capabilities. These competences reflect both individual skills and experiences as well as distinctive ways of doing things inside firms. To the extent that such competences are difficult to imitate and are effectively deployed and redeployed in the marketplace (reflecting dynamic capabilities), they can provide the foundations for competitive advantage.

The essence of the firm is its ability to create, transfer, assemble, integrate, and exploit knowledge assets. Knowledge assets underpin competences, and competences in turn underpin the firm's product and service offerings to the market. The firm's capacity to sense and seize opportunities, to reconfigure its knowledge assets, competencies, and complementary assets, to select appropriate organization forms, and to allocate resources astutely and price strategically all constitute its dynamic capabilities.

The knowledge perspective presented here requires us to stress the entrepreneurial rather than the administrative side of corporate governance. In high-technology industries, firms are not so much organizations designed to minimize transactions costs—although this they do—but organizational structures capable of shaping and reshaping clusters of assets in the distinct and unique combinations needed to serve ever-changing customer needs. Accordingly, boundary issues (such as vertical integration) are not determined by transactions cost considerations alone. Rather, they are strongly influenced by tacit knowledge and imitability/replicability considerations. Even setting aside strategic and transaction cost issues, the tacit component of knowledge cannot frequently

be transferred absent the transfer of personnel and organizational systems/
routines. Tacit knowledge and its transfer properties help determine the boundaries of the firm and may well swamp transaction costs considerations.

Competitive advantage can be attributed not only to the ownership
of knowledge assets and other assets complementary to them, but also to the
ability to combine knowledge assets with other assets needed to create value.
Knowing what assets to develop, and what to abandon, is a critical element in
the success equation. Dynamic capabilities are critical if knowledge assets are
to support sustainable competitive advantage.[35]

Thus, the competences/capabilities view of the firm sees the proper
boundaries of the firm and governance structure being determined not only
with reference to transactions costs, but also with reference to technological
and knowledge concerns. The boundaries of the firm, and future integration
and outsourcing opportunities, must clearly be made with reference to learning
and knowledge issues as well as transaction cost economics.

The emphasis on the development and exploitation of knowledge assets
shifts the focus of attention from cost minimization to value maximization. Governance decisions involve both questions of what assets to build inside the firm
versus accessing externally, as well as how to organize internally. This perspective thus complements transaction cost economics.

Conclusion

Knowledge, competence and related intangibles have emerged as the key
drivers of competitive advantage in developed nations. This is not just because of
the importance of knowledge itself, but because of the rapid expansion of goods
and factor markets, leaving intangible assets as the main basis of competitive
differentiation in many sectors. There is implicit recognition of this with the
growing emphasis being placed on the importance of intangible assets, reputation, customer loyalty, and technological know-how.

While there is some recognition of these changes, there is perhaps a failure to recognize just how deep these issues go. The value-enhancing challenges
facing management are gravitating away from the administrative and towards
the entrepreneurial. This is not to denigrate the importance of administration,
but merely to indicate that better administration is unlikely to be where the
economic "rents" (superior profits) reside. Indeed, if one looks at the sources of
wealth creation today, they are markedly different from what they were barely
two decades ago. The key sources of wealth creation at the dawn of the new
millennium will lie with new enterprise formation; the renewal of incumbents;
the exploitation of technological know-how, intellectual property, and brands;
and the successful development and commercialization of new products and
services.

The implications for management are clearly quite considerable. New forms of business organization—and new management styles that enable intangibles to be developed and dynamic capabilities to be practiced—are clearly critical. There is now sufficient experience with new network organizations and with alliances to sensitize management to the richness of the organizational menu that is now available. Moreover, modern information technology clearly enables a greater variety of transactional structures than was hitherto thought possible. What is apparent is the need to focus on developing a deeper understanding of imitability and replicability issues with respect to intangibles and the role of markets in undermining traditional forms of competitive advantage.

The extension of markets and the growth of competition is a great benefit to the consumer and society. However, the post-war evolution of markets has powerful strategic implications for how and where firms position themselves to build competitive advantage. This does not appear to be well appreciated. It is no longer in product markets but in intangibles assets where advantage is built and defended. There is no such thing as a privileged product market position—unless it rests on some upstream intangible asset. The focus of strategy analysis must change, and is changing, as indicated by the burgeoning literature in strategic management on the resource-based theory of the firm.[36] Managers who figure this out are likely to be well positioned to build and maintain competitive advantage in the next millennium. They must recognize that in open unregulated markets, the domains in which value can be built are likely to be more and more confined. Perhaps Andy Grove is right after all when he warns that "only the paranoid survive."

Notes

1. D.J. Teece, "The Market for Know-How and the Efficient International Transfer of Technology," *Annuals of the American Association of Political and Social Sciences* (November 1981), pp. 81-86.
2. S. Kuznets, *Modern Economic Growth: Rate, Structure, Spread* (New Haven, CT: Yale University Press, 1966).
3. These included the late Edwin Mansfield, Richard Nelson, Chris Freeman, Sidney Winter, Paul David, Nathan Rosenberg, Giovanni Dosi, and David Mowery.
4. See P. Romer, "What Determines the Rate of Growth and Technological Change," World Bank Working Papers, WPS 279, World Bank, 1989.
5. I. Nonaka and H. Takeuchi, *The Knowledge Creating Company* (New York, NY: Oxford University Press, 1995).
6. M. Miller, *Merton Miller on Derivatives* (London: John Wiley & Sons, 1997).
7. P. Grindley and D.J. Teece, "Managing Intellectual Capital: Licensing and Cross-Licensing in Semiconductors and Electronics," *California Management Review*, 39/2 (Winter 1997): 8-41.
8. That's not to say that these are not opportunities to take bets against the market, but such bets represent asset plays by investors which ought not be thought of as a foundation for competitive advantage, as gains need not require involvement in operations of any kind.
9. Teece (1981), op. cit.
10. B. Arthur, "Competing Technologies: An Overview," in G. Dosi et al., eds., *Technical Change and Economic Theory* (London: Frances Pinter, 1988).
11. D.J. Teece, G. Pisano, and A. Shuen, "Dynamic Capabilities and Strategic Management," *Strategic Management Journal*, 18/7 (1997): 509-533.

12. Following Dataquest, we define SLI as an integrated circuit that contains a compute engine, memory, and logic on a single chip and has more than 100,000 utilized gates. Two types of SLI devises can be recognized: ASICs (application-specific integrated circuits) that are sold to a single user, and ASSPs (application-specific standard product) that are sold to more than one user.

13. Dataquest, *ASIC's Worldwide*, December 18, 1995.

14. Fumio Kodama, *Analyzing Japanese High Technologies* (London: Pinter, 1991).

15. "A Dynamic Mix of Chips and Biotech," *Forbes*, January 26, 1996, pp. 76-81.

16. Teece (1981), op. cit., p. 84.

17. For analysis of the sources of innovation, see D.J. Teece, "Firm Organization, Industrial Structure, and Technological Innovation," *Journal of Economic Behavior and Organization*, 31 (1996): 193-224.

18. This section is based on Teece (1981), op. cit., p. 82-84.

19. These ideas are developed further in C.E. Shannon and W. Weaver, *The Mathematical Theory of Communication* (Chicago, IL: University of Illinois Press, 1949). I am grateful to Max Boisot for drawing them to my attention.

20. For example, we could identify innovation that were architectural or non architectural, competency enhancing or competency destroying.

21. This section is based in part on Teece, Pisano and Shuen, op cit.

22. D.J. Teece, "Technology Transfer by Multinational Firms: The Resource Cost of Transferring Technological Know-how," *The Economic Journal*, 87 (1977): 242-261.

23. S.A. Lippman and R.P. Rumelt, "Demand Uncertainty and Investment in Industry-Specific Capital," *Industrial and Corporate Change*, 1/1 (1992): 235-262.

24. R. Nelson and S. Winter, *An Evolutionary Theory of Economic Change* (Cambridge, MA: Harvard University Press, 1982).

25. D.J. Teece, "Towards an Economic Theory of the Multiproduct Firm," *Journal of Economic Behavior and Organization*, 3 (1982): 39-63.

26. M.E. Porter, *The Competitive Advantage of Nations* (New York, NY: Free Press, 1990).

27. See K. Clark and T. Fujimoto, *Product Development Performance: Strategy, Organization, and Management in the World Auto Industries* (Cambridge, MA: Harvard Business School Press, 1991).

28. Nelson and Winter, op. cit.

29. Competences may in turn be embedded in other corporate assets, including assets complementary to knowledge assets.

30. S. Winter, "Knowledge and Competence as Strategic Assets," in D. Teece, ed., *The Competitive Challenge: Strategies for Industrial Innovation and Renewal* (New York, NY: Harper & Row, Ballinger Division, 1987).

31. This isn't necessary for broad level integration of physical components, where the bundling of intellectual property in products simplifies intellectual property transactions.

32. D.J. Teece, *The Multinational Corporation and the Resource Cost of International Technology Transfer* (Cambridge, MA: Ballinger, 1976), p. 48.

33. W.M. Cohen and D.A. Levinthal, "Absorption Capacity: A New Perspective on Learning and Innovation," *Administrative Sciences Quarterly*, 35 (1990): 128-152.

34. D. Mowery, "Firm Structure, Government Policy, and the Organization of Industrial Research," *Business History Review*, 58 (1984): 504-531.

35. The astute management of the value in a firm's competence/knowledge base is a central issue in strategic management. D.J. Teece, "Profiting from Technological Innovation," *Research Policy*, 15/6 (1986): 285-305. The firm must therefore be understood not just in terms of its competences, but also in terms of its dynamic capabilities and the ability to orchestrate internal and external assets so as to capture value. Dynamic capabilities reflect the entrepreneurial side of management. Incentives as well as the formal and informal structure of the firm are all elements of governance affecting dynamic capabilities. These elements together help define the firm as we know it. Accordingly, competitive advantage flows from both management and structure.

36. For an excellent compendium, see Nicolai Foss, ed., *Resources, Firms and Strategies: A Reader in the Resource-Based Perspective* (New York, NY: Oxford University Press, 1997).

Strategic Management Journal, Vol. 18:7, 509–533 (1997)

DYNAMIC CAPABILITIES AND STRATEGIC MANAGEMENT

DAVID J. TEECE[1]*, GARY PISANO[2] and AMY SHUEN[3]
[1]*Haas School of Business, University of California, Berkeley, California, U.S.A.*
[2]*Graduate School of Business Administration, Harvard University, Boston, Massachusetts, U.S.A.*
[3]*School of Business, San Jose State University, San Jose, California, U.S.A.*

The dynamic capabilities framework analyzes the sources and methods of wealth creation and capture by private enterprise firms operating in environments of rapid technological change. The competitive advantage of firms is seen as resting on distinctive processes (ways of coordinating and combining), shaped by the firm's (specific) asset positions (such as the firm's portfolio of difficult-to-trade knowledge assets and complementary assets), and the evolution path(s) it has adopted or inherited. The importance of path dependencies is amplified where conditions of increasing returns exist. Whether and how a firm's competitive advantage is eroded depends on the stability of market demand, and the ease of replicability (expanding internally) and imitatability (replication by competitors). If correct, the framework suggests that private wealth creation in regimes of rapid technological change depends in large measure on honing internal technological, organizational, and managerial processes inside the firm. In short, identifying new opportunities and organizing effectively and efficiently to embrace them are generally more fundamental to private wealth creation than is strategizing, if by strategizing one means engaging in business conduct that keeps competitors off balance, raises rival's costs, and excludes new entrants. © 1997 by John Wiley & Sons, Ltd.

INTRODUCTION

The fundamental question in the field of strategic management is how firms achieve and sustain competitive advantage.[1] We confront this question here by developing the dynamic capabilities approach, which endeavors to analyze the sources of wealth creation and capture by firms. The development of this framework flows from a recognition by the authors that strategic theory is replete with analyses of firm-level strategies for sustaining and safeguarding extant competitive advantage, but has performed less well with

respect to assisting in the understanding of how and why certain firms build competitive advantage in regimes of rapid change. Our approach is especially relevant in a Schumpeterian world of innovation-based competition, price/performance rivalry, increasing returns, and the 'creative destruction' of existing competences. The approach endeavors to explain firm-level success and failure. We are interested in both building a better theory of firm performance, as well as informing managerial practice.

In order to position our analysis in a manner that displays similarities and differences with existing approaches, we begin by briefly reviewing accepted frameworks for strategic management. We endeavor to expose implicit assumptions, and identify competitive circumstances where each paradigm might display some relative advantage as both a useful descriptive and normative theory of competitive strategy. While numerous theories have been advanced over the past

Key words: competences; capabilities; innovation; strategy; path dependency; knowledge assets

*Correspondence to: David J. Teece, Institute of Management, Innovation and Organization, Haas School of Business, University of California, Berkeley, CA 94720–1930, U.S.A.
[1] For a review of the fundamental questions in the field of strategy, see Rumelt, Schendel, and Teece (1994).

Received 17 April 1991
Final revision received 4 March 1997

two decades about the sources of competitive advantage, many cluster around just a few loosely structured frameworks or paradigms. In this paper we attempt to identify three existing paradigms and describe aspects of an emerging new paradigm that we label dynamic capabilities.

The dominant paradigm in the field during the 1980s was the competitive forces approach developed by Porter (1980). This approach, rooted in the structure–conduct–performance paradigm of industrial organization (Mason, 1949; Bain, 1959), emphasizes the actions a firm can take to create defensible positions against competitive forces. A second approach, referred to as a strategic conflict approach (e.g., Shapiro, 1989), is closely related to the first in its focus on product market imperfections, entry deterrence, and strategic interaction. The strategic conflict approach uses the tools of game theory and thus implicitly views competitive outcomes as a function of the effectiveness with which firms keep their rivals off balance through strategic investments, pricing strategies, signaling, and the control of information. Both the competitive forces and the strategic conflict approaches appear to share the view that rents flow from privileged product market positions.

Another distinct class of approaches emphasizes building competitive advantage through capturing entrepreneurial rents stemming from fundamental firm-level efficiency advantages. These approaches have their roots in a much older discussion of corporate strengths and weaknesses; they have taken on new life as evidence suggests that firms build enduring advantages only through efficiency and effectiveness, and as developments in organizational economics and the study of technological and organizational change become applied to strategy questions. One strand of this literature, often referred to as the 'resource-based perspective,' emphasizes firm-specific capabilities and assets and the existence of isolating mechanisms as the fundamental determinants of firm performance (Penrose, 1959; Rumelt, 1984; Teece, 1984; Wernerfelt, 1984).[2] This perspective

recognizes but does not attempt to explain the nature of the isolating mechanisms that enable entrepreneurial rents and competitive advantage to be sustained.

Another component of the efficiency-based approach is developed in this paper. Rudimentary efforts are made to identify the dimensions of firm-specific capabilities that can be sources of advantage, and to explain how combinations of competences and resources can be developed, deployed, and protected. We refer to this as the 'dynamic capabilities' approach in order to stress exploiting existing internal and external firm-specific competences to address changing environments. Elements of the approach can be found in Schumpeter (1942), Penrose (1959), Nelson and Winter (1982), Prahalad and Hamel (1990), Teece (1976, 1986a, 1986b, 1988) and in Hayes, Wheelwright, and Clark (1988): Because this approach emphasizes the development of management capabilities, and difficult-to-imitate combinations of organizational, functional and technological skills, it integrates and draws upon research in such areas as the management of R&D, product and process development, technology transfer, intellectual property, manufacturing, human resources, and organizational learning. Because these fields are often viewed as outside the traditional boundaries of strategy, much of this research has not been incorporated into existing economic approaches to strategy issues. As a result, dynamic capabilities can be seen as an emerging and potentially integrative approach to understanding the newer sources of competitive advantage.

We suggest that the dynamic capabilities approach is promising both in terms of future research potential and as an aid to management endeavoring to gain competitive advantage in increasingly demanding environments. To illustrate the essential elements of the dynamic capabilities approach, the sections that follow compare and contrast this approach to other models of strategy. Each section highlights the strategic

---

[2] Of these authors, Rumelt may have been the first to self-consciously apply a resource perspective to the field of strategy. Rumelt (1984: 561) notes that the strategic firm 'is characterized by a bundle of linked and idiosyncratic resources and resource conversion activities.' Similarly, Teece (1984: 95) notes: 'Successful firms possess one or more forms of intangible assets, such as technological or managerial know-

how. Over time, these assets may expand beyond the point of profitable reinvestment in a firm's traditional market. Accordingly, the firm may consider deploying its intangible assets in different product or geographical markets, where the expected returns are higher, if efficient transfer modes exist.' Wernerfelt (1984) was early to recognize that this approach was at odds with product market approaches and might constitute a distinct paradigm of strategy.

insights provided by each approach as well as the different competitive circumstances in which it might be most appropriate. Needless to say, these approaches are in many ways complementary and a full understanding of firm-level, competitive advantage requires an appreciation of all four approaches and more.

MODELS OF STRATEGY EMPHASIZING THE EXPLOITATION OF MARKET POWER

Competitive forces

The dominant paradigm in strategy at least during the 1980s was the competitive forces approach. Pioneered by Porter (1980), the competitive forces approach views the essence of competitive strategy formulation as 'relating a company to its environment . . . [T]he key aspect of the firm's environment is the industry or industries in which it competes.' Industry structure strongly influences the competitive rules of the game as well as the strategies potentially available to firms.

In the competitive forces model, five industry-level forces—entry barriers, threat of substitution, bargaining power of buyers, bargaining power of suppliers, and rivalry among industry incumbents—determine the inherent profit potential of an industry or subsegment of an industry. The approach can be used to help the firm find a position in an industry from which it can best defend itself against competitive forces or influence them in its favor (Porter, 1980: 4).

This 'five-forces' framework provides a systematic way of thinking about how competitive forces work at the industry level and how these forces determine the profitability of different industries and industry segments. The competitive forces framework also contains a number of underlying assumptions about the sources of competition and the nature of the strategy process. To facilitate comparisons with other approaches, we highlight several distinctive characteristics of the framework.

Economic rents in the competitive forces framework are monopoly rents (Teece, 1984). Firms in an industry earn rents when they are somehow able to impede the competitive forces (in either factor markets or product markets) which tend to drive economic returns to zero. Available strategies are described in Porter (1980). Competitive strategies are often aimed at altering the firm's position in the industry *vis-à-vis* competitors and suppliers. Industry structure plays a central role in determining and limiting strategic action.

Some industries or subsectors of industries become more 'attractive' because they have structural impediments to competitive forces (e.g., entry barriers) that allow firms better opportunities for creating sustainable competitive advantages. Rents are created largely at the industry or subsector level rather than at the firm level. While there is some recognition given to firm-specific assets, differences among firms relate primarily to scale. This approach to strategy reflects its incubation inside the field of industrial organization and in particular the industrial structure school of Mason and Bain[3] (Teece, 1984).

Strategic conflict

The publication of Carl Shapiro's 1989 article, confidently titled 'The Theory of Business Strategy,' announced the emergence of a new approach to business strategy, if not strategic management. This approach utilizes the tools of game theory to analyze the nature of competitive interaction between rival firms. The main thrust of work in this tradition is to reveal how a firm can influence the behavior and actions of rival firms and thus the market environment.[4] Examples of such moves are investment in capacity (Dixit, 1980), R&D (Gilbert and Newberry, 1982), and advertising (Schmalensee, 1983). To be effective, these strategic moves require irreversible commitments.[5] The moves in question will have no effect if they can be costlessly undone. A key idea is that by manipulating the market environment, a firm may be able to increase its profits.

---

[3] In competitive environments characterized by sustainable and stable mobility and structural barriers, these forces may become the determinants of industry-level profitability. However, competitive advantage is more complex to ascertain in environments of rapid technological change where specific assets owned by heterogeneous firms can be expected to play a larger role in explaining rents.

[4] The market environment is all factors that influence market outcomes (prices, quantities, profits) including the beliefs of customers and of rivals, the number of potential technologies employed, and the costs or speed with which a rival can enter the industry.

[5] For an excellent discussion of committed competition in multiple contexts, see Ghemawat (1991).

This literature, together with the contestability literature (Baumol, Panzar, and Willig, 1982), has led to a greater appreciation of the role of sunk costs, as opposed to fixed costs, in determining competitive outcomes. Strategic moves can also be designed to influence rivals' behavior through signaling. Strategic signaling has been examined in a number of contexts, including predatory pricing (Kreps and Wilson, 1982a, 1982b) and limit pricing (Milgrom and Roberts, 1982a, 1982b). More recent treatments have emphasized the role of commitment and reputation (e.g., Ghemawat, 1991) and the benefits of firms simultaneously pursuing competition and cooperation[6] (Brandenburger and Nalebuff, 1995, 1996).

In many instances, game theory formalizes long-standing intuitive arguments about various types of business behavior (e.g., predatory pricing, patent races), though in some instances it has induced a substantial change in the conventional wisdom. But by rationalizing observed behavior by reference to suitably designed games, in explaining everything these models also explain nothing, as they do not generate testable predictions (Sutton, 1992). Many specific game-theoretic models admit multiple equilibrium, and a wide range of choice exists as to the design of the appropriate game form to be used. Unfortunately, the results often depend on the precise specification chosen. The equilibrium in models of strategic behavior crucially depends on what one rival believes another rival will do in a particular situation. Thus the qualitative features of the results may depend on the way price competition is modeled (e.g., Bertrand or Cournot) or on the presence or absence of strategic asymmetries such as first-mover advantages. The analysis of strategic moves using game theory can be thought of as 'dynamic' in the sense that multiperiod analyses can be pursued both intuitively and formally. However, we use the term 'dynamic' in this paper in a different sense, referring to situations where there is rapid change in technology and market forces, and 'feedback' effects on firms.[7]

We have a particular view of the contexts in which the strategic conflict literature is relevant to strategic management. Firms that have a tremendous cost or other competitive advantage *vis-à-vis* their rivals ought not be transfixed by the moves and countermoves of their rivals. Their competitive fortunes will swing more on total demand conditions, not on how competitors deploy and redeploy their competitive assets. Put differently, when there are gross asymmetries in competitive advantage between firms, the results of game-theoretic analysis are likely to be obvious and uninteresting. The stronger competitor will generally advance, even if disadvantaged by certain information asymmetries. To be sure, incumbent firms can be undone by new entrants with a dramatic cost advantage, but no 'gaming' will overturn that outcome. On the other hand, if firms' competitive positions are more delicately balanced, as with Coke and Pepsi, and United Airlines and American Airlines, then strategic conflict is of interest to competitive outcomes. Needless to say, there are many such circumstances, but they are rare in industries where there is rapid technological change and fast-shifting market circumstances.

In short, where competitors do not have deep-seated competitive advantages, the moves and countermoves of competitors can often be usefully formulated in game-theoretic terms. However, we doubt that game theory can comprehensively illuminate how Chrysler should compete against Toyota and Honda, or how United Airlines can best respond to Southwest Airlines since Southwest's advantage is built on organizational attributes which United cannot readily replicate.[8] Indeed, the entrepreneurial side of strategy—how significant new rent streams are created and protected—is largely ignored by the game-theoretic approach.[9] Accordingly, we find that the approach, while important, is most relevant

---

[6] Competition and cooperation have also been analyzed ouside of this tradition. See, for example, Teece (1992) and Link, Teece and Finan (1996).
[7] Accordingly, both approaches are dynamic, but in very different senses.

[8] Thus even in the air transport industry game-theoretic formulations by no means capture all the relevant dimensions of competitive rivalry. United Airlines' and United Express's difficulties in competing with Southwest Airlines because of United's inability to fully replicate Southwest's operation capabilities is documented in Gittel (1995).
[9] Important exceptions can be found in Brandenburger and Nalebuff (1996) such as their emphasis on the role of complements. However, these insights do not flow uniquely from game theory and can be found in the organizational economics literature (e.g., Teece, 1986a, 1986b; de Figueiredo and Teece, 1996).

when competitors are closely matched[10] and the population of relevant competitors and the identity of their strategic alternatives can be readily ascertained. Nevertheless, coupled with other approaches it can sometimes yield powerful insights.

However, this research has an orientation that we are concerned about in terms of the implicit framing of strategic issues. Rents, from a game-theoretic perspective, are ultimately a result of managers' intellectual ability to 'play the game.' The adage of the strategist steeped in this approach is 'do unto others before they do unto you.' We worry that fascination with strategic moves and Machiavellian tricks will distract managers from seeking to build more enduring sources of competitive advantage. The approach unfortunately ignores competition as a process involving the development, accumulation, combination, and protection of unique skills and capabilities. Since strategic interactions are what receive focal attention, the impression one might receive from this literature is that success in the marketplace is the result of sophisticated plays and counterplays, when this is generally not the case at all.[11]

In what follows, we suggest that building a dynamic view of the business enterprise— something missing from the two approaches we have so far identified—enhances the probability of establishing an acceptable descriptive theory of strategy that can assist practitioners in the building of long-run advantage and competitive flexibility. Below, we discuss first the resource-based perspective and then an extension we call the dynamic capabilities approach.

MODELS OF STRATEGY EMPHASIZING EFFICIENCY

Resource-based perspective

The resource-based approach sees firms with superior systems and structures being profitable not because they engage in strategic investments

that may deter entry and raise prices above long-run costs, but because they have markedly lower costs, or offer markedly higher quality or product performance. This approach focuses on the rents accruing to the owners of scarce firm-specific resources rather than the economic profits from product market positioning.[12] Competitive advantage lies 'upstream' of product markets and rests on the firm's idiosyncratic and difficult-to-imitate resources.[13]

One can find the resources approach suggested by the earlier preanalytic strategy literature. A leading text of the 1960s (Learned *et al.*, 1969) noted that 'the capability of an organization is its demonstrated and potential ability to accomplish against the opposition of circumstance or competition, whatever it sets out to do. Every organization has actual and potential strengths and weaknesses; it is important to try to determine what they are and to distinguish one from the other.' Thus what a firm can do is not just a function of the opportunities it confronts; it also depends on what resources the organization can muster.

Learned *et al.* proposed that the real key to a company's success or even to its future development lies in its ability to find or create 'a competence that is truly distinctive.'[14] This literature also recognized the constraints on firm behavior and, in particular, noted that one should not assume that management 'can rise to any occasion.' These insights do appear to keenly anticipate the resource-based approach that has since emerged, but they did not provide a theory or systematic framework for analyzing business strategies. Indeed, Andrews (1987: 46) noted that 'much of what is intuitive in this process is yet to be identified.' Unfortunately, the academic literature on capabilities stalled for a couple of decades.

New impetus has been given to the resource-based approach by recent theoretical developments in organizational economics and in the theory of strategy, as well as by a growing

---

[10] When closely matched in an aggregate sense, they may nevertheless display asymmetries which game theorists can analyze.
[11] The strategic conflict literature also tends to focus practitioners on product market positioning rather than on developing the unique assets which make possible superior product market positions (Dierickx and Cool, 1989).

[12] In the language of economics, rents flow from unique firm-specific assets that cannot readily be replicated, rather than from tactics which deter entry and keep competitors off balance. In short, rents are Ricardian.
[13] Teece (1982: 46) saw the firm as having 'a variety of end products which it can produce with its organizational technology.'
[14] Elsewhere Andrews (1987: 47) defined a distinctive competence as what an organization can do particularly well.

body of anecdotal and empirical literature[15] that highlights the importance of firm-specific factors in explaining firm performance. Cool and Schendel (1988) have shown that there are systematic and significant performance differences among firms which belong to the same strategic group within the U.S. pharmaceutical industry. Rumelt (1991) has shown that intraindustry differences in profits are greater than interindustry differences in profits, strongly suggesting the importance of firm-specific factors and the relative unimportance of industry effects.[16] Jacobsen (1988) and Hansen and Wernerfelt (1989) made similar findings.

A comparison of the resource-based approach and the competitive forces approach (discussed earlier in the paper) in terms of their implications for the strategy process is revealing. From the first perspective, an entry decision looks roughly as follows: (1) pick an industry (based on its 'structural attractiveness'); (2) choose an entry strategy based on conjectures about competitors' rational strategies; (3) if not already possessed, acquire or otherwise obtain the requisite assets to compete in the market. From this perspective, the process of identifying and developing the requisite assets is not particularly problematic. The process involves nothing more than choosing rationally among a well-defined set of investment alternatives. If assets are not already owned, they can be bought. The resource-based perspective is strongly at odds with this conceptualization.

From the resource-based perspective, firms are heterogeneous with respect to their resources/capabilities/endowments. Further, resource endowments are 'sticky:' at least in the short run, firms are to some degree stuck with what they have and may have to live with what they lack.[17] This stickiness arises for three reasons. First, business development is viewed as an extremely complex

process.[18] Quite simply, firms lack the organizational capacity to develop new competences quickly (Dierickx and Cool, 1989). Secondly, some assets are simply not readily tradeable, for example, tacit know-how (Teece, 1976, 1980) and reputation (Dierickx and Cool, 1989). Thus, resource endowments cannot equilibrate through factor input markets. Finally, even when an asset can be purchased, firms may stand to gain little by doing so. As Barney (1986) points out, unless a firm is lucky, possesses superior information, or both, the price it pays in a competitive factor market will fully capitalize the rents from the asset.

Given that in the resources perspective firms possess heterogeneous and sticky resource bundles, the entry decision process suggested by this approach is as follows: (1) identify your firm's unique resources; (2) decide in which markets those resources can earn the highest rents; and (3) decide whether the rents from those assets are most effectively utilized by (a) integrating into related market(s), (b) selling the relevant intermediate output to related firms, or (c) selling the assets themselves to a firm in related businesses (Teece, 1980, 1982).

The resource-based perspective puts both vertical integration and diversification into a new strategic light. Both can be viewed as ways of capturing rents on scarce, firm-specific assets whose services are difficult to sell in intermediate markets (Penrose, 1959; Williamson, 1975; Teece, 1980, 1982, 1986a, 1986b; Wernerfelt, 1984). Empirical work on the relationship between performance and diversification by Wernerfelt and Montgomery (1988) provides evidence for this proposition. It is evident that the resource-based perspective focuses on strategies for exploiting existing firm-specific assets.

However, the resource-based perspective also invites consideration of managerial strategies for developing new capabilities (Wernerfelt, 1984). Indeed, if control over scarce resources is the source of economic profits, then it follows that such issues as skill acquisition, the management of knowledge and know-how (Shuen, 1994), and learning become fundamental strategic issues. It is in this second dimension, encompassing skill acquisition, learning, and accumulation of organizational and intangible or 'invisible' assets (Itami

---

[15] Studies of the automobile and other industries displayed differences in organization which often underlay differences amongst firms. See, for example, Womack, Jones, and Roos, 1991; Hayes and Clark, 1985; Barney, Spender and Reve, 1994; Clark and Fujimoto, 1991; Henderson and Cockburn, 1994; Nelson, 1991; Levinthal and Myatt, 1994.

[16] Using FTC line of business data, Rumelt showed that stable industry effects account for only 8 percent of the variance in business unit returns. Furthermore, only about 40 percent of the dispersion in industry returns is due to stable industry effects.

[17] In this regard, this approach has much in common with recent work on organizational ecology (e.g., Freeman and Boeker, 1984) and also on commitment (Ghemawat, 1991: 17–25).

---

[18] Capability development, however, is not really analyzed.

and Roehl, 1987), that we believe lies the greatest potential for contributions to strategy.

The dynamic capabilities approach: Overview

The global competitive battles in high-technology industries such as semiconductors, information services, and software have demonstrated the need for an expanded paradigm to understand how competitive advantage is achieved. Well-known companies like IBM, Texas Instruments, Philips, and others appear to have followed a 'resource-based strategy' of accumulating valuable technology assets, often guarded by an aggressive intellectual property stance. However, this strategy is often not enough to support a significant competitive advantage. Winners in the global marketplace have been firms that can demonstrate timely responsiveness and rapid and flexible product innovation, coupled with the management capability to effectively coordinate and redeploy internal and external competences. Not surprisingly, industry observers have remarked that companies can accumulate a large stock of valuable technology assets and still not have many useful capabilities.

We refer to this ability to achieve new forms of competitive advantage as 'dynamic capabilities' to emphasize two key aspects that were not the main focus of attention in previous strategy perspectives. The term 'dynamic' refers to the capacity to renew competences so as to achieve congruence with the changing business environment; certain innovative responses are required when time-to-market and timing are critical, the rate of technological change is rapid, and the nature of future competition and markets difficult to determine. The term 'capabilities' emphasizes the key role of strategic management in appropriately adapting, integrating, and reconfiguring internal and external organizational skills, resources, and functional competences to match the requirements of a changing environment.

One aspect of the strategic problem facing an innovating firm in a world of Schumpeterian competition is to identify difficult-to-imitate internal and external competences most likely to support valuable products and services. Thus, as argued by Dierickx and Cool (1989), choices about how much to spend (invest) on different possible areas are central to the firm's strategy. However, choices about domains of competence are influenced by past choices. At any given point in time, firms must follow a certain trajectory or path of competence development. This path not only defines what choices are open to the firm today, but it also puts bounds around what its internal repertoire is likely to be in the future. Thus, firms, at various points in time, make long-term, quasi-irreversible commitments to certain domains of competence.[19]

The notion that competitive advantage requires both the exploitation of existing internal and external firm-specific capabilities, and developing new ones is partially developed in Penrose (1959), Teece (1982), and Wernerfelt (1984). However, only recently have researchers begun to focus on the specifics of how some organizations first develop firm-specific capabilities and how they renew competences to respond to shifts in the business environment.[20] These issues are intimately tied to the firm's business processes, market positions, and expansion paths. Several writers have recently offered insights and evidence on how firms can develop their capability to adapt and even capitalize on rapidly changing environments.[21] The dynamic capabilities approach seeks to provide a coherent framework which can both integrate existing conceptual and empirical knowledge, and facilitate prescription. In doing so, it builds upon the theoretical foundations provided by Schumpeter (1934), Penrose (1959), Williamson (1975, 1985), Barney (1986), Nelson and Winter (1982), Teece (1988), and Teece *et al.* (1994).

TOWARD A DYNAMIC CAPABILITIES FRAMEWORK

Terminology

In order to facilitate theory development and intellectual dialogue, some acceptable definitions are desirable. We propose the following.

---

[19] Deciding, under significant uncertainty about future states of the world, which long-term paths to commit to and when to change paths is the central strategic problem confronting the firm. In this regard, the work of Ghemawat (1991) is highly germane to the dynamic capabilities approach to strategy.

[20] See, for example, Iansiti and Clark (1994) and Henderson (1994).

[21] See Hayes *et al.* (1988), Prahalad and Hamel (1990), Dierickx and Cool (1989), Chandler (1990), and Teece (1993).

Factors of production

These are 'undifferentiated' inputs available in disaggregate form in factor markets. By undifferentiated we mean that they lack a firm-specific component. Land, unskilled labor, and capital are typical examples. Some factors may be available for the taking, such as public knowledge. In the language of Arrow, such resources must be 'nonfugitive.'[22] Property rights are usually well defined for factors of production.

Resources[23]

Resources are firm-specific assets that are difficult if not impossible to imitate. Trade secrets and certain specialized production facilities and engineering experience are examples. Such assets are difficult to transfer among firms because of transactions costs and transfer costs, and because the assets may contain tacit knowledge.

Organizational routines/competences

When firm-specific assets are assembled in integrated clusters spanning individuals and groups so that they enable distinctive activities to be performed, these activities constitute organizational routines and processes. Examples include quality, miniaturization, and systems integration. Such competences are typically viable across multiple product lines, and may extend outside the firm to embrace alliance partners.

Core competences

We define those competences that define a firm's fundamental business as core. Core competences must accordingly be derived by looking across the range of a firm's (and its competitors) products and services.[24] The value of core competences can be enhanced by combination with the appropriate complementary assets. The degree

to which a core competence is distinctive depends on how well endowed the firm is relative to its competitors, and on how difficult it is for competitors to replicate its competences.

Dynamic capabilities

We define dynamic capabilities as the firm's ability to integrate, build, and reconfigure internal and external competences to address rapidly changing environments. Dynamic capabilities thus reflect an organization's ability to achieve new and innovative forms of competitive advantage given path dependencies and market positions (Leonard-Barton, 1992).

Products

End products are the final goods and services produced by the firm based on utilizing the competences that it possesses. The performance (price, quality, etc.) of a firm's products relative to its competitors at any point in time will depend upon its competences (which over time depend on its capabilities).

Markets and strategic capabilities

Different approaches to strategy view sources of wealth creation and the essence of the strategic problem faced by firms differently. The competitive forces framework sees the strategic problem in terms of industry structure, entry deterrence, and positioning; game-theoretic models view the strategic problem as one of interaction between rivals with certain expectations about how each other will behave;[25] resource-based perspectives have focused on the exploitation of firm-specific assets. Each approach asks different, often complementary questions. A key step in building a conceptual framework related to dynamic capabilities is to identify the foundations upon which distinctive and difficult-to-replicate advantages can be built, maintained, and enhanced.

A useful way to vector in on the strategic elements of the business enterprise is first to identify what is not strategic. To be strategic, a

---

[22] Arrow (1996) defines fugitive resources as ones that can move cheaply amongst individuals and firms.
[23] We do not like the term 'resource' and believe it is misleading. We prefer to use the term firm-specific asset. We use it here to try and maintain links to the literature on the resource-based approach which we believe is important.
[24] Thus Eastman Kodak's core competence might be considered imaging, IBM's might be considered integrated data processing and service, and Motorola's untethered communications.

[25] In sequential move games, each player looks ahead and anticipates his rival's future responses in order to reason back and decide action, i.e., look forward, reason backward.

capability must be honed to a user need[26] (so there is a source of revenues), unique (so that the products/services produced can be priced without too much regard to competition) and difficult to replicate (so profits will not be competed away). Accordingly, any assets or entity which are homogeneous and can be bought and sold at an established price cannot be all that strategic (Barney, 1986). What is it, then, about firms which undergirds competitive advantage?

To answer this, one must first make some fundamental distinctions between markets and internal organization (firms). The essence of the firm, as Coase (1937) pointed out, is that it displaces market organization. It does so in the main because inside the firms one can organize certain types of economic activity in ways one cannot using markets. This is not only because of transaction costs, as Williamson (1975, 1985) emphasized, but also because there are many types of arrangements where injecting high-powered (market like) incentives might well be quite destructive of cooperative activity and learning.[27] Inside an organization, exchange cannot take place in the same manner that it can outside an organization, not just because it might be destructive to provide high-powered individual incentives, but because it is difficult if not impossible to tightly calibrate individual contribution to a joint effort. Hence, contrary to Arrow's (1969) view of firms as quasi markets, and the task of management to inject markets into firms, we recognize the inherent limits and possible counterproductive results of attempting to fashion firms into simply clusters of internal markets. In particular, learning and internal technology transfer may well be jeopardized.

Indeed, what is distinctive about firms is that they are domains for organizing activity in a nonmarket-like fashion. Accordingly, as we discuss what is distinctive about firms, we stress competences/capabilities which are ways of organizing and getting things done which cannot be accomplished merely by using the price system

to coordinate activity.[28] The very essence of most capabilities/competences is that they cannot be readily assembled through markets (Teece, 1982, 1986a; Zander and Kogut, 1995). If the ability to assemble competences using markets is what is meant by the firm as a nexus of contracts (Fama, 1980), then we unequivocally state that the firm about which we theorize cannot be usefully modeled as a nexus of contracts. By 'contract' we are referring to a transaction undergirded by a legal agreement, or some other arrangement which clearly spells out rights, rewards, and responsibilities. Moreover, the firm as a nexus of contracts suggests a series of bilateral contracts orchestrated by a coordinator. Our view of the firm is that the organization takes place in a more multilateral fashion, with patterns of behavior and learning being orchestrated in a much more decentralized fashion, but with a viable headquarters operation.

The key point, however, is that the properties of internal organization cannot be replicated by a portfolio of business units amalgamated just through formal contracts as many distinctive elements of internal organization simply cannot be replicated in the market.[29] That is, entrepreneurial activity cannot lead to the immediate replication of unique organizational skills through simply entering a market and piecing the parts together overnight. Replication takes time, and the replication of best practice may be illusive. Indeed, firm capabilities need to be understood not in terms of balance sheet items, but mainly in terms of the organizational structures and managerial processes which support productive activity. By construction, the firm's balance sheet contains items that can be valued, at least at original market prices (cost). It is necessarily the case, therefore, that the balance sheet is a poor shadow of a firm's distinctive competences.[30]

---

[26] Needless to say, users need not be the current customers of the enterprise. Thus a capability can be the basis for diversification into new product markets.
[27] Indeed, the essence of internal organization is that it is a domain of unleveraged or low-powered incentives. By unleveraged we mean that rewards are determined at the group or organization level, not primarily at the individual level, in an effort to encourage team behavior, not individual behavior.

[28] We see the problem of market contracting as a matter of coordination as much as we see it a problem of opportunism in the fact of contractual hazards. In this sense, we are consonant with both Richardson (1960) and Williamson (1975, 1985).
[29] As we note in Teece *et al.* (1994), the conglomerate offers few if any efficiencies because there is little provided by the conglomerate form that shareholders cannot obtain for themselves simply by holding a diversified portfolio of stocks.
[30] Owners' equity may reflect, in part, certain historic capabilities. Recently, some scholars have begun to attempt to measure organizational capability using financial statement data. See Baldwin and Clark (1991) and Lev and Sougiannis (1992).

That which is distinctive cannot be bought and sold short of buying the firm itself, or one or more of its subunits.

There are many dimensions of the business firm that must be understood if one is to grasp firm-level distinctive competences/capabilities. In this paper we merely identify several classes of factors that will help determine a firm's distinctive competence and dynamic capabilities. We organize these in three categories: processes, positions, and paths. The essence of competences and capabilities is embedded in organizational processes of one kind or another. But the content of these processes and the opportunities they afford for developing competitive advantage at any point in time are shaped significantly by the assets the firm possesses (internal and market) and by the evolutionary path it has adopted/inherited. Hence organizational processes, shaped by the firm's asset positions and molded by its evolutionary and co-evolutionary paths, explain the essence of the firm's dynamic capabilities and its competitive advantage.

Processes, positions, and paths

We thus advance the argument that the competitive advantage of firms lies with its managerial and organizational processes, shaped by its (specific) asset position, and the paths available to it.[31] By managerial and organizational processes, we refer to the way things are done in the firm, or what might be referred to as its routines, or patterns of current practice and learning. By position we refer to its current specific endowments of technology, intellectual property, complementary assets, customer base, and its external relations with suppliers and complementors. By paths we refer to the strategic alternatives available to the firm, and the presence or absence of increasing returns and attendant path dependencies.

Our focus throughout is on asset structures for which no ready market exists, as these are the only assets of strategic interest. A final section

focuses on replication and imitation, as it is these phenomena which determine how readily a competence or capability can be cloned by competitors, and therefore distinctiveness of its competences and the durability of its advantage.

The firm's processes and positions collectively encompass its competences and capabilities. A hierarchy of competences/capabilities ought to be recognized, as some competences may be on the factory floor, some in the R&D labs, some in the executive suites, and some in the way everything is integrated. A difficult-to-replicate or difficult-to-imitate competence was defined earlier as a distinctive competence. As indicated, the key feature of distinctive competence is that there is not a market for it, except possibly through the market for business units. Hence competences and capabilities are intriguing assets as they typically must be built because they cannot be bought.

Organizational and managerial processes

Organizational processes have three roles: coordination/integration (a static concept); learning (a dynamic concept); and reconfiguration (a transformational concept). We discuss each in turn.

Coordination/integration. While the price system supposedly coordinates the economy,[32] managers coordinate or integrate activity inside the firm. How efficiently and effectively internal coordination or integration is achieved is very important (Aoki, 1990).[33] Likewise for external coordination.[34] Increasingly, strategic advantage requires the integration of external activities and technologies. The growing literature on strategic

---

[31] We are implicitly saying that fixed assets, like plant and equipment which can be purchased off-the-shelf by all industry participants, cannot be the source of a firm's competitive advantage. In asmuch as financial balance sheets typically reflect such assets, we point out that the assets that matter for competitive advantage are rarely reflected in the balance sheet, while those that do not are.

[32] The coordinative properties of markets depend on prices being "sufficient" upon which to base resource allocation decisions.
[33] Indeed, Ronald Coase, author of the pathbreaking 1937 article 'The nature of the firm,' which focused on the costs of organizational coordination inside the firm as compared to across the market, half a century later has identified as critical the understanding of 'why the costs of organizing particular activities differs among firms' (Coase, 1988: 47). We argue that a firm's distinctive ability needs to be understood as a reflection of distinctive organizational or coordinative capabilities. This form of integration (i.e., inside business units) is different from the integration between business units; they could be viable on a stand-alone basis (external integration). For a useful taxonomy, see Iansiti and Clark (1994).
[34] Shuen (1994) examines the gains and hazards of the technology make-vs.-buy decision and supplier codevelopment.

alliances, the virtual corporation, and buyer–supplier relations and technology collaboration evidences the importance of external integration and sourcing.

There is some field-based empirical research that provides support for the notion that the way production is organized by management inside the firm is the source of differences in firms' competence in various domains. For example, Garvin's (1988) study of 18 room air-conditioning plants reveals that quality performance was not related to either capital investment or the degree of automation of the facilities. Instead, quality performance was driven by special organizational routines. These included routines for gathering and processing information, for linking customer experiences with engineering design choices, and for coordinating factories and component suppliers.[35] The work of Clark and Fujimoto (1991) on project development in the automobile industry also illustrates the role played by coordinative routines. Their study reveals a significant degree of variation in how different firms coordinate the various activities required to bring a new model from concept to market. These differences in coordinative routines and capabilities seem to have a significant impact on such performance variables as development cost, development lead times, and quality. Furthermore, Clark and Fujimoto tended to find significant firm-level differences in coordination routines and these differences seemed to have persisted for a long time. This suggests that routines related to coordination are firm-specific in nature.

Also, the notion that competence/capability is embedded in distinct ways of coordinating and combining helps to explain how and why seemingly minor technological changes can have devastating impacts on incumbent firms' abilities to compete in a market. Henderson and Clark (1990), for example, have shown that incumbents in the photolithographic equipment industry were sequentially devastated by seemingly minor innovations that, nevertheless, had major impacts on how systems had to be configured. They attribute these difficulties to the fact that systems-level or 'architectural' innovations often require new routines to integrate and coordinate engineering tasks. These findings and others sug-

gest that productive systems display high interdependency, and that it may not be possible to change one level without changing others. This appears to be true with respect to the 'lean production' model (Womack *et al.*, 1991) which has now transformed the Taylor or Ford model of manufacturing organization in the automobile industry.[36] Lean production requires distinctive shop floor practices and processes as well as distinctive higher-order managerial processes. Put differently, organizational processes often display high levels of coherence, and when they do, replication may be difficult because it requires systemic changes throughout the organization and also among interorganizational linkages, which might be very hard to effectuate. Put differently, partial imitation or replication of a successful model may yield zero benefits.[37]

---

[35] Garvin (1994) provides a typology of organizational processes.

[36] Fujimoto (1994: 18–20) describes key elements as they existed in the Japanese auto industry as follows: 'The typical volume production system of effective Japanese makers of the 1980s (e.g., Toyota) consists of various intertwined elements that might lead to competitive advantages. Just-in-Time (JIT), Jidoka (automatic defect detection and machine stop), Total Quality Control (TQC), and continuous improvement (Kaizen) are often pointed out as its core subsystems. The elements of such a system include inventory reduction mechanisms by Kanban system; levelization of production volume and product mix (heijunka); reduction of 'muda' (non-value adding activities), 'mura' (uneven pace of production) and muri (excessive workload); production plans based on dealers' order volume (genyo seisan); reduction of die set-up time and lot size in stamping operation; mixed model assembly; piece-by-piece transfer of parts between machines (ikko-nagashi); flexible task assignment for volume changes and productivity improvement (shojinka); multi-task job assignment along the process flow (takotei-mochi); U-shape machine layout that facilitates flexible and multiple task assignment, on-the-spot inspection by direct workers (tsukurikomi); fool-proof prevention of defects (poka-yoke); real-time feedback of production troubles (andon); assembly line stop cord; emphasis on cleanliness, order and discipline on the shop floor (5-S); frequent revision of standard operating procedures by supervisors; quality control circles; standardized tools for quality improvement (e.g., 7 tools for QC, QC story); worker involvement in preventive maintenance (Total Productive Maintenance); low cost automation or semi-automation with just-enough functions); reduction of process steps for saving of tools and dies, and so on. The human-resource management factors that back up the above elements include stable employment of core workers (with temporary workers in the periphery); long-term training of multi-skilled (multi-task) workers; wage system based in part on skill accumulation; internal promotion to shop floor supervisors; cooperative relationships with labor unions; inclusion of production supervisors in union members; generally egalitarian policies for corporate welfare, communication and worker motivation. Parts procurement policies are also pointed out often as a source of the competitive advantage.

[37] For a theoretical argument along these lines, see Milgrom and Roberts (1990).

The notion that there is a certain rationality or coherence to processes and systems is not quite the same concept as corporate culture, as we understand the latter. Corporate culture refers to the values and beliefs that employees hold; culture can be a *de facto* governance system as it mediates the behavior of individuals and economizes on more formal administrative methods. Rationality or coherence notions are more akin to the Nelson and Winter (1982) notion of organizational routines. However, the routines concept is a little too amorphous to properly capture the congruence amongst processes and between processes and incentives that we have in mind. Consider a professional service organization like an accounting firm. If it is to have relatively high-powered incentives that reward individual performance, then it must build organizational processes that channel individual behavior; if it has weak or low-powered incentives, it must find symbolic ways to recognize the high performers, and it must use alternative methods to build effort and enthusiasm. What one may think of as styles of organization in fact contain necessary, not discretionary, elements to achieve performance.

Recognizing the congruences and complementarities among processes, and between processes and incentives, is critical to the understanding of organizational capabilities. In particular, they can help us explain why architectural and radical innovations are so often introduced into an industry by new entrants. The incumbents develop distinctive organizational processes that cannot support the new technology, despite certain overt similarities between the old and the new. The frequent failure of incumbents to introduce new technologies can thus be seen as a consequence of the mismatch that so often exists between the set of organizational processes needed to support the conventional product/service and the requirements of the new. Radical organizational re-engineering will usually be required to support the new product, which may well do better embedded in a separate subsidiary where a new set of coherent organizatonal processes can be fashioned.[38]

Learning. Perhaps even more important than integration is learning. Learning is a process by which repetition and experimentation enable tasks to be performed better and quicker. It also enables new production opportunities to be identified.[39] In the context of the firm, if not more generally, learning has several key characteristics. First, learning involves organizational as well as individual skills.[40] While individual skills are of relevance, their value depends upon their employment, in particular organizational settings. Learning processes are intrinsically social and collective and occur not only through the imitation and emulation of individuals, as with teacher–student or master–apprentice, but also because of joint contributions to the understanding of complex problems.[41] Learning requires common codes of communication and coordinated search procedures. Second, the organizational knowledge generated by such activity resides in new patterns of activity, in 'routines,' or a new logic of organization. As indicated earlier, routines are patterns of interactions that represent successful solutions to particular problems. These patterns of interaction are resident in group behavior, though certain subroutines may be resident in individual behavior. The concept of dynamic capabilities as a coordinative management process opens the door to the potential for interorganizational learning. Researchers (Doz and Shuen, 1990; Mody, 1993) have pointed out that collaborations and partnerships can be a vehicle for new organizational learning, helping firms to recognize dysfunctional routines, and preventing strategic blindspots.

Reconfiguration and transformation. In rapidly changing environments, there is obviously value in the ability to sense the need to reconfigure the firm's asset structure, and to accomplish the necessary internal and external transformation (Amit and Schoemaker, 1993; Langlois, 1994). This requires constant surveillance of markets and technologies and the willingness to adopt best practice. In this regard, benchmarking is of con-

---

[38] See Abernathy and Clark (1985).

[39] For a useful review and contribution, see Levitt and March (1988).

[40] Levinthal and March, 1993. Mahoney (1992) and Mahoney and Pandian (1995) suggest that both resources and mental models are intertwined in firm-level learning.

[41] There is a large literature on learning, although only a small fraction of it deals with organizational learning. Relevant contributors include Levitt and March (1988), Argyris and Schon (1978), Levinthal and March (1981), Nelson and Winter (1982), and Leonard-Barton (1995).

siderable value as an organized process for accomplishing such ends (Camp, 1989). In dynamic environments, narcissistic organizations are likely to be impaired. The capacity to reconfigure and transform is itself a learned organizational skill. The more frequently practiced, the easier accomplished.

Change is costly and so firms must develop processes to minimize low pay-off change. The ability to calibrate the requirements for change and to effectuate the necessary adjustments would appear to depend on the ability to scan the environment, to evaluate markets and competitors, and to quickly accomplish reconfiguration and transformation ahead of competition. Decentralization and local autonomy assist these processes. Firms that have honed these capabilities are sometimes referred to as 'high-flex'.

Positions

The strategic posture of a firm is determined not only by its learning processes and by the coherence of its internal and external processes and incentives, but also by its specific assets. By specific assets we mean for example its specialized plant and equipment. These include its difficult-to-trade knowledge assets and assets complementary to them, as well as its reputational and relational assets. Such assets determine its competitive advantage at any point in time. We identify several illustrative classes.

Technological assets. While there is an emerging market for know-how (Teece, 1981), much technology does not enter it. This is either because the firm is unwilling to sell it[42] or because of difficulties in transacting in the market for know-how (Teece, 1980). A firm's technological assets may or may not be protected by the standard instruments of intellectual property law. Either way, the ownership protection and utilization of technological assets are clearly key differentiators among firms. Likewise for complementary assets.

Complementary assets. Technological innovations require the use of certain related assets to produce and deliver new products and services.

Prior commercialization activities require and enable firms to build such complementarities (Teece, 1986b). Such capabilities and assets, while necessary for the firm's established activities, may have other uses as well. These assets typically lie downstream. New products and processes either can enhance or destroy the value of such assets (Tushman, Newman, and Romanelli, 1986). Thus the development of computers enhanced the value of IBM's direct sales force in office products, while disk brakes rendered useless much of the auto industry's investment in drum brakes.

Financial assets. In the short run, a firm's cash position and degree of leverage may have strategic implications. While there is nothing more fungible than cash, it cannot always be raised from external markets without the dissemination of considerable information to potential investors. Accordingly, what a firm can do in short order is often a function of its balance sheet. In the longer run, that ought not be so, as cash flow ought be more determinative.

Reputational assets. Firms, like individuals, have reputations. Reputations often summarize a good deal of information about firms and shape the responses of customers, suppliers, and competitors. It is sometimes difficult to disentangle reputation from the firm's current asset and market position. However, in our view, reputational assets are best viewed as an intangible asset that enables firms to achieve various goals in the market. Its main value is external, since what is critical about reputation is that it is a kind of summary statistic about the firm's current assets and position, and its likely future behavior. Because there is generally a strong asymmetry between what is known inside the firm and what is known externally, reputations may sometimes be more salient than the true state of affairs, in the sense that external actors must respond to what they know rather than what is knowable.

Structural assets. The formal and informal structure of organizations and their external linkages have an important bearing on the rate and direction of innovation, and how competences and capabilities co-evolve (Argyres, 1995; Teece, 1996). The degree of hierarchy and the level of vertical and lateral integration are elements of

---

[42] Managers often evoke the 'crown jewels' metaphor. That is, if the technology is released, the kingdom will be lost.

firm-specific structure. Distinctive governance modes can be recognized (e.g., multiproduct, integrated firms; high 'flex' firms; virtual corporations; conglomerates), and these modes support different types of innovation to a greater or lesser degree. For instance, virtual structures work well when innovation is autonomous; integrated structures work better for systemic innovations.

Institutional assets. Environments cannot be defined in terms of markets alone. While public policies are usually recognized as important in constraining what firms can do, there is a tendency, particularly by economists, to see these as acting through markets or through incentives. However, institutions themselves are a critical element of the business environment. Regulatory systems, as well as intellectual property regimes, tort laws, and antitrust laws, are also part of the environment. So is the system of higher education and national culture. There are significant national differences here, which is just one of the reasons geographic location matters (Nelson, 1994). Such assets may not be entirely firm specific; firms of different national and regional origin may have quite different institutional assets to call upon because their institutional/policy settings are so different.

Market (structure) assets. Product market position matters, but it is often not at all determinative of the fundamental position of the enterprise in its external environment. Part of the problem lies in defining the market in which a firm competes in a way that gives economic meaning. More importantly, market position in regimes of rapid technological change is often extremely fragile. This is in part because time moves on a different clock in such environments.[43] Moreover, the link between market share and innovation has long been broken, if it ever existed (Teece, 1996). All of this is to suggest that product market position, while important, is too often overplayed. Strategy should be formulated with regard to the more fundamental aspects of firm performance, which we believe are rooted in competences and capabilities and shaped by positions and paths.

Organizational boundaries. An important dimension of 'position' is the location of a firm's boundaries. Put differently, the degree of integration (vertical, lateral, and horizontal) is of quite some significance. Boundaries are not only significant with respect to the technological and complementary assets contained within, but also with respect to the nature of the coordination that can be achieved internally as compared to through markets. When specific assets or poorly protected intellectual capital are at issue, pure market arrangements expose the parties to recontracting hazards or appropriability hazards. In such circumstances, hierarchical control structures may work better than pure arms-length contracts.[44]

Paths

Path dependencies. Where a firm can go is a function of its current position and the paths ahead. Its current position is often shaped by the path it has traveled. In standard economics textbooks, firms have an infinite range of technologies from which they can choose and markets they can occupy. Changes in product or factor prices will be responded to instantaneously, with technologies moving in and out according to value maximization criteria. Only in the short run are irreversibilities recognized. Fixed costs—such as equipment and overheads—cause firms to price below fully amortized costs but never constrain future investment choices. 'Bygones are bygones.' Path dependencies are simply not recognized. This is a major limitation of microeconomic theory.

The notion of path dependencies recognizes that 'history matters.' Bygones are rarely bygones, despite the predictions of rational actor theory. Thus a firm's previous investments and

---

[43] For instance, an Internet year might well be thought of as equivalent to 10 years on many industry clocks, because as much change occurs in the Internet business in a year that occurs in say the auto industry in a decade.

[44] Williamson (1996: 102–103) has observed, failures of coordination may arise because 'parties that bear a long term bilateral dependency relationship to one another must recognize that incomplete contracts require gap filling and sometimes get out of alignment. Although it is always in the collective interest of autonomous parties to fill gaps, correct errors, and affect efficient realignments, it is also the case that the distribution of the resulting gains is indeterminate. Self-interested bargaining predictably obtains. Such bargaining is itself costly. The main costs, however, are that transactions are maladapted to the environment during the bargaining interval. Also, the prospect of ex post bargaining invites ex ante prepositioning of an inefficient kind.'

its repertoire of routines (its 'history') constrain its future behavior.[45] This follows because learning tends to be local. That is, opportunities for learning will be 'close in' to previous activities and thus will be transaction and production specific (Teece, 1988). This is because learning is often a process of trial, feedback, and evaluation. If too many parameters are changed simultaneously, the ability of firms to conduct meaningful natural quasi experiments is attenuated. If many aspects of a firm's learning environment change simultaneously, the ability to ascertain cause–effect relationships is confounded because cognitive structures will not be formed and rates of learning diminish as a result. One implication is that many investments are much longer term than is commonly thought.

The importance of path dependencies is amplified where conditions of increasing returns to adoption exist. This is a demand-side phenomenon, and it tends to make technologies and products embodying those technologies more attractive the more they are adopted. Attractiveness flows from the greater adoption of the product amongst users, which in turn enables them to become more developed and hence more useful. Increasing returns to adoption has many sources including network externalities (Katz and Shapiro, 1985), the presence of complementary assets (Teece, 1986b) and supporting infrastructure (Nelson, 1996), learning by using (Rosenberg, 1982), and scale economies in production and distribution. Competition between and amongst technologies is shaped by increasing returns. Early leads won by good luck or special circumstances (Arthur, 1983) can become amplified by increasing returns. This is not to suggest that first movers necessarily win. Because increasing returns have multiple sources, the prior positioning of firms can affect their capacity to exploit increasing returns. Thus, in Mitchell's (1989) study of medical diagnostic imaging, firms already controlling the relevant complementary assets could in theory start last and finish first.

In the presence of increasing returns, firms can compete passively, or they may compete strate-gically through technology-sponsoring activities.[46] The first type of competition is not unlike biological competition amongst species, although it can be sharpened by managerial activities that enhance the performance of products and processes. The reality is that companies with the best products will not always win, as chance events may cause 'lock-in' on inferior technologies (Arthur, 1983) and may even in special cases generate switching costs for consumers. However, while switching costs may favor the incumbent, in regimes of rapid technological change switching costs can become quickly swamped by switching benefits. Put differently, new products employing different standards often appear with alacrity in market environments experiencing rapid technological change, and incumbents can be readily challenged by superior products and services that yield switching benefits. Thus the degree to which switching costs cause 'lock-in' is a function of factors such as user learning, rapidity of technological change, and the amount of ferment in the competitive environment.

Technological opportunities. The concept of path dependencies is given forward meaning through the consideration of an industry's technological opportunities. It is well recognized that how far and how fast a particular area of industrial activity can proceed is in part due to the technological opportunities that lie before it. Such opportunities are usually a lagged function of foment and diversity in basic science, and the rapidity with which new scientific breakthroughs are being made.

However, technological opportunities may not be completely exogenous to industry, not only because some firms have the capacity to engage in or at least support basic research, but also because technological opportunities are often fed by innovative activity itself. Moreover, the recognition of such opportunities is affected by the

---

[45] For further development, see Bercovitz, de Figueiredo, and Teece, 1996.

[46] Because of huge uncertainties, it may be extremely difficult to determine viable strategies early on. Since the rules of the game and the identity of the players will be revealed only after the market has begun to evolve, the pay-off is likely to lie with building and maintaining organizational capabilities that support flexibility. For example, Microsoft's recent about-face and vigorous pursuit of Internet business once the Net-Scape phenomenon became apparent is impressive, not so much because it perceived the need to change strategy, but because of its organizational capacity to effectuate a strategic shift.

organizational structures that link the institutions engaging in basic research (primarily the university) to the business enterprise. Hence, the existence of technological opportunities can be quite firm specific.

Important for our purposes is the rate and direction in which relevant scientific frontiers are being rolled back. Firms engaging in R&D may find the path dead ahead closed off, though breakthroughs in related areas may be sufficiently close to be attractive. Likewise, if the path dead ahead is extremely attractive, there may be no incentive for firms to shift the allocation of resources away from traditional pursuits. The depth and width of technological opportunities in the neighborhood of a firm's prior research activities thus are likely to impact a firm's options with respect to both the amount and level of R&D activity that it can justify. In addition, a firm's past experience conditions the alternatives management is able to perceive. Thus, not only do firms in the same industry face 'menus' with different costs associated with particular technological choices, they also are looking at menus containing different choices.[47]

Assessment

The essence of a firm's competence and dynamic capabilities is presented here as being resident in the firm's organizational processes, that are in turn shaped by the firm's assets (positions) and its evolutionary path. Its evolutionary path, despite managerial hubris that might suggest otherwise, is often rather narrow.[48] What the firm can do and where it can go are thus rather constrained by its positions and paths. Its competitors are likewise constrained. Rents (profits) thus tend to flow not just from the asset structure of the firm and, as we shall see, the degree of its imitability, but also by the firm's ability to reconfigure and transform.

The parameters we have identified for determining performance are quite different from those in the standard textbook theory of the firm, and in the competitive forces and strategic conflict

approaches to the firm and to strategy.[49] Moreover, the agency theoretic view of the firm as a nexus of contracts would put no weight on processes, positions, and paths. While agency approaches to the firm may recognize that opportunism and shirking may limit what a firm can do, they do not recognize the opportunities and constraints imposed by processes, positions, and paths.

Moreover, the firm in our conceptualization is much more than the sum of its parts—or a team tied together by contracts.[50] Indeed, to some extent individuals can be moved in and out of organizations and, so long as the internal processes and structures remain in place, performance will not necessarily be impaired. A shift in the environment is a far more serious threat to the firm than is the loss of key individuals, as individuals can be replaced more readily than organizations can be transformed. Furthermore, the dynamic capabilities view of the firm would suggest that the behavior and performance of particular firms may be quite hard to replicate, even if its coherence and rationality are observable. This matter and related issues involving replication and imitation are taken up in the section that follows.

Replicability and imitatability of organizational processes and positions

Thus far, we have argued that the competences and capabilities (and hence competitive advantage) of a firm rest fundamentally on processes, shaped by positions and paths. However, competences can provide competitive advantage and generate rents only if they are based on a collection of routines, skills, and complementary assets that are difficult to imitate.[51] A particular set of routines can lose their value if they support a competence which no longer matters in the marketplace, or if they can be readily replicated or emulated by competitors. Imitation occurs when firms discover and simply copy a firm's organizational routines and procedures. Emulation occurs when firms

---

[47] This is a critical element in Nelson and Winter's (1982) view of firms and technical change.
[48] We also recognize that the processes, positions, and paths of customers also matter. See our discussion above on increasing returns, including customer learning and network externalities.

[49] In both the firm is still largely a black box. Certainly, little or no attention is given to processes, positions, and paths.
[50] See Alchian and Demsetz (1972).
[51] We call such competences distinctive. See also Dierickx and Cool (1989) for a discussion of the characteristics of assets which make them a source of rents.

discover alternative ways of achieving the same functionality.[52]

Replication

To understand imitation, one must first understand replication. Replication involves transferring or redeploying competences from one concrete economic setting to another. Since productive knowledge is embodied, this cannot be accomplished by simply transmitting information. Only in those instances where all relevant knowledge is fully codified and understood can replication be collapsed into a simple problem of information transfer. Too often, the contextual dependence of original performance is poorly appreciated, so unless firms have replicated their systems of productive knowledge on many prior occasions, the act of replication is likely to be difficult (Teece, 1976). Indeed, replication and transfer are often impossible absent the transfer of people, though this can be minimized if investments are made to convert tacit knowledge to codified knowledge. Often, however, this is simply not possible.

In short, competences and capabilities, and the routines upon which they rest, are normally rather difficult to replicate.[53] Even understanding what all the relevant routines are that support a particular competence may not be transparent. Indeed, Lippman and Rumelt (1992) have argued that some sources of competitive advantage are so complex that the firm itself, let alone its competitors, does not understand them.[54] As Nelson and Winter (1982) and Teece (1982) have explained, many organizational routines are quite tacit in nature. Imitation can also be hindered by the fact few routines are 'stand-alone;' coherence may require that a change in one set of routines in one part of the firm (e.g., production) requires changes in some other part (e.g., R&D).

Some routines and competences seem to be attributable to local or regional forces that shape firms' capabilities at early stages in their lives. Porter (1990), for example, shows that differences in local product markets, local factor markets, and institutions play an important role in shaping competitive capabilities. Differences also exist within populations of firms from the same country. Various studies of the automobile industry, for example, show that not all Japanese automobile companies are top performers in terms of quality, productivity, or product development (see, for example, Clark and Fujimoto, 1991). The role of firm-specific history has been highlighted as a critical factor explaining such firm-level (as opposed to regional or national-level) differences (Nelson and Winter, 1982). Replication in a different context may thus be rather difficult.

At least two types of strategic value flow from replication. One is the ability to support geographic and product line expansion. To the extent that the capabilities in question are relevant to customer needs elsewhere, replication can confer value.[55] Another is that the ability to replicate also indicates that the firm has the foundations in place for learning and improvement. Considerable empirical evidence supports the notion that the understanding of processes, both in production and in management, is the key to process improvement. In short, an organization cannot improve that which it does not understand. Deep process understanding is often required to accomplish codification. Indeed, if knowledge is highly tacit, it indicates that underlying structures are not well understood, which limits learning because scientific and engineering principles cannot be as systematically applied.[56] Instead, learning is confined to proceeding through trial and error, and the

---

[52] There is ample evidence that a given type of competence (e.g., quality) can be supported by different routines and combinations of skills. For example, the Garvin (1988) and Clark and Fujimoto (1991) studies both indicate that there was no one 'formula' for achieving either high quality or high product development performance.

[53] See Szulanski's (1995) discussion of the intrafirm transfer of best practice. He quotes a senior vice president of Xerox as saying 'you can see a high performance factory or office, but it just doesn't spread. I don't know why.' Szulanski also discusses the role of benchmarking in facilitating the transfer of best practice.

[54] If so, it is our belief that the firm's advantage is likely to fade, as luck does run out.

[55] Needless to say, there are many examples of firms replicating their capabilities inappropriately by applying extant routines to circumstances where they may not be applicable, e.g., Nestle's transfer of developed-country marketing methods for infant formula to the Third World (Hartley, 1989). A key strategic need is for firms to screen capabilities for their applicability to new environments.

[56] Different approaches to learning are required depending on the depth of knowledge. Where knowledge is less articulated and structured, trial and error and learning-by-doing are necessary, whereas in mature environments where the underlying engineering science is better understood, organizations can undertake more deductive approaches or what Pisano (1994) refers to as 'learning-before-doing.'

leverage that might otherwise come from the application of scientific theory is denied.

Imitation

Imitation is simply replication performed by a competitor. If self-replication is difficult, imitation is likely to be harder. In competitive markets, it is the ease of imitation that determines the sustainability of competitive advantage. Easy imitation implies the rapid dissipation of rents.

Factors that make replication difficult also make imitation difficult. Thus, the more tacit the firm's productive knowledge, the harder it is to replicate by the firm itself or its competitors. When the tacit component is high, imitation may well be impossible, absent the hiring away of key individuals and the transfers of key organization processes.

However, another set of barriers impedes imitation of certain capabilities in advanced industrial countries. This is the system of intellectual property rights, such as patents, trade secrets, and trademarks, and even trade dress.[57] Intellectual property protection is of increasing importance in the United States, as since 1982 the legal system has adopted a more pro-patent posture. Similar trends are evident outside the United States. Besides the patent system, several other factors cause there to be a difference between replication costs and imitation costs. The observability of the technology or the organization is one such important factor. Whereas vistas into product technology can be obtained through strategies such as reverse engineering, this is not the case for process technology, as a firm need not expose its process technology to the outside in order to benefit from it.[58] Firms with product technology, on the other hand, confront the unfortunate circumstances that they must expose what they have got in order to profit from the technology. Secrets

are thus more protectable if there is no need to expose them in contexts where competitors can learn about them.

One should not, however, overestimate the overall importance of intellectual property protection; yet it presents a formidable imitation barrier in certain particular contexts. Intellectual property protection is not uniform across products, processes, and technologies, and is best thought of as islands in a sea of open competition. If one is not able to place the fruits of one's investment, ingenuity, or creativity on one or more of the islands, then one indeed is at sea.

We use the term appropriability regimes to describe the ease of imitation. Appropriability is a function both of the ease of replication and the efficacy of intellectual property rights as a barrier to imitation. Appropriability is strong when a technology is both inherently difficult to replicate and the intellectual property system provides legal barriers to imitation. When it is inherently easy to replicate and intellectual property protection is either unavailable or ineffectual, then appropriability is weak. Intermediate conditions also exist.

CONCLUSION

The four paradigms discussed above are quite different, though the first two have much in common with each other (strategizing) as do the last two (economizing). But are these paradigms complementary or competitive? According to some authors, 'the resource perspective complements the industry analysis framework' (Amit and Schoemaker, 1993: 35). While this is undoubtedly true, we think that in several important respects the perspectives are also competitive. While this should be recognized, it is not to suggest that there is only one framework that has value. Indeed, complex problems are likely to benefit from insights obtained from all of the paradigms we have identified plus more. The trick is to work out which frameworks are appropriate for the problem at hand. Slavish adherence to one class to the neglect of all others is likely to generate strategic blindspots. The tools themselves then generate strategic vulnerability. We now explore these issues further. Table 1 summarizes some similarities and differences.

---

[57] Trade dress refers to the 'look and feel' of a retail establishment, e.g., the distinctive marketing and presentation style of The Nature Company.

[58] An interesting but important exception to this can be found in second sourcing. In the microprocessor business, until the introduction of the 386 chip, Intel and most other merchant semi producers were encouraged by large customers like IBM to provide second sources, i.e., to license and share their proprietary process technology with competitors like AMD and NEC. The microprocessor developers did so to assure customers that they had sufficient manufacturing capability to meet demand at all times.

Table 1. Paradigms of strategy: Salient characteristics

Paradigm	Intellectual roots	Representative authors addressing strategic management questions	Nature of rents	Rationality assumptions of managers	Fundamental units of analysis	Short-run capacity for strategic reorientation	Role of industrial structure	Focal concern
(1) Attenuating competitive forces	Mason, Bain	Porter (1980)	Chamberlinean	Rational	Industries, firms, products	High	Exogenous	Structural conditions and competitor positioning
(2) Strategic conflict	Machiavelli, Schelling, Cournot, Nash, Harsanyi, Shapiro	Ghemawat (1986) Shapiro (1989) Brandenburger and Nalebuff (1995)	Chamberlinean	Hyper-rational	Firms, products	Often infinite	Endogenous	Strategic interactions
(3) Resource-based perspectives	Penrose, Selznick, Christensen, Andrews	Rumelt (1984) Chandler (1966) Wernerfelt (1984) Teece (1980, 1982)	Ricardian	Rational	Resources	Low	Endogenous	Asset fungibility
(4) Dynamic capabilities perspective	Schumpeter, Nelson, Winter, Teece	Dosi, Teece, and Winter (1989) Prahalad and Hamel (1990) Hayes and Wheelwright (1984) Dierickx and Cool (1989) Porter (1990)	Schumpeterian	Rational	Processes, positions, paths	Low	Endogenous	Asset accumulation, replicability and inimitability

Efficiency vs. market power

The competitive forces and strategic conflict approaches generally see profits as stemming from strategizing—that is, from limitations on competition which firms achieve through raising rivals' costs and exclusionary behavior (Teece, 1984). The competitive forces approach in particular leads one to see concentrated industries as being attractive—market positions can be shielded behind entry barriers, and rivals costs can be raised. It also suggests that the sources of competitive advantage lie at the level of the industry, or possibly groups within an industry. In text book presentations, there is almost no attention at all devoted to discovering, creating, and commercializing new sources of value.

The dynamic capabilities and resources approaches clearly have a different orientation. They see competitive advantage stemming from high-performance routines operating 'inside the firm,' shaped by processes and positions. Path dependencies (including increasing returns) and technological opportunities mark the road ahead. Because of imperfect factor markets, or more precisely the nontradability of 'soft' assets like values, culture, and organizational experience, distinctive competences and capabilities generally cannot be acquired; they must be built. This sometimes takes years—possibly decades. In some cases, as when the competence is protected by patents, replication by a competitor is ineffectual as a means to access the technology. The capabilities approach accordingly sees definite limits on strategic options, at least in the short run. Competitive success occurs in part because of policies pursued and experience and efficiency obtained in earlier periods.

Competitive success can undoubtedly flow from both strategizing and economizing,[59] but along with Williamson (1991) we believe that 'economizing is more fundamental than strategizing .... or put differently, that economy is the best strategy.'[60] Indeed, we suggest that, except

in special circumstances, too much 'strategizing' can lead firms to underinvest in core competences and neglect dynamic capabilities, and thus harm long-term competitiveness.

Normative implications

The field of strategic management is avowedly normative. It seeks to guide those aspects of general management that have material effects on the survival and success of the business enterprise. Unless these various approaches differ in terms of the framework and heuristics they offer management, then the discourse we have gone through is of limited immediate value. In this paper, we have already alluded to the fact that the capabilities approach tends to steer managers toward creating distinctive and difficult-to-imitate advantages and avoiding games with customers and competitors. We now survey possible differences, recognizing that the paradigms are still in their infancy and cannot confidently support strong normative conclusions.

Unit of analysis and analytic focus

Because in the capabilities and the resources framework business opportunities flow from a firm's unique processes, strategy analysis must be situational.[61] This is also true with the strategic conflict approach. There is no algorithm for creating wealth for the entire industry. Prescriptions they apply to industries or groups of firms at best suggest overall direction, and may indicate errors to be avoided. In contrast, the competitive forces approach is not particularly firm specific; it is industry and group specific.

Strategic change

The competitive forces and the strategic conflict approach, since they pay little attention to skills, know-how, and path dependency, tend to see

[59] Phillips (1971) and Demsetz (1974) also made the case that market concentration resulted from the competitive success of more efficient firms, and not from entry barriers and restrictive practices.
[60] We concur with Williamson that economizing and strategizing are not mutually exclusive. Strategic ploys can be used to disguise inefficiencies and to promote economizing outcomes, as with pricing with reference to learning curve costs. Our view of economizing is perhaps more expansive than

Williamson's as it embraces more than efficient contract design and the minimization of transactions costs. We also address production and organizational economies, and the distinctive ways that things are accomplished inside the business enterprise.
[61] On this point, the strategic conflict and the resources and capabilities are congruent. However, the aspects of 'situation' that matter are dramatically different, as described earlier in this paper.

strategic choice occurring with relative facility. The capabiliies approach sees value augmenting strategic change as being difficult and costly. Moreover, it can generally only occur incrementally. Capabilities cannot easily be bought; they must be built. From the capabilities perspective, strategy involves choosing among and committing to long-term paths or trajectories of competence development.

In this regard, we speculate that the dominance of competitive forces and the strategic conflict approaches in the United States may have something to do with observed differences in strategic approaches adopted by some U.S. and some foreign firms. Hayes (1985) has noted that American companies tend to favor 'strategic leaps' while, in contrast, Japanese and German companies tend to favor incremental, but rapid, improvements.

Entry strategies

Here the resources and the capabilities approaches suggest that entry decisions must be made with reference to the competences and capabilities which new entrants have, relative to the competition. Whereas the other approaches tell you little about where to look to find likely entrants, the capabilities approach identifies likely entrants. Relatedly, whereas the entry deterrence approach suggests an unconstrained search for new business opportunities, the capabilities approach suggests that such opportunities lie close in to one's existing business. As Richard Rumelt has explained it in conversation, 'the capabilities approach suggests that if a firm looks inside itself, and at its market environment, sooner or later it will find a business opportunity.'

Entry timing

Whereas the strategic conflict approach tells little abut where to look to find likely entrants, the resources and the capabilities approach identifies likely entrants and their timing of entry. Brittain and Freeman (1980) using population ecology methodologies argued that an organization is quick to expand when there is a significant overlap between its core capabilities and those needed to survive in a new market. Recent research (Mitchell, 1989) showed that the more industry-specialized assets or capabilities a firm possesses, the more likely it is to enter an emerging techni-

cal subfield in its industry, following a technological discontinuity. Additionally, the interaction between specialized assets such as firm-specific capabilities and rivalry had the greatest influence on entry timing.

Diversification

Related diversification—that is, diversification that builds upon or extends existing capabilities—is about the only form of diversification that a resources/capabilities framework is likely to view as meritorious (Rumelt, 1974; Teece, 1980, 1982; Teece *et al.*, 1994). Such diversification will be justifiable when the firms' traditional markets decline.[62] The strategic conflict approach is likely to be a little more permissive; acquisitions that raise rivals' costs or enable firms to effectuate exclusive arrangements are likely to be seen as efficacious in certain circumstances.

Focus and specialization

Focus needs to be defined in terms of distinctive competences or capability, not products. Products are the manifestation of competences, as competences can be molded into a variety of products. Product market specialization and decentalization configured around product markets may cause firms to neglect the development of core competences and dynamic capabilities, to the extent to which competences require accessing assets across divisions.

The capabilities approach places emphasis on the internal processes that a firm utilizes, as well as how they are deployed and how they will evolve. The approach has the benefit of indicating that competitive advantage is not just a function of how one plays the game; it is also a function of the 'assets' one has to play with, and how these assets can be deployed and redeployed in a changing market.

---

[62] Cantwell shows that the technological competence of firms persists over time, gradually evolving through firm-specific learning. He shows that technological diversification has been greater for chemicals and pharmaceuticals than for electrical and electronic-related fields., and he offers as an explanation the greater straight-ahead opportunities in electrical and electronic fields than in chemicals and pharmaceuticals. See Cantwell (1993).

Future directions

We have merely sketched an outline for a dynamic capabilities approach. Further theoretical work is needed to tighten the framework, and empirical research is critical to helping us understand how firms get to be good, how they sometimes stay that way, why and how they improve, and why they sometimes decline.[63] Researchers in the field of strategy need to join forces with researchers in the fields of innovation, manufacturing, and organizational behavior and business history if they are to unlock the riddles that lie behind corporate as well as national competitive advantage. There could hardly be a more ambitious research agenda in the social sciences today.

ACKNOWLEDGEMENTS

Research for this paper was aided by support from the Alfred P. Sloan Foundation through the Consortium on Competitiveness and Cooperation at the University of California, Berkeley. The authors are grateful for helpful comments from two anonymous referees, as well as from Raffi Amit, Jay Barney, Joseph Bower, Henry Chesbrough, Giovanni Dosi, Sumantra Goshal, Pankaj Ghemawat, Connie Helfat, Rebecca Henderson, Dan Levinthal, Richard Nelson, Margie Peteraf, Richard Rosenbloom, Richard Rumelt, Carl Shapiro, Oliver Williamson, and Sidney Winter. Useful feedback was obtained from workshops at the Haas School of Business, the Wharton School, the Kellogg School (Northwestern), the Harvard Business School, and the International Institute of Applied Systems Analysis (IIASA) in Vienna, the London School of Economics, and the London Business School.

REFERENCES

Abernathy, W. J. and K. Clark (1985). 'Innovation: Mapping the winds of creative destruction', *Research Policy*, 14, pp. 3–22.

---

[63] For a gallant start, see Miyazaki (1995) and McGrath *et al.* (1996). Chandler's (1990) work on scale and scope, summarized in Teece (1993), provides some historical support for the capabilities approach. Other relevant studies can be found in a special issue of *Industrial and Corporate Change* 3(3), 1994, that was devoted to dynamic capabilities.

Alchian, A. A. and H. Demsetz (1972). 'Production, information costs, and economic organization', *American Economic Review*, 62, pp. 777–795.

Amit, R. and P. Schoemaker (1993). 'Strategic assets and organizational rent', *Strategic Management Journal* 14(1), pp. 33–46.

Andrews, K. (1987). *The Concept of Corporate Strategy* (3rd ed.). Dow Jones-Irwin, Homewood, IL.

Aoki, M. (1990). 'The participatory generation of information rents and the theory of the firm'. In M. Aoki, B. Gustafsson and O. E. Williamson (eds.), *The Firm as a Nexus of Treaties*. Sage, London, pp. 26–52.

Argyres, N. (1995). 'Technology strategy, governance structure and interdivisional coordination', *Journal of Economic Behavior and Organization*, 28, pp. 337–358.

Argyris, C. and D. Schon (1978). *Organizational Learning*. Addison-Wesley, Reading, MA.

Arrow, K. (1969). 'The organization of economic activity: Issues pertinent to the choice of market vs. nonmarket allocation'. In *The Analysis and Evaluation of Public Expenditures: The PPB System, 1*. U.S. Joint Economic Committee, 91st Session. U.S. Government Printing Office, Washington, DC, pp. 59–73.

Arrow, K. (1996) 'Technical information and industrial structure', *Industrial and Corporate Change*, 5(2), pp. 645–652.

Arthur, W. B. (1983). 'Competing technologies and lock-in by historical events: The dynamics of allocation under increasing returns', working paper WP-83-90, International Institute for Applied Systems Analysis, Laxenburg, Austria.

Bain, J. S. (1959). *Industrial Organization*. Wiley, New York.

Baldwin, C. and K. Clark (1991). 'Capabilities and capital investment: New perspectives on capital budgeting', Harvard Business School working paper #92–004.

Barney, J. B. (1986). 'Strategic factor markets: Expectations, luck, and business strategy', *Management Science* 32(10), pp. 1231–1241.

Barney, J. B., J.-C. Spender and T. Reve (1994). *Crafoord Lectures*, Vol. 6. Chartwell-Bratt, Bromley, U.K. and Lund University Press, Lund, Sweden.

Baumol, W., J. Panzar and R. Willig (1982). *Contestable Markets and the Theory of Industry Structure*. Harcourt Brace Jovanovich, New York.

Bercovitz, J. E. L., J. M. de Figueiredo and D. J. Teece (1996). 'Firm capabilities and managerial decision-making: A theory of innovation biases'. In R. Garud, P. Nayyar and Z. Shapira (eds), *Innovation: Oversights and Foresights*. Cambridge University Press, Cambridge, U.K. pp. 233–259.

Brandenburger, A. M. and B. J. Nalebuff (1996). *Co-opetition*. Doubleday, New York.

Brandenburger, A. M. and B. J. Nalebuff (1995). 'The right game: Use game theory to shape strategy', *Harvard Business Review*, 73(4), pp. 57–71.

Brittain, J. and J. Freeman (1980). 'Organizational proliferation and density-dependent selection'. In J. R. Kimberly and R. Miles (eds.), *The Organizational*

Life Cycle. Jossey-Bass, San Francisco, CA, pp. 291–338.

Camp, R. (1989). *Benchmarking: The Search for Industry Best practices that Lead to Superior Performance*. Quality Press, Milwaukee, WI.

Cantwell, J. (1993). 'Corporate technological specialization in international industries'. In M. Casson and J. Creedy (eds.), *Industrial Concentration and Economic Inequality*. Edward Elgar, Aldershot, pp. 216–232.

Chandler, A.D., Jr. (1966). *Strategy and Structure*. Doubleday, Anchor Books Edition, New York.

Chandler, A. D., Jr. (1990). *Scale and Scope: The Dynamics of Industrial Competition*. Harvard University Press, Cambridge, MA.

Clark, K. and T. Fujimoto (1991). *Product Development Performance: Strategy, Organization and Management in the World Auto Industries*. Harvard Buiness School Press, Cambridge, MA.

Coase, R. (1937). 'The nature of the firm', *Economica*, **4**, pp. 386–405.

Coase, R. (1988). 'Lecture on the Nature of the Firm, III', *Journal of Law, Economics and Organization*, **4**, pp. 33–47.

Cool, K. and D. Schendel (1988). 'Performance differences among strategic group members', *Strategic Management Journal*, **9**(3), pp. 207–223.

de Figueiredo, J. M. and D. J. Teece (1996). 'Mitigating procurement hazards in the context of innovation', *Industrial and Corporate Change*, **5**(2), pp. 537–559.

Demsetz, H. (1974). 'Two systems of belief about monopoly'. In H. Goldschmid, M. Mann and J. F. Weston (eds.), *Industrial Concentration: The New Learning*. Little, Brown, Boston, MA, pp. 161–184.

Dierickx, I. and K. Cool (1989). 'Asset stock accumulation and sustainability of competitive advantage', *Management Science*, **35**(12), pp. 1504–1511.

Dixit, A. (1980). 'The role of investment in entry deterrence', *Economic Journal*, **90**, pp. 95–106.

Dosi, G., D. J. Teece and S. Winter (1989). 'Toward a theory of corporate coherence: Preliminary remarks', unpublished paper, Center for Research in Management, University of California at Berkeley.

Doz, Y. and A. Shuen (1990). 'From intent to outcome: A process framework for partnerships', INSEAD working paper.

Fama, E. F. (1980). 'Agency problems and the theory of the firm', *Journal of Political Economy*, **88**, pp. 288–307.

Freeman, J. and W. Boeker (1984). 'The ecological analysis of business strategy'. In G. Carroll and D. Vogel (eds.), *Strategy and Organization*. Pitman, Boston, MA, pp. 64–77.

Fujimoto, T. (1994). 'Reinterpreting the resource-capability view of the firm: A case of the development-production systems of the Japanese automakers', draft working paper, Faculty of Economics, University of Tokyo.

Garvin, D. (1988). *Managing Quality*. Free Press, New York.

Garvin, D. (1994). 'The processes of organization and management', Harvard Business School working paper #94–084.

Ghemawat, P. (1986). 'Sustainable advantage', *Harvard Business Review*, **64**(5), pp. 53–58.

Ghemawat, P. (1991). *Commitment: The Dynamics of Strategy*. Free Press, New York.

Gilbert, R. J. and D. M. G. Newberry (1982). 'Preemptive patenting and the persistence of monopoly', *American Economic Review*, **72**, pp. 514–526.

Gittell, J. H. (1995). 'Cross functional coordination, control and human resource systems: Evidence from the airline industry', unpublished Ph.D. thesis, Massachusetts Institute of Technology.

Hansen, G. S. and B. Wernerfelt (1989). 'Determinants of firm performance: The relative importance of economic and organizational factors', *Strategic Management Journal*, **10**(5), pp. 399–411.

Hartley, R. F. (1989). *Marketing Mistakes*. Wiley, New York.

Hayes, R. (1985). 'Strategic planning: Forward in reverse', *Harvard Business Review*, **63**(6), pp. 111–119.

Hayes, R. and K. Clark (1985). 'Exploring the sources of productivity differences at the factory level'. In K. Clark, R. H. Hayes and C. Lorenz (eds.), *The Uneasy Alliance: Managing the Productivity-Technology Dilemma*. Harvard Business School Press, Boston, MA, pp. 151–188.

Hayes, R. and S. Wheelwright (1984). *Restoring our Competitive Edge: Competing Through Manufacturing*. Wiley, New York.

Hayes, R., S. Wheelwright and K. Clark (1988). *Dynamic Manufacturing: Creating the Learning Organization*. Free Press, New York.

Henderson, R. M. (1994). 'The evolution of integrative capability: Innovation in cardiovascular drug discovery', *Industrial and Corporate Change*, **3**(3), pp. 607–630.

Henderson, R. M. and K. B. Clark (1990). 'Architectural innovation: The reconfiguration of existing product technologies and the failure of established firms', *Administrative Science Quarterly*, **35**, pp. 9–30.

Henderson, R. M. and I. Cockburn (1994). 'Measuring competence? Exploring firm effects in pharmaceutical research, *Strategic Management Journal*, Summer Special Issue, **15**, pp. 63–84.

Iansiti, M. and K. B. Clark (1994). 'Integration and dynamic capability: Evidence from product development in automobiles and mainframe computers', *Industrial and Corporate Change*, **3**(3), pp. 557–605.

Itami, H. and T. W. Roehl (1987). *Mobilizing Invisible Assets*. Harvard University Press, Cambridge, MA.

Jacobsen, R. (1988). 'The persistence of abnormal returns', *Strategic Management Journal*, **9**(5), pp. 415–430.

Katz, M. and C. Shapiro (1985). 'Network externalities, competition and compatibility', *American Economic Review*, **75**, pp. 424–440.

Kreps, D. M. and R. Wilson (1982a). 'Sequential equilibria', *Econometrica*, **50**, pp. 863–894.

Kreps, D. M. and R. Wilson (1982b). 'Reputation and imperfect information', *Journal of Economic Theory*, **27**, pp. 253–279.

Langlois, R. (1994). 'Cognition and capabilities:

Opportunities seized and missed in the history of the computer industry', working paper, University of Connecticut. Presented at the conference on Technological Oversights and Foresights, Stern School of Business, New York University, 11–12 March 1994.

Learned, E., C. Christensen, K. Andrews and W. Guth (1969). *Business Policy: Text and Cases*. Irwin, Homewood, IL.

Leonard-Barton, D. (1992). 'Core capabilities and core rigidities: A paradox in managing new product development', *Strategic Management Journal*, Summer Special Issue, **13**, pp. 111–125.

Leonard-Barton, D. (1995). *Wellsprings of Knowledge*. Harvard Business School Press, Boston, MA.

Lev, B. and T. Sougiannis (1992). 'The capitalization, amortization and value-relevance of R&D', unpublished manuscript, University of California, Berkeley, and University of Illinois, Urbana–Champaign.

Levinthal, D. and J. March (1981). 'A model of adaptive organizational search', *Journal of Economic Behavior and Organization*, **2**, pp. 307–333.

Levinthal, D. A. and J. G. March (1993). 'The myopia of learning', *Strategic Management Journal*, Winter Special Issue, **14**, pp. 95–112.

Levinthal, D. and J. Myatt (1994). 'Co-evolution of capabilities and industry: The evolution of mutual fund processing', *Strategic Management Journal*, Winter Special Issue, **15**, pp. 45–62.

Levitt, B. and J. March (1988). 'Organizational learning', *Annual Review of Sociology*, **14**, pp. 319–340.

Link, A. N., D. J. Teece and W. F. Finan (October 1996). 'Estimating the benefits from collaboration: The Case of SEMATECH', *Review of Industrial Organization*, **11**, pp. 737–751.

Lippman, S. A. and R. P. Rumelt (1992) 'Demand uncertainty and investment in industry-specific capital', *Industrial and Corporate Change*, **1**(1), pp. 235–262.

Mahoney, J. (1995). 'The management of resources and the resources of management', *Journal of Business Research*, **33**(2), pp. 91–101.

Mahoney, J. T. and J. R. Pandian (1992). 'The resource-based view within the conversation of strategic management', *Strategic Management Journal*, **13**(5), pp. 363–380.

Mason, E. (1949). 'The current state of the monopoly problem in the U.S.', *Harvard Law Review*, **62**, pp. 1265–1285.

McGrath, R. G., M-H. Tsai, S. Venkataraman and I. C. MacMillan (1996). 'Innovation, competitive advantage and rent: A model and test', *Management Science*, **42**(3), pp. 389–403.

Milgrom, P. and J. Roberts (1982a). 'Limit pricing and entry under incomplete information: An equilibrium analysis', *Econometrica*, **50**, pp. 443–459.

Milgrom, P. and J. Roberts (1982b). 'Predation, reputation and entry deterrence', *Journal of Economic Theory*, **27**, pp. 280–312.

Milgrom, P. and J. Roberts (1990). 'The economics of modern manufacturing: Technology, strategy, and organization', *American Economic Review*, **80**(3), pp. 511–528.

Mitchell, W. (1989). 'Whether and when? Probability and timing of incumbents' entry into emerging industrial subfields', *Administrative Science Quarterly*, **34**, pp. 208–230.

Miyazaki, K. (1995). *Building Competences in the Firm: Lessons from Japanese and European Optoelectronics*. St. Martins Press, New York.

Mody, A. (1993). 'Learning through alliances', *Journal of Economic Behavior and Organization*, **20**(2), pp. 151–170.

Nelson, R. R. (1991). 'Why do firms differ, and how does it matter?' *Strategic Management Journal*, Winter Special Issue, **12**, pp. 61–74.

Nelson, R. R. (1994). 'The co-evolution of technology, industrial structure, and supporting institutions', *Industrial and Corporate Change*, **3**(1), pp. 47–63.

Nelson, R. (1996). 'The evolution of competitive or comparative advantage: A preliminary report on a study', WP-96-21, International Institute for Applied Systems Analysis, Laxemberg, Austria.

Nelson, R. and S. Winter (1982). *An Evolutionary Theory of Economic change*. Harvard University Press, Cambridge, MA.

Penrose, E. (1959). *The Theory of the Growth of the Firm*. Basil Blackwell, London.

Phillips, A. C. (1971). *Technology and Market Structure*. Lexington Books, Toronto.

Pisano, G. (1994). 'Knowledge integration and the locus of learning: An empirical analysis of process development', *Strategic Management Journal*, Winter Special Issue, **15**, pp. 85–100.

Porter, M. E. (1980). *Competitive Strategy*. Free Press, New York.

Porter, M. E. (1990). *The Competitive Advantage of Nations*. Free Press, New York.

Prahalad, C. K. and G. Hamel (1990). 'The core competence of the corporation', *Harvard Business Review*, **68**(3), pp. 79–91.

Richardson, G. B. H. (1960, 1990). *Information and Investment*. Oxford University Press, New York.

Rosenberg, N. (1982). *Inside the Black Box: Technology and Economics*. Cambridge University Press, Cambridge, MA

Rumelt, R. P. (1974). *Strategy, Structure, and Economic Performance*. Harvard University Press, Cambridge. MA.

Rumelt, R. P. (1984). 'Towards a strategic theory of the firm'. In R. B. Lamb (ed.), *Competitive Strategic Management*. Prentice-Hall, Englewood Cliffs, NJ, pp. 556–570.

Rumelt, R. P. (1991). 'How much does industry matter?', *Strategic Management Journal*, **12**(3), pp. 167–185.

Rumelt, R. P., D. Schendel and D. Teece (1994). *Fundamental Issues in Strategy*. Harvard Business School Press, Cambridge, MA.

Schmalensee, R. (1983). 'Advertising and entry deterrence: An exploratory model', *Journal of Political Economy*, **91**(4), pp. 636–653.

Schumpeter, J. A. (1934). *Theory of Economic Development*. Harvard University Press, Cambridge, MA.

Schumpeter, J. A. (1942). *Capitalism, Socialism, and Democracy*. Harper, New York.

Shapiro, C. (1989). 'The theory of business strategy', *RAND Journal of Economics*, 20(1), pp. 125–137.

Shuen, A. (1994). 'Technology sourcing and learning strategies in the semiconductor industry', unpublished Ph.D. dissertation, University of California, Berkeley.

Sutton, J. (1992). 'Implementing game theoretical models in industrial economies', In A. Del Monte (ed.), *Recent Developments in the Theory of Industrial Organization*. University of Michigan Press, Ann Arbor, MI, pp. 19–33.

Szulanski, G. (1995). 'Unpacking stickiness: An empirical investigation of the barriers to transfer best practice inside the firm', *Academy of Management Journal*, Best Papers Proceedings, pp. 437–441.

Teece, D. J. (1976). *The Multinational Corporation and the Resource Cost of International Technology Transfer*. Ballinger, Cambridge, MA.

Teece, D. J. (1980). 'Economics of scope and the scope of the enterprise', *Journal of Economic Behavior and Organization*, 1, pp. 223–247.

Teece, D. J. (1981). 'The market for know-how and the efficient international transfer of technology', *Annals of the Academy of Political and Social Science*, 458, pp. 81–96.

Teece, D. J. (1982). 'Towards an economic theory of the multiproduct firm', *Journal of Economic Behavior and Organization*, 3, pp. 39–63.

Teece, D. J. (1984). 'Economic analysis and strategic management', *California Management Review*, 26(3), pp. 87–110.

Teece, D. J. (1986a). 'Transactions cost economics and the multinational enterprise', *Journal of Economic Behavior and Organization*, 7, pp. 21–45.

Teece, D. J. (1986b). 'Profiting from technological innovation', *Research Policy*, 15(6), pp. 285–305.

Teece, D. J. 1988. 'Technological change and the nature of the firm'. In G. Dosi, C. Freeman, R. Nelson, G. Silverberg and L. Soete (eds.), *Technical Change and Economic Theory*. Pinter Publishers, New York, pp. 256–281.

Teece, D. J. (1992). 'Competition, cooperation, and innovation: Organizational arrangements for regimes of rapid technological progress', *Journal of Economic Behavior and Organization*, 18(1), pp. 1–25.

Teece, D. J. (1993). 'The dynamics of industrial capitalism: Perspectives on Alfred Chandler's *Scale and Scope* (1990)', *Journal of Economic Literature*, 31(1), pp. 199–225.

Teece, D. J. (1996) 'Firm organization, industrial structure, and technological innovation', *Journal of Economic Behavior and Organization*, 31, pp. 193–224.

Teece, D. J. and G. Pisano (1994). 'The dynamic capabilities of firms: An introduction', *Industrial and Corporate Change*, 3(3), pp. 537–556.

Teece, D. J., R. Rumelt, G. Dosi and S. Winter (1994). 'Understanding corporate coherence: Theory and evidence', *Journal of Economic Behavior and Organization*, 23, pp. 1–30.

Tushman, M. L., W. H. Newman and E. Romanelli (1986). 'Convergence and upheaval: Managing the unsteady pace of organizational evolution', *California Management Review*, 29(1), pp. 29–44.

Wernerfelt, B. (1984). 'A resource-based view of the firm', *Strategic Management Journal*, 5(2), pp. 171–180.

Wernerfelt, B. and C. Montgomery (1988). 'Tobin's Q and the importance of focus in firm performance', *American Economic Review*, 78(1), pp. 246–250.

Williamson, O. E. (1975). *Markets and Hierarchies*. Free Press, New York.

Williamson, O. E. (1985). *The Economic Institutions of Capitalism*. Free Press, New York.

Williamson, O. E. (1991). 'Strategizing, economizing, and economic organization', *Strategic Management Journal*, Winter Special Issue, 12, pp. 75–94.

Williamson, O. E. (1996) *The Mechanisms of Governance*. Oxford University Press, New York.

Womack, J., D. Jones and D. Roos (1991). *The Machine that Changed the World*. Harper-Perennial, New York.

Zander, U. and B. Kogut (1995). 'Knowledge and the speed of the transfer and imitation of organizational capabilities: An empirical test', *Organization Science*, 6(1), pp. 76–92.

Dynamic capabilities, competence and the behavioral theory of the firm

J. Lamar Pierce, Christopher S. Boerner and David J. Teece

1 INTRODUCTION

Among the scores of articles and books that have helped to shape how economists conceptualize organizations, Richard Cyert and James March's *A Behavioral Theory of the Firm* stands in a class by itself. It is difficult to overstate the influence this work has had on our understanding of the internal organization, operations, and performance of firms. Paramount among Cyert and March's achievements was their effort to open up the world of economics to organization theory. Whereas the economics profession had once viewed itself as somehow removed from other social science disciplines, Cyert and March (along with their colleagues in the Carnegie School) put economics in touch with research in sociology, political science, social psychology and law. In doing so, they distilled new and important insights into the structure and performance of economic organizations, and made internal organization, decision making, and the behavior of firms a subject of serious enquiry. As Oliver Williamson observes, 'The *Behavioral Theory of the Firm* joined economics and organization theory to pry open what had been a black box, in order to examine the business firm in more operationally engaging ways' (Williamson 1996, p. 23).

While the influence of Cyert and March on subsequent work in economics, notably transaction cost and agency theory, is well established, one significant aspect of this work that is frequently overlooked is the role it has played in the development of theories of firm strategy, particularly those relating to the importance of firm competencies and dynamic capabilities. These theories, which focus on the internal characteristics and differential abilities of firms to adapt to and exploit changing environments, draw upon Cyert and March and related literature. While the behavioral theory of the firm provides no proposal for managers seeking to change firm behavior, noting that firms 'solve pressing problems rather than develop long-run strategies' (1963, p. 119), it has unquestionably provided rich insight into business and corporate strategy. This chapter identifies the elements of *A Behavioral Theory* critical in the development of these approaches, and establishes the extent of its influence by showing the epistemological lineage between them.

In the next section we review the key aspects of *A Behavioral Theory of the Firm* that relate to firm strategy. Section 3 traces how these concepts have been applied and extended in various theories of firm strategy. Particular attention is paid to the role Cyert and March's work has played in subsequent work on firm competencies (Section 4) and capabilities (Section 5). The final section provides concluding remarks and directions for future research.

Reprinted with permission from *The Economics of Choice, Change and Organization: Essays in Memory of Richard M. Cyert* (Edward Elgar, 2002), edited by Mie Augier and James G. March, pp. 81–95.

2   THE BEHAVIORAL THEORY OF THE FIRM

When Cyert and March's work appeared in 1963, the utility of conceptualizing the firm as a production function had already been repeatedly challenged in the academic literature. While scholars such as Ronald Coase, Herbert Simon, and Edith Penrose had put forward building blocks for a new approach, the neoclassical view of the firm still predominated. The assumptions of the neoclassical view were that the firm enjoyed perfect information and certainty about environmental outcomes, it suffered no control or adaptability problems, it maximized profit, and it suffered no dysfunctional internal resource allocation problems. Its strategies and performance were predictable, it manufactured and assembled tangible components, and it sold its output in final product markets. These assumptions provided for a very simple and manageable treatment of the firm which could be integrated into neoclassical price theory; but it was not a good abstraction of a firm's internal organization.[1] Indeed, the neoclassical model failed to recognize firm heterogeneity, strategic behavior, and performance.

Meanwhile, early organizational theorists had focused on the internal characteristics that accounted for this diversity of organization. Sociological and social psychological approaches examined the decision-making processes, efficiency of individuals and small groups, and the coordination of effort (Gouldner 1954; Blau 1955; Argyris 1960; Likert 1961). While the work of organizational theorists had yielded insights into the decision processes employed by humans and in organizations, they had failed to relate this understanding specifically to the context of the firm. Their theories did not address the unique environmental and decision variables facing this particular form of organization.

Thus while the work of organizational theorists formed a basis for analysing the structure and actions of organizations, they had by no means developed a theory of the firm. Endeavoring to fill this void, Cyert and March set out to develop a theory that 'takes (1) the firm as its basic unit, (2) the prediction of firm behavior with respect to such decisions as price, output, and resource allocation as its objective, and (3) an explicit emphasis on the actual process of organizational decision making as its basic research commitment' (1963, p. 19). Against these goals, the shortfalls of earlier theories are clear. Although the neoclassical view addresses (1) and (2), it fails to approach the actual processes of condition (3). Likewise, organizational theory satisfies (1) and (3), yet fails to predict the components of firm behavior in (2). Cyert and March sought to create a theory that met all these challenges and, in doing so, develop the language necessary for a robust theoretical discussion of the firm.

Cyert and March argue that a behavioral theory of the firm requires attention to organizational goals, expectations, choice, and control. Only through these characteristics can one truly understand how firms function. Their subtheory on organizational goals focuses on how coalitions of individuals bargain to determine the goals of the greater organization. While the goals of individuals within a coalition may be disparate, so long as the resources available are greater than the demands of the members, the coalition, and thus the organization, will be feasible. At any given time, organizations will have numerous goals pertaining to each of the diverse decision variables facing them. These goals must address a variety of subjects including sales, market share, profit, inventory, and production levels.

Organizational expectations focus on how a firm gathers and interprets information from its environment. Unlike the traditional theory of expectations, Cyert and March do not assume that firms are able to gather all the relevant information and perfectly calculate expected outcomes.

Firms are heterogeneous entities without perfect knowledge of potential costs, returns, and probability distributions. The search for and processing of information is not simply another use for firm resources. Search is initially unsystematic, with commitments to action occurring early in the search process. The intensity of the search increases as the implementation of the action nears. Firms use rather simple computations to process the gathered information, since the gamut of alternative actions is not readily available. Feasibility and improvement on current procedures are the necessary hurdles for the implementation of new procedures. In addition, the analysis of information and the calculation of expectation in the firm is inherently biased, either through the hopes and aspirations of individuals or subunits, or through the bargaining needs of any coalition. Finally, communication is not perfect within the organization. Communication may be biased, and individuals may attempt in their communication to eliminate this bias. Information therefore cannot flow seamlessly through the firm without distortion, manipulation, and misunderstanding.

Cyert and March present the firm as adaptively rational, where its learning and behavior are conditioned by its experience. The adaptive nature of the firm is focused in the firm's learning and memory, which are operationalized in the form of standard operating procedures and decision rules. These standard operating procedures include general choice procedures and specific operating procedures. General choice procedures address three principles: avoid uncertainty, maintain the rules, and use simple rules. These general choice procedures have been learned through the firm's past environmental conditions and internal constraints. Consequently, general choice procedures tend to be extremely stable in the long run and change only with considerable pressure.

Specific standard operating procedures also change slowly, but can be adjusted with concentrated effort. These procedures are the unique characteristics of the firm, which define and determine how the firm reacts to stimuli and situations. Some of these procedures may be codified to achieve consistency in organizational protocol, but other procedures may be tacit in nature. Standard operating procedures can therefore entail everything from the temperature at which coffee is served in a restaurant to the tacit search of applications for basic research. These specific standard operating procedures highly differentiate even those firms producing similar products by creating embedded differences in every common task they perform. Procedures are highly fixed and difficult to change, and therefore represent dissimilarities relatively invulnerable to market transactions.

The four major types of specific standard operating procedures are task performance rules, continuing records and reports, information handling rules, and plans. Task performance rules deal with the specification of methods for accomplishing a variety of tasks, including pricing, and production and accounting procedures. These rules need to be consistent within the organization in order to facilitate coordination between units performing indelibly linked tasks. If units are unable to understand and predict how complementary tasks will be performed, they may hinder one another with conflicting decisions. Task performance rules strictly define the parameters within which one can accomplish a task. This may include production line tasks as well as more complicated engineering and design solutions. These rules are persistent, though they may change as new ideas and rules are brought in with labor movement.

Continuing records and reports concern the documentation and codification of all elements of business operations important to the firm. Records and reports are the way in which a firm controls its procedures and predicts future outcomes and environments. They also control how information is stored and disseminated throughout the firm, an element critical to the firm's ability to monitor adherence to standard procedures. Recording procedures also determine the level of codification of standard operating procedures, a concept extremely important in the replicability and imitability of all procedures. In a related fashion, information handling rules define how the firm absorbs, transmits, and exports information. These procedures dictate what information the firm will perceive in its outside environment, which is critical to its ability to recognize opportunity and potential threats. The transmission of information influences how different components of the firm assimilate outside information, and whether or not this information is analysed and applied within the firm. These procedures have wide-ranging effects for technology adoption and process improvements. Technological spillovers from outside the firm and among intrafirm organizations are dependent on the codified and tacit procedures for information transmission and dissemination. Firms unable to effectively gain outside knowledge and share process improvements will innovate with limited success and will be slow to adapt to a changing environment. These procedures also relate to information leaving the firm, or potentially its protection of intellectual property. Clearly the firm does not want its innovations distributed among its competitors, therefore it will establish strict protocols regarding confidentiality and information releases.

Plan procedures define how resources will be allocated, including both short-run and long-run budgets and expenditures. These procedures have significant influences on the firm's long-run success in that they determine which aspects of the organization will receive priority support. Research and development funding is an integral part of a firm's ability to evolve and grow, and plan procedures dictate the relative support these activities will receive. A firm whose plan procedures do not support innovation is unlikely to survive over long periods of time. More specifically, what types and areas of research and development are supported will tend to determine the firm's potential evolution. Plan procedures can define the firm's intent and ability to innovate and evolve its dynamic capabilities in particular directions.

3   THE BEHAVIORAL THEORY OF THE FIRM AND STRATEGY

While *A Behavioral Theory* provided a revolutionary view of the internal characteristics of the firm, strategic and managerial considerations were not the focus of attention. The goal was not to explain market behavior, but rather to understand decisions and actions inside the firm. Cyert and March believed that organizations were incapable of following specific, unified objectives. Such specific objectives are critical to the establishment of corporate strategy, and without this ability, managers could influence the direction of the firm only marginally. Any objectives agreed upon by a management coalition would inevitably be highly ambiguous goals, enfeebling the ability of a top manager or entrepreneur to truly control the direction of the firm. Cyert and March argued that while 'individuals have goals; collectivities of people do not' (1992, p. 30), and thus the firm could not have well-defined objectives.

Premised on this weak (or the absence of) leadership, *A Behavioral Theory* posits that the firm's strategies and learning processes are short term in focus with adaptations induced by crises. Management is unable to reconfigure internal resources because of the immutability of standard operating procedures and the ambiguity of coalition goals. In his discussion of firm strategy, Oliver Williamson notes that in Cyert and March 'the firm resembles a fire department more than a strategic actor' (1999, p. 14). The firm is focused on finding solutions to immediate problems, not on longer-term strategic options. Although *A Behavioral Theory* 'can not articulate a serious policy proposal for changing the behavior pattern' (Cyert and March 1963, p. 297), it nevertheless provides a greater understanding of the limitations to strategic action. The understanding of how routines and path dependency limit and enable the firm to solve problems was an important step in the development of the strategy literature.

Diverse fields have benefited from *A Behavioral Theory*'s diligent integration of economics and organizational theory. Since the publishing of this book, numerous approaches to understanding the nature of the firm have emerged, most recently theories regarding the importance of various internal firm competencies and capabilities. While this still-emerging literature has helped to reshape our understanding of the nature of the firm, many of its basic insights can be traced to Cyert and March's work in *A Behavioral Theory*.

Perhaps the most basic contribution of Cyert and March to this literature is their recognition of the fundamental importance of firm heterogeneity. Their work presents the firm as a complex organization defined by its unique goals, expectations, and standard operating procedures. Because each firm is uniquely defined by these aspects, firms are heterogeneous and thus not easily modeled. This heterogeneity creates inequalities in both short- and long-term performance, as each firm's unique characteristics make it better or worse suited than its rivals to succeed in a given environment. Cyert and March's analysis of the internal organization of the firm eliminates the possibility of the neoclassical competitive market. A market will never reach equilibrium with identical firms earning the same minimal level of profits. Diversity in firm standard operating procedures within an industry will inevitably produce differential results among competitors, heterogeneity that cannot be explained by industry-level effects. This performance heterogeneity has been subsequently examined and verified by several empirical studies (Jacobson 1988; Hansen and Wernerfelt 1989). Cool and Schendel (1988) have shown that there are systematic and significant differences in performance among firms belonging to the same strategic group within the US pharmaceutical industry. Additionally, Rumelt (1991) found intra-industry profit heterogeneity to be greater than inter-industry differences in profits, suggesting the relative importance of firm-related sources of performance. In a sense, Cyert and March's assertions about the importance of firm characteristics have been verified.

The idea that firms are fundamentally heterogeneous, in terms of their internal knowledge, skills and resources, is at the heart of the field of strategic management. Cyert and March's work in *A Behavioral Theory* was an important step toward understanding this heterogeneity. Their move to develop a complete theory of the firm that explicitly recognized firm differences undercut the prevailing neoclassical assumptions that had so hindered the creation of a useful theory of the firm. Most subsequent economic theories of firm strategy are consequently intellectual descendants of Cyert and March's early efforts.

4 THE BEHAVIORAL THEORY AND FIRM COMPETENCIES

With the aid of Cyert and March's recognition that firms are fundamentally heterogeneous, scholars began working to better understand the nature and origins of this heterogeneity and its implications for firm performance. Early work by Penrose (1959), Rubin (1973), Andrews (1971) and Learned et al. (1969) drew attention to the importance of internal firm resources and skills. Andrews's (1971) classic text on strategy, for example, centered on the resource position of firms. Those internal firm resources, which are unique or superior relative to those of rival firms, may be a source of lasting competitive advantage provided they are matched appropriately to environmental opportunities. Likewise, Learned et al. (1969, p. 179) emphasize the importance of internal firm resources, noting:

> [T]he capability of an organization is its demonstrated and potential ability to accomplish against the opposition of circumstance or competition, whatever it sets out to do. Every organization has actual and potential strengths and weaknesses; it is important to try to determine what they are and to distinguish one from the other.

These ideas serve as the foundation for an important early model of firm strategy, the resource-based view of the firm.

The resource-based approach to firm strategy portrays firms as a collection of tangible and intangible assets, resources or competencies, which are tied to the firm and are difficult for others to imitate. Teece (1988) describes a firm's competencies as a set of differentiated technological skills, complementary assets and organizational routines that provide the basis for a firm's competitive capacities in one or more businesses. Externally, these competencies may be perceived as a firm's skill in a particular product area. However, a competence is the ability of a firm to solve organizational and technical problems, and thus is not limited to a specific set of products.[2] Indeed, firms frequently possess competencies that extend into multiproduct space. Examples of firm-specific competencies include employment of skilled personnel, in-house knowledge of technology, operating routines and trade contacts (Wernerfelt 1984). These resources arise primarily through organizational learning (Nelson and Winter 1982). As a result, they are closely tied to the products and markets in which the firm has historically been active. These resources enable firms to have markedly lower costs or to offer higher-quality products and performance than competitors. To the extent that resource endowments are 'sticky', firms with superior competencies will tend to be more profitable than competitors.

To be considered a source of competitive advantage, an organizational competence must meet three conditions: it must be heterogeneously distributed within an industry; it must be difficult to purchase on the market; and it must be difficult or impossible to imitate. Considerable discussion in the literature suggests that high-technology competencies are particularly likely to meet these conditions since such capabilities are frequently based on tacit knowledge and are subject to considerable uncertainty regarding quality and performance (Dosi 1982; Nelson and Winter 1982). As a result, high-technology competencies are likely to be difficult to acquire through straightforward market transactions or easily transfer internally to new uses (Teece 1982; Mowery 1983). The same features that make the market transfer of technology competencies difficult also limit the ability of other firms to imitate these competencies. The non-replicable nature of many technology competencies is the cornerstone of their strategic importance.

Teece et al. (1994) divide a firm's organizational competence into three components: (i) allocative competence – the decisions involving what to produce and how to price it; (ii) transactional competence – decisions on whether to make or to buy, and whether to do so alone or in a partnership; and (iii) administrative competence – how to design organizational structures and policies to enable efficient performance. Additionally, they define technical competence as the ability to design and develop products and processes, and as the ability to operate facilities effectively. Technical competencies, which also include learning, typically have significant tacit components, making them relatively safe from replication. These competencies reside largely in the organizational routines that contain a firm's collective knowledge. Nelson and Winter (1982) established an extensive discussion of routines in their evolutionary theory of the firm. Routines are patterns of interactions representing solutions to particular problems resident in group behavior, and can only be partially codified, due to their inherently tacit dimension. Routines can be both static and dynamic. Static routines allow the firm to replicate certain previously performed tasks, and although they are generally stable, improvements and mutations will always occur with repetition. Dynamic routines are those that seek new product and process innovations and are generally aimed at learning. These routines are heavily embedded in the research and development a firm pursues. As both Nelson and Winter (1982) and Teece (1982) argue, routines can be highly tacit in nature. This makes replication or imitation of them extremely difficult, and renders them non-contractable in an intermediary market.

Nelson and Winter's work also emphasizes the routine as the organizational memory. They assert that organizations learn by doing, and this knowledge is stored in the routines of the firm. In their view of the firm, information flows into the organization from the external environment. Members interpret this information and react by invoking routines that were successful in the past. Their performance generates information recognized by others, who interpret it and invoke the associated routine. Members of the organization are thus continually reacting to both external and internal information. The routines of the organization are self-sustaining, in that their repetition strengthens their existence in the firm. It is the conformity to these routines that can pose a problem for the organization. As the firm's environment changes, routines will continue to persist even though they may no longer be effective at solving the relevant problems. This persistence is dangerous if it makes the firms unable to adapt to a new environment. Firms will tend to select inputs that are compatible with internal routines rather than alter the routine to fit new alternative inputs.

The resource-based view of firm strategy, as defined above, builds on and extends many core concepts first addressed by Cyert and March in *A Behavioral Theory*. The categorization of competencies by Teece et al. (1997) as allocative, transactional, administrative and technical is directly related to Cyert and March's discussion of standard operating procedures. While Cyert and March do not address the make versus buy decision, the remainder of the competencies discussed in Teece et al. have parallels in the task performance rules, records and reports, information-handling rules, and plans procedures presented in 1963. The allocative competence from Teece would be found in the task performance rules and plans procedures of Cyert and March. Procedures for how to produce the good are task performance rules, while how much of the good to produce is jointly dependent on the budgetary allocation of plans and the more micro-level decisions of task performance rules. Even though the make/buy decision of transactional competence is not discussed in Cyert and March, it could be implicitly included in the allocation of resources to subunits included in plans procedures.[3] Teece's organizational competence cannot be distinctly placed in the procedure categorization of Cyert and March, but rather refers to procedures throughout their specific standard operating procedures. The same can be stated for technical competence, though innovation is not heavily discussed in *A Behavioral Theory*. The ability to accomplish those innovations sparked by problems encountered in production, however, could be specifically placed in task performance and information rules.

Teece et al. (1997) have taken the concept of specific standard operating procedures from Cyert and March and advanced it, placing these procedures in more relevant groupings and adding important specific dimensions such as the make/buy decision, external ties, and technology. They have better clarified the importance of cross-firm differences in these procedures by grouping them in categories of strategic relevance. Most importantly, they have shown the importance of these procedures in the firm's ability to achieve a sustainable competitive advantage. This lays the foundation for the strategic element, missing in *A Behavioral Theory*. However, many of the building blocks can be found in Cyert and March's original work.

In addition, the non-marketable nature of internal firm competencies is hinted at in the early Cyert and March. One aspect of their discussion of standard operating procedures is that these procedures are intimately linked to the firm itself. Indeed, they suggest that these procedures define a given firm by dictating its handling of information, its learning, its operations, and its range of possible actions. The success or failure of a given firm is closely tied to these procedures, as are the directions the firm takes. These procedures are woven into the firm's organizational structure, and thus are not readily transferable or replicable by other firms. Attempts by other firms to develop or adopt new or observed procedures will inevitably be hindered by the entrenchment of existing procedures meant to be replaced. The path-dependent nature of standard operating procedures makes their elimination as difficult as their integration or creation. Competencies that are no longer relevant to the firm's environment are equally as recalcitrant, as they are composed of these entrenched procedures. The extreme embeddedness of competencies therefore makes them unmarketable among organizations.

The concept of organizational routines found in the resource-based view is also directly related to Cyert and March's discussion in 1963. Routines are discussed by Nelson and Winter in much the same way as their predecessors defined procedures, in terms of repetitive patterns of activity in an organization. As in *A Behavioral Theory*, Nelson and Winter present routines as being relatively self-sustaining and static, despite a dynamic environment. Both treatises agree that these routines/procedures define how the firm will treat information and how it will solve observable problems. They also concur that organizational learning is accomplished through and embedded in routines/procedures. The routines/procedures of the firm are therefore deeply rooted in history and difficult to change. They are unique to the firm and inherently simplifying processes. The importance of Cyert and March's examination of standard operating procedures is evident in Nelson and Winter, which in turn greatly influences much of the work in the resource-based view of the firm.

Evidence has shown that routines and internal coordination play a critical role in firm performance. Several papers have sought to document how firm-level competencies, based in routines and procedures, determine differential firm performance. The importance of the integration and coordination of internal activity has been found to be very important to the firm (Aoki 1990). This coordination is also clearly important for relationships with outside suppliers and partners (Shuen 1994). Evidence of the importance of the organization of production is also available. Garvin's (1988) air conditioner plant study found that quality performance was driven by special organizational routines, rather than by capital investment or the level of automation. The importance of coordinating routines is also found by Clark and Fujimoto (1991) in the automobile industry. Differences in the coordinative routines in new model development was responsible for considerable variance in development cost, lead times, and quality. The importance of these routines is evident in studies of Japanese manufacturing by Womack et al. (1991) and Fujimoto (1994). These studies of lean manufacturing indicated not only the importance of these routines but also the difficulty of replicating them. They validate Cyert and March's early assertion of standard operating procedures as key foundations of firm behavior.

5   THE BEHAVIORAL THEORY AND DYNAMIC CAPABILITIES

While the resource-based theory is a relatively static approach toward firm strategy, it does discuss the implications of the nature of firm competencies toward long-run survival and strategy. This long-run view has been further addressed by the dynamic capabilities literature, which studies firms' abilities to adapt to and exploit a changing environment. The dynamic capabilities theory of the firm seeks to explain how firms achieve and sustain competitive advantage despite an ever-changing environment. Building on the resource-based, transaction-cost, and evolutionary theories of the firm, dynamic capabilities argues that a firm gains competitive advantage through internal routines or standard operating procedures that define the firm's processes. Routines, which are patterns of interactions representing successful solutions to specific problems, are deeply conditioned by its history, and not readily changed or developed. They are endemic to the firm, observed in group behavior, and highly subject to path dependency. These routines are defined as how tasks are accomplished, how problems are solved, and how knowledge is learned, and are not tangibly identifiable or necessarily codified. They are the firm's patterns of current practice and its organizational learning.

Dynamic capabilities 'emphasizes the key role of strategic management in appropriately adapting, integrating, and re-configuring internal and external organizational skills, resources, and functional competencies toward a changing environment' (Teece and Pisano 1994, p. 57). The firm's strategic dimensions are constrained by available paths, its current position, and its organizational processes or routines. The available paths represent the firm's opportunities and strategic alternatives. Firms are in part tied to their past and current positions, unable to choose from the infinite array of technologies and markets in existence. Firms typically are only capable of successful learning in areas or ways close to those it currently employs (Teece 1988). The marginal cost of gaining further knowledge in known areas is usually much less than innovating in unrelated fields (Cohen and Levinthal 1990). Thus firms will tend to innovate close in to areas they know well. A firm is not an infinitely malleable entity, but rather is an organization capable of limited change at significant cost. The past and current activities of the firm will powerfully influence the technological paths available to it, in that breakthroughs in related areas will be more readily identifiable and exploitable to the firm (Dosi 1982). The research areas currently focused on as well as the firm's ties to outside innovations will define which technological advances are potentially available for their development and use. Additionally, management's ability to identify and choose among these opportunities will determine the firm's capability in adapting to and exploiting changing technologies.

The firm's current position is defined by its intellectual property, supplier relations, strategic alliances, and endowment of technology. As in the resource-based view, tradable and readily transferable assets represent no concrete competitive advantage. These assets therefore are often tacit knowledge assets, ones deeply embedded in the routines and processes of the firm (Teece 1981). Other assets, such as the firm's location and financial position, can also determine its available strategic options. Those assets that are difficult to replicate or imitate, however, form the key competencies of the firms, and dynamic capabilities are those competencies that allow the firm to respond to and exploit changing market environments.

The organizational processes or routines of the firm can be partly viewed in how efficient the firm is in the integration of its internal activities and its external ties. These routines govern how information is gathered and processed, aspects critical to innovation and problem solving. Routines exist in how the firm relates to its suppliers, and how information is gathered from external sources. The coordination of separate groups within the firm is routinized in the practices of management, as are research and development processes, fields, and goals. The incentives and controls within the firm are critical routines defining its position and future paths.

Some of the most important routines within the firm involve learning. In the dynamic capabilities view, learning in the firm is an inherently organizational process. While individual skills and knowledge can contribute critically to the organization, learning processes are intrinsically social and collective. The coordination of search procedures and communication are necessary for effective learning, and the current routines determine how and what a firm can process. Additionally, the organizational knowledge gained from learning is stored in the new routines and logic of the organization. The existing processes for locating, identifying, and integrating important information into the firm will guide the trajectory of the firm's learning. As discussed in Cyert and March, and Nelson and Winter (1982), learning by the firm is largely determined by these routines and is thus highly path dependent in nature.

Although existing routines are largely determinant of the firm's learning trajectory, the firm may still have difficulty harnessing competencies based in these routines for specific strategic adaptations. The firm may wish to apply its highly successful routines toward other aspects of its organization. Replication of successful routines allows the firm to engage in geographic and product line expansion, and may help it better understand the routines in order to modify and improve them. The capabilities created by routines may be difficult to understand because they involve tacit knowledge and production and research processes not readily observable or codified. The tacit nature of these processes may be impossible to replicate, even by the firm itself, and the firm's ability to replicate its routines may be inevitably hampered by its inability to identify them. Lippman and Rumelt (1982) have argued that some sources of competitive advantage are so transparent that the firm itself cannot identify them. Even if the firm can identify its routines, it may not wholly understand them, or may find them inseparably linked to other specific routines (Teece 1976). Thus attempting to apply these routines in strategic initiative may be improbable.

When the firm is unable to replicate its successful routines, its competitors are even more unlikely to imitate them successfully. When routines are highly tacit, imitation will likely be impossible, as competitors have no ability to observe internal procedures. When competitors are able to observe and imitate competence-forming routines, however, the firm may be able to protect itself with intellectual property rights. Although intellectual property rights, such as patents, are highly observable, they are mostly limited to product technologies. Process technologies, or the routines endemic in the firm's production, are not readily observable, and thus cannot be easily imitated. Such routines may be difficult to replicate as well, but allow no window of observation for the potential imitator.

The critical aspects of dynamic capabilities are the ability of the firm to identify the changing market environment, to sense the opportunity, then to seize it. The ability of the firm to sense the need and the opportunity and then accomplish the necessary transformation is the essence of dynamic capability, and creates significant value (Amit and Schoemaker 1993; Langlois

1994). Part of this ability is dependent on the firm's ability to locate and assimilate information from its environment. The location and integration of this information is grounded in part on the firm's search and information-processing routines, manifested in research and development and the firm's existing ties to the outside environment. Not only must the firm discover new paths through its own and others' research, it must also recognize the importance of these paths. Past experience conditions the feasible alternatives management is likely to perceive (Teece et al. 1997). Firms not only face different costs associated with particular technologies, but they also face different perceived technological choices (Nelson and Winter 1982).

The firm must also be able to reconfigure its organization and assets before its competitors upon recognition of a new opportunity or environmental shift. Despite the assertion of managers, the firm's evolutionary path is rather narrow, and the alternative directions available to the firm are limited by its positions and previous path. The width of the potential path determines the number of options from which a firm can choose. The ability of the firm to follow the chosen path successfully is of equal importance in these capabilities. Key characteristics and routines of the firm will determine its ability to locate opportunities and accomplish the necessary adjustments, and will directly determine the extent of its dynamic capabilities. In particular, the ability to locate and address them is an inherently entrepreneurial function, not an administrative one.

The analysis of relatively static firms in dynamic environments is a key contribution of *A Behavioral Theory*, one which is a starting-point for the development of the dynamic capabilities literature. Cyert and March argue and establish the inherent rigidity of the firm, stating that the alteration and modification of the organization is extremely difficult, even over long periods of time. The standard operating procedures that are critical to the firm's operation cannot be immediately modified. These procedures are built from the entirety of the firm's history, dependent on its previous path and determinant of the future. Even if the firm's information-handling procedures identify an attractive alternative set of goals and expectations, it may be unable to alter standard operating procedures that evolved to serve previous firm goals. A firm's ability to identify alternate choices is intrinsically linked to its past as well. Cyert and March state repeatedly that a firm's search patterns and behavior are heavily biased, such that the information gathered and the opportunities recognized will indelibly be dependent on past and current behavior. The idea that 'history matters' is crucial to the dynamic capabilities literature, which views this history dependence as the driving force in long-run performance heterogeneity.

Dynamic capabilities stresses that the inherently rigid firm is forever challenged with metamorphosing market and technological characteristics. Firms must recognize these changes, identify new opportunities and appropriate adaptations, and successfully mutate toward the new environment. The internal routines or procedures of the firm help determine their ability to identify and accomplish this change. The entrepreneurial capacity of the organization to sense and then seize opportunities is critical to its dynamic capabilities.

A more specific application of Cyert and March in the dynamic capabilities literature is the importance of routines in identifying and exploiting opportunities. Cyert and March intently focus on the critical influence of standard operating procedures in the unique character of the firm, and stress their role in firms' abilities to identify and adapt to changes in their environment. While they portray all firms as sharing the same basic principles of general choice procedure (uncertainty avoidance, rules maintenance, simple rules), they argue that each firm has specific standard operating procedures that define the direction of constantly recurring activities. These procedures provide consistency within the firm and directly influence organizational decisions. Specific standard operating procedures dictate how the firm conducts all of its operations, from the mundane to technologically sophisticated. They also direct how the firm integrates, records, reports, locates, and utilizes the information necessary to identify potential problems and solutions. In addition, they influence the firm's strategic behavior in the allocation of its limited resources among potential alternative uses. Standard operating procedures make a firm unique, both in its static nature and in its dynamic capabilities. They are what define the competencies of the organization, made up of the routines that define its ability to integrate resources and produce products. Routines are also what limit the firm in its ability to adapt to its dynamic environment, for in giving stability to the organization, they limit its flexibility. In the words of Cyert and March, 'these procedures change slowly' (1992, p. 122) and the differential ability to accelerate this rate can determine the survival of the firm.

The dynamic capabilities literature develops the concept of standard operating procedures in discussing the importance of routines in firm performance. A firm's dynamic capabilities depend on two dimensions: its ability to identify opportunities, and its ability to change the firm's organizational structure to accommodate and exploit them. Both of these dimensions are evident in *A Behavioral Theory of the Firm*. The firm's ability to identify opportunities lies in its standard operating procedures for handling and processing information and in innovation realized from its task performance rules. These procedures, deemed routines in later literature, determine in which arenas the firm will be searching. The routines of the firm are its managerial and organizational processes, and search routines will increase the probability of recognizing some opportunities but will eliminate others. Search routines, as in Cyert and March, will depend on the past successes of the firm and its current and future expected problems. Under this acknowledgment of firms' unique search routines, we should expect technological and market strategies to suffer from path dependency. The search routines, founded in past successes and failures, help determine new directions for the firms to take.

Cyert and March also identify firms' differential procedures for processing and evaluating information. This heterogeneity is addressed by the dynamic capabilities literature as critical to the recognition of ripe opportunities. Firms may locate the information necessary to identify a new opportunity, but their processing routines may limit their ability to understand the potential benefits or application of the knowledge. Some firms can be expected to have information-processing routines completely incapable of identifying new directions, while others will be able to know the importance of their discovery immediately. Some firms have the entrepreneurial capacity to respond; some do not. Cyert and March discuss how each firm will have different ways of integrating new knowledge, locating it in different media and locations. The sources of this information will not be uniform across firms, and therefore organizations will have biased and filtered knowledge about their environment and potential opportunities. The firm's task performance procedures will influence its ability to realize learning by doing. Certain manufacturing procedures will tend to produce more innovation in reducing the cost and increasing the speed of production. Heterogeneity in firm task performance procedures will create differential levels of innovation potential from simply performing routines. These firm-specific routines will not only lend certain firms greater potential for efficiency improvements, but will also give them the opportunity for radical innovations. In essence, task performance procedures can provide another mode for identifying potential opportunities, and can thus be determinant of a firm's dynamic capabilities.

Cyert and March's work is also important in the second critical aspect of dynamic capabilities – the ability of the firm to adapt to and exploit opportunities. The path-dependent nature of standard operating procedures is firmly rooted in *A Behavioral Theory*, and is voiced even more loudly in Nelson and Winter (1982). Procedures and routines develop from years of problem-solving behavior in the organization, and are self-reinforcing characteristics. They are extremely difficult to change and determinant of future paths. The inherent heterogeneity of these routines across firms ensures that some firms will be better able to adapt their procedures to changes in their environment, an aspect critical in dynamic capabilities. The basis for the exploitation aspect of dynamic capabilities is firmly established in the work of Cyert and March, and inherited through the evolutionary theory of Nelson and Winter.

6   CONCLUSION

As is shown in this chapter, *A Behavioral Theory of the Firm* has richly contributed to a tradition of literature culminating in theories on firm competence and dynamic capabilities. The focus of Cyert and March on the heterogeneity of firm characteristics was critical to the development of these theories. Less critical but still important was the portrayal of a rigid firm in a dynamic environment. The standard operating procedures detailed in their work formed the basis for the firm routines of Nelson and Winter (1982), which in turn led to the explication of firm competence and dynamic capabilities. The conceptualization of how firms identify opportunities and adapt to exploit them is implicitly tied to procedures explained by Cyert and March.

It is important to note that while *A Behavioral Theory* cannot itself be classified as a study of firm strategy, it is nevertheless the starting point for numerous advances in this field. The literature discussed here by no means adequately summarizes the impact in economics and organization theory. Moreover, *A Behavioral Theory* is by no means the sole contribution of Cyert and March. Both Richard Cyert and James March have provided important later contributions to the theory of the firm, and more specifically to the field of strategy. Yet their 1963 classic remains critical to the modern understanding of the nature and behavior of the firm.

NOTES

1. Economists such as Friedman (1953) argued that whether or not the model accurately represented the firm was irrelevant so long as its predictive value was high.
2. A firm's competencies, as defined by Teece, are typically implicitly or explicitly *assumed* in economic theory. As such, competencies are viewed as widely and freely distributed among firms, thus giving limited insight into heterogeneity, organizational structure or firm performance.
3. The clearly-defined dichotomy of make/buy in the strategy literature, however, should likely be attributed to Williamson's (1975) work and the transaction cost literature that followed it.

REFERENCES

Amit, R. and P. Schoemaker (1993), 'Strategic assets and organizational rent', *Strategic Management Journal*, **14**, 33–46.
Andrews, Kenneth R. (1971), *The Concept of Corporate Strategy*, Homewood, IL: Dow Jones-Irwin.
Aoki, Masahiko (1990), 'Toward an economic model of the Japanese firm', *Journal of Economic Literature*, **28**, 1–27.

66 J. L. Pierce, C. S. Boerner & D. J. Teece

Argyris, C. (1960), *Understanding Organizational Behavior*, Homewood, IL: Dorsey.

Blau, P. (1955), *Dynamics of Bureaucracy*, Chicago: University of Chicago Press.

Clark, Kim B. and T. Fujimoto (1991), *Product Development Performance: Strategy, Organization and Management in the World Auto Industries*, Cambridge, MA: Harvard Business School Press.

Cohen, Wesley M. and Daniel A. Levinthal (1990), 'Absorptive capacity: a new perspective on learning and innovation' *Administrative Science Quarterly*, **35**, 569–96.

Cool, K. and D. Schendel (1988), 'Performance differences among strategic group members', *Strategic Management Journal*, **9**, 207–23.

Cyert, Richard M. and James G. March (1963), *A Behavioral Theory of the Firm*, Englewood Cliffs, NJ: Prentice-Hall.

Cyert, Richard M. and James G. March (1992), *A Behavioral Theory of the Firm*, 2nd edn, Cambridge, MA: Blackwell Business.

Dosi, G. (1982), Technological paradigms and technological trajectories: a suggested interpretation of the determinants and directives of technological change', *Research Policy*, **11**, 147–62.

Friedman, Milton (1953), *Essays in Positive Economics*, Chicago: University of Chicago Press.

Fujimoto, T. (1994), *Reinterpreting the Resource-capability View of the Firm: A Case of the Development-production Systems of the Japanese Automakers*, Tokyo: University of Tokyo Press.

Garvin, David A. (1988), *Managing Quality*, New York: Free Press.

Gouldner, A. (1954), *Patterns of Industrial Bureaucracy*, Glencoe, IL: Free Press.

Hansen, G. and B. Wernerfelt (1989), 'Determinants of firm performance: the relative importance of economic and organizational factors', *Strategic Management Journal*, **10**, 399–411.

Jacobson, R. (1988), 'The persistence of abnormal returns', *Strategic Management Journal*, **9**, 415–30.

Langlois, R. (1994), 'Cognition and capabilities: opportunities seized and missed in the history of the computer industry', Conference on Technological Oversights and Foresights, Stern School of Business, New York University.

Learned, E., C. Christensen, K. Andrews and W. Guth (1969), *Business Policy: Text and Cases*, Homewood, IL: Irwin.

Likert, R. (1961), *New Patterns of Management*, New York: McGraw-Hill.

Lippman, S. and R. Rumelt (1982), 'Uncertain imitability: an analysis of interfirm difference in efficiency under competition', *Bell Journal of Economics*, **13**, 413–38.

Mowery, D. (1983), 'The relationship between intrafirm and contractual forms of industrial research in American manufacturing, 1900–1940', *Explorations in Economic History*, **20**, 351–74.

Nelson, R.R. and S.G. Winter (1982), *An Evolutionary Theory of Economic Change*, Cambridge: Belknap Press.

Penrose, Edith T. (1959), *The Theory of the Growth of the Firm*, Oxford: Basil Blackwell.

Peteraf, M. (1993), 'The cornerstones of competitive advantage: a resource-based view', *Strategic Management Journal*, **14**, 179–91.

Rubin, P.H. (1973), 'The expansion of firms', *Journal of Political Economy*, **81**, 936–49.

Rumelt, Richard P. (1991), 'How much does industry matter?', *Strategic Management Journal*, **12**, 167–85.

Shuen, Amy (1994), 'Technology sourcing and learning strategies in the semiconductor industry', PhD Dissertation Walter A. Haas School of Business, University of California, Berkeley.

Teece, D.J. (1976), *The Multinational Corporation and the Resource Cost of International Technology Transfer*, Cambridge, MA: Ballinger.

Teece, David J. (1981), 'The market for know-how and the efficient international transfer of technology', *Annals of the American Association of Political and Social Sciences*, November, 81–6.

Teece, David J. (1982), 'Towards an economic theory of the multiproduct firm, *Journal of Economic Behavior and Organization*, **3**, 39–63.

Teece, David J. (1988), 'Technological change and the nature of the firm', in G. Dosi, C. Freeman, R. Nelson, G. Silverberg and L. Soete (eds), *Technical Change and Economic Theory*, London and New York: Pinter, 256–81.

Teece, D., R. Rumelt, G. Dosi and S. Winter (1994), 'Understanding Corporate Coherence: Theory and Evidence', *Journal of Economic Behavior and Organization*, **23**, (1), pp. 1–30.

Teece, David J. and Gary Pisano (1994), 'The dynamic capabilities of firms: an introduction', *Industrial and Corporate Change*, **3**, 537–56.

Teece, D.J., G. Pisano and A. Shuen (1997),'Dynamic capabilities and strategic management, *Strategic Management Journal*, **18**, 509–33.

Wernerfelt, Birger (1984), 'A resource-based view of the firm', *Strategic Management Journal*, **12**, 75–94.

Williamson, Oliver E. (1975), *Markets and Hierarchies*, New York: Free Press.

Williamson, Oliver E. (1996), *The Mechanisms of Governance*, New York: Oxford University Press.

Williamson, Oliver E. (1999), 'Strategy research: governance and competence perspectives', Working Paper BPP-74, Haas School of Business, University of California, Berkeley.

Womack, J., D. Jones and D. Roos (1991), *The Machine That Changed the World*, New York: Harper-Perennial.

mir vol. 47, 2007/2, pp. 175–192

mir
Management
International Review
© Gabler Verlag 2007

Mie Augier/David J. Teece

Dynamic Capabilities and Multinational Enterprise: Penrosean Insights and Omissions

Abstract and Key Results

- Penrose's legacy is a curious one. Much cited, but little read, her work is recognized as one of the main intellectual foundations for modern resource based theories of business strategy and theories of organizational routines and capabilities.

- However, Penrose did not aim to contribute to the field of strategy; her goal was to advance understanding of the nature of the firm and its growth. Nevertheless, there are important insights in Penrose's work that have implications for international business and for strategy.

- We discuss some of the implications of Penrose's work as well as its limitations. We also briefly discuss the usefulness of adopting a "Penrosean" capability perspective in multinational enterprise (MNE) strategy analysis.

- The dynamic capabilities framework puts entrepreneurial management into the theory of multinational enterprise, a task Penrose left untouched.

Key Words

Penrose, Multinational Enterprise, Strategy Analysis, Strategic Management, Entrepreneurship, Dynamic Capabilities

Authors

Mie Augier, Post-doctoral Fellow, Graduate School of Business, Stanford University, Stanford, California, USA.
David J. Teece, Mitsubishi Bank Professor of International Business and Finance, Institute of Management, Innovation and Organization, Haas School of Business, University of California, Berkeley, Berkeley, California, USA.

Manuscript received December 2004, revised June 2005, final version received January 2006.

Introduction

Edith Penrose's many and varied contributions to business studies deserve recognition. In her later years, she focused on the oil industry and on multinational enterprises (MNEs).[1] In this paper, we note some of her earlier contributions which helped initiate important streams of research, including the resource based theory of the firm. Her influence has also extended to new streams of research on dynamic capabilities and entrepreneurship. We discuss some implications for MNEs of the dynamic capabilities framework.

In her most important scholarly journey, Edith Penrose set out to develop a theory of the growth of the firm. Indeed, this was the title of her now well-known 1959 treatise.[2] Along the way she made several other astute observations about firms that turned out to be provocative to scholars interested in the theory of the firm and business strategy. It is these observations – particularly the notion that the firm is best thought of as a bundle of resources – which now constitute her better-known legacy.

The Resource Based Theory of the Firm

Penrose defined the internal resources of the firm as "the productive services available to a firm from its own resources, particularly the productive services available from management with experience within the firm" (p. 5). She presents the firm as an "autonomous administrative planning unit, the activities of which are interrelated and are coordinated" by management (pp. 15 et seq.). "A firm is more than an administrative unit; it is a collection of productive resources the disposal of which between uses and over time is determined by administrative decision – the physical resources of the firm consist of tangible things – there are also human resources available in a firm – strictly speaking, it is never resources themselves that are the 'inputs' in the productive process, but only the services that they render" (pp. 24 et seq.).

Put succinctly, Edith Penrose saw the firm as a "pool of resources the utilization of which is organized in an administrative framework. In a sense, the final products being produced by a firm at any given time merely represent one of several ways in which the firm could be using its resources" (pp. 149 et seq.).

As with the dynamic capabilities approach (which we shall discuss later), Penrose was enlightened enough to see a role in economic theory not only for managers but for entrepreneurs. "A theory of the growth of firms is essentially an examination of the changing productive opportunities of firms..." (pp. 31 et seq.). Penrose furthermore saw the business environment as an «image» in the entrepreneur's mind. This is an important insight about entrepreneurship as well as leadership (and the importance of having an entrepreneurial element in leadership). Innovation is very much about the ability of the entrepreneur to look at markets, technologies and business models and to interpret them "differently". Being able to see market and technological opportunities through different lenses (and in new ways) is an important entrepreneurial capability. It enables one to see opportunities that others might miss.

Penrose also recognized that as managers embrace growth, they are forced to decentralize, thereby shifting responsibility down the hierarchy. "New men are brought in and the existing personnel of the firm all gain further experience" (p. 52).[3] Critically, "many of the productive services created through an increase in knowledge that occurs as a result of experience gained in the operation of the firm as time passes will remain unused if the firm fails to expand" (p. 54). These unused resources aren't manifested in the form of idleness, but "in the concealed form of unused abilities" (p. 54). Penrose therefore saw the capacities of management – not exhaustion of technologically based economies of scale – as setting the limit to which a firm could grow. In her view, there was always a limit to the amount of expansion any firm, no matter how large, could undertake in a given period.[4]

It was the unused capacities of management, coupled with the tangibility of certain resources, which also enabled diversification in the Penrosian firm. Industrial R&D could assist by drawing firms into entirely new areas, particularly if the firm focused on more generic R&D activities. Sales and marketing relationships could also be leveraged to support the roll out of new products (pp. 116 et seq.).

Edith Penrose's ideas influenced the work of Teece (1980, 1982) on diversification. In particular, Teece (1982) built on Penrose's observation that "[o]f all outstanding characteristics of business firms, perhaps the most inadequately treated in economic analysis is the diversification of their activities" (Penrose 1959, p. 104) in outlining a theory of the multi-product firm. This in turn alerted the strategy field to her work on resources, impacting Wernerfelt (1984) and others. But it wasn't so much her claim that managers learn and develop unused capacities that has received the most attention in recent years.[5] Rather, it was her representation of the firm as a pool of resources that has caught the imagination of scholars in the field of business strategy.

However, what Penrose precisely meant by resources remains rather vague.[6] Moreover, the Penrosian view that growth is fueled primarily by underutilized managerial capabilities can be challenged.[7] In particular, enterprise growth can be attributed to market and technological factors as well as to the strong financial rewards that both managers and shareholders receive as the business enterprise grows. Growth also flows from investment in R&D, as pointed out by several business historians and economists.[8]

From the perspective of modern (strategic) management, a missing dimension in Penrose is an understanding of the basis for competitive advantage. Penrose implicitly adopts a profit-seeking framework; but other than a very general discussion of the competitive strength of small and large firms, she does not address the question of how firms develop competitive advantage. While she does recognize the importance of managerial skills, she underplays the role of intangible assets, though they are mentioned.[9] In this sense, she is not "modern"; but she was ahead of her time in many ways, not least of which is that she did recognize the importance of the entrepreneurial activities of management. However, this was only mentioned in passing, and the importance of managerial action in sensing and seizing emerging opportunities and managing threats.

The importance of knowledge assets is also underplayed. This ought not be surprising since the world Penrose was observing was one in which there were still significant barriers to trade and investment, and in such environments know-how is less critical as a factor in determining competitive advantage (Teece 2000, Chapter 1). Outsourcing and off shoring debates were not center stage in the early post war economy which was her laboratory.

Nevertheless, the Penrosian conceptualization of the firm remains relevant. Her insights remain good starting points for developing a theory of the firm, and for understanding the role of the manager. Her perspective is compatible with the recent emphasis on the importance of routines and processes. Routines and processes can be thought of as providing underutilized capacity that management can leverage for growth.

Penrose and the Theory of Dynamic Capabilities

As noted, and with the benefit of hindsight, Penrose appears to have underplayed growth driven by the entrepreneurial elements of management. She seems to recognize that know-how can be used to convert physical assets to different uses.[10] The firm, she said, was "both an administrative organization and a collection of productive resources, both human and material" (p. 320). The services rendered by these resources are the primary inputs into a firm's production processes and are firm specific in the sense that they are a function of the knowledge and experience that the firm has acquired over time. This is in essence a recognition of the path-dependent nature of organizational processes and routines and their roles in carrying knowledge (later emphasized by Cyert and March (1963) and Nelson and Winter (1982).[11]

When services that are currently going unused are applied to new lines of business, these services can also function as a growth engine for the firm through diversification (Teece 1980, 1982). Learning likewise enables the organization to use its resources more efficiently. As a result, even firms that have weak balance sheets may nevertheless be able to grow as managerial capacity is freed up for new uses as a result of managerial and organizational learning.[12] Penrose appears to be articulating a weak form of what is now referred to as the dynamic capabilities approach.

The dynamic capabilities approach seeks to provide a coherent (and evolutionary) framework for how firms develop competitive advantage, and maintain it over time. In essence, dynamic capabilities are about identifying the foundations that undergird long run enterprise growth and prosperity. First outlined in working papers (Teece/Pisano/Shuen 1990), and then published in Teece and Pisano (1994) and in Teece, Pisano and Shuen (1997),[13] the dynamic capabilities approach builds upon the theoretical foundations provided by Schumpeter (1934), Williamson (1975, 1985), Cyert and March (1963), Rumelt (1984), Nelson and Winter (1982), Teece (1982) and Teece and Pisano (1994). As discussed above, it is consistent with certain elements of Penrose's framework too. If one can explain the foundations of long run profitability, one is quite some distance down the road to a theory of the growth of the enterprise. This was of course Penrose's ambition.

Dynamic capabilities refer to the (inimitable) capacity firms have to shape, reshape, configure and reconfigure the firm's asset base so as to respond to changing technologies and markets. Dynamic capabilities relate to the firm's ability to proactively adapt in order to generate and exploit internal and external *firm specific competences,* and to address the firm's *changing environment* (Teece/Pisano/Shuen 1997). As Collis (1994) and Winter (2003) note, one element of dynamic capabilities is that they govern the rate of change of ordinary capabilities.[14] If a firm possesses resources/competences but lacks dynamic capabilities, it has a chance to make a competitive return for a short period, but superior returns cannot be sustained. It may earn Ricardian (quasi) rents, but such quasi rents will be competed away, often rather quickly. It cannot earn Schumpeterian rents because it hasn't built the capacity to be continually innovative. Nor is it likely to be able to earn monopoly (Porterian) rents since these require market power coupled with exclusive behavior or strategic manipulation (Teece/Pisano/Shuen 1997). Dynamic capabilities thus not only include an organization's (non-imitable) ability to sense changing customer needs, technological opportunities, and competitive developments; but also its ability to adapt to – and possibly even to shape – the business environment in a timely and efficient manner. A significant element of intentionality is involved.

The development and astute management of intangible assets/intellectual capital is now central to sustained enterprise competitiveness, requiring new conceptual frameworks for business and economic analysis. As former U.S. Federal Reserve Chairman Alan Greenspan remarked, "we must begin the important work of developing a framework capable of analyzing the growth of an economy increasingly dominated by conceptual products".[15] Dynamic capability theory is a framework that is well equipped to meet this challenge (Teece 2006b).

Penrose's framework is consistent with elements of the dynamic capabilities framework. Her emphasis on the fungible nature of resources obviously provides scope for the notion that a firm's competencies can be reshaped. But as noted, her framework was bereft of considerations of competitive advantage.[16] The whole inimitability story is missing.[17] Nor did she emphasize the role of the changing environment and the constant need to improve and renew capabilities. She saw learning as an opportunity, not a necessity. She also underplayed the resource allocation role of management. She recognized the importance of entrepreneurship but did not develop this concept much nor did she show how entrepreneurship could be important to the erection of new markets.

Other Growth Issues and the Penrose Effect

We have emphasized Penrose's contribution to the resource-based theory of the firm. Some of her ideas are consistent with the dynamic capabilities framework; yet until two decades ago when strategy scholars picked up on this work (Teece 1982), Penrose's emphasis on fungible resources had not received much attention in either the economics or the strategic management literature. Rather, it was her work on constraints on firm level growth and on the role of learning that received attention. While she recognized how the fungible nature of a firm's resources could create the foundation for lateral enterprise expansion, it was her emphasis on the administrative and managerial constraints on growth that captured the attention of scholars.

Penrose argued that the human resources required for firm growth and the management of change are firm specific. As a corollary, at any moment in time these resources are constrained by their internal availability. Put differently, managerial capacity cannot be expanded indefinitely and at will. Rather, expansion requires the recruitment and development of additional high-level human resources.[18] Accordingly, the level of current efficiency will, beyond a point, diminish with the rate of change in size.

The above constraints on firm growth became known as the "Penrose effect". Both microeconomic and macroeconomic scholars recognized the Penrose effect in the 1960s. These scholars incorporated Penrosean thinking into their work (e.g. Marris 1964, Uzawa 1969). However, as noted above, we think the more enduring legacy will be Penrose's conceptualization of the firm as a bundle of (quasi fungible) resources.

Interestingly, the Economic Journal (1961) predicted that the "Theory of the Growth of the Firm" would be an influential book; however, that influence has been far greater in the field of strategy than in the field of economics. Economists in the main are resistant to her teachings, as they imply the total inadequacy of the neoclassical theory of the firm.[19]

Entrepreneurship, Enterprise Design, and the Role of Markets

As implicitly recognized by Penrose, firms need to be viewed as human organizations, not computer controlled machines. As such, firms must confront challenges in the realm of organizational design including imperfect incentive alignment, imperfect governance, and bureaucratic decision-making. Organizations facilitate decisions because they constrain the set of alternatives as well as the relevant parameters to be considered. Organizations can be rendered more effective and efficient by improving the ways in which those limits are defined and imposed (Simon 1947, March/Simon 1958).

While Penrose may have recognized the human element in organizations, she did not really explore issues of organizational *design*. As noted by Herbert Simon, "[d]esign calls for initiative, focus of attention on major problems, search for alternatives. One cannot choose the best, one cannot even satisfice, until one has alternatives to choose from." Nowhere is this clearer than in the *entrepreneurial* activities of organizations. As Simon has observed: "Especially in the case of new or expanding firms, the entrepreneur does not face an abstract capital market. He or she exerts much effort to induce potential investors to share the company's views (often optimistic) about its prospects. This executive is much closer to Schumpeter's entrepreneur [and to the Penrosian manager] than to the entrepreneur of current neoclassical theory. Whether the firm expands or contracts is determined not just by how its customers respond to it, but by how insightful, sanguine and energetic its owners and managers are about its opportunities – by how much they possess of the "animal spirits" that Keynes was obliged to introduce into his account of the trade cycle (Nelson/Winter 1982)." (1991, pp. 35 et seq.) These factors go beyond the managerial elements highlighted by Penrose. Arguably, they are more important.

One example of the importance of design is in the development of the "architecture" of a business firm. This element of design is embedded in part in management's choice of (or creation of) a business model. A business model defines the manner in which a business enterprise delivers value to customers, entices customers to pay for value, and converts those payments to profit. It reflects the firm-specific assumptions about what customers want and how an enterprise can be profitable as a result of the value delivered. The business model determines: (1) how the revenue and cost structure of business is to be "designed" and then possibly "redesigned" to meet customer needs; (2) the ways in which the resources are to be assembled and the relevant market segments can be identified; (3) the mechanisms through which value can be created and captured. The purpose of a business model is to "articulate" the value proposition, identify targeted market segments, define the structure of the value chain, and estimate the cost structure and profit potential (Chesbrough/ Rosenbloom 2002, pp. 533 et seq.). In short, a business model is a plan for the financial and organizational "architecture" of a business that makes valid assumptions about costs, scale, and customer and competitor behavior. It outlines the contours of the solution required to win in the market place. Getting the business model right is critical to the success of a new business; adjusting and/or improving the model is likely to be critical for continued success. However, the importance of "business models" has been largely neglected in the management and economics literature, at least until recently. A firm's capacity to create, adjust, hone and replace business models is a critical building block of this firm's dynamic capabilities.

Design issues are also important when considering the *changing nature and dynamics* of international business. In recent decades, increased globalization, and in particular outsourcing and off shoring, appear to have gained momentum. However, while globalization has expanded, it is by no means "complete". Precisely because cross-border integration is incomplete (i.e., the world is characterized by semi-globalization) the study of international business and multinational enterprise remains an important scholarly activity.[20] Otherwise, mainstream strategy and management content would suffice for international business too. Because of incomplete integration and differences in business environments, locational factors and institutional differences must be taken into account. Such differences do not merely indicate the presence of barriers to the internationalization of business; they can also be beneficial to MNEs.

In recent decades, the MNE has been shaped by three key developments critical to its nature and scope: (i) the simultaneous increase in both the outsourcing and the off-shoring of production, (ii) the emergence of a distributed and open innovation model, i.e. not only production and manufacturing are being outsourced, but so is innovation, and, (iii) the development of low cost information and computer technology, which enables small firms to perform transactions, and adopt business models, previously only available to large enterprises. For instance, internet-based companies such as Amazon, eBay, Google, and Yahoo make it possible for small businesses to reach global markets that were previously inaccessible, except at considerable cost. This has led to the emergence of what might be thought of as "mini"-multinationals, sometimes employing only a handful of workers, and using internet-based technology to anchor the coordination of their global activities. In short, information and computer technology has enabled efficient global operations for very small as well as small, medium, and large enterprises. Small enterprises in particular may be launched from multiple jurisdictions – rendering the home/host country dichotomy irrelevant from the time of organizational founding. Also, these mini-multinationals are often founded by individuals collaborating across boundaries, and they exhibit MNE characteristics from their birth. Designing and orchestrating the business model and organizational structure of such firms has become increasingly complex. In the realm of the external environment, markets for such expanding firms must be "seized" and, sometimes, created.

Although Penrose did recognize the importance of creating markets as a result of entrepreneurship, she did not address the *simultaneous* role of entrepreneurs in creating markets and designing organizations.[21] An essential characteristic of organizations/firms is that they embody knowledge, which can't be easily bought and sold. Sometimes, the only way to capitalize on knowledge is to start a firm and build the necessary complementary assets (Teece 1986).[22] Profit flows from innovation, buttressed by the development of complementary technologies, and the astute deployment of complementary assets.

Penrose's work differs from Coase's (1937), in terms of the rationale for the firm's existence and expansion. She does not assume that "in the beginning there were markets". Her perspective is more in keeping with Simon's (1991) perspective that "in the beginning there were firms"; entrepreneurs create new markets by starting entrepreneurial organizations because the relevant external capabilities simply aren't there (cf. Langlois 1992).[23]

Penrose emphasized entrepreneurial imagination and the non-market nature of entrepreneurial knowledge. She noted that it is: "evident that such management [entrepreneurship] cannot be hired in the market place" (p. 45). A few decades earlier Frank Knight (1921) perceptively linked the existence of firms to entrepreneurs seizing opportunities for profit in the face of uncertainty: "It is ... true uncertainty which ... gives the characteristic form of 'enterprise' to economic organization as a whole and accounts for the peculiar income of the entrepreneur" (1921, p. 232).[24]

Her vision of entrepreneurship is very close to that of Frank Knight. She emphasized entrepreneurship as explicitly an organizational phenomenon: "The productive activities of ... a firm are governed by what we shall call its 'productive opportunity', which comprises all of the productive possibilities that its 'entrepreneurs' can see and take advantage of " (p. 31). Entrepreneurs have "intimate knowledge of the resources, structure, history, operations and personnel of the firm" (p. 54).

There are other ideas in strategic management that were not directly anticipated by Penrose, perhaps in part because she did not self-consciously endeavor to provide normative frameworks for managers. Hence, her neglect of certain issues now considered important to the field of management today should not be construed as a criticism, but merely as an observation. One such example is the idea that markets need to be developed. It is common in economics to assume that markets exist. As Arrow (1974) observed: "Although we are not usually explicit about it, we really postulate that when a market could be created, it would be." If it is not, this reflects market failure, and such failure can in turn be attributed to "transaction costs" or "adverse selection". The absence of certain insurance markets is a typical example. As a general rule, economics suggests that markets fail because inputs or outputs are not priced properly. For example, gasoline that pollutes is consumed "too much" because the costs of using it are not fully internalized. Arrow (1956) and Arrow and Debreu (1959) do discuss the absence of fully developed contingent claims markets, but in the main such lacunae are explained by the absence of demand, or just simply transaction costs.

Moreover, in commercializing new technologies, pioneering entrepreneurs often find that formal market research and expert forecasts, however sophisticated from a methodological perspective, fail to predict which new markets will come into existence, and where and when these markets will actually materialize. Christensen (1997), Mintzberg (1994) and others have documented a wide variety of cases that illustrate this unpredictability in business. Human history also attests to this unpredictability in other areas – such as Columbus' discovery of the New World or the fall of the Berlin Wall.

There is little in economics to suggest that markets can be shaped by the purposeful decisions of managers, i.e. by firms. Penrose chose not to develop that point either. For her theory of the growth of the firm, markets were not specifically treated. However, firm behavior shapes markets just as markets shape firm behavior and firm growth. Consistent with this view, Herbert Simon argued that perhaps we should not assume an explanation is needed of why *firms* actually exist. Simon uses the illustration of a visitor from Mars approaching earth observing economic exchanges, with organizations appearing as green areas, and market transactions as red lines in between. What does the visitor see? Organizations, green areas, would be dominant. We live in an "organization economy" rather than a "market economy", and organizations are more ubiquitous than market transactions; even more so if we go back in history (Simon 1991). Simon suggests that the more natural question to ask than the Coasian one, is "why do markets exist"? Instead of focusing on theories to explain the existence of firms, Simon raises questions such as, why do particular organizational forms (such as professional services firms) exist, and how should they be structured? How do these organizational forms relate to broader processes of (technological, cultural, etc.) change in the modern economy? What motivates people in real organizations (authority, rewards, loyalty, identification, coordination)? These are issues to be addressed by strategic management in the future; not all of these are Penrosian themes sensu stricto.

Dynamic Capabilities, Resources and Competitive Advantage: Implications for MNEs

While Penrose may not have fully developed the capability concept, the subsequent development of the (dynamic) capabilities approach can be usefully applied to MNEs. Somewhat under-researched in mainstream MNE theory (at least as far as internalization theory is concerned), has been consideration of the importance and the particulars of the firm's managerial and organizational capabilities, although this is now being addressed.[25] To the extent that notions of organizational capability have been around for decades, and have received much attention recently, more efforts to embed the capability concept into MNE theory would appear useful so as to align more closely academic research on the MNE and strategic management theory.

As discussed above, Edith Penrose had provided elements of a resource-based/ capabilities perspective. She viewed the firm as an administrative organization, and as a pool of production resources: "At all times there exist, within every firm, pools of unused productive resources and these together with the changing knowledge of management, create a productive opportunity which is unique to each firm. Unused productive services are, for the enterprising firm, at the same time a challenge to innovate, an incentive to expand, and a source of competitive advantage". (Penrose 1960, p. 2). As Pitelis (2000) notes, unused resources are critical to Penrose's theory of internal or "organic"/endogenous enterprise expansion.

Penrose certainly did not overplay, from a theoretical perspective, the international aspects of large corporations, believing that the differences do not, in fact, require theoretical distinction (1987, p. 56). However, she did note that: "the managerial, technological, or financial contribution from the parent may be considerable and generally make new real resources available to the local economy", (1968, p. 43).

The general framework advanced by dynamic capability theory sees difficulty-to-imitate and globally exercised dynamic capabilities (and resources) as foundational to the competitive advantage of MNEs.[26] The greater the diversity and rate of change in business environments, the more critical dynamic capabilities become for the MNE's financial performance.

Some observers have identified a modality of competition, referred to as hypercompetition. It is a modality "characterized by intense and rapid competitive moves, in which competitors must move quickly to build [new] advantages and erode the advantages of their rivals" (D'Aveni/Gunther 1994, pp. 217 et seq.). Hypercompetition appears to be the result of rapid innovation, globalization, and deregulation. Dynamic capabilities are likely to be essential to the survival of MNE in industries and environments characterized as hypercompetitive.

As noted above, it is necessary that the MNE build capabilities that are "sustainable" i.e. inimitable. Inimitability is more likely to occur in the presence of "isolating mechanisms" and "tight appropriability regimes" (Rumelt 1987; Teece 1986, 2000).[27] When the appropriability regime is "tight", differential performance can be more readily sustained, at least for some length of time.[28]

The dynamic capabilities perspective on the MNE addresses more than simply the need for rapid innovation, adaptation, and flexibility. It also identifies the importance of proactive entrepreneurial behavior shaping the MNE's footprint. In the presence of significant gaps between the cost structures and growth rates of national economies, the MNE's ability to respond to – and shape – the changing kaleidoscope of opportunities at home and abroad is critical to success. Outsourcing and off-shoring activities to foreign subsidiaries and alliance partners, involves establishing quality control and product/service evaluation protocols on a global basis.

Indeed, dynamic capabilities are resident in a firm's processes and routines as well as within the firm's top management team. Maintaining dynamic capabilities within the MNE requires continuous entrepreneurial activity on a global scale. Entrepreneurial activity is different from – but related to – managerial activity. It is about understanding opportunities, getting things started, and finding new and better ways of putting things together. It is about coordinating on a global basis the assembly of disparate and usually co-specialized resources, getting "approvals" for non-routine activities, sensing business opportunities, and finding ways to deploy capabilities globally as well as locally. We have come to associate the entrepreneur with the individual who starts a new business providing a new or improved product or service. Such action is clearly entrepreneurial; but the entrepreneurial function required in the MNE context should not be thought of as confined to new enterprise startup activities.

The replication of capabilities involves transferring or redeploying competences (technological or organizational) from one concrete economic setting to another. Since productive knowledge is usually embodied, the transfer of skill cannot be accomplished by simply transmitting information. Only in those instances where all relevant knowledge is fully codified and understood can replication be collapsed into a simple problem of information transfer. Too often, the contextual dependence of original performance in the home market is poorly appreciated, so unless the MNE has already replicated its systems of productive knowledge in other markets, the act of replication is likely to be difficult (Teece 1976). Indeed, replication and transfer are often impossible absent the transfer of people, though this can be minimized if investments are made to convert tacit knowledge to codified knowledge. Often, however, this is simply not possible.

In short, competences and capabilities, and the routines upon which they rest, are usually rather difficult to replicate. Even understanding what all the relevant routines are that support a particular competence may not be transparent. Indeed, Lippman and Rumelt (1982) have argued that some sources of competitive advantage are so complex that the firm itself, let alone its competitors, does not understand them.[29] As Nelson and Winter (1982) and Teece (1981, 1982) have explained, many organizational routines are quite tacit in nature. Imitation can also be hindered by the fact that few routines are 'stand-alone'; coherence may require that a change in one set of routines in one part of the firm (e.g. production) be accompanied by changes in some other part (e.g. R&D).

Some routines and competences seem to be attributable to local or regional forces that shape firms' capabilities at early states in their lives. Porter (1990), for example, shows that differences in local product markets, local factor markets, and institutions play an important role in shaping competitive capabilities. Differences also exist within populations of firms from the same country. Various studies of the automobile industry, for example, show that not all Japanese automobile companies are top performers in terms of quality, productivity, or product development (see, for example, Clark/Fujimoto 1991). The role of firm-specific history has been highlighted as a critical factor explaining such firm-level (as opposed to regional or national-level) differences (Nelson/Winter 1982).[30] Replication in a different context may thus be rather difficult.[31]

At least two types of strategic value flow from replication. One is the ability to support geographic expansion, and has been emphasized here. The other is the ability to support product line expansion. To the extent that the capabilities in question are relevant to customer needs elsewhere, replication can confer value.[32] Another is that the ability to replicate also indicates that the enterprise has the foundations in place for learning and improvement. Considerable empirical evidence supports the notion that the understanding of processes, both in production and in management, is the key to process improvement. In short, an organization cannot improve that which it does not understand.

Factors that make replication difficult also make imitation difficult. Thus, when the MNE's productive knowledge is more tacit, it becomes harder for the MNE itself to replicate it, and for competitors to imitate it. When the tacit component is high, imitation may well be impossible, absent the hiring away of key individuals and the transfer of key organizational processes.

In conclusion, the concept of dynamic capabilities, when applied to the MNE, highlights organizational and managerial competences, critical to achieve superior performance. Key ingredients are difficult-to-replicate routinized processes, the basic manner in which a business is designed, as well as the decision frames, heuristics and protocols that enable MNEs to avoid poor investment choices and embrace astute ones. Once assets are within management's orbit, their effective utilization and continuous orchestration on a global basis becomes essential. Indeed, orchestration directed at achieving new combinations and new asset co-alignments is central to the dynamic capabilities framework. Preventing imitation and internal rent dissipation are key elements too.

Lying at the heart of dynamic capabilities are several fundamental management/ organizational skills including: (1) learning and innovation processes; (2) business "design" competence (what business model to employ); (3) investment allocation decision heuristics; (4) asset orchestration, bargaining and transactional competence, and (5) efficient governance and incentive alignment (Teece 2006). Buttressing these is an understanding of the processes of imitation and the strategies and processes that can be used to protect intellectual property. Widely diffused managerial and organizational competence cannot be core elements of an MNE's dynamic capabilities.

Note that dynamic capabilities flow from more than just learning and technological accumulation. This is not meant to downplay the importance of technological accumulation. Technological innovation and learning remain important mechanisms by which firms build from specific (technological) capabilities. However, in a world where the global outsourcing of R&D is common (Teece/Pisano/Shan 1988, Chesbrough 2003) it becomes problematic to rely too much on in house R&D as the sole foundation of competitive advantage. Orchestrating a global portfolio of technological assets inside and outside the enterprise is now essential.

The dynamic capabilities framework relegates an MNE's administrative competence to secondary importance, unless such competence is embedded in distinct and difficult to replicate business processes. Stable administrative functions can typically be outsourced to multiple vendors. Of course, there may well be circumstances where administration is complex, novel, and difficult to imitate in which case it can be the source of competitive advantage.

The distinct skills, which constitute an MNE's dynamic capabilities cannot generally be bought or "outsourced"; they must be built, or at least assembled. Once co-specialized assets are assembled, they must be skillfully orchestrated on a global basis. Such orchestration skills require astute decision-making on a global basis and an entrepreneurial capacity built into the management team. These skills and processes are instrumental to long-run enterprise performance and cannot be outsourced without loss of competitive advantage. They lie at the core of the MNE's capabilities. MNEs possessing dynamic capabilities are able to quickly respond to – and shape – evolving technologies and marketplaces. Accordingly, such firms should exhibit superior enterprise performance over multiple product life cycles.

While Penrose did not anticipate most and certainly not all elements critical to successful international expansion, she did play an important role by being an important inspiration to dynamic capabilities. Her search for a theory of the growth of the firm is in some measure answered by the dynamic capabilities framework.

Conclusion

Within the field of strategic management, Penrose's work has often been extensively cited while also being mis-characterized. What is needed is careful scholarship, initiated by a careful reading of her work, especially the Theory of the Growth of the Firm. In this paper, we have discussed some of her insights relevant to strategic management, entrepreneurship, international business, and industrial organization. We have also indicated certain limitations to her framework and analyses. A critical reading of her writings can nevertheless provide fresh insights to economics and management.

Acknowledgements

We are grateful to Giovanni Dosi, Richard Nelson, Christos Pitelis, Alain Verbeke and two anonymous referees for comments on earlier drafts; to the Kauffmann Foundation, the Sloan Foundation and the Lester Center for Entrepreneurship & Innovation for support and to Frances Darnley and Patricia Lonergan for skillful assistance.

Endnotes

1 For an extensive coverage of Penrose's overall contribution, see Penrose and Pitelis (1999).

2 Less well known, but also elaborating the theme of the growth of the firm, is her case study of the Hercules Powder Company, published in 1960. It was originally intended for inclusion in the Theory of the Growth of the Firm but was omitted to keep down the size of the book though the case study was designed to illustrate the theory outlined in the book.

3 This has subsequently come to be known as the "Penrose Effect".

4 In her own words, describing the limits of growth as being generated by the same dynamics underlying the growth process itself: "[B]ecause the very nature of a firm as an administrative and planning organization requires that the existing responsible officials of the firm at least know and approve, even if they do not in detail control, all aspects of the plans and operations of the firm ... the capacities of the existing managerial personnel of the firm necessarily set a limit to the expansion of that firm in any given period of time, for it is self-evident that such management cannot be hired in the market place" (p. 45). Note the emphasis on the missing markets for management – we shall return to that issue later in this paper in sections 4 and 5.

5 This is discussed in more detail in section 4 below.

6 Teece, Pisano, and Shuen (1997) tried to tighten this by defining resources as firm specific assets that are difficult if not impossible to imitate. Trade secrets and certain specialized production facilities are examples. These assets are difficult to transfer because of transfer and transaction costs, amplified in the presence of tacit knowledge.

7 The flip side of this is of course that a firm's growth is limited by the capabilities of its incumbent management (the "Penrose Effect" discussed later).

8 Moreover the use of "excess resources" may involve positive costs, see Pitelis (2002).

9 At least industrial R&D is discussed along with customer relationships.

10 As Penrose writes: "For physical resources the range of services inherent in any given resource depends on the physical characteristics of the resource, and it is probably safe to assume that at any given time the known productive services inherent in a resource do not exhaust the full potential of the resource... The possibilities of using services change with changes in knowledge... there is a close connection between the type of knowledge possessed by the personnel in the firm and the services obtainable from its material resources" (1959, p. 76).

11 The links between Penrose and Cyert & March are discussed in Pitelis (2006).

12 Teece's paper on the multiproduct firm (Teece 1982) was the first to apply Penrose's ideas to strategic management issues. This paper focused on developing further Penrose's idea that human capital in firms is usually not entirely 'specialized' and can therefore be (re)deployed to allow the firm's diversification into new products and services. He also extended the Penrosian notion that firms' possess excess resources which can be used for diversification. Later, Wernerfelt (1984) cites Penrose for "the idea of looking at firms as a broader set of resources ... [and] the optimal growth of the firm involves a balance between exploitation of existing resources and development of new ones".

13 This explains why references to dynamic capabilities began before the publication of this paper. In the early to mid 90's, the working paper versions were quoted. See for instance Mahoney and Pandian (1992).

14 For the particulars on the specific nature of different types of dynamic capabilities, see Teece (2006b).

15 Chairman Alan Greenspan also noted recently, "over the past half century, the increase in the value of raw materials has accounted for only a fraction of the overall growth of U.S. gross domestic product (GDP). The rest of that growth reflects the embodiment of ideas in products and services that consumers value. This shift of emphasis from physical materials to ideas as the core of value creation appears to have accelerated in recent decades" (Remarks of Alan Greenspan, Stanford Institute for Economic Policy Research 2004).

16 See also Rugman and Verbeke (2002).

17 Except perhaps for her discussion on "impregnable bases" see Pitelis (2004).

18 As an example, consider Google's expansion of online network advertising into new markets around the world. According to Google's CEO Eric Schmidt, this is limited only by the speed at which the company can hire local staff, "set up bank accounts and collect the money". "Google sees no limit to global drive", Financial Times, February 3, 2005, p. 17.

19 See also Penrose and Pitelis (1999).

20 See also Rugman and Verbeke (2004).

21 The dynamic process of market creation is illustrated in Penrose's study of the Hercules Powder Company where she talks about "the creation of consumer demand as a consequence of entrepreneurial desire to find a use for available productive resources" (Penrose 1960, p. 9).

22 That was essentially also what Frank Knight had in mind: "The receipt of profit in a particular case may be argued to be the result of superior judgment. But it is judgment of judgment, especially one's own judgment, and in an individual case there is no way of telling good judgment from good luck, and a succession of cases sufficient to evaluate the judgment or determine its probable value transforms the profit into a wage. ... If ... capacities were known, the compensation for exercising them can be competitively imputed and is a wage; only, in so far as they are unknown or known only to the possessor himself, do they give rise to a profit" (1921, p. 311). For a discussion of Knight's theory of the firm, see Langlois and Cosgel (1993).

23 She did also recognize the role of intentionality, an important part of entrepreneurship, as reflected in her early contributions to the debate in the American Economic Review about biological analogies.

24 His full argument is as follows: "With uncertainty entirely absent, every individual being in possession of perfect knowledge, there would be no occasion for anything of the nature of responsible management or control of productive activities. ... its [business firm's] existence in the world is a direct result of the fact of uncertainty" (p. 271).

25 See, for example, the various contributions by Rugman and Verbeke (2001, 2003 and 2005). In addition, others have emphasized management expertise in the theory of the MNE e.g. Hood and Young (1979, p. 56) in discussing firm-specific factors, reference management expertise. Indeed, they state clearly (p. 92) that "large corporations do possess, and lay much store by, acquired managerial experience through which profit opportunities are diagnosed. Such experience is an important dimension of an MNE's comparative advantage". The framework developed here endeavors to specify what particular management expertise is likely to be critical.

26 For applications of Penrose's ideas to the MNE, see Pitelis (2000, 2004), Dunning (2003), Rugman and Verbeke (2002, 2004) and various contributions in this special issue.

27 In addition to the importance of intellectual property rights protection, the tacit nature of know-how, and the inherent difficulty of technology transfer, another factor is the importance of the unique coalignment of specific assets. Specific assets may not simply be ubiquitously available.

28 Competitive advantages are continuously eroded by actions of other players that lead again to higher levels of competition and the need to react faster. In the end, these dynamic interactions between firm learning and adaptation, on the one hand, and higher levels of competition and selection, on the other hand, can cancel each other out. This is often dubbed an 'arms race' or 'the Red Queen effect' (Kaufman 1995) after the comment to Alice in Wonderland: "it takes all the running you can do to keep in the same place" (Carroll 1946). Companies adapt faster and faster, but as a consequence of the resulting increase in competition, they do not make any progress. When isolating mechanisms are operative and appropriability regimes are tight, Red Queen effects can be overcome.

29 If so, the firm's advantage is likely to fade, as luck does run out.

30 See also Bartlett and Ghoshal (1989), Rugman and Verbeke (2005).

31 See for example, Rugman and Verbeke (2004).

32 Needless to say, there are many examples of firms replicating their capabilities inappropriately by applying extant routines to circumstances where they may not be applicable e.g. Nestle's transfer of developed-country marketing methods for infant formula to the Third World (Hartley 1989). A key strategic need is for firms to screen capabilities for their applicability to new environments.

References

Alchian, A., Uncertainty, Evolution, and Economic Theory, *Journal of Political Economy*, 58, 3, 1950, pp. 211–222.

Alchian, A., Biological Analogies in the Theory of the Firm: Comment, *American Economic Review*, 43, 4, 1953, pp. 600–603.

Bartlett, C./Ghoshal, S., *Managing Across Borders: The Transnational Solution*, Boston, MA: Harvard Business School Press 1989.

Chesbrough, H./Rosenbloom, R. S., The Role of the Business Model in Capturing Value from Innovation: Evidence from Xerox Corporation's Technology, *Industrial and Corporate Change*, 11, 3, 2002, pp. 529–555.

Chesbrough, H., *Open Innovation: The New Imperative for Creating and Profiting from Technology*, Boston: Harvard Business School Press 2003.

Christensen, C. M., *The Innovator's Dilemma: When New Technologies Cause Great Firms to Fail*, Boston, MA: Harvard Business School Press 1997.

Collis, D. J., Research Note: How Valuable are Organisational Capabilities?, *Strategic Management Journal*, 15, Winter Special Issue, 1994, pp. 143–152.

Cyert, R./March, J.G., *A Behavioral Theory of the Firm*, Englewood Cliffs: Prentice Hall 1963.

D'Aveni, R. A./Gunther, R., *Hypercompetition: Managing the Dynamics of Strategic Maneuvering*, New York: The Free Press 1994.

Dunning, J. H., The Contribution of Edith Penrose to International Business Scholarship, *Management International Review*, 43, 1, 2003, pp. 3–19.

Hood, N./Young, S., *The Economics of Multinational Enterprise*, London: Longman 1979.

Jacobides, M., The Architecture of Organizational Capabilities, *Industrial and Corporate Change*, forthcoming.

Knight, F., *Risk, Uncertainty and Profit*, Boston, MA: Houghton Mifflin 1921.

Langlois, R., Transactions-cost Economics in Real Time, *Industrial and Corporate Change*, 1, 1, 1992, pp. 99–127.

Langlois, R./Cosgel, M., Frank Knight on Risk, Uncertainty, and the Firm, *Economic Inquiry*, 31, 3, 1993, pp. 456–465.

Loasby, B., *Choice, Complexity and Ignorance*, Oxford: Oxford University Press 1976.

Loasby, B., *The Mind and Method of the Economist*, Cheltenham: Edward Elgar 1989.

March, J.G./Simon, H.A., *Organizations*, New York: Wiley 1958.

Marshall, A., *Principles of Economics*, London: McMillan 1925.

Marris, R.L., *The Economic Theory of Managerial Capitalism*, New York: Free Press of Glencoe 1964.

Mintzberg, H., *The Rise and Fall of Strategic Planning*, New York: Free Press 1994.

Nelson, R./Winter, S.G., *An Evolutionary Theory of Economic Change*, Cambridge: Belknap Press 1982.

Penrose, E., Biological Analogies in the Theory of the Firm, *American Economic Review*, 42, 6, 1952, pp. 804–819.

Penrose, E., Biological Analogies in the Theory of the Firm: Rejoinder, *American Economic Review*, 43, 4, 1953, pp. 603–609.

Penrose, E. T., *The Theory of the Growth of the Firm*, 3rd edition, Oxford: Oxford University Press 1959/1995.

Penrose, E., The Growth of the Firm: A Case Study: The Hercules Powder Company, *Business History Review* 34, 1, 1960, pp. 1–23.

Penrose, P./Pitelis, C. N., Edith Elura Tilton Penrose: Life, Contribution and Influence, *Contributions to Political Economy*, 18, 1, 1999, pp. 3–22.

Pitelis, C., A Theory of the (Growth of the) Transnational Firm: A Penrosian Perspective, *Contributions to Political Economy*. 19, 2000, p. 71–79.

Pitelis, C. N. (ed.), *The Growth of the Firm: The Legacy of Edith Penrose*, Oxford: Oxford University Press 2002.

Pitelis, C. N., Edith Penrose and the Resource-based View of (International) Business Strategy, *International Business Review*, 13, 4, 2004, pp. 523–532.

Pitelis, C., A Note on Cyert and March (1963) and Penrose (1959): A Case for Synergy, Organization Science Special Issue, 'A Behavioral Theory of the Firm? 40 Years and Counting', Submission 2006.

Rugman, A./Verbeke, A., A Final Word on Edith Penrose, *Journal of Management Studies*, 41, 1, 2004, pp. 205–217.

Rugman, A. M./Verbeke, A., A Note on the Transnational Solution and the Transaction Cost Theory of Multinational Strategic Management, *Journal of International Business Studies*, 23, 4, 1992, pp.761–71.

Rugman, A. M./Verbeke, A., Subsidiary-specific Advantages in Multinational Enterprises, *Strategic Management Journal*, 22, 3, 2001, pp. 237–250.

Rugman, A. M./Verbeke, A., Edith Penrose's Contribution to the Resource-based View of Strategic Management, *Strategic Management Journal*, 23, 2002, pp. 769–780.

Rugman, A. M./Verbeke, A., Extending the Theory of the Multinational Enterprise: Internalization and Strategic Management Perspectives, *Journal of International Business Studies*, 34, 2, 2003, pp. 125–137.

Rugman, A. M./Verbeke, A., A Perspective on Regional and Global Strategies of Multinational Enterprises, *Journal of International Business Studies*, 35, 1, 2004, pp. 3–18.

Rumelt, R., Towards a Strategic Theory of the Firm, in Lamb, R. B. (ed.), *Competitive Strategic Management*, Englewood Cliffs, NJ: Prentice Hall 1984.

Rumelt, R./Schendel, D./Teece, D., Introduction, in Rumelt, R./Schendel, D./Teece, D. (eds.), *Fundamental Issues in Strategy*, Boston: Harvard Business School Press 1994.

Schumpeter, J., *The Theory of Economic Development*, Cambridge: Harvard University Press 1934.

Simon, H. A., Organizations and Markets, *Journal of Economic Perspectives*, 5, 2, 1991, pp. 25–44.

Simon, H.A., Strategy and Organizational Evolution, *Strategic Management Journal*, 14, Winter Special Issue, 1993, pp.131–142.

Teece, D., The Market for Know-how and the Efficient International Transfer of Technology, *The Annals of the Academy of Political and Social Science*, 458, 1981, pp. 81–96.

Teece, D., Towards an Economic Theory of the Multiproduct Firm, *Journal of Economic Behavior and Organization*, 3, 1, 1982, pp. 39–63.

Teece, D., *Managing Intellectual Capital*, Oxford: Oxford University Press 2000.

Teece, D., Reflections on the Hymer Thesis, *International Business Review*, 15, 2, 2006, pp. 124–139.

Teece, D., *Explicating Dynamic Capabilities*, Seminar held at the Judge Business School, Cambridge May 2006.

Teece, D./Pisano, G., The Dynamic Capabilities of Firms: An Introduction, *Industrial and Corporate Change*, 3, 3, 1994, pp. 537–556.

Teece, D./Pisano, G./Shuen, A., Dynamic Capabilities and Strategic Management, *Strategic Management Journal*, 18, 7, 1997, pp. 537–533.

Uzawa, H., Time Preference and the Penrose Effect in a Two-Class Model of Economic Growth, *Journal of Public Economy*, 77, 4, 1969, pp. 628–652.

Wernerfelt, B., A Resource-based View of the Firm, *Strategic Management Journal*, 5, 2, 1984, pp. 171–180.

Williamson, O. E., *Markets and Hierarchies: Analysis and Antitrust Implications*, New York: Free Press 1975.

Williamson, O. E., *The Economic Institutions of Capitalism*, New York: Free Press 1985.

Winter, S., Understanding Dynamic Capabilities, *Strategic Management Journal*, 24, 10, 2003, pp. 991–995.

Managers, Markets, and Dynamic Capabilities

Introduction

The concept of dynamic capabilities highlights organizational and managerial competences. Key ingredients of dynamic capabilities include organizational processes directed toward learning and innovation, the basic manner in which a business is designed, as well as the decision frames and heuristics that inform firms' investment choices over time. Once assets come within the orbit of management rather than the market, their effective utilization and orchestration becomes essential. Indeed, orchestration directed at achieving new combinations and co-alignment of assets is central to the dynamic capabilities framework. Such orchestration requires astute decision making and entrepreneurial capacity. Managers play a critical role in such orchestration and therefore have particular importance for dynamic capabilities.

Dynamic capabilities of all types perform an economic function: they affect how well business enterprises function within an economic system. An analysis of dynamic capabilities would be incomplete if it did not address this economic function. In this chapter, we analyze what economic theory and logic does and does not tell us about (strategic) managers in general and the asset orchestration function that they perform in particular. We also suggest promising directions for an economic theory of the firm that incorporates the dynamic capabilities of managers in a central way. This economic approach to understanding the managerial processes that underpin dynamic capabilities complements the following chapter, which focuses on organizational research on managerial and organizational processes. Together these two chapters provide a backdrop for the empirical analyses of managerial and organizational dynamic capabilities in subsequent chapters.

Understanding the Fundamental Economic Problems "Solved" by Strategic Managers

It is an understatement to say that economic theory underplays the role of the manager; in fact, the strategic manager simply does not exist in any recognizable

Reprinted with permission from *Dynamic Capabilities: Understanding Strategic Change in Organizations* (Blackwell Publishing, 2007), by Constance E. Helfat, Sydney Finkelstein, Will Mitchell, Margaret A. Peteraf, Harbir Singh, David J. Teece and Sidney G. Winter, pp. 19–29.

form. True, shareholders appoint agents (managers) to stewardship roles in the enterprise, but economic theory says little about what executives actually do and the economic function, if any, that they perform.[1] Sometimes executives manage workers through the employment relationship; but otherwise the executive in economic theory is rather a lackluster being who is almost completely invisible, and doesn't really perform an economic function, other than standing in for the owner/investor.

At least one well-known economist has commented on this lacuna. William Baumol notes that in economic theory:

"There is no room for enterprise or initiative. The management group becomes a passive calculator that reacts mechanically to changes imposed on it by fortuitous external developments over which it does not exert, and does not even attempt to exert, any influence. One hears of no clever ruses, ingenious schemes, brilliant innovations, of no charisma or of any of the other stuff of which outstanding entrepreneurship is made; one does not hear of them because there is no way in which they can fit into the model." (Baumol, 1968: 67)

The cavalier treatment of entrepreneurship and management in economics stems in part from a failure to understand the importance of managing organizations, and the absence of well-developed and well-functioning markets for intangibles and other idiosyncratic assets, particularly those of the co-specialized variety. Because markets are often viewed, at least in the neoclassical paradigm, as working rather frictionlessly, the special role that managers play in transactions and in asset deployment, business model design, strategy formulation and implementation, and leadership seems quite unnecessary. In a perfectly competitive world with homogeneous inputs and outputs and technology that are ubiquitously available for all, the functions identified above aren't needed. The manager is left simply as a calculator, setting marginal revenue equal to marginal cost. Of course, if this is all managers do, a reasonably simple software program and a set of rules for the organization would void the need for managers and management.

On closer examination, however, executive management performs several distinctive and important roles, which help the economic system overcome special problems, problems that might otherwise result in "market failures." That is, but for the actions of astute managers, competitive markets wouldn't function very well. Moreover, business organizations couldn't function either. Seven particular classes of economic functions can be assigned in economic theory to management. They are: 1) orchestrating co-specialized assets; 2) selecting organizational/governance modes and associated incentive systems; 3) designing business models; 4) nurturing change (and innovation) processes/routines; 5) making investment choices; 6) providing leadership, vision, and motivation to employees; and 7) designing and implementing controls and basic operations. None of these functions can be performed well, if at

---

[1] Oliver Williamson has noted that supplying a coherent theory of effective coordination and resource allocation, and of entrepreneurship and technical progress is a "tall order" (Williamson, 1991: 19). This chapter endeavors to make progress towards this goal, which has important ramifications for management theory and the theory of the firm. It implies a very different set of economic activities as the essence of the enterprise than the literature has heretofore featured.

all, by computers or by naked market processes. Managers are needed to make markets work well, and to make organizations function properly.

The first six classes of decisions are "strategic" and/or entrepreneurial and must be performed astutely for firms to compete effectively. They relate to issues of strategic "fit" between the company and its competitive environment, as well as between and amongst the assets that comprise the resource base of the firm. We do not discuss the seventh set of decisions at length in this chapter, as it focuses on more operational issues. The management skills required for successful execution of operational decisions are conceptually different from those required for strategic management. The fact that they are not at the essential core of this book does not make them unimportant. Operational capabilities can provide a strong point of differentiation and advantage for a particular company. Nevertheless, we largely ignore these considerations in this chapter, which focuses on strategic management in general and decisions around resource allocation and asset alignment in particular.

If managers did not perform strategic functions within and among business enterprises, the entire adjustment and resource allocation function in the economy would fall on the price system. However, it is also generally accepted that a complete set of contingent claims markets does not exist, and even when markets do exist, trading volumes are often thin. If certain assets are rarely if ever bought and sold, then how can the economic system be restructured and assets brought into alignment?

The economics literature contains some general recognition that "internal organization" solves the problem. Exactly how internal organization solves the problem is never explained very well, if at all. Williamson and others have suggested that, with internal organization, "managerial fiat" allocates resources. Unfortunately, the extant literature doesn't go much further. In this chapter, we seek to identify the functions of the executive that matter in a fundamental economic sense, and with regard to dynamic capabilities in particular. In this manner, we may better understand the distinctive role of managerial activity.

Asset Orchestration (In the Face of Thin Markets)

In early management scholarship, Chester Barnard and others stressed the role of management in limiting conflict and effectuating cooperation inside the firm. Barnard saw formal organization and the business firm as a system of consciously coordinated activities of two or more persons. In Barnard's view, achieving successful cooperation should by no means be taken for granted, as it is by no means the norm. As he notes, "most cooperation fails in the attempt, or dies in infancy, or is short lived" (Barnard, 1938: 5). The particular functions of management that Barnard recognizes include control, supervision, and administration (Barnard, 1938: 6), which are operational activities that relate to the business of keeping an organization functioning. Although these (managerial) functions must be performed, they ignore the importance of the strategic functions that managers perform in dynamic environments.[2]

---

[2] It is perhaps of interest to note that Barnard's perspectives were no doubt shaped by his experience as an executive in the Bell System. Barnard served as President of New Jersey Bell. At the time, it was a regulated telephone company.

Today, many of the firm's assets are intangibles, and flexibility, entrepreneurship, and adjustment and adaptation to competition and changing consumer needs is paramount. We address these functions in more detail below.

General considerations regarding asset orchestration

One of the most touted virtues of a private enterprise economy is its ability to achieve the coordination of disparate actors external to the enterprise itself – both consumers and producers – without central planners (Hayek, 1945). The price system of course serves as the mechanism that supposedly facilitates coordination. Prices act as signals of scarcity or abundance. Consumers adjust to price increases by reducing consumption; producers react to the same signal by increasing production, and the market clears. This simple mechanism means that a good deal of resource allocation can take place via market mechanisms – quickly and efficiently. Prices rise and resources will move to the higher valued activity; ditto when prices fall. Commodity markets usually behave in this fashion; and if all markets were commodity like, then the role and importance of (strategic) management would be limited.

A very large proportion of goods, assets, and services, however, are not exchanged in open, organized, and well-developed markets. For many transactions – forward, contingent, term, and spot – markets do not exist or are occasional at best. In these circumstances, markets are "thin," offering limited liquidity for asset holders. Assets are not automatically allocated to their first best use. As we discuss below, this creates the opportunity for managers to use the firm's financial and other resources to build value inside firms. These functions are also socially desirable in most instances because they assist in aligning certain types of complementary assets – alignment which is necessary for systemic innovation and enhanced competition. If the economic system fails in these functions, firm performance and the economy at large will suffer.

Thin markets are exposed to transactional complexity and contractual hazards; or even if not exposed to hazards, may experience liquidity discounts – the difference between "bid" and "ask" prices is likely to be large. Frequently, transactions in these markets don't occur at all because the services that an idiosyncratic asset provides may be difficult to describe, to define, and to access. If the asset is a competence, the valuation may be difficult to assess if the value of the competence depends on complementary and/or co-specialized assets owned by the seller, the buyer, or third parties. All of this is to say that certain assets tend to be built rather than bought (because there may not be a market) and to be deployed and redeployed inside the firm rather than sold (because sale in a market is not a good way to extract value). Because assets are bundled together and often tightly linked inside incumbent firms, it may be difficult to obtain assets in the desired configurations through asset purchase or sale in mergers and acquisitions. This is not to say that mergers and acquisitions (M&A) are not an important component of asset reconfiguration. Indeed, Capron, Dussauge, and Mitchell (1998) argue that market failures that constrain the exchange of discrete resources create incentives to use mergers and acquisitions in order to accomplish asset reconfiguration. Put differently, asset purchases/sales are often infeasible, absent purchasing or selling corporate entities in which many such assets are bundled together.

A striking example of thin or nonexistent markets is the market for know-how and for intangible assets more generally. As Teece (1981) noted more than two decades ago, "unassisted markets are seriously faulted as institutional devices for facilitating trading in many kinds of technological and managerial know-how. The imperfections in the market for know-how for the most part can be traced to the nature of the commodity in question." The same is true with respect to intellectual property and other intangibles. Mutually beneficial trades frequently don't happen because the property rights may be poorly defined (fuzzy),[3] the asset difficult to transfer, or its use difficult to meter. When arm's-length market trading is impaired, internal resource allocation and asset transfer within the firm achieves greater significance. This is of course a managerially directed activity.

Accordingly, resource allocation inside the firm substitutes and complements resource allocation by markets when markets for particular assets are thin or non-existent. Relatedly, because of co-specialization, or because of differing perceptions about future demand and technological innovation, or because of differing asset positions of buyer and seller, there may be wide disparities between how the existing owner of an asset values it and the manner in which another agent or potential owner might value it.

Because many intangible assets are idiosyncratic, they may be more valuable when they can co-evolve in a coordinated way with other assets. The ability to assemble unique configurations of co-specialized assets therefore can enhance value. In short, managers often create great value by assembling particular constellations of assets inside an enterprise, because by employing such assets, they frequently can produce highly differentiated and innovative goods and services that consumers want. This process of assembling and orchestrating particular constellations of assets for economic gain is a fundamental function of management.

Effectuating systemic innovation (Teece, 2000) provides a good example of asset orchestration. Systemic innovation occurs when deep co-specialization exists between parts of a system requiring in turn the tight coordination across subsystems for innovation to occur. Systemic innovation contrasts with autonomous innovation, in which technological development can occur without immediate and direct co-ordination with other elements of a system.

Consider the automobile. New types of tires (such as tubeless tires, and later radial tires) have over time been developed without immediate regard for other developments in the automobile. Notwithstanding that some "components" can be developed independent of other parts of the system, it is frequently the case that innovation in one component will facilitate innovation elsewhere. For example, radial tires permitted cars to be designed for higher speeds, without compromising safety.

Systemic innovation, on the other hand, almost always requires common managerial control of the parts for success, since innovation activity must be highly coordinated

---

[3] See Teece (2000) for a discussion of the fuzzy boundaries associated with intellectual property rights.

Thin markets →

           Need for internal resource *allocation* →

                      Strategic managers required

Thin markets in the presence of change →

           Need for internal resource *reconfiguration* →

                      Strategic managers who build, align, and
                                  adapt co-specialized assets

Figure 2.1 Thin markets and strategic managers

across subsystems. Contractual mechanisms will rarely suffice to achieve the necessary coordination between or amongst firms (Teece, 1980; 1988b). For instance, the Lockheed L1011 wide-bodied aircraft's late entry into the market was caused by the inability of Rolls-Royce to develop the RB211 engine on time – and the aircraft design was co-specialized to the new, still undeveloped, engine. Indeed, the failure of Rolls-Royce to develop the RB211 on time was a major contributing factor not only to the slow launch of the L1011, but also to the bankruptcy of the Lockheed Corporation.

In short, fuzzy property rights (as with intangibles), appropriability issues, and co-specialization are among the reasons why asset markets can be thin. This renders market transactions difficult. Whenever this occurs, managers have a distinctive role that differs from the role of traders and arbitrageurs.

Asset Orchestration Versus Coordination and Adaptation

Coordination as an economic problem is only necessary because of change (Hayek, 1945). In a static environment, a short period of "set up" would be required to organize economic activity; but absent change in consumer tastes or technology, economic agents (both traders and managers) would sort out the optimal flows of goods and services (together with methods of production). Thereafter, there would be no need for their services.

Now introduce change. If there were a complete set of forward and contingent claims markets, adjustments would occur automatically; absent a complete set of futures and contingent claims markets, there is the need for economic agents to engage in trading activities, and for managers/entrepreneurs to "integrate, build, and reconfigure internal and external competences to address rapidly changing environments" (Teece, Pisano, and Shuen, 1997). That is why what Adner and Helfat (2003) termed "dynamic managerial capabilities" hold particular importance.

> **Dynamic managerial capability** *is the capacity of managers to purposefully create, extend, or modify the resource base of an organization.*
> Dynamic managerial capabilities include **asset orchestration**.

Coordinating and adapting effectively to changing environments (Cyert and March, 1963) is an important managerial function that is an element of a firm's dynamic capabilities. Barnard (1938) and Richardson (1960) developed this theme early. Chester Barnard viewed the firm fundamentally as a structure to achieve coordination and adaptation. But as Williamson (1995) observes, Barnard did not compare the firm with markets in terms of their coordinative or adaptive capabilities. As noted above, one key difference is that the firm, by employing astute managers and good incentive design, can achieve coordination and adaptation with respect to nontraded or thinly traded assets; the market on the other hand enables rapid adaptation with respect to assets that are actively traded in thick markets.

However, the strategic management function involves much more than "coordination" and "adaptation." The functions of the (strategic) executive go well beyond what Barnard and Williamson identified. In particular, "coordination" and "adaptation" as management functions do not fully capture the essence of critical managerial activity in dynamic markets. Such managerial activity involves, inter alia, orchestrating complementary and co-specialized assets, inventing and implementing new business models, and making astute investment choices (including with regard to R&D and M&A) in situations of uncertainty and ambiguity.[4] Nor do traditional perspectives convey the importance of asset alignment, opportunity identification, and accessing critical co-specialized assets. These are all important managerial functions that create value.

Put another way, the importance of strategic management stems in a fundamental sense from what can be thought of as "market failures."[5] The "market failures" arise not just from high transaction costs and contractual incompleteness.[6] Rather, they have to do with the thinness of asset markets, and the need to identify, "build," align, adapt, and coordinate activities and assets, especially complementary/co-specialized assets. Managers perform these important functions in the economic system.

G. B. Richardson (1960) has remarked on the information problems associated with achieving coordination and investment decisions. However, he focused on industry-level coordination of investment. He identified situations where limited information about competitors' investment decisions may impede efficient investment. In contrast, the essential coordination task identified here involves assembling and reassembling often idiosyncratic firm assets (including through strategic alliances with other firms).

---

[4] Milgrom and Roberts (1990: 525) also note that "non-convexities and significant complementarities provide a reason for explicit coordination between functions such as marketing and production."

[5] The use of the term "market failure" is only relative to the theoretical norm of absolute static and dynamic efficiency. Of course, a (private) enterprise economic system as a whole achieves an efficient allocation of resources, as strategic managers and the organization they lead are an inherent part of the economic system. However, the framework does highlight the fact that management systems and corporate governance must function well for a private enterprise market-oriented system to function well.

[6] To the extent that transaction costs are relevant, they are of the dynamic variety (see Langlois, 1992).

Asset orchestration
→ A fundamental function of management
→ Particularly important in dynamic settings
→ Assembling and "orchestrating" configurations of co-specialized assets

Needless to say, the proficient achievement of the necessary coordination by no means occurs automatically. Decision makers need information about changing consumer needs and technology. Such information is not always available; or if it is available, decision makers must collect information, analyze it, synthesize it, and act on it inside the firm. Situations are dealt with in many ways, sometimes by creating rules, which specify how the organization will respond to the observations made (March and Simon, 1958). If this path is chosen, then rules may become codified and routinely applied (Casson, 2000: 129) whenever certain changes are detected.[7] However, such rules need to be periodically revised, which entails dynamic capabilities.

The coordinating and resource allocating activities performed by managers shape markets[8] as much as markets shape the business enterprise (Chandler, 1990; Simon, 1993). Put simply, the business enterprise and markets co-evolve. Managers shape this co-evolution. The need for asset coordination and orchestration and associated investment choices is a fundamental economic problem that the firm's managers help address. In this regard, the evolutionary fitness of a business enterprise may be endogenous to its technical fitness. By using technically proficient asset orchestration capabilities, managers may be able to shape the external environment to the firm's advantage, leading to evolutionary fitness.

The emergence/development of competitive markets is thus important for strategic management. As markets become developed and highly efficient, managers have less room to build competitive advantage (Barney, 1986). The emergence of competitive intermediate product markets in petroleum and chemicals, for example,

Figure 2.2   Co-evolution of markets and the business enterprise

[7]   Casson argues that rule making is entrepreneurial, but that rule implementation is routine, and is characterized by managerial and administrative work.
[8]   For example, both Priceline and eBay set out to alter the structure of existing markets, and to some extent did so.

has been identified as a major leveler in global competition (Teece, 2000). Competitive advantage is illusory when all markets are highly competitive. However, change and technological innovation create new market opportunities. As long as idiosyncratic assets abound, this will create thin market situations and provide opportunities for competitive advantage.

Towards a Dynamic Capabilities (Economic) Theory of the Firm

Ronald Coase in his classic (1937) article on the nature of the firm described firms and markets as alternative modes of governance, the choice between them made so as to minimize transaction costs. The boundaries of the firm were set by bringing transactions into the firms so that at the margin the internal costs of organizing equilibrated with the costs associated with transacting in the market.

Initiated by Coase's (1937) seminal paper, a substantial literature has emerged on the relative efficiencies of firms and markets. This literature, greatly expanded by Oliver Williamson (1975; 1985) and others, has come to be known as transaction cost economics. It analyzes the relative efficiencies of markets and internal organization, as well as intermediate forms of organization such as strategic alliances.

Contractual difficulties associated with asset specificity are at the heart of the relative efficiency calculations in transaction cost economics. When specific assets are needed to support efficient production, then the preferred organizational mode is internal organization. Vertical and other forms of integration are preferred over contractual arrangements when efficient production requires investors to make irreversible investments in specific assets. The structures used to support transactions are referred to as governance modes. Internal organization (doing things inside the firm) is one such governance mode.

The dynamic capabilities approach is very consistent with Coase in some ways but not others. It is accepted that it is useful to think of the firm and markets as alternative modes of governance. Relatedly, the selection of what to organize (manage) internally versus via alliances versus the market depends on the nontradability of assets and what Langlois has termed "dynamic transactions costs."

But it is not enough to convert the notion of nontradability entirely into the concept of "transaction costs," defined by Arrow (1969: 48) as the "costs of running the economic system." Others have tried to operationalize the concept of transaction costs, with Alchian and Demsetz (1972) proposing technological nonseparabilities and Williamson (1985) focusing on specific assets. There is indeed a strong relationship between specific assets and nontraded or thinly traded assets.

However, there are reasons why assets are not traded (or are thinly traded) that do not relate to asset specificity. For instance, the land on the corner of Park Avenue and 59th Street in New York City rarely comes onto the market. The ability to write highly creative and efficient software for computer operating systems is not widely distributed. Brands that signal particular values (e.g. Lexus) are likewise thinly traded. Uniqueness and asset specificity aren't quite the same. In addition, the concept of co-specialization is important (Teece, 1986). Assets that are co-specialized to each

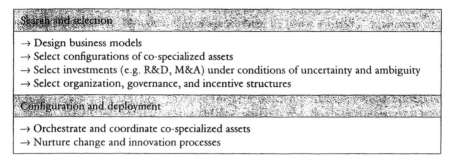

Figure 2.3 Elements of asset orchestration

other need to be employed in conjunction, often inside the firm.[9] This isn't the
emphasis of Coase, Alchian and Demsetz, or of Williamson.

Assembling co-specialized assets inside the firm in the dynamic capabilities framework is not done primarily to guard against opportunism and recontracting hazards,
although in some cases that may be important. Instead, because effective coordination and alignment of these assets/resources is difficult to achieve through the price
system, special value can accrue to achieving good alignment within the firm. This is
different from what Barnard (1938) has suggested with his emphasis on the functions
of the executive as rooted in cooperative adaptation of a conscious and deliberate
kind. Here the focus is on the "orchestration" of co-specialized assets by strategic
managers. It is a proactive process designed to: 1) keep co-specialized assets in
value-creating co-alignment, 2) select new co-specialized assets to be developed
through the investment process, and 3) divest or run down co-specialized assets that
no longer help yield value. Rather than stressing opportunism (although opportunism surely exists and must be guarded against), the emphasis in dynamic capabilities
is on change processes, inventing and reinventing the architecture of the business,
asset selection, and asset orchestration.

One might reasonably ask the reasons for this significant difference in emphasis.
Clearly, in dynamic capabilities, a comparative institutional framework is adopted.
"Small numbers" bargaining is at the core, as in Williamson (1975). However, the
emphasis on dynamic capabilities is not just on protecting value, but also on creating
it. Barnard wouldn't naturally see the importance of this emphasis, because his
laboratory was the regulated Bell operating companies.

Alchian and Demsetz and Williamson have all emphasized opportunistic free riding. Indeed, their human actors are assumed to be boundedly rational, self-interest
seeking, opportunistic, and full of guile. The dynamic capabilities framework adds
other (arguably less ubiquitous) traits of human nature: 1) intrapreneurship and
entrepreneurship, and 2) foresight and acumen. Williamson appears to recognize

---

[9] Dynamic capabilities centrally concern the strategic management function, which tran-
scends the question of optimal firm boundaries. Value can be created by astutely organizing
assets both inside and outside the firm. In this sense, one should not expect a theory of
dynamic capabilities to uniquely provide a theory of the firm.

that such skills ought to influence the theory of economic organization, when he quotes businessman Rolf Sprecket: "Whenever I see something badly done, or not done at all, I see an opportunity to make a fortune." Williamson comments: "Those instincts, if widely operative, will influence the practice and ought to influence the theory of economic organization" (1999: 1089). This statement opens the door to dynamic capabilities.

There are other differences as well. Williamson makes the transaction the unit of analysis; in dynamic capabilities, the currency of interest includes complementary and co-specialized assets. The utility of transaction cost economics and related frameworks to make–buy–ally decisions and related governance decisions are not in dispute. But transaction cost economics leaves us without an understanding of the distinctive role of strategic management. Executives must not only choose governance modes (as between market arrangements, alliances, and internal organization), but they must also understand how to design and implement different governance structures, and to coordinate investment activities.

Just as the governance of markets is not preordained by the economic system, nor is the selection of governance modes. Many elements of internal organization, business model design, and alliance structure require managers to select and design methods of governance. For example, as chapter 5 explains in more detail, a relational capability for alliances includes selection and design of alliance governance. Again, dynamic capabilities come to the fore.

Conclusion

In this chapter, we have argued that any robust economic theory of the firm must include a primary role for strategic managers and their dynamic capabilities. Critical dynamic managerial capabilities include asset orchestration, frequently involving co-specialized and complementary assets within the resource base of an organization. Not only must managers assemble these bundles of resources, but also they must design appropriate governance and incentive structures.

Part II

INTELLECTUAL CAPITAL, TECHNOLOGY TRANSFER, AND ORGANIZATIONAL LEARNING

An Economics Perspective on Intellectual Capital[1]

Mie Augier

Stanford University

David J. Teece

Haas School of Business, University of California, Berkeley

> Technological advance, resting in the new knowledge and occurring accidentally or mechanically, seems to be the only possible offset to this "natural" tendency to diminishing returns.
>
> Frank H. Knight, "Diminishing Returns from Investments," *Journal of Political Economy*

Introduction

Business organizations employ knowledge. They generate and process information, formulate plans and strategies, make decisions, monitor behavior and experiences, and learn, create, and use know-how. Although economists have traditionally modeled firms as employing capital, labor, and other factors of production to increase output—possibly with exogenous technical change as a shift parameter in the production function—it is increasingly realized within the economics profession that knowledge and intellectual capital (IC) are the primary creators of value in the economy (i.e., the creation and use of intangible rather than tangible [physical] assets are the keys to wealth creation), and technological change is not exogenous but, in fact, generated in large measure by firms themselves. As Peter Drucker suggested: "The traditional factors of production—land, labor and capital—have not disappeared. But they have become secondary. Knowledge is becoming the only meaningful resource" (1993, p. 42).

Economists and management it was probally scholars (as well as scholars from other disciplines) have done much to advance our understanding of the central issues around intellec-tual capital. While classical economists were aware of the role of technology and knowledge in economic growth, Schumpeter who brought innovation to the fore. Unfortunately, Schumpeterian economics until quite recently was ignored by mainstream economists. Notable exceptions to this include Paul David, Giovanni Dosi, Chris Freeman, Zvi Griliches, Edwin Mansfield, David Mowery, Richard

---

[1] We are indebted to Bernard Marr for encouragement and suggestions and to Patricia Lonergan for skillful assistance.

Nelson, Nathan Rosenberg, Sidney Winter, and occasionally Kenneth Arrow and Robert Solow. These economists took innovation issues seriously, and while small in number, they initiated several streams of research that helped build a rich understanding of the economics of technological change. In recent years, business economists and management scholars added considerably to the understanding of technological change and intellectual capital.

In short, economists provided early insights into many of the issues around knowledge and technological innovation. As an example, at least since Arrow (1962), knowledge has been well appreciated (among economists) for its "public good" characteristics (i.e., the nonrivalrous nature of consumption) because of high levels of nonexcludability. The attributes of knowledge have been used to explain, for instance, why imitation can (but need not be) easy, why diffusion of new technologies depends on the mobility of engineers and scientists, and why know-how markets do not work well (Teece 1977a, 1981a). Also, more-recent research on the generation of new knowledge made it possible to understand the role of technological externalities and the positive feedback effects on technological innovation (David, 1993).

Despite the development of important insights by a few economists, it is unfortunately the case that the production and utilization of technological and organizational knowledge is still handled in a rather cavalier way within mainstream (neoclassical) economic theory. The challenges posed by technological change for economic theory have been recognized since at least Frank Knight (1921), but it wasn't until Teece (1981a, 1986), Nelson and Winter (1982), and Nonaka (1991) that issues such as the tacit nature of much technological and organizational knowledge came to be widely recognized and the ramifications explored.[2] Because of the tacit (i.e., difficult or costly to articulate) nature of know-how, those practicing a technique may be able to do so with great facility, but they may not be able to transfer the skill to others without demonstration and involvement.

The growing recognition of the importance of knowledge and intangible assets, their tacit nature, and the desire to understand what creates competitive advantages at both the level of the firm and the level of the economy has stimulated many diverse (but not always consistent) streams of research on technological innovation and knowledge management. The intention of this chapter is to review some of the key insights and contributions to the economics and management of intellectual capital. The following section focuses on the organization of research and development (R&D) and the production of new technology. The next section outlines classical contributions to understanding the role of knowledge in the economy and the increasing awareness of the importance of innovation. The section after that surveys central concepts in the economies of knowledge and intellectual property as they exist in the literature today. Then we highlight the measurement issues and review some of the relevant recent empirical literature on intangibles before the chapter concludes.

---

[2] Frank Knight is an often-neglected advocate for the fact that technological change makes economic predictions difficult; as he stated: "The most fundamentally and irretrievably uncertain phases or factors of progress are those which amount essentially to the increase of knowledge as such. This description evidently holds for the improvement of technological processes and the forms of business organization and for the discovery of new natural resources. Here it is a contradiction in terms to speak of anticipation, in an accurate and detailed sense, for to anticipate the advance would be to make it at once" (Knight 1921, p. 318).

Organizing Research and Development and Knowledge Production Activities

Intellectual assets created by businesses are developed through learning, experience, and at least since the early twentieth century, of course, organized industrial research and development (R&D) activities. R&D encompasses several different activities that can occur in any order. Basic research is aimed purely at the creation of new scientific and technical knowledge. Its purpose is to advance understanding of phenomena. Its core foundations are usually quite abstract. Applied research is designed to implement new scientific and technical knowledge, which is expected to have a practical but not necessarily a commercial payoff. While basic research is aimed at new knowledge for its own sake, the goal of applied research is practical and has utility. In development, the new knowledge is embedded in a product or process and honed for commercial application. Boundaries among these activities are quite fuzzy, and the manner in which they have been organized and linked has changed over time (Teece, 1989). For almost a century and a half, organized research activities have placed an important (although ever changing) role.

The first organized research laboratory in the United States was established by Thomas Edison in 1876. In 1886, Arthur D. Little, an applied scientist, started his enterprise, which became a major technical services, consulting organization to other enterprises. Eastman Kodak (1893), B. F. Goodrich (1895), General Electric (1900), Dow (1900), Dupont (1902), Goodyear (1909), and American Telephone & Telegraph (1907) followed soon thereafter. The industrial laboratory constituted a significant departure from an earlier period of U.S. history, when innovation was largely the work of independent inventors like Eli Whitney (the cotton gin), Samuel Morse (telegraph), Charles Goodyear (vulcanization of rubber), and Cyrus McCormick (the reaper).

The founding of formal R&D programs and laboratories stemmed in part from competitive threats, which necessitated a more proactive strategy toward innovation. For instance, AT&T at first followed the telegraph industry's practice of relying on the market for technological innovation. However, the expiration of the major Bell patents and the growth of large numbers of independent telephone companies helped stimulate AT&T to organize Bell Labs. Competition likewise drove George Eastman to established laboratories at Kodak Park in Rochester, New York, to counteract efforts by German dyestuff and chemical firms to enter into the manufacture of fine chemicals, including photographic chemicals and film.

During the early years of the twentieth century, the number of research labs grew dramatically. By World War I, perhaps as many as 100 industrial research laboratories were in the United States. The number tripled during that war, and industrial R&D even maintained its momentum during the Depression. R&D activity conducted in centralized laboratories of American business enterprises increased still further during World War II and maintained momentum through the 1950s and the 1960s. Significant breakthroughs included the transistor, electronic computing, synthetic fibers, and lasers.

By the early 1970s, however, management was beginning to lose faith in the science-driven view of industrial research and technological innovation, primarily because few blockbuster products emerged from the research funded during the 1950s, 1960s, and 1970s. As a result of this and other factors, from the mid-1970s on, there has been a marked change in organization and strategy, as both industry and government have come to recognize that the classical form of R&D organization, with centralized research and a science-driven culture, was simply not working, in part because new technology was not getting into new products and processes soon enough and imitation rates had increased. Foreign competitors began undermining the traditional markets of many U.S. firms.

Many firms realized that extracting value from intellectual capital is a much more-complicated and risky process than extracting value from physical capital. Many were confronted by the paradox of being leaders in R&D and the creation of intangibles but laggards in capturing value from their investments. The fruit of much R&D was being appropriated by domestic and foreign competitors, and much technology was wasting away in many research laboratories. In telecommunications, Bell Lab's contribution to the economy at large far outstripped its contribution to AT&T. Xerox Corporation's Palo Alto Research Center made stunning contributions to the economy in the area of the personal computer, local area networks, and the graphical user interface that became the basis of Apple's Macintosh computer. Xerox shareholders were well served, too, but most of the benefits ended up in the hands of Xerox's competitors.

By the 1980s and 1990s, a new model for organizing research became apparent. First, R&D activity came to be decentralized inside large corporations themselves, with the aim to bring it closer to the users. Intel, the world leader in microprocessors, spent over $1 billion per year on R&D but had no separate R&D laboratory. Rather, development was conducted in the manufacturing facilities. It did not invest in fundamental research at all, except possibly through its funding of university research. It did, however, participate actively in the development and sharing of new process knowledge through its funding of Sematech.

Second, many companies were looking to the universities for much of their basic or fundamental research, maintaining close associations with the science and engineering departments at the major research universities. Indeed, over the century, the percentage of academic research funded by industry grew from 2.7% in 1960 to 6.8% in 1995. However, strong links between university research and industrial research are limited primarily to electronics (especially semiconductors), chemical products, medicine, and agriculture. For the most part, university researchers are insufficiently versed in the particulars of specific product markets and customer needs to configure products to the needs of the market. Moreover, in many sectors, the cost of research equipment is so high that universities simply cannot participate.

Third, corporations embraced alliances involving R&D, manufacturing, and marketing to get products to market quicker and leverage off complementary assets already in place elsewhere. (It is important to note, however, that outsourcing R&D is a complement, not a substitute, to in-house R&D.) Outsourcing and codevelopment arrangements had become common by the 1980s and 1990s (e.g., Pratt & Whitney's codevelopment programs for jet engines), as the costs of product development increased and the antitrust laws were modified to recognize the benefits of cooperation on R&D and related activities. The National Cooperative Research Act of 1984 and its amendment in 1993 provided greater clarity with respect to the likely positive antitrust treatment of cooperative efforts relating to technological innovation and its commercialization. Cooperation was also facilitated by the emergence of capable potential partners in Europe and Japan.

These developments meant that, at the end of the twentieth century, research and development and the creation and exploitation of intangible assets was being conducted in quite a different manner from the early decades of the century. Many corporations closed their central research laboratories or dramatically scaled back, including Westinghouse, RCA, AT&T, and Unocal, to name just a few. Alliances and cooperative efforts of all kinds were of much greater importance in both developing and commercializing new knowledge.

Importantly, a transformation in industry structure brought about through venture-capital-funded startups was well underway. New business enterprises, or "startups," were in part the cause for the decline of research laboratories; but in many ways the startups still depended on the organized R&D labs for their birthright. Beginning in the late 1970s, the organized venture capital industry, providing funding for new enterprise development, rose to significance. This was particularly true in industries such as biotech and information services. While venture capital in one form or another has been around for much of the twentieth century—the Rockefellers, Morgans, Mellons, Vanderbilts, Hilmans, and other significant families had been funding entrepreneurs for quite some time—institutional sources of money, including pension funds and university endowments, had become significant sources by the 1980s. This dramatically increased the funds available, as well as the professionalism by which "the money" provided guidance to a new breed of entrepreneurs, eager to develop and market new products incorporating new technology.

As a result, venture funded startups proliferated in many sectors. While, in the 1970s, Apple Computer significantly "bootstrapped" (although it did take modest venture funding from Arthur Rock and others) itself into the personal computer industry, in the 1980s, Compaq and others received much larger infusions of venture capital to get started in the personal computer industry. In biotechnology, venture funding also grew to great significance. However, it is extremely unusual for venture funds to support the efforts of companies making investments in early stage research. Rather, venture funding tends to be focused more on exploiting intangibles, less in creating them. Successful startups frequently begin with a product or process concept (and often personnel) that has been "incubated" to some level in a research program of an already established firm. Nevertheless, the phenomena of venture funding is significant, as it is now a very important channel by which intangible assets are employed and new products and processes brought to market.

The Economics of Knowledge: Some Historical Roots

Antecedents

The inclusion of knowledge as a factor in the study of modern economic growth was advanced by post-World War II scholars studying the sources of productivity improvement in the U.S. economy. However, the linkage of knowledge to economic performance in fact had been made much earlier. Issues of knowledge externalities and learning were present in Smith (1776) and Marshall (1925); the tacit nature of knowledge had been recognized by Hayek (1945) and Knight (1921); and Schumpeter (1943) focused on entrepreneurship, the organization of innovation, and innovation-driven competition.[3] These antecedents are given only a cursory and selective review in what follows.

Adam Smith was aware of the importance of learning and knowledge for economic growth. His now famous discussion of the pin factory demonstrated how repeated

---

[3] As Schumpeter noted, "The fundamental impulse that sets and keeps the capitalist engine in motion comes from the new consumers' goods, the new methods of production or transportation, the new markets, the new forms of industrial organization that capitalist enterprise creates" (Schumpeter, 1943, p. 83).

exposure to individual tasks in the pin-making process enabled workers to increase production. As he wrote,

> The great increase of the quantity of work which, in consequence of the division of labor, the same number of people are capable of performing, is owing to three different circumstances; first, to the increase of individual dexterity in every particular workman; secondly, to the saving of time which is commonly lost in passing from one species of work to another; and lastly, to the invention of a great number of machines which facilitate and abridge labour. (Smith 1776, p. 112).

In other words, learning by doing increases output from individual skills in part because of product innovations. Wealth and growth in Smith is a coevolutionary process, in which growing markets support the division of labor.[4] In effect, Smith recognized that the division of labor and increasing returns follows from organizational change and learning. Others recognized that the capacity for individuals and organizations to create and absorb new knowledge is important (Loasby 2004). These elements were subsequently developed further in theories of the firm by Edith Penrose (1959), Nelson and Winter (1982), Teece (1982, 1984), and others.

Another important contribution by a classical economist to the economics of knowledge was Alfred Marshall's early discussion of "external economies" arising from the interaction between industrial districts. He recognized that positive externalities were available to all firms in a given industry. Marshall thus flagged early on the importance of spillover and appropriability issues. Others agreed. For instance, Allyn Young noted that, "not all of the economies which are properly to be called external can be accounted for by adding up the internal economies of all the separate firms" (Young 1928, p. 528).

However, while ideas relating to the study of innovation were mentioned by the classical economists, they provided no in-depth analysis or analytical apparatus to help us better understand the particulars of technological innovation and the creation and commercialization of intellectual capital and other intangibles. A rather limited number of economists, including Nelson and Winter, Abramovitz, Kuznets, Mansfield, and Rosenberg, kept the study of innovation alive and added to our understanding of knowledge generation, storage, and use.

Knowledge (know-how) and information (know-of) are related but analytically separate concepts. Nevertheless, it is important to recognize that issues surrounding ignorance and asymmetric information did receive attention. For instance, Simon (1955, 1978) studied the impact of bounded rationality, and Akerlof and others studied the impact of limited information on market failure. In particular, Simon criticized assumptions of perfect information and unlimited computational capacity and aimed to replace the assumption of global rationality with an assumption more in correspondence with how humans (and other choosing organisms) made decisions, their computational limitations, and how they accessed information in their current environments (1955, p. 99).

Furthermore, the injection of the entrepreneur into economic theory by Knight (1921), Schumpeter (1934), and others was also clearly significant; but as with innovation and learning, not much analytical structure was provided for analyzing the role

---

[4] As Young (1928) wrote: "Adam Smith's dictum amounts to the theorem that the division of labour depends in large part upon the division of labour . . . change becomes progressive and propagates itself in a cumulative way" (p. 533).

of knowledge in organizations in a detailed way, and so conceptual development of issues related to intangibles failed to become mainstream.

This left economics as a field being perhaps the first of the social sciences to flag the importance of innovation to economic and social development; yet economic theory was extremely slow to incorporate this understanding into its mainstream. Most economists preferred to ignore the subject, as it tended to make economic modeling more difficult. Static rather than (technologically) dynamic models held the attention of the profession for quite a number of decades.[5]

Innovation and Economic Growth

The notion that innovation is not just an important phenomenon but the primary driver of economic growth was long suspected by classical economists.[6] Economic historians consistently recognized the importance of knowledge (e.g., Kuznets 1967, Abramovitz 1962) and kept knowledge on stage in the study of economic growth.[7] As discussed previously, outlines of modern theories of technological change and growth are of Smithian origins. Considerable additional impetus to the importance of innovation and intangible assets came when Solow (1957) provided the important calculation that 87.5% of the growth in output in the United States between the years of 1909 and 1949 could be ascribed to technological improvements alone. The "Solow residual" was not just substantial, it appeared to be of overwhelming importance. However, one early reaction was to try and explain the "residual" by reference to improvements in the quality of the capital stock.[8]

Indeed, growth theorists did not take the full import of empirical studies by productivity/growth scholars seriously for quite some time. Nicholas Kaldor argued for the existence of a "technical progress" function: Per-capita income was a function of

---

[5] The use of mathematic modeling in economics has been debated for centuries, at least in part because excessive formalism often undermines dynamics (Nelson and Winter 1982; Teece 1984). Alfred Marshall for instance wrote to a student and colleague: "(1) Use mathematics as a shorthand language, rather than as an engine of inquiry. (2) Keep to them till you have done. (3) Translate into English. (4) Then illustrate by examples that are important in real life. (5) Burn the mathematics. (6) If you can't succeed in 4, burn 3." (in Krugman 1998). Debreu's textbook of course promotes a different view: "The theory of value is treated here with the standards of rigor of the contemporary formalist school of mathematics" (1959, p. x). The problem is that the rigor of mathematics undermines the empirical validity of the theory. Nelson and Winter (1982) distinguish between "formal" and "appreciative" theorizing in economics, with appreciative referring to empirically relevant and applied work.

[6] See, for instance, Schumpeter (1943): "The essential point to grasp is that in dealing with capitalism we are dealing with an evolutionary process. . . . The fundamental impulse that sets and keeps the capitalist engine in motion comes from the new consumer goods, the new methods of production or transportation, the new forms of industrial organization that capitalist enterprise creates. . . . In the case of retail trade the competition that matters arises not from additional shops of the same type, but from the department store, the chain store, the mail-order house and the super market, which are bound to destroy those pyramids sooner or later. Now a theoretical construction which neglects this essential element of the case neglects all that is most typically capitalist about it; even if correct in logic as well as in fact, it is like Hamlet without the Danish Prince."

[7] Kuznets remarked, "all empirical knowledge, all scientifically tested information, no matter how abstract and remote it may seem, is potentially applicable in economic production" (1967, p. 61).

[8] Solow argues, for instance, that increased capital-intensive investment embodies new machinery and new ideas as well as increased learning for even further economic progress.

per-capita investment. In a series of important studies, Edward Denison (1962), Zvi Griliches (1963), and Dale W. Jorgensen and Zvi Griliches (1967) argued that there were errors in measurement in the early growth work. One such error, it was argued, was that the Solow residual actually was substantially less than first estimated, because if technical progress usually arrives "embodied" in new capital goods, then a lot more growth can be ascribed to simply the "qualitative growth" of capital inputs.

Further progress began to be made when Kenneth Arrow argued that the level of the "learning" coefficient is a function of cumulative investment (i.e., past gross investment) (Arrow 1962). Arrow recognized that because new machines are more productive versions of those in existence, capital investment not only induces labor productivity through augmenting the capital stock (as in Kaldor) but also improves productivity through the use of higher-quality capital, where quality improvement stems from innovation.

Despite a burst of inquiry in the immediate postwar period, interest by growth theorists in innovation was minimal in the 1960s, 1970s, and 1980s and macroeconomists in general pursued business cycle and rational expectation issues. Interest in growth was renewed in the mid-1980s, in particular with Paul Romer's 1986 article on "Increasing Returns and Long Run Growth." This article heralded the emergence of the "new growth theory."

Innovation and intangibles are now somewhat recognized by growth theorists. In particular, Romer described the macroeconomic importance of intellectual assets and growth (Romer 1993):

> Every generation has perceived limits to growth that finite resources and undesirable side effects would pose if no new recipes or ideas were discovered. And every generation has underestimated the potential for finding new recipes and ideas. We consistently fail to grasp how many ideas remain to be discovered. The difficulty is the same one we have with compounding. Possibilities do not add up. They multiply. (p. 3)

The *new* in the new growth theory, compared to the classical Solow model (Solow 1957), is that long-term growth is explained, not by the growth of the population, but by knowledge accumulation. Knowledge generates increasing returns and growth, in part because of its public good characteristic.

One central insight is the effects of the positive externalities of technological knowledge. As Romer (1986, p. 1003) remarks, "The creation of new knowledge by one firm is assumed to have a positive external effect on the production possibilities of other firms, because knowledge cannot be perfectly patented or kept secret." Because of zero (or close to zero) marginal costs of using new knowledge and lower costs of using existing knowledge to lower the costs of producing new knowledge, there is dynamic scale economics in knowledge accumulation, an insight arguably already provided by the classical economists. Assuming only partial excludability, the "new growth theory" showed that there could be positive externalities from (private) knowledge accumulation efforts. In short, the "new growth theorists" began to pay attention to what the classical economists and a small group of business economists and business historians had been saying for decades. Nevertheless, the new growth theory does represent progress.

In short, widespread recognition of the importance of innovation and intangibles in both economic theory and growth theory has been very slow in coming. Moreover, mainstream theory is still not particularly insightful with respect to the causes and nature of technological progress and learning. The reason for this is the inherent limitations of neoclassical theorizing, and its inability so far to incorporate such phenomena as the tacit nature of knowledge, the role of entrepreneurship, and the importance of disequilibrium (Simon 1978; Teece and Winter 1984).

Firm-Level Developments

For quite some time, microeconomic analysis has been out in front of macro-economics with respect to the study of intellectual capital. Eclectic approaches to the study of innovation at the firm have been pursued with vigor by a few economists and several notable social scientists at least since 1950. In particular, evolutionary ideas of technological change have become widespread. For example, one can reference the early Nelson and Winter work on technological change (1977, 1982) and the early work of Teece (1977a, 1977b) and Dosi (1982) on technology transfer and techno-logy paradigms.

Microeconomic work on spillovers and appropriability has proceeded unabated since Alfred Marshall. Teece (1986), Rosenberg and Steinmueller (1988), and Mansfield (1988) noted the importance of externalities and "spillovers" and studied processes of technology transfer. "Spillovers" may be generated by rival firms, univer-sities, and government research organizations. Indeed, March and Simon (1958) argued earlier that organizations may learn by imitating or borrowing from their rivals.

Also, knowledge spillovers are important at the intraorganizational level, and research suggests that a firm's innovative performance is strongly influenced by knowledge generated outside the firm's formal R&D (Mansfield 1968; Teece 1992; Chesbrough 2003). Teece (1986) developed the concept of appropriability regimes to explicitly recognized industry- and firm-level differences in appropriability.

Microeconomic studies focused on issues relating to creating and maintaining a competitive advantage at the firm level. Issues around learning and intangibles have become especially salient. Whereas learning in neoclassical theory was mainly about productivity gains in human capital resulting from increasing quality or speed of job performance as a result of previous experience in a given task (Arrow 1962) or expe-rience improving individual skills and productivity through investing experience in training (Becker 1964), organizational learning theorists emphasized competency traps in learning and the coevolution and adaptation of individual and organizational learn-ing (March 1991).

Issues in (organizational) learning are central to the recent economics of intellec-tual capital (Teece, Boerner and Macher 2001). Learning enables businesses to modify and develop new technologies, structures, and operating practices in the face of changing economic conditions. It also enables the creation of intangible assets as the basis for creating sustainably competitive advantages.

This literature also produced insights into the complex nature of technology devel-opment. Developing a new product or process is a highly uncertain venture, entailing the interaction of a host of frequently complex technological and market factors (Kline and Rosenberg, 1986). Successful new product development involves bringing to-gether knowledge from a variety of sources and effectively meeting performance crite-ria that differ across multiple dimensions (Patel and Pavitt, 1998).

Increasingly, researchers recognized that knowledge is frequently embedded in busi-ness processes and "routines." As Nelson and Winter (1982, p. 106) point out, "skills, organization and 'technology' are intimately intertwined in a functioning routine, and it is difficult to say exactly where one aspect ends and another begins." This suggests that the "cospecialization" of "complementary assets" (Teece 1986) and activities is thus not just about physical assets, it also embraces interconnectedness and close coupling between knowledge and physical assets.

Nelson and Winter's work on routines began to explore the internal process by which firms learn and develop new, strategically relevant competencies. Research examining the dynamic nature of the capabilities of the business firm further developed these issues.

First outlined in Teece and Pisano (1994) and elaborated in Teece, Pisano, and Shuen (1997), the dynamic capabilities approach to the business firm and strategy builds on the theoretical foundations provided by Schumpeter (1934); Penrose (1959); Williamson (1975, 1985); Cyert and March (1963); Rumelt (1984); Nelson and Winter (1982); Teece (1982); and Teece and Pisano (1994). In particular, it is consistent with the Schumpeterian view that the emergence of new products and processes results from "new combinations" of knowledge. In a similar vein, it is argued in the dynamic capabilities approach that competitive success arises from the continuous development and reconfiguration of firm-specific assets (Teece and Pisano 1994; Teece et al. 1997). Whereas Penrose and the resource-based scholars recognize the competitive importance of firm-specific capabilities, researchers of the dynamic capabilities approach attempt to outline specifically how organizations develop and renew internal competencies. Therefore, the latter approach is concerned with a subset of a firm's overall capabilities, namely, those that allow firms to create new knowledge and invest in the commercialization of new technologies. As these developments suggest, intellectual capital and intangible assets have become increasingly important and discussed in the literature. We turn to some of the recent developments in the sections that follow. Consistent with several authoritative definitions of intellectual capital (for instance, OECD), we use the term as referring to organizational and individual human capital (knowledge) and nonmonetary assets that can be used to generate wealth.

Central Concepts in the Economics of Knowledge and Intellectual Property

As seen already, classical economists laid the foundation for much of the work on the economics of knowledge and intellectual capital in a business context. While progress has been slow, what now exists in economic theory and business studies is an important set of concepts routinely employed to study the role of intellectual capital in business performance. These concepts are critical to the formulation of technology strategy. In what follows, we outline some of the new wisdom on the role of knowledge and intangible assets more generally.

The Nature of Knowledge

Understanding the very nature of knowledge itself and other intangible assets remains perplexing. Know-how is not a physical commodity—it is arguably not a commodity at all. Accordingly, new concepts, language, and terminology had to be developed so that one could begin to understand and grasp the fundamental nature of knowledge. Key concepts that have been developed over the years and accepted into the literature include what follows.

Codified versus Tacit

Tacit knowledge is that knowledge which is difficult to articulate in a way that is meaningful and understood.[9] It is often hard to explain to others things one knows intuitively. The fact that we know more than we can tell speaks to the tacit dimension of knowledge. Moreover, stand-alone codified knowledge (knowledge that can be written down such as blueprints, formulas, or computer code) need not convey much meaning. This is more akin to information than knowledge.

Consider how to sail a yacht. It can be readily explained by simple mechanics. But if one gives such instruction and puts the student into a sailing dinghy with a good breeze afoot, for sure the dinghy will soon be capsized. The transfer of codified knowledge is insufficient. Tacit knowledge built with just a few hours of real experience—how to hold the mainsheet, where to put one's weight, just how to "point" as the wind shifts, and the like—is critical to establish even a modest level of proficiency.

There appears to be a simple but powerful relationship between the codification of knowledge and the cost of its transfer. Simply stated, the more a given item of knowledge or experience has been codified, the more economically at least part of it can be transferred. This is a purely technical property that depends on the ready availability of channels of communication suitable for the transmission of well-codified information, for example, printing, radio, telegraph, and data networks. Whether information so transferred is considered meaningful by those who receive it depends on whether they are familiar with the code selected as well as the different contexts in which it is used (Shannon and Weaver 1949).

Tacit knowledge is slow and costly to transmit. Ambiguities abound and can be overcome only when communication takes place face to face. Errors or interpretation can be corrected by prompt personal feedback.

The transmission of codified knowledge, on the other hand, does not require face-to-face contact and often can be carried out largely by impersonal means, such as when one computer "talks" to another or a technical manual is passed from one individual to another. Messages are better structured and less ambiguous if they can be transferred in codified form.

Observable versus Nonobservable in Use

Much technology is available for public examination and reverse engineering the moment the product that embodies it is sold into the market. This is simply an unavoidable consequence of engaging in commerce; reverse engineering and copying, with or without improvements, is the harsh reality that must often be faced. For example, a new CT scanner, laser printer, or microprocessor is available for conceptual imitation and reverse engineering once it has been released into the market. The technology behind new products typically is ascertainable and, absent patents, may well be imitable.

Process technology, however, is often different. You cannot easily find out the manufacturing process by which something was made simply by inspecting the product. Rarely is the "signature" of a process ascertainable through reverse engineering. While clues about a manufacturing process may sometimes be gleaned by closely inspecting the product, much about process technology can be protected if the owners

---

[9] The classical insights on the nature of tacit knowledge are provided by Hayek (1945) and Polyani (1962) and early applications to the study of technology, including Teece (1981a).

of the process technology are diligent in protecting the trade secrets used in the factory. In short, absent patents, process technology is inherently more protectable than product technology.

Positive versus Negative Knowledge

Technological innovation involves considerable uncertainty. Research efforts frequently go down what turns out to be a blind alley. It is well recognized that a discovery (positive knowledge) can focus research on promising areas of inquiry, thereby avoiding blind alleys. However, it is frequently forgotten that negative knowledge—knowledge of failures ("this approach doesn't work")—is also valuable, as it can help steer resources into more promising avenues. For this reason, firms often find it desirable to keep their failures as well as their successes secret, even setting to one side issues of embarrassment.

The Paradigmatic Nature of Technological Innovation

One of the best modern contributions to understanding technological change comes from Dosi's analogy between technological evolution and Thomas Kuhn's view on scientific evolution: "In broad analogy with the Kuhnian definition of a 'paradigm', we shall define a 'technological paradigm' as 'model' and a 'pattern' of solution of selected technological problems, based on selected principles derived from the natural sciences and on selected material technologies" (Dosi 1982, p. 152). Even more Kuhnian is the view that a technological paradigm is constituted by the existence of an "exemplar" and a set of heuristics for elaborating the relevant paradigm. The broad characteristics of technological evolution begins with a preparadigmatic phase, where product design and technology is flexible, then a paradigmatic phase follows with the emergence of a standard.[10]

Intangible Assets, Tangible Assets, and Intellectual Property

Knowledge assets are simply one class of intangible assets; they differ from tangible assets in several important respects. These are summarized in Table 1.1.

First, knowledge has aspects of what economists refer to as public goods; as discussed earlier, consumption by one individual does not reduce the amount left for another. This is especially true for scientific knowledge. One engineer's use of Newton's laws does not subtract from the ability of others to use the same laws. However, the distinction erodes quickly as one moves toward industrial knowledge and away from scientific knowledge. While multiple use need not take away from knowledge—indeed, it may well be augmented—the economic value may well decline with simultaneous use by multiple entities. This is saying little more than the obvious. Imitators can dramatically lower the market value of knowledge by augmenting its supply in the market.

Competition simply drives down the price of knowledge, even though its utility has not declined. In a related manner, while knowledge does not wear out like most physical assets (tractors, trucks, refrigerators, and disk drives), it is frequently exposed to rapid depreciation because of the creation of new knowledge. Therefore, leading edge

---

[10] Dosi's use of technological paradigms as a frame for understanding technological change can also accommodate the insights of dominating designs, technological regimes, and so forth. See Dosi (1982) for details.

Table 1.1

Differences between Intangible Assets and Tangible Assets		
	Knowledge (Intangible) Assets	**Physical (Tangible) Assets**
Publicness	Use by one party need not prevent use by another	Use by one party prevents simultaneous use by another
Depreciation	Does not "wear out" but usually depreciates rapidly	Wears out; may depreciate quickly or slowly
Transfer costs	Hard to calibrate (increases with the tacit portion)	Easier to calibrate (depends on transportation and related costs)
Property rights	Limited (patents, trade secrets, copyrights, trademarks, etc.) and fuzzy, even in developed countries	Generally comprehensive and clearer, at least in developed countries
Enforcement of property rights	Relatively difficult	Relatively easy

products in the computer industry are often obsolete in a matter of months, not years. In fact, the depreciation may be so radical that a technological breakthrough drops the value of current practice technology to zero, or very nearly so.

An important difference between intangible and tangible assets is the availability and enforceability of property rights. Physical assets (land, cars, yachts, etc.) are generally well protected. Ownership is relatively easy to define, and the "boundaries" of the property can be clearly delineated. Whether theft has occurred is relatively easy to ascertain, and in many jurisdictions, there is a decent chance of getting police assistance in property recovery if the asset is of significant value—not so with intangibles.

It may be natural to think that the different forms of intellectual property (patents, trade secrets, trademarks, copyrights, etc.) as providing similar ownership rights, with readily available protection against theft and misuse; but this is not so. There can be "holes" and "gaps" in intellectual property coverage, and ascertaining whether trespass or theft has occurred can be difficult. Moreover, patents and copyrights eventually expire and cannot be extended. This is generally not so for physical assets.

Patents, trade secrets, and trademarks provide protection for different mediums in different ways. The strongest form of intellectual property is the patent. A valid patent provides rights for exclusive use by the owner, although depending on the scope of the patent, it may be possible to invent around it, albeit at some cost. Trade secrets provide no rights of exclusion over any knowledge domain, but they protect covered secrets in perpetuity. Trade secrets can well augment the value of a patent position. Different knowledge mediums quality for different types of intellectual property protection. The degree that intellectual property keeps imitators at bay may also depend on other external factors, such as regulations, which may block or limit the scope for invent-around alternatives.[11]

---

[11] Contributions to the discussions of patent and patent protection include the early survey data from Mansfield, Schwartz and Wagner (1981) and Levin et al. (1987). An extension and discussion of these studies can be found in Schankerman (1998).

Replicability, Imitability, and Appropriability of Knowledge

The economic value of knowledge depends not just on its ultimate utility, but on the ease of transfer and replication. If it can be replicated, it can be "scaled" and applied in new contexts. Replicability is closely related to transferability. If it can be transferred, from one geography to another or from one product market context to a different one, then it can potentially yield more value. But the catch is that, if it can be readily transferred, it is also prone to being lost to competitors.

Replication

The replication of know-how involves transferring or redeploying competences from one economic setting to another. Since productive knowledge is typically embodied, this cannot be accomplished by simply transmitting information. Only in those instances where all relevant knowledge is fully codified and understood can replication be collapsed into a simple problem of information transfer. Too often, the contextual dependence of original performance is poorly appreciated, so unless firms have replicated their systems of productive knowledge on many prior occasions, the act of replication is likely to be difficult (Teece 1993). Indeed, replication and transfer are often impossible without the transfer of people, although this can be minimized if investments are made to convert tacit knowledge to codified knowledge. However, such transfer may not be possible.

In short, knowledge assets are normally rather difficult to replicate. Even understanding the relevant routines that support a particular competence may not be transparent. Indeed, Lippman and Rumelt (1982) have argued that some sources of competitive advantage are so complex that the firm itself, let alone its competitors, does not understand them.

Imitation can also be hindered by the fact that few routines work well in all contexts. Therefore, imitating a part of what a competitor does may not enhance performance at all. Understanding the overall causal structure of organization and superior performance is often critical to successful imitation and replication. This observation provides the foundation for the concept of uncertain imitability (Lippman and Rumelt 1982). Because key performance factors in an organization are not understood (externally and possibly internally as well), replicating observable attributes is no guarantee of success.

At least two types of benefits flow to the firm from expertise in replication if it can be achieved. One is simply the ability to support geographic and product line expansion ("scalability"). To the extent that the organizational capabilities in question are relevant to the customer needs elsewhere, replication can confer value. Another is that the ability to replicate indicates that the firm has the foundations in place for learning and improvement.

Second, understanding processes, in both production and in management, is the key to process improvement; an organization cannot improve what it does not understand. Deep process understanding is often required to accomplish codification and replication. Indeed, if knowledge is highly tacit, it indicates that the phenomenon may not be well understood, except at an experiential level. When knowledge is tacit, the rate of learning may be limited because scientific and engineering principles cannot be systematically applied. Instead, learning is confined to proceeding through trial and error, and the amplification to learning that might otherwise come from the application of modern science is denied.

Table 1.2

Appropriatability Regimes for Knowledge Assets		
Intellectual Property Rights	**Inherent Replicability**	
	Easy	**Hard**
Tight	Weak	Moderate
Loose	Moderate	Strong

Imitation

Imitation is simply replication performed by a competitor. If self-replication is difficult, imitation is likely to be even harder. In competitive markets, the ease of imitation determines the sustainability of a competitive advantage. Easy imitation leads to the rapid dissipation of supernormal profits.

Factors that make replication difficult also make imitation difficult. Therefore, the more tacit the firm's productive knowledge, the harder it is to replicate, by the firm itself or by its competitors. When the tacit component is high, imitation may well be impossible, absent the hiring away of key individuals and the transfer of key organizational processes.

In advanced industrial countries, intellectual property rights may impede imitation of certain capabilities. These rights present a formidable imitation barrier in particular contexts. Several other factors, in addition to the patent system, cause the difference between replication costs and imitation costs. The observability of the technology or the organization is one such important factor. As mentioned earlier, while insight into product technology can be obtained thorough strategies such as reverse engineering, this is not the case for process technology, as the firm need not expose its process technology to the outside to benefit from it. Firms with product technology, on the other hand, confront the unfortunate circumstances that they must expose what they have to complete a sale. Secrets, therefore, are more easily protected if there is no need to expose them in contexts where competitors can learn about them.

Appropriability

Appropriability is a function of the nature of knowledge, ease of replication, and efficiency of intellectual property rights as a barrier to imitation. Appropriability is strong when a technology is both inherently difficult to replicate and the intellectual property system provides legal barriers to imitation. As shown in Table 1.2, the owners of valuable intangibles that are inherently easy to replicate might enjoy different layers of "protection," depending on the inherent ease of replication and the availability and .effectuality of intellectual property protection; without these, appropriability is weak.[12]

---

[12] A description of the results of an inquiry into appropriability conditions in manufacturing industries is found in Levin et al. (1987). Their data and discussion are consistent with the views discussed here.

The Distinction between Innovation and Intellectual Property

Much confusion has been caused by ignoring the significant distinction between an innovation and the intellectual property that embodies it. The latter is merely a legal right (more precisely, a collection of various legal rights, some procedural and some substantive).

An inventor develops, say, a new technology for cracking petroleum. The technology exists when it has been developed and tested. But it becomes covered by intellectual property only once it is legally recognized as such: In the case of patents, this occurs when a particular country's patent office recognizes the inventor's application and grants a patent. An issued patent is presumed valid, but its ultimate validity is never established until it is challenged and upheld in a court of law. This distinction between the innovation and legal "intellectual property" rights is most readily seen when the property right grant expires. Beethoven's copyright in his compositions has long since expired. But Beethoven's creations live on. An innovation may be just as valuable to society, in the sense that it represents an advance over the available alternative technologies, the day after the patent on that innovation expires as it was the day before the patent expired. But the legal rights of the innovator are radically different before and after the expiration date; after that date, the innovator has no right to exclude others from using the innovation. The private value falls, but the social value does not decline and may in fact increase.

One other key distinction is that the innovation and the legal rights are often not coextensive. An innovator may obtain legal rights over only part of the totality of the innovation. Confusion can sometimes arise when individuals seek to assess the value of the "technology" per se, rather than the value of the patent rights, namely, the right to exclude others from using the patented aspects of the technology. If the two are sold together, it may not matter. When they are not, it does.

Capturing Value from Intellectual Capital

As mentioned earlier, extracting value from intangible capital is a much more complicated and risky process than extracting value from tangible (physical) capital. Intellectual property, standing alone, generates little or no value to the final consumer. A patent, for instance, is merely a piece of paper that conveys the right to exclude others. The vast majority of patents are never practiced. Rather, value typically arises only after inventions are embedded in devices, which are then combined with other (complementary) assets to produce a product or service sold in a market.

To take a simple example, merely coming up with an idea for a new semiconductor device or even obtaining a patent or copyright on a design for a better semiconductor device does not generate economic value. Value is generated only when some entity combines an invention or a new design with the manufacturing, marketing, after-sale support, and other capabilities necessary to actually produce and sell semiconductors. Complementary assets typically assist in the extraction of value from intellectual property. Such assets generate a return that is analytically separate from the intellectual property itself.

In short, frequently, significant hurdles must be cleared and significant risks undertaken before an innovative idea can be successfully commercialized. Often, the individual(s) or firm(s) that supplies the necessary complementary assets and skills needed to commercialize the innovation or that takes the necessary risks is not the inventor. When this is the case, the gains from innovation get split not only with the consumer but also with the owners of the relevant complementary assets. Getting the commercialization strategy right is therefore very important, as discussed in Teece (1986).

Appropriability Regimes

A fundamental reason why innovators with good, marketable ideas fail to open up markets successfully is that they operate in an environment where appropriability is weak. This constrains their ability to capture the economic benefits arising from their ideas. The two most important environmental factors conditioning this are the efficacy of legal protection mechanisms and the nature of technology (Teece 1986).

It is well known that patents do not generally block competitors. Rarely, if ever, do patents confer perfect appropriability, although they afford considerable advantage in some industries, such as with new chemical products and rather simple mechanical inventions (Levin et al. 1987). Very often, patents can be "invented around" (Mansfield et al. 1988; Mansfield 1986). They are especially ineffective at protecting process innovations. Often patents provide little protection because the legal and financial requirements for upholding their validity or proving their infringement are high.

The degree of legal protection a firm enjoys is not necessarily a "god given" attribute. The inventor's own intellectual property strategy enters the equation. The inventor of a core technology need not only seek to patent the innovation but can also seek complementary patents on new features or manufacturing processes and possibly on designs.

Of course, the more fundamental is the invention, the better the chances that a broad patent will be granted and granted in multiple jurisdictions. It must be recognized that exclusionary rights are not fully secured by the mere issuance of a patent. While a patent is presumed to be valid in many jurisdictions, validity is never firmly established until a patent has been upheld in court. The strongest patents are those that are broad in scope and have already been upheld in court.

In some industries, particularly where the innovation is embedded in processes, trade secrets are a viable alternative to patents. Trade secret protection is possible, however, only if a firm can put its product before the public and still keep the underlying technology secret. Usually only chemical formulas and industrial-commercial processes can be protected as trade secrets after they are "out."

The degree to which knowledge about an innovation is tacit or easily codified also affects the ease of imitation. Tacit knowledge, by definition, is difficult to articulate and, so, hard to pass on unless those who possess the know-how can demonstrate it to others. It is also hard to protect using intellectual property law. Codified knowledge is easier to transmit and receive and more exposed to industrial espionage. On the other hand, it is often easier to protect using the instruments of intellectual property law. Appropriability regimes can be divided into "weak" (innovations are difficult to protect because they can be easily codified and legal protection of intellectual property is ineffective) and "strong" (innovations are easy to protect because knowledge about them is tacit or they are well protected legally). Despite recent efforts to strengthen the protection of intellectual property, strong appropriability is the exception rather than the rule. This has been so for centuries and will never be substantially different in democratic societies, where the migration of individuals and ideas faces few governmental constraints.

Standards and Timing Issues

The success of the strategies, methods, and procedures by which innovators endeavor to develop new technology and capture value from it are frequently severely affected by factors over which they may have little control. Standards and timing issues are among such factors.

Standard issues are particularly important when technologies must work closely together as a coupled or intertwined "system." Examples include telecommunications and computer equipment (interconnection is usually required) or even photocopiers (all the aftermarket products, such as paper and toner, must conform to certain standards for the machine to work or at least work well).

These factors lead to efforts by companies to promote proprietary standards (when they believe they have a good chance of success) or open standards when the success of a competitor's proprietary standard is of greater concern. Many factors affect a firm's success, or lack thereof, in establishing standards. Achieving overall critical mass is frequently an issue, particularly when the phenomenon of two-sided (or multisided) markets is at issue (Rochet and Tirole 2004; Evans 2003). When standards are at issue, success may beget further success and dominant standards emerge. When customers adopt a standard, they implicitly (and sometimes explicitly) abandon others. Inasmuch as innovations are often developed around existing or prospective standards, the rise and decline of certain standards is likely to have an impact on competitive outcomes.

Other Issues

A plethora of research by economists working in intellectual capital or related fields (like management and organization) is endeavoring to come to grips with the economics and management of intellectual capital. This chapter has barely scratched the surface of existing contributions. It is also selective. Omitted areas clearly worthy of mention, had space permitted, are important empirical work on patents and trends in patent activity, R&D and venture capital funding, licensing and cross-licensing issues, and technology transfer. Some of these topics are covered elsewhere (e.g., Teece 1977a, 1977b; Grindley and Teece 1997). These omissions are not meant to signal their unimportance.

Measurement Issues: Accounting and Market Metrics (Tobin's Q)

It is undisputed that the creation of intangible assets and intellectual capital is a source of economic growth and productivity enhancement. It is also undisputed that private enterprise businesses, in the aggregate, generate value from various investments, including investments aimed at creating valuable technological assets. Quite simply, firms would stop investing in R&D unless they continued to perceive that, as a result, such research generates an acceptable rate of return; and venture capitalists would be unable to raise money if they could not deliver the prospect of a positive return, commensurate with the risk. But quantifying the value of intangibles and the returns they generate is not easy. It is also a very important matter, for several reasons. First, it is extremely hard to manage assets that one cannot describe or measure. One has difficulties, not only in setting priorities, but in determining success or failure in asset management activities. Also, if intangibles are not measured correctly, an organization might appear to be doing poorly when it fact it is simply investing in intangibles. Accounting practices in the United States and elsewhere do not recognize many forms of intangibles, and this renders accounting data of limited value and causes discrepancies to emerge between the market value and the book value of the business enterprise.

In recent decades, scholars embarked on inquiries as to the quantitative importance of intangibles and their impact on the performance of the business enterprise. Four performance measures have received attention: (1) market value, as established in (public) capital markets; (2) gross margins; (3) patents; and (4) direct measures of innovation, such as innovation counts. The last is deeply imbued with judgmental assessment and is dealt with only in a cursory fashion here.

Stock Market Valuations

If the stock market is strongly efficient, the market value of a company is at all times equal to its fundamental value, where the fundamental value is defined as the expected present discounted value of future payments to shareholders. Assuming further the absence of market power, adjustment costs, and debt and taxes, then under the efficient market thesis, a company's value as determined by investors' pricing decisions equates to enterprise value, that is, the replacement cost of its assets. Put differently, the ratio of its market value to the replacement cost of capital, known as *Tobin's Q*, should equal 1.

An inference is that if the market value of the firm is greater than the replacement cost of its tangible assets, the difference must reflect the value of intangibles. Furthermore, since accounting standards require a very conservative treatment of intangibles, corporate balance sheets of publicly traded companies are believed, in the main, to capture tangible assets. Because intangibles are not properly reflected on balance sheets, researchers argue that the informativeness of financial information is compromised.

Nevertheless, the difference between market value and the replacement cost of tangible assets on the balance sheet has come to be used as a proxy for the value of intangibles. However, absent specification of what these intangibles are, it is very difficult to disaggregate and assign values to particular intangibles. Moreover, the inference that the difference between a firm's market value and the replacement cost of its physical assets represents the value of its intangibles requires the assumption of "strong form" market efficiency (where prices reflect all information, public as well as private), but this may be difficult to accept if investors lack good information about the firm's intangibles.

However, researchers have begun to explore the empirical relevance of (stock) market values. For instance, studies have established that investors regard R&D expenditures as a significant value-enhancing activity, presumably because they build (intangible) technological assets (Chan, Kesinger, and Martin 1992). Also, econometric studies that explore relationships between market-to-book ratios and R&D-to-sales ratios show positive, statistically significant associations (see Hirchez and Weygandt 1985). The evidence is clear that investors view R&D, on average, as value enhancing. Moreover, the magnitude of the contribution for the investing enterprise appears considerably higher than the cost of capital.

Gross Margins

Another approach utilizes accounting data, in particular gross margins (the difference between revenues and cost of goods sold), to assess how investment in intangibles affects performance. One basic approach, offered by Hand and Lev (2003), is to use econometric analysis and to regress the current-year dollar gross margin on the current and lagged R&D, advertising, and general and administrative expenses. Hand and Lev's analysis yielded several findings (p. 304): over the period 1980–2000, the mean yearly NPV (the present value of an investment's future net cash flows minus the initial investment) of $1.00 spent on R&D, advertising, and personnel were $0.35, $0.24, and $0.14, respectively. Scale also mattered, at least for R&D and advertising activities. Based on their findings, Hand concludes, "overall, my findings support the view that R&D and advertising intangibles have emerged over the past 20 years to become a critical means by which firms today create value and that one mechanism of value creation is that of increasingly profitable returns-to-scale" (Hand and Lev, p. 304).

Patent and Patent Citation Counts

The issuance of patents and the size of a firm's patent portfolio are also measures, albeit noisy ones, of innovative output. Because of the skewness in patent values—many patents are quite worthless but a few extremely valuable—it has turned out to be necessary to impose some at least crude measure of quality to make sense of the data. The most common measure of quality is the number of citations to a patent included in other subsequent patent applications. A number of studies demonstrated that quality-adjusted patents capture some element of the firm's R&D asset value. For instance, Hall, Jaffee, and Trajtenberg (2000) show that citation accepted patent counts help explain Tobin's Q values.

Innovation Counts

Another way to measure innovative output is directly, that is, to map significant technological innovations, then assign them to the particular firms responsible for their creation and commercialization. While this approach is superior at one level—it actually highlights innovation rather than say R&D expenditure (expenditure measures the cost of inputs into innovative activities)—it suffers from the lack of comparability; that is, there is no easy way to compare innovations and quantify their significance, except possibly through panels of experts who make qualitative judgments.[13]

Organizational Capital

The primary focus in this very short survey of measurement issues has been on technological assets. However, it is well recognized that organizational innovation is as significant (if not more so) than technological innovation in creating value. A. H. Cole asserted that, "if changes in business procedures and practices were patentable, the contribution of business change to the economic growth of the nation would be as widely recognized as the influence of mechanical inventions" (1968, pp. 61–62).

As an example, consider Henry Ford's invention of the moving assembly line. This was unquestionably one of the greatest innovations in the automobile industry, with ramifications for other industries, too. However, this invention was not technological,

---

[13] Very few studies of this kind have been done. The most notable study was done by Mansfield (1968), where he examined innovation in the petroleum industry. This study was extended and updated by Teece (1977b).

it was organizational. The Ford Motor Company's entire system of production had to be modified to accommodate it.

Another organizational innovation was the adaptation of the M-form structure. The transition from corporations organized in a unitary structure to corporations organized in a decentralized, profit-center-oriented multidivisional structure had a salutary effect on business performance. In a study of the adaptation of this new structure in the petroleum industry (Armour and Teece 1978), the innovation was shown to produce a statistically significant improvement in return on equity of approximately 2 percentage points during the diffusion period 1955–1968. A subsequent study (Teece 1981b) of the pairwise differential performance of the two leading firms in a number of industries yielded a similar finding. This study, which used a sample of the largest firms and most important U.S. industries, found that the M-form innovation displayed a statistically significant improvement in firm performance amounting to 2.37% and 1.22% for return on equity and return on assets, respectively. These results held while the innovation was being diffused. Both studies support the insights from Chandler (1966) and Williamson (1975) on the importance of organizational innovation and organizational design on economic performance.

Also, the diffusion path of the M-form innovation was not unlike diffusion paths associated with technological innovations. Teece (1980) argued that such similarities between the diffusion processes affecting technological and administration or organizational innovations indicates the broader potential of insights from the economics of technological change literature. Indeed, we may see more-recent work examining issues regarding the relationship between organizations and performance as contributors to this stream of ideas in the Mansfield/Teece tradition.

More recently, other (indirect) measures of the impact of organizational innovation have been attempted. Brynjolfsson and Yang, 1999, showed that a $1.00 investment in computers has about a $10.00 impact on market value. This has been interpreted to reflect positive results from new business processes the installation of enterprise software frequently requires. The authors' explanation is as follows: "our deduction is that the main portion of computer related intangible assets comes from the new business processes, new organizational structure and new market strategies—computer use is complementary to new workplace organization—Wal-Mart's main assets are not the computer software and hardware, but the intangible business processes they have built around those computer systems" (1999, p. 30).

Furthermore, recent evidence (Morck and Yeung 2003) supports earlier work (Teece 1982), indicating that know-how transfer inside firms (across jurisdictions and product space) enhances value. In the earlier study, internal technology transfer processes were seen as more efficient and effective than arm's-length transfers across organizational boundaries. Morck and Yeung's work supports this analysis by showing a positive contribution of diversification to value when it is aimed at scaling intangibles.

Conclusion

Knowledge and other intangible assets have emerged as key to business performance in the economic system. The development, ownership, and use of intellectual capital also helps explain wealth creation and levels of living around the globe. This is not just because of the importance of knowledge itself but because of expansion and competition in the goods and factor markets. These developments left intangible assets as the main basis for competitive differentiation in many sectors of the economy. There is implicit recognition of this, with the growing emphasis being placed by scholars on the importance of intangible assets, reputation, loyalty, and technological knowledge. Although many foundational insights were provided by classical economists (and some neoclassical economists), the Dosi/Mansfield/Nelson/Teece/Winter tradition provided key elements of the analytical and conceptual framework put forward here for analyzing and applying those early ideas to issues of knowledge and intellectual capital. Recent work further advances this tradition and lays an expanded foundation for the further understanding of the economics and management of intellectual capital.

References

Armour, H., and D. Teece. 1978. "Organizational Structure and Economic Performance: A Test of the Multidivisional Hypothesis." *Bell Journal of Economics 9*, no. 2: 106–122.

Abramovitz, M. 1962. "Economic Growth in the United Sates." *American Economic Review 52*: 762–782.

Arrow, K. 1962. "The Economic Implications of Learning by Doing." *Review of Economic Studies 29*: 155–173.

Becker, G. 1964. *Human Capital*. New York: Columbia University Press.

Brynjolfsson, E., and S. Yang. 1999. "The Intangible Costs and Benefits of Computer Investments: Evidence From Financial Markets." Working Paper, Sloan School, Massachusetts Institute of Technology, Cambridge, MA.

Chan, S., J. Kesinger, and J. Martin. 1992. "The Market Rewards Promising R&D." *Journal of Applied Corporate Finance 5*: 59–62.

Chandler, A. 1966. *Strategy and Structure*. Boston: Harvard Business School Press,.

Chesbrough, H. 2003. *Open Innovation: The New Imperative for Creating and Profiting from Technology*. Cambridge, MA: Harvard University Press.

Cole, A. H. 1968. "The Entrepreneur, Introductory Remarks." *American Economic Review 58*, no. 2: 60–63.

Cyert, R., and J. G. March. 1963. *A Behavioral Theory of the Firm*. Englewood Cliffs, NJ: Prentice-Hall.

David, P. 1993. "Path-Dependency and Predictability in Dynamic Systems with Local Network Externalities." In: *Technology and the Wealth of Nations*, ed. D. Forey and C. Freeman, London: Pinter.

Denison, E. G. 1962. *The Sources of Economic Growth in the United States and the Alternatives before Us*. New York: Committee on Economic Development.

Debreu. G. 1959. *Theory of Value*. New Haven, CT: Yale University Press.

Dosi, G. 1982. "Technological Paradigms and Technological Trajectories. A Suggested Interpretation of the Determinants and Directions of Technical Change." *Research Policy 11*: 147–162.

Drucker, P. 1993. *Post-Capitalist Society*. New York: HarperBusiness.

Evans, D. 2004. "The Antitrust Economics of Multi Sided Platform Markets." *Yale Journal of Regulation* forthcoming.

Freeman, C. 1982. *The Economics of Industrial Innovation*. London: Pinter Publishers.

Griliches, Z. 1963. "The Sources of Measured Productivity Growth: United States Agriculture, 1940–60." *Journal of Political Economy 71*: 331–346.

Grindley, P., and D. Teece. 1997. "Managing Intellectual Capital: Licensing and Cross-Licensing in Semiconductors and Electronics." *California Management Review 39*, no. 2: 8–41.

Hahn, F., and C. Matthews. 1964. "The Theory of Economic Growth: A Survey." *Economic Journal 74*: 779–902.

Hall, B., A. Jaffee, and M. Trajtenberg. 2000. "Market Value and Patent Citations: A First Look." Working Paper. National Bureau of Economic Research, Cambridge, MA.

Hand, J., and B. Lev. 2003. *Intangible Asset Values, Measures, Risks*. Oxford: Oxford University Press.

Hayek, F. A. 1945. "Economics and Knowledge," *Individualism and Economic Order*. Chicago: University of Chicago Press.

Hirschez, M., and J. Weygandt. 1985. "Amortization Policy for Advertising and R&D Expenditure." *Journal of Accounting Research* 23, no. 10: 326–335.

Jorgensen, D., and Z. Griliches. 1967. "The Explanation of Productivity Change." *Review of Economic Studies* 34: 249–283.

Kline, S., and N. Rosenberg. 1986. "An overview of innovation." In: *The Positive Sum Strategy*, ed. R. Landau and N. Rosenberg, pp. 275–305. Washington, DC: National Academy Press.

Knight, F. 1921. *Risk, Uncertainty and Profit*. Cambridge, UK: Riverside Press.

———. 1944. "Diminishing Returns from Investments." *Journal of Political Economy* 52: 26–47.

Krugman, P. 1998. "Two Cheers for Formalism." *Economic Journal* 108: 1829–1836.

Kuznets, S. 1967. *Toward a Theory of Economic Growth*. New York: Norton.

Levin, R., C. Klevorick, R. Nelson, and S. G. Winter. 1987. "Appropriating the Returns from Industrial Research and Development." *Brookings Papers on Economic Activity*, 1987, no. 3: 783–820.

Lippman, S., and R. Rumelt. 1982. "Uncertain Imitability: An Analysis of Interfirm Differences in Efficiency under Competition." *Bell Journal of Economics* 13: 418–438.

Mansfield, E. 1968. *The Economics of Technological Change*. New York: W. W. Norton.

———. 1988. "The Speed and Cost of Industrial Innovation in Japan and the United States External vs. Internal Technology." *Management Science*. 34, no. 10: 1157–1168.

———, R. John, R. Anthony, W. Samuel, and B. George. 1977. "Social and Private Rates of Return from Industrial Innovations." *Quarterly Journal of Economics* 91: 221–240.

———, M. Schwartz, and S. Wagner. 1981. "Imitation Costs and Patents: An Empirical Study." *The Economic Journal* 91: 907–918.

Loasby, B. 2004. "Evolution and the Human Mind." Paper Presented at the Schumpeter Society Conference, Milan, 2004.

Mansfield, E. 1986. "Patents and Innovation: An Empirical Study." *Management Science* 32: 173–181.

March, J. G. 1991. "Exploration and Exploitation in Organizational Learning." *Organization Science* 2: 71–87.

———, and H. A. Simon 1958. *Organizations*. New York: Wiley.

Marshall, A. 1890. *Principles of Economics*. London: MacMillan.

———. 1925. *Industry and Trade*. London: MacMillan.

Morck, R., and B. Yeung. 2003. "Why Firms Diversify: Internalization vs. Agency Behavior." Intangible Assets, SSRC Working Paper.

Nelson, R. R., and S. G. Winter. 1977. "Dynamic Competition and Technical Progress." In: *Economic Progress, Private Values, and Public Policy: Essays in Honor of William Fellner*, ed. B. Balassa and R. R. Nelson. Amsterdam: North-Holland.

Nelson, R., and S. G. Winter 1982. *An Evolutionary Theory of Economic Change*. Cambridge, MA: Belknap Press.

Nonaka, I. 1991. "The Knowledge-Creating Company." *Harvard Business Review* 69, no. 6: 96–104.

Patel, P., and K. Pavitt. (1998). "The Wide (and Increasing) Spread of Technological Competencies in the World's Largest Firms: A Challenge to Conventional Wisdom." In: *The Dynamic Firm: The Role of Technology, Strategy, Organization, and Regions*, ed. A. D. Chandler, P. Hagström, and Ö. Sölvell, pp. 192–212. Oxford: Oxford University, Press.

Penrose E. 1959. *The Theory of the Growth of the Firm*. Oxford: Blackwell.

Polyani, M. 1962. *The Tacit Dimension*. New Haven, CT: Yale University Press.

Rochet, J., and J. Tirole. 2004. "Multisided Markets: An Overview." Working Paper, MIT, Boston, MA.

Romer, P. 1986. "Increasing Returns and Long Run Growth." *Journal of Political Economy* 94: 1002–1037.

————. 1993. "Economic Growth." In: *The Fortune Encyclopedia of Economics*, ed. D. Henderson. New York: Time Warner Books.

————. 1990. "Endonenous Technological Change." *Journal of Political Economy* 98: 71–102.

Rosenberg, N., and W. E. Steinmuller. 1988. "Why Are Americans Such Poor Imitators?" *American Economic Review* 78, no. 2: 229–234.

Rumelt, R. 1984. "Towards a Strategic Theory of the Firm." In: *Competitive Strategic Management*, ed. R. B. Lamb. Englewood Cliffs, NJ: Prentice-Hall.

Schankerman, M. 1998. "How Valuable Is Patent Protection? Estimates by Technology Field." *Rand Journal of Economics* 29, no. 1: 77–107.

Schumpeter, J. 1934. *The Theory of Economic Development.* Cambridge, MA: Harvard University Press.

————. 1943. *Capitalism, Socialism, and Democracy.* New York: Harper and Brothers.

Shannon, C., and W. Weaver. 1949. *A Mathematical Theory of Communication.* Urbana: University of Illinois Press.

Simon, H. A. 1955. "A Behavioral Model of Rational Choice." *Quarterly Journal of Economics* 69: 99–118.

————. 1978. "Rationality as Process and as Product of Thought." *American Economic Review* 68, no. 2: 1–16.

Smith, A. 1776. *An Inquiry into the Nature and Causes of the Wealth of Nations.* London: Methuen and Co., Ltd.

Solow, R. 1956. "A Contribution to the Theory of Economic Growth." *Quarterly Journal of Economics* 70, no. 1: 65–94.

————. 1957. "Technical Change and the Aggregate Production Function." *Review of Economics and Statistics* 39: 312–320.

————. 1994. "Perspectives on Growth Theory." *Journal of Economic Perspectives.*

Teece, D. 1977a. "Technology Transfer by Multinational Firms: The Resource Cost of Transferring Technological Know-How." *The Economic Journal* 87: 242–261.

————. 1977b. *R&D in Energy: Implications of Petroleum Industry Reorganization.* Stanford, CA: Stanford University Institute for Energy Studies.

————. 1980. "The Diffusion of an Administrative Innovation." *Institute of Management Sciences* 26, no. 5: 464–470.

————. 1981a. "The Market for Know-How and the Efficient International Transfer of Technology." *Annals of the Academy of Political and Social Science*: 81–96.

————. 1981b. "Internal Organization and Economic Performance: An Empirical Analysis of the Profitability of Principal Firms." *Journal of Industrial Economics* 30, no. 2: 173–199.

————. 1982. "Towards an Economic Theory of the Multiproduct Firm." *Journal of Economic Behavior and Organization* 3: 39–63.

————. 1984. "Economic Analysis and Strategic Management." *California Management Review* 26, no. 3: 87–110.

————. 1986. "Profiting from Technological Innovation." *Research Policy* 15, no. 6: 285–305.

————. 1989. "Inter-Organizational Requirements of the Innovation Process." *Managerial and Decision Economics*, Special Issue: 35–42.

————. 1992. "Competition, Cooperation, and Innovation: Organizational Arrangements for Regimes of Rapid Technological Progress." *Journal of Economic Behavior and Organization* 18, no. 1: 1–25.

————. 1993. "The Dynamics of Industrial Capitalism: Perspectives on Alfred Chandler's Scale and Scope (1990)." *Journal of Economic Literature.*

————, and G. Pisano 1994. "The Dynamic Capabilities of Firms: An Introduction." *Industrial and Corporate Change* 3: 3.

————, C. Boerner, and J. Macher. 2001. "A Review and Assessment of Organizational Learning in Economic Theories." In: *Handbook of Organizational Learning and Knowledge.* ed. M. Dierkers, A. B. Antal, J. Child, and I. Nonaka. NY: Oxford University Press.

————, G. Pisano, and A. Shuen 1997. "Dynamic Capabilities and Strategic Management." *Strategic Management Journal* 18, no. 7: 509–533.

————, and S. G. Winter. 1984. "The Limits of Neoclassical Theory in Management Education." *American Economic Review* 74, no. 2: 116–121.

Williamson, O. E. 1975. *Markets and Hierarchies: Analysis and Antitrust Implications.* New York: The Free Press.

————. 1985. *The Economic Institutions of Capitalism.* New York: The Free Press.

Young, A. 1928. "Increasing Returns and Economic Progress." *Economic Journal* 38: 527–542.

Technology and Technology Transfer: Mansfieldian Inspirations and Subsequent Developments

David J. Teece

ABSTRACT. This paper discusses the foundational work and ideas of Edwin Mansfield to the economics of technological change and innovation, and introduces some of the recent work in the field. I argue that much of the recent work on patenting, technology strategy and the economics of knowledge has roots to the early Mansfield contributions, and that he should be recognized as a pioneer for these recent developments.

Key words: economics of innovation, knowledge, intangible assets, R&D management

JEL Classification: O32, O34, L10

1. Introduction

At least since Joseph Schumpeter, scholars have struggled to understand the nature and the dynamics of the economics of technical change. Edwin Mansfield was born into that struggle and was for many decades a true pioneer in the study of the economics of technological change. His early books including 'The Economics of Technological Change' (1968), and 'Technological Change: An Introduction to a Vital Area of Modern Economics' (1971) summarize his early insights and display his passionate desire to wake up the field of economics to a critical area of research. He undoubtedly was the leader in the study of the nature of industrial research in America, certainly during the period of his active scholarship, and arguably to this day.

Although both classical economists and 'modern' economists such as Solow, Nelson, David, Rosenberg, and Kuznets had recognized the

Director, Institute of Management
Innovation and Organization Professor
Haas School of Business
University of California
Berkeley, U.S.A.

importance of innovation and understood it's key role in economic growth and wealth creation, it was not until Mansfield that anyone had performed serious empirical studies of industrial research. Mansfield provided leading insights into issues such as the role of academic and basic research in increasing innovation and productivity, the diffusion of technological innovations, the private and social returns to innovation, and the role of patents and the patent system. With great wisdom, Mansfield chose areas of study that have emerged as being critically important to managers and policy makers.

However, Ed Mansfield showed considerable frustration with modern economics and the work of economic theorists. Indeed, by the 1970s Ed openly displayed almost a disdain for modern economic theory because of the field's infatuation with static analysis, and its abject failure to embrace the study of technology and technological change.

As one of Ed Mansfield's students, I must first acknowledge my huge dept to him personally and intellectually. As a graduate student at Penn in the early 1970s, I was fortunate to end up in his Ph.D. class on the economics of technological change. He opened my eyes to a set of issues for which I had no previous exposure. Because I had a background in international trade and finance and economic development, he encouraged me to study technology transfer. No one at that time, including Ed, knew much about the topic. We learned together, with Ed sending me into the field to collect data and absorb what I could from corporate R&D managers, from licensing executives, and from the experiences of the international departments of the Fortune 500. Some of my findings, along

 Journal of Technology Transfer, 30 1/2, 17–33, 2005
© *2005 Springer Science+Business Media, Inc. Manufactured in The Netherlands.*

with my reflections on those findings, are discussed in Section 3.

Besides developing a substantive understanding of technology transfer, I learned quite a lot methodologically from Ed. He was a well-recognized statistician with a good nose for data. He was comfortable working with small samples. He let the data, not theory, lead him to answers. In fact, much of my work and methodological approaches can be seen as combining Mansfield's insights and approaches with other traditions, in particular transaction cost economics, and evolutionary and behavioral theory.

In the rest of this paper I shall describe in more detail the intellectual influence of Ed Mansfield on my work on the economics of technological change and technology transfer. I shall track some of the recent developments with respect to these early ideas and mention how recent work builds on the early Mansfield studies. In doing so I hope to demonstrate that his influence was substantial, and that his legacy in the field deserves more recognition. If Schumpeter founded the study of the economics of innovation,[1] then Mansfield was the first to give it empirical meaning at the micro level.

2. Mansfield's vision and early work

One of many lessons that I learned from Mansfield—and he in turn was undoubtedly shaped by his early years at Carnegie Mellon University (which in the late 1950s and early 1960s when Mansfield was there had scholars such as Herb Simon, Dick Cyert, Jim March, Franco Modigliani and Bill Cooper, among others)—was the importance of interdisciplinary research. As a young graduate student, I wanted to believe that the hard problems of the world were solvable. I came to realize with Ed's help that this would require a multidisciplinary approach. Mansfield always made the case for interdisciplinary research. In his later years he wrote:

"[the economics of technological change] remains an area where there is particular need for people who are comfortable working in, and drawing on, a variety of disciplines. Very few problems of any consequence can be solved within the confines of a single discipline. It continues to require persons

who have a lively interest in both basic and applied work, and who are able to use each to enrich the other. It is still an area needing people who like to work on ill-defined problems where little is known and nothing is tidy, but where the rewards for even a partial solution are very high. Those with such attributes should be encouraged to enter this field because the opportunities continue to be enormous. While a lot more is known now than 40 years ago, the truth is that economists have only scratched the surface' (Mansfield, 1995, p. xxi)."

This was the mantra Mansfield had been advancing to his students for over 20 years. It was good advice, although risky for a young economist to follow. Ed was keenly aware how little was known about innovation and industrial research. Mansfield, like March and Simon and the Carnegie School, was ahead of his time, substantively and methodologically. Half a century later David Kreps would write: 'I am increasingly convinced that economists should—and will—have to change large pieces of the paradigm that has kept us relatively monolithic for the past 50 years. We'll increasingly look like and work with our colleagues in the other.. social sciences' (2004). Were David Kreps a Mansfield student, he would have realized this much earlier.

Thinking outside the box of conventional economics was particularly necessary when it came to issues of the economics of technical change. For one thing, neoclassical economics can not address issues of change other than comparative statics (Machlup, 1967) because even adjustments to equilibrium are outside the domain of neoclassical economics. As a result, neoclassical theory can not really deal with issues of innovation. Ed recognized this, but few others did.[2]

Mansfield's methodological response was always to start first with observation (influenced, perhaps, by the 'problem driven' research that was present at Carnegie). He encouraged me—as well as his other students and colleagues—to collect data in the field. This was extremely wise. Late in life he reflected on this method, in the introduction to the two volumes of collected papers of his:

"In general, my approach has been to try to get a reasonably solid empirical footing before attempting to model complex phenomena about which very little is known; to keep the theoretical apparatus as simple, transparent and robust as possible;

to collect data directly from firms (and other economic units) carefully tailored to shed light on the problem at hand (rather than to try to adapt readily available general-purpose data, which often is hazardous), and to check the results as thoroughly as possible with technologists, executives, government officials and others who are close to whatever phenomenon is being studied'. (Mansfield, 1995, p. ix)."

'It was', Mansfield continued, 'a privilege and a great pleasure to have contributed to the formation and growth of this young field, which is now a major and vibrant sector of economics' (1995, p. ix). Similarly, I must say it was a privilege and a great pleasure to study under Mansfield, and help advance understanding of technological change and technology transfer. I only wish many more scholars had followed Ed's lead. The field would be further ahead had they done so.

My own work in technology transfer (and technological change in general) took Mansfield's advice to heart: it was interdisciplinary in the sense that it endeavored to reach out to other disciplines (although there was not much at the time to reach out to); and it tried to be methodologically rigorous. I will first summarize this work and then link it to recent developments in the economics and management of knowledge (including industrial knowledge). In particular, I shall focus on issues relating to the nature of knowledge and the importance of intellectual capital and intellectual property.

3. The economics of (international) technology transfer

In the early 1970s, literature on (international) technology transfer was basically non-existent. Indeed, to the extent that there was a literature, the focus was on the challenges of transferring know-how from the laboratory into practice. Indeed, there was almost no conceptual apparatus available to help one think through the issues.

The doctoral thesis I wrote under Ed Mansfield was an early effort to understand technology transfer. It truly involved writing on a clean sheet of paper. Doing research in an area where there had been almost no scholarly exploration is a daunting task, even to an established scholar, let

alone a graduate student.But as Ed explained, it was sometimes a little easier to receive recognition if you were the first into a field or a new subject matter area. This has been my research strategy and my comparative advantage ever since.

My doctoral thesis, published as a book (Teece, 1976) and as journal articles (Teece, 1977a, b) was ably guided by Ed.[3] It was the first, and I believe the only study to date directed at measuring the costs associated with the (international) transfer of industrial knowledge. The topic was important because scholars at the time really had no idea as to what was the true state of affairs. Many economic theorists treated technology transfer as though it was costless—and while good intuition might suggest that the process was somewhat costly, there were no empirical studies to settle the issue. It's not like it was a hotly debated issue—the zero transfer cost assumption was made, and just not challenged. Undoubtedly, there are instances where assuming zero transfer cost is a sufficiently good approximation. For instance, once certain scientific knowledge is published, it can sometimes be absorbed at low cost by other scientists knowledgeable in the field. But there were no studies at the time with respect to the transfer and absorption costs associated with replicating industrial knowledge in different contexts.

Mansfield's instinct was that technology was expensive to transfer; and his instinct turned out to be well founded. However, what my dissertation study did unearth was that there was a learning curve with respect to technology transfer—the more experience (as measured by number of transfers) a transferor had at replicating a particular technology, the lower the cost of transfer/replication. The data showed that industrial enterprises simply got better at the transfer process the more they worked on it—so long as the technology in question did not change very much, and the environment to which it was transferred was familiar. Put differently, if companies could 'freeze' designs and transfer technology only to familiar 'places', in familiar configurations, then replication costs would decline with each instance of replication (replication is a topic returned to in Section 4 'Replicability, imitabililty, and appropriability of knowledge').

A rather counterintuitive finding of my study was that the costs of international technology transfer were sometimes (although not generally) less than the costs of domestic transfer. This result follows naturally if either (i) skills abroad are better than skills at home/or (ii) the factor (resource) cost of offshore skills are cheaper than equivalent domestic skills (these two factors mean that absorption costs could be lower abroad).

Another implicit finding of my study—which with three decades of refection I can now appreciate much better—is that learning industrial knowledge often involves expensive lessons. Industrial knowledge cannot generally be transferred just with the transfer of blueprints or even the transfer of people. It frequently involves the actual running (i.e. operating) of industrial facilities in a quasi-experimental way before yields/performance become acceptable. 'Switching on' a plant, however, can be a very expensive operation if non-marketable (i.e. substandard) products are produced during the startup period. This can lead to the waste of large amounts of resources, and cost overruns associated with the replication of manufacturing plants.

Indeed, some of the anecdotes I remember from my field research relate to the horrific expenses that Rolm and Haas experienced in starting up chemical (industrial) processes in the U.K. Differences in materials and environmental factors often led to surprising cost overruns, particularly if a technology was transferred and embedded in a plant configuration which had not already been tested and validated close to the home R&D facility. Another way to state this is that learning how to apply and reapply industrial knowledge can be costly—and in my study tens of millions of dollars of cost overruns in a technology transfer project were not uncommon, especially if a technology not properly understood was transferred prematurely. Upon reflection, this remains an important insight.

My doctoral dissertation study actually endeavored to measure various components of transfer costs. I endeavored to measure not just from the actual costs of transfer activities, but also the costs flowing from the consequences of poorly executed transfer activities. For many years I felt awkward about my results because my methodology included project startup costs

as part of transfer (replication) costs. However, upon further reflection, I'm increasingly comfortable with this definition. The results simply drive home that transfer costs can be high because of the 'knock on' effects if replication/transfer is not properly accomplished. This is a lesson worth remembering. Put differently, the failure to achieve smart transfer can have very serious cost implications.

Needless to say, these insights required scores of interviews to develop. I remain forever grateful for Ed Mansfield's mandate that I do field research. I'm also grateful to scores of unnamed executives who gave of their time without recognition or reward, and to the Penfield Traveling Fellowship in International Affairs and Lettres (at the University of Pennsylvania) which provided the financing for me to travel throughout the U.S., interview executives, and collect data. The process itself was insightful and valuable.[4]

After I had completed my doctoral dissertation, an independent of my own efforts, a literature began to emerge on the nature of knowledge. For some reason, I did not know of Polyani (1966) even by the time I had finished by Ph.D My dissertation would have displayed better conceptual underpinnings had I been a bit more aware of the concept of tacit knowledge, and Polyani's teachings. It was too early to benefit from Nelson and Winter's work, but I have subsequently learned that they were incubating similar ideas.

Indeed, post-1980 there has been a flowering of work on the nature of know-how and the problems of replication. In what follows I introduce some of the learning which has emerged in the last 25 years on the nature of innovation—and knowledge replication/transfer, some of it having been leveraged off of Mansfield's early contributions.

4. Summarizing elements of received wisdom on replication and transfer

Developing an understanding of knowledge and intangible assets, critical to the formulation of technology strategy and the management of R&D. I will endeavor to summarize some of this literature below, and where appropriate make connections to some of Ed's contributions.

Understanding the nature of knowledge and other intangible assets remains perplexing.

Know-how, whether scientific or industrial, is not a physical commodity—it is arguably not a commodity at all. Accordingly, new concepts, language and terminology have had to be developed so that one can begin to understand and grasp the fundamental nature of knowledge. Key concepts that have developed over the years and accepted into the literature are outlined below.

Ed Mansfield's early efforts to come to grips with technology transfer benefited from the field research done at Penn. He was amongst the first to note:

> "Economists sometimes assume that technology is like a sheaf of blueprints and that all one has to do is ship off the right set of papers. Unfortunately, it isn't that simple or costless. For one thing, the available evidence, both recent and for earlier periods, indicates that publications and reports are a much less effective way of transferring technology than the movement of people. To transfer 'know-how', much of which is not written down in any event, there is frequently no substitute for person-to-person training and assistance, some of which may have to go on for extensive periods of time' (Mansfield, 1975, p. 373)."

We can address these issues better now, leveraging off of the work of many who either walked in Ed's footsteps, or were fellow travelers. Important concepts that help in the understanding of innovation and technology transfer include the following:

Codified/tacit knowledge

Tacit knowledge is (as Mansfield hints) that knowledge which is difficult to write down in a way that is meaningful and readily understood.[5] It is often hard to explain to others things which one only knows intuitively (Polyani, 1966; Teece 1981). The fact that we know more than we can tell speaks to the tacit dimension of knowledge. Moreover, stand-alone codified knowledge—knowledge which can be written down such as blueprints, formulas, or computer code—need not convey much meaning. It's more akin to information than knowledge.

Consider how to sail a yacht. It can be readily written down and explained by simple mechanics. But if one simply provides 'the book' and puts the student into a sailing dinghy with a good breeze afoot, for sure the dinghy will soon be capsized. The transfer of codified knowledge is insufficient. Tacit knowledge built with just a few hours of real experience—how to hold the main-sheet, where to put ones weight, just how to 'point' as the wind shifts, etc.—is critical to establish even a modest level of proficiency.

It is now recognized that there is a simple but powerful relationship between the codification of knowledge and the cost of its transfer. Simply stated, the more a given item of knowledge or experience has been codified, the more economically at least that part of it can be transferred. This is a purely technical property that depends on the ready availability of channels of communication suitable for the transmission of well-codified information—for example, printing, radio, telegraph, and data networks. However, it has long been recognized that whether information so transferred will be considered meaningful by those who receive it will depend on whether they are familiar with the code selected as well as the different contexts in which it is used (Shannon and Weaver, 1949).

Tacit knowledge is especially slow and costly to transmit (Teece, 1976, 1977, 1981a). Ambiguities abound and can be overcome only when communications take place in face-to-face situations. Errors or interpretation can be corrected by a prompt use of personal feedback. Mansfield (1975) pointed to the differences between types of (technology) transfer in the context of the transfer of know-how.

Other scholars have built on the earlier Mansfield and Teece work on technology transfer, and have shown that knowledge does not necessarily flow easily, even from unit to another within the firm (Grant, 1996; Szulanski, 1996).

The transmission of codified knowledge, on the other hand, does not necessarily require face-to-face contact and can often be carried out largely by impersonal means, such as when one computer 'talks' to another, or when a technical manual is passed from one individual to another. Messages are better structured and less ambiguous if they can be transferred in codified form.

Observable(not-observable) in use

Much technology is available for public examination and reverse engineering can be enabled the moment the product which embodies it is sold into the market. This is simply an unavoidable consequence of engaging in commerce; reverse engineering and copying, with or without improvements, is the harsh reality that must often be faced. For example, a new CT scanner, laser printer, or microprocessor is available for conceptual imitation and reverse engineering once it has been released in the market. The technology behind new products is typically ascertainable and, absent patents, may well be immitable.[6] In the studies conducted by Mansfield and his colleagues (Mansfield *et al.*, 1982, Chapter 2) reverse engineering was the most frequent channel by which technology leaked out.

Process technology, however, is often different. You can not easily find out the manufacturing process by which something was made simply by inspecting the product. It is rare that the 'signature' of a process is ascertainable through reverse engineering. While clues about a manufacturing process may sometimes be gleaned by closely inspecting the product, much about process technology can be protected if the owners of process technology are diligent in protecting the trade secrets used in the factory. In short, absent patents, process technology is inherently more protectable than product technology.

Positive/negative knowledge

Technological innovation involves considerable uncertainty. Research efforts frequently go down what turns out to be a blind alley. It is well recognized that a discovery (positive knowledge) can focus research on promising areas of inquiry, thereby avoiding blind alleys. However, it is frequently forgotten that negative knowledge —knowledge of failures ('this approach does not work')—is also valuable, as it can help steer resource allocation into more promising avenues. For this reason, firms often find it desirable to keep their failures as well as their successes secret, even setting to one side issues of embarrassment.

The paradigmatic nature of technological innovation

One of the best modern contributions to understanding technological change comes from Dosi's analogy between technological evolution and Thomas Kuhn's view on scientific evolution.'In broad analogy with the Kuhnian definition of a 'paradigm', we shall define a 'technological paradigm' as 'model' and a 'pattern' of solution of selected technological problems, based on selected principles derived from the natural sciences and on selected material technologies' (Dosi, 1982, p. 152). Even more Kuhnian is the view that a technological paradigm is constituted by the existence of an 'exemplar' and a set of heuristics for elaborating the relevant paradigm. The broad characteristics of technological evolution begin with a pre-paradigmatic phase where product design and technology is flexible, then a paradigmatic phase follows with the emergence of a standard.[7]

Intangible assets, tangible assets, and intellectual property

Knowledge assets are simply one class of intangible assets; they differ from tangible assets in several important respects. These are summarized in Figure 1.

First, knowledge has aspects of what economists refer to as public goods—when consumption by one individual does not reduce the amount left for another. This is especially true for scientific knowledge. One engineer's use of Newton's laws does not subtract from the ability of others to use the same laws. However, the distinction erodes quickly as one moves towards

CHARACTERISTICS	KNOW-HOW/ IP	PHYSICAL COMMODITIES
1. Recognition of trading opportunities	Inherently difficult	Posting frequent
2. Disclosure of attributes	Relatively difficult	Relatively easy
3. Property Rights	Limited [patents, trade secrets, copyright, etc.]	Broad
4. Item of Sale	License	Measurable units
5. Variety	Heterogeneous	Homogeneous
6. Unit of consumption	Often Unclear	$, Value, weight
Inherent tradability:	Low	High

Figure 1. Inherent tradeability of different assets.

industrial knowledge and away from scientific knowledge. While multiple use need not take away from knowledge—indeed it may well be augmented—the economic value may well decline with simultaneous use by multiple entities. This is saying little more than the obvious. Imitators can dramatically lower the market value of knowledge by augmenting its supply in the market.

Competition simply drives down the price of knowledge, even though its utility has not declined. Relatedly, while knowledge does not wear out as do most physical assets (like tractors, trucks, refrigerators, and disk drives), it is frequently exposed to rapid depreciation because of the creation of new knowledge. Thus leading edge products in the computer industry are often obsolete in a matter of months, not years. In fact, the depreciation may be so radical that a technological breakthrough drops the value of current practice technology to zero, or very nearly so.

An important difference between intangible and tangible assets is the availability and enforceability of property rights. Physical assets (land, cars, yachts, etc.) are generally well protected. Ownership is relatively easy to define, and the 'boundaries' of the property can be clearly delineated. Whether theft has occurred is relatively easy to ascertain, and in many jurisdictions there is a decent chance of getting police assistance in property recovery if the asset is of significant value. Not so with intangibles.

It may be natural to think that the different forms of intellectual property (patents, trade secrets, trademarks, copyrights, etc.) as providing similar ownership rights, with readily available protection against theft and misuse; but this is not so. There can be 'holes' and 'gaps' in intellectual property coverage,[8] and ascertaining whether trespass or theft has occurred can be difficult. Moreover, patents and copyrights eventually expire and cannot be extended. This is generally not so for physical assets.

Patents, trade secrets, trademarks provide protection for different mediums in different ways. The strongest form of intellectual property is the patent. The importance of patents for innovation was recognized by Mansfield (1986): 'The patent system', he noted, 'is at the heart of our nation's

policies toward technological innovation. Consequently, it is of widespread interest to managers, management scientists, and economists, among others' (1986, p. 173).

A valid patent provides rights for exclusive use by the owner, although depending on the scope of the patent it may be possible to invent around it, albeit at some cost. Trade secrets do not provide rights of exclusion over any knowledge domain, but they do protect covered secrets in perpetuity. Trade secrets can well augment the value of a patent position. Different knowledge mediums quality for different types of intellectual property protection. The degree that intellectual property keeps imitators at bay may also depend on other external factors, such as regulations, which may block or limit the scope for invent-around alternatives.[9]

Replicability, imitability, and appropriability of knowledge

The economic value of knowledge depends not just on its ultimate utility, but on the ease of transfer and replicability. If it can be replicated it can be 'scaled' and applied in new contexts. Replicability is closely related to transferability. If it can be transferred, from one geography to another, or from one product market context to a different one, then technology can potentially yield more value. But the catch is that if it can be readily transferred, it is often also prone to being lost to ones competitors through easy imitation (see Section 'Imitation').[10]

Replication

The replication of know how involves transferring or redeploying competences from one economic setting to another. Since productive knowledge is typically embodied, this cannot be accomplished by simply transmitting information. Only in those instances where all relevant knowledge is fully codified and understood can replication be collapsed into a simple problem of information transfer. Too often, the contextual dependence of original performance is poorly appreciated, so unless firms have replicated their systems of productive knowledge on many prior occasions, the act of replication is likely to be difficult (Teece,

1977a, 1993). Indeed, replication and transfer are often impossible without the transfer of people, though this can be minimized if investments are made to convert tacit knowledge to codified knowledge. However, this may not be possible.

In short, knowledge assets are normally rather difficult to replicate. Even understanding the relevant routines that support a particular competence may not be transparent. Indeed, Lippman and Rumelt (1982) have argued that some sources of competitive advantage are so complex that the firm itself, let alone its competitors, does not understand them.

Imitation can also be hindered by the fact that few routines work well in all contexts. Thus, imitating a part of what a competitor does may not enhance performance at all. Understanding the overall causal structure of processes, organization and superior performance is often critical to successful imitation and replication. This observation provides the foundation for the concept of uncertain immitability (Lippman and Rumelt, 1982). Because key performance factors in an organization are not understood (externally and possibly internally as well), replicating observable attributes is not guarantee of success.

At least two types of benefits flow to the firm from expertise in replication if it can be achieved. One is simply the ability to support geographic and product line expansion ('scalability'). To the extent that the organizational capabilities in question are relevant to the customer needs elsewhere, replication can confer value. Another is that the ability to replicate indicates that the firm has the foundations in place for learning and improvement.

Secondly, understanding processes, both in production and in management, is the key to process improvement; an organization cannot improve what it does not understand. Deep process understanding is often required to accomplish codification and replication. Indeed, if knowledge is highly tacit, it indicates that the phenomenon may not be well understood, except at an experiential level. When knowledge is tacit, the rate of learning may be limited because scientific and engineering principles cannot be systematically applied. Instead, learning is confined to proceeding through trial-and-error, and the amplification to learning that might otherwise

come from the application of modern science is denied.

Imitation

Imitation is simply replication performed by a competitor. If self-replication is difficult, imitation is likely to be even harder. In competitive markets, it is the ease of imitation that determines the sustainability of competitive advantage. Easy imitation leads to the rapid dissipation of supernormal profits.

Factors that make replication difficult also make imitation difficult. Thus, the more tacit the firm's productive knowledge, the harder is replication by the firm itself, or by it's competitors. When the tacit component is high, imitation may well be impossible, absent the hiring away of key individuals and the transfer of key organizational processes.

In advanced industrial countries, intellectual property rights may impede imitation of certain capabilities.[11] Nevertheless, imitation lags tend to be short (Mansfield *et al.*, 1982, Chapter 2). These rights present a formidable imitation barrier in certain particular contexts. Several other factors, in addition to the patent system, cause there to be a difference between replication costs and imitation costs. The observability of the technology or the organization is one such important factor. As mentioned earlier, while insight into product technology can be obtained thorough strategies such as reverse engineering, this is not the case for process technology, as the firm need not expose its process technology to the outside in order to benefit from it. Firms with product technology, on the other hand, confront the unfortunate circumstances that they must expose what they have got in order to complete a sale. Secrets are thus more protectable if there is no need to expose them in contexts where competitors can learn about them.

Appropriability

Appropriability is a function of both the nature of knowledge, ease of replication, and the efficiency of intellectual property rights as a barrier to imitation. Appropriability is strong when a technology is both inherently difficult to replicate and intellectual property systems provides legal barriers to imitation. As shown in Figure 2, there are different layers of 'protection' which owners of valuable intangibles might enjoy. If technology is inherently easy to replicate and the intellectual property protection is either unavailable or ineffectual, then appropriability is weak.[12]

Much confusion has been caused by ignoring the significant distinction between an innovation and the intellectual property which embodies that innovation. The latter is merely a legal right (or, more precisely, a collection of various legal rights, some procedural, and some substantive).

An inventor develops say, a new technology for cracking petroleum. The technology exists when it has been developed and tested. But it only becomes covered by intellectual property once it is legally recognized as such—in the case of patents, when a particular country's patent office recognizes the inventor's application and grants a patent. An issued patent is presumed to be valid, but its ultimate validity is never established until it is challenged, and validity subsequently upheld in a court of law.

The distinction between the innovation and legal 'intellectual property' rights is most readily seen when the property right grant expires. Beethoven's copyright in his compositions has long since expired. But Beethoven's creations live on.

INTELLECTUAL PROPERTY RIGHTS	INHERENT REPLICABILITY: EASY	INHERENT REPLICABILITY: HARD
LOOSE	WEAK	MODERATE
TIGHT	MODERATE	STRONG

Figure 2. Appropriability regimes for knowledge assets.

An innovation may be just as valuable to society—in the sense that it represents an advance over the available alternative technologies—the day after the patent on that innovation expires as it was the day before the patent expires. But the legal rights of the innovator are radically different before and after the expiration date; after that date, the innovator has no right to exclude others from using the innovation. The private value falls, but the social value does not decline, and may in fact increase.

One other key distinction is that the innovation and the legal rights are often not coextensive. An innovator may only obtain legal rights over part of the totality of the innovation. Confusion can sometimes arise when individuals seek to assess the value of the 'technology' *per se*, rather than the value of the patent rights—namely, the right to exclude others from using the patented aspects of the technology. If the two are sold together it may not matter. When they are not, it does.

5. Capturing value from intellectual capital

As mentioned earlier, extracting value from intangible capital is a much more complicated and risky process than extracting value from tangible (physical) capital. Intellectual property, standing alone, generates little or no value to the final consumer. A patent, for instance, is merely a piece of paper that conveys the right to exclude others. The vast majority of patents are never practiced. Rather, value typically arises only after inventions are embedded in devices which are then combined with other (complementary) assets to produce a product or service which is sold in a market.

To take a simple example: merely coming up with an idea for a new semiconductor device, or even obtaining a patent or copyright on a design for a better semi-conductor device, does not generate economic value. What generates value is when some entity combines an invention or a new design with the manufacturing, marketing, after sales support and other capabilities that are necessary to actually produce and sell semiconductors. Complementary assets typically assist in the extraction of value from intellectual property. Such assets generate a return which is analytically separate from the intellectual property itself.

In short, there are often significant hurdles that have to be cleared, and significant risks that must be undertaken, before an innovative idea can be successfully commercialized. Often, the individual(s) or firm(s) which supplies the necessary complementary assets and skills needed in order to commercialize the innovation, or which takes the necessary risks, are not the same as the inventor. When this is the case, the gains from innovation get split not only with the consumer, but also with the owners of the relevant complementary assets. Getting the commercialization strategy right is thus very important, as discussed in Teece (1986).

Appropriability regimes

One of the most fundamental reasons why innovators with good marketable ideas fail to open up markets successfully is that they are operating in an environment where appropriability is weak. This constrains their ability to capture the economic benefits arising from their ideas. As shown in Figure 2, the two most important environmental factors conditioning this are the efficacy of legal protection mechanisms and the nature of technology (including it's inherent replicability).

It is well known that patents do not generally block competitors. As Mansfield taught (1985, 1988), they can often (but not always) be worked around. Rarely, if ever, do patents confer perfect appropriability, although they do afford considerable advantage in some industries, such as with new chemical products, pharmaceuticals, and rather simple mechanical inventions (Levin *et al.*, 1987). They are especially ineffective at protecting process innovations. Often patents provide little protection because the legal and financial requirements for upholding their validity or for proving their infringement are high.

The degree of legal protection a firm enjoys is not necessarily a 'god given' attribute. The inventor's own intellectual property strategy itself enters the equation. The inventor of core technology need not only seek to patent the innovation itself, but can also seek complementary patents on new features and/or manufacturing processes, and possibly on designs.

Of course, the more fundamental the invention, the better the chances that a broad patent will be granted, and granted in multiple jurisdictions. It must be recognized that exclusionary rights are not fully secured by the mere issuance of a patent. While a patent is presumed to be valid in many jurisdictions, validity is never firmly established until a patent has been upheld in court. The strongest patents are those that are broad in scope, and have already been upheld in court.

In some industries, particularly where the innovation is embedded in processes, trade secrets are a viable alternative to patents. Trade secret protection is possible, however, only if a firm can put its product before the public and still keep the underlying technology secret. Usually only chemical formulas and industrial-commercial processes can be protected as trade secrets after they' are 'out'.

The degree to which knowledge about an innovation is tacit or easily codified also affects the ease of imitation. Tacit knowledge is, by definition, difficult to articulate and so is hard to pass on unless those who possess the know-how can demonstrate it to others. It is also hard to protect using intellectual property law. Codified knowledge is easier to transmit and receive and is more exposed to industrial espionage. On the other hand, it is often easier to protect using the instruments of intellectual property law.

As shown in Figure 2, appropriability regimes can be divided into 'weak' (innovations are difficult to protect because they can be easily codified and legal protection of intellectual property is ineffective) and 'strong' (innovations are easy to protect because knowledge about them is tacit and/or they are well protected legally). Despite recent efforts to strengthen the protection of intellectual property, strong appropriability is the exception rather than the rule. This has been so for centuries, and it will never be substantially different in democratic societies, where the migration of individuals and ideas face few governmental constraints.

The success of the strategies, methods, and procedures by which innovators endeavor to develop new technology and capture value from it are frequently severely impacted by factors over which it may have little control. Standards and timing issues are amongst such factors.

Standard issues are particularly important when technologies must work closely together as a coupled or intertwined 'system'. Examples include telecommunications and computer equipment (interconnection is usually required) or even photocopiers—the 'aftermarket' products e.g. paper, toner must all conform to certain standards for the machine to work, or at least work well.

These factors lead to efforts by companies to promote proprietary standards (when they believe they have a good chance of success) or open standards when it's the success of a competitor's proprietary standard which is of greater concern. There are many factors which impact a firm's success, or lack thereof, in establishing standards. Achieving overall critical mass is frequently an issue, particularly when the phenomenon of two sided (or multisided) markets is at issue (Evans 2003; Rochet and Tirole, 2004). When standards are at issue, success may beget further success and dominant standards may emerge. When customers adopt a standard, they implicitly (and sometimes explicitly) abandon others. Inasmuch as innovations are often developed around existing or prospective standards, the rise and decline of certain standards is likely to have an impact on competitive outcomes, and possibly also on the value of technology.

6. Valuation issues: accounting and market metrics

It is undisputed that the creation of intangible assets and intellectual capital are sources of economic growth and productivity enhancement. It is also undisputed that private enterprise businesses in aggregate generate value from various investments, including investments aimed at creating valuable technological assets. Quite simply, firms would stop investing in R&D unless they continued to perceive that as a result they were generating an acceptable rate of return; and

venture capitalists would not be able to raise money if they could not deliver the prospect of a positive return, commensurate with the risk.

Quantifying the value of intangibles and the returns they generate isn't easy.[13] However, as Mansfield recognized that it is a very important matter. One reason is that it's extremely hard to manage assets that you cannot describe or measure. Not only will one have difficulties in setting priorities, but one will also have difficulty determining success and/or failure in asset management activities. Also, if intangibles are not measured correctly, it might appear that an organization is doing poorly when it fact it is simply investing in intangibles. Accounting practices in the U.S. and elsewhere do not recognize many forms of intangibles, and this renders accounting data of limited value, and causes discrepancies to emerge between the market value and the book value of the business enterprise. Finally, to the extent that social returns exceed private, there is a case for government policies favoring innovation.

In recent decades, scholars have extended Mansfield's early work and embarked on inquiries as to the quantitative importance of intangibles, and their impact on the performance of the business enterprise. Four performance measures have received attention: (1) internal rates of return, as measured by the examination of the R&D portfolios of individual firms (2) market value, as established in (public) stock markets (3) gross margins (4) patents (5) direct measures of innovation such as innovation counts. The latter is deeply imbued with judgmental assessment and will only be dealt with in a cursory fashion.

Internal (private and social) rates of return

Ed Mansfield was the pioneer in demonstrating empirically that private rates of return from investment in R&D were in the double digits for selected industrial enterprises, but that the social rates of return were many times the private rates of return. The latter findings were the first clear measurement of spillovers associated with R&D. These results have been cited extensively in the past. They undergrid the case for government support of R&D, and for policies that favor innovation. In an important paper, Mansfield and his co-authors (1977) made perhaps the first study of the social returns from a sample of industrial innovations, using a model that measured the social benefits from innovations. Social benefits included both the profits of the innovator plus the benefits to consumers due to reduction in prices due to the innovation. The median social rate of return for the 17 innovations reported in the study was 50%; about twice the median private return.

Two follow-up studies supported by the NSF supported and even strengthened Mansfield's findings. They showed that the median social rate of return to be 70% and the median private rate of return to be 36 (Mansfield himself reflected on these findings and subsequent studies in his 1991 paper, 'Social Returns from R&D: Findings, Methods and Limitations'). Moreover, several other studies have confirmed and extended the ideas and results, including two papers in the proceedings of the AER by Scherer (1983) and Piekarz (1983). Piekarz also discusses some of the policy issues associated with Mansfield's (and other's) findings. The findings support the case that government policy should favor innovation.

Stock market valuations

If the stock market is strongly efficient, the market value of a company is at all times equal to it's fundamental value, where fundamental value is defined as the expected present discounted value of future payments to shareholders. Assuming further the absence of market power, adjustment costs, and debt and taxes, then under the efficient market thesis a company's value as determined by investors pricing decisions will equate to enterprise value—that is, the replacement cost of it's assets. Put differently, the ratio of it's market value to the replacement cost of capital—known as Tobin's Q—should equal 1.

An inference is that if the market value of the firm is greater than the replacement cost of it's tangible assets, the difference must reflect the value of intangibles. Furthermore, since accounting standards require a very conservative treatment of intangibles, corporate balance sheets of publicly traded companies are believed to in the main capture tangible assets. Because intangibles

are not properly reflected on balance sheets, researchers argue that the informativeness of financial information is compromised.

Nevertheless, the difference between market value and the replacement cost of tangible assets on the balance sheet has come to be used as a proxy for the value of intangibles. However, absent specification of what these intangibles are, it is very difficult to disaggregate and assign values to particular intangibles. Moreover, the inference that the difference between a firm's market value and the replacement cost of it's physical assets represents the value of it's intangibles require the assumption of 'strong form' market efficiency (where prices reflect all information, public as well as private)—but this may be difficult to accept if investors do not have good information about the firm's intangibles.

Nevertheless, researchers have begun to explore the empirical relevance of (stock) market values. For instance, studies have established that investors regard R&D expenditures as a significant value enhancing activity, presumable because they build (intangible) technological assets (Chan *et al.*, 1992). Also, econometric studies that explore relationships between market-to-book ratios and R&D-to-sales ratios show positive and statistically significant associations (see Hirchey and Weyganat, 1985). The evidence is clear that investors view R&D as on average as being value enhancing. Moreover, the magnitude of the contribution for the investing enterprise appears considerably higher than the cost of capital.

Gross margins

Another approach utilizes accounting data, and in particular gross margins (the differences between revenues and cost of goods sold), to assess how investment in intangibles affects performance. One basic approach offered by Hand (2003) is to use econometric analysis and to regress current year dollar gross margin on current and lagged R&D, advertising, and general and administrative expenses. Hand's analysis yielded several findings (p. 304): over the period 1980–2000, the mean yearly NPV of $1.00 spent on R&D, advertising, and personnel were $0.35, $0.24, and $0.14, respectively. Scale also mattered, at least for R&D and advertising activities. Based on his findings, Hand concludes:

'Overall, my findings support the view that R&D and advertising intangibles have emerged over the past 20 years to become a critical means by which firms today create value and that one mechanism of value creation is that of increasingly profitable returns-to-scale' (Hand, p. 304).

Patent and patent citation counts

The issuance of patents, and the size of a firm's patent portfolio, is also a measure, albeit a noisy one, of innovative output. Because of the skewness in patent values—many patents are quite worthless, but a few extremely valuable—it has turned out to be necessary to impose some at least crude measure of quality in order to make sense of the data. The most common measure of quality is the number of citations to a patent included in other subsequent patent applications. A number of studies have demonstrated that quality adjusted patents capture some element of the firm's R&D asset value. For instance, Hall *et al.* (2000) show that citation accepted patent counts help explain Tobin's Q values.

Innovation counts

Another way to measure innovative output is directly i.e. to map significant technological innovations, and then to assign them to particular firms responsible for their creation and commercialization. While this approach is at one level superior—it actually highlights innovation rather than say R&D expenditure (expenditure measures the cost of inputs into innovative activities)—it suffers from the lack of comparability i.e. there is no easy way to compare innovations, and to quantify their significance, except possibly through panels of experts who make qualitative judgments.[14]

Organizational capital

The primary focus in this very short survey of measurement issues has been on technological assets. However, it is well recognized that organizational innovation is as significant (if not more so) than technological innovation in creating

value. Cole has asserted that 'if changes in business procedures and practices were patentable, the contribution of business change to the economic growth of the nation would be as widely recognized as the influence of mechanical inventions (1968, p. 61–62).

As an example, consider Henry Ford's invention of the moving assembly line. This was unquestionably one of the greatest innovations in the automobile industry, with ramification for other industries too. However, this invention was not technological, it was organizational. The Ford Motor Company's entire system of production had to be modified to accommodate it.

Another organizational innovation was the adaptation of the M-Form structure. The transition from corporations organized in a unitary structure to corporations organized in a decentralized profit center oriented multidivisional structure had a salutary effect on business performance. In a study of the adaptation of this new structure in the petroleum industry (Armour and Teece, 1978) the innovation was shown to produce a statistically significant improvement in return on equity of approximately two percentage points during the diffusion period 1955 – 1968. A subsequent study (Teece, 1981b) of the pair wise differential performance of the two leading firms in a number of industries yielded a similar finding. This study, which used a sample of the largest firms and most important U.S. industries, that the M-form innovation displayed a statistically significant improvement in firm performance amounting to 2.37 and 1.22% for return on equity and return on assets, respectively. These results held while the innovation was being diffused. Both studies support the insights from Chandler (1968) and Williamson (1975) on the importance of organizational innovation and organizational design on economic performance.

Also, the diffusion path of the M-Form innovation was not unlike diffusion paths that Mansfield identified for technological innovations. Teece (1980) argued that such similarities between the diffusion processes affecting technological and administration/organizational innovations indicates the broader potential of insights from the economics of technological change literature. Indeed, we may see recent work examining issues regarding the relationship between organizations and performance as contributors to this stream of ideas in the Mansfield/Teece tradition.

Recently, other (indirect) measures of the impact of organizational innovation have been attempted. Brynjolfsson and Yang (1999), have showed that a $1.00 investment in computers has about a $10.00 impact on market value. This has been interpreted to reflect positive results from new business processes which the installation of enterprise software frequently requires. The author's explanation is as follows:

'Our deduction is that the main portion of computer related intangible assets comes from the new business processes, new organizational structure and new market strategies—computer use is complementary to new workplace organization—Wal-Mart's main assets are not the computer software and hardware, but the intangible business processes they have built around those computer systems (1999, p. 30).

Furthermore, recent evidence (Morck and Yeung, 2003) supports earlier work (Teece, 1982) indicating that know-how transfer inside firms (across jurisdictions and product space) is value enhancing. In this earlier study, internal technology transfer processes were seen as more efficient and effective than arms length transfers across organizational boundaries. Morck and Yeung's recent work supports this analysis by showing a positive contribution of diversification to value when it is aimed at scaling intangibles.

7. The multinational firm, internalization, and R&D activity

My work with Ed on international technology transfer also helped lay the foundations for new thinking on the distinctive role of the multinational firm. While it is true that knowledge need not move freely inside the firm, as Szulanski and others have demonstrated, it generally does move easier inside firms than between unrelated entities. This is not only because it is easier to marshal the necessary transfer of people internally, but also because of common language and control the latter softening intellectual property ('leakage') concerns. Shared values and goals inside the firm also assist technology transfer, at least when they exist.

In the 1950s and 1960s, and 1970s, Hymer (1976) and others were trumpeting that the multinational firm was an instrument for exploiting monopoly power, in part through the manner in which it exploited technology developed at home. The Mansfield–Teece–Williamson tradition, focusing on the multinational firm as a relatively efficient mechanism for transferring technology,[15] was a significant counterpoint to the Hymer argument. Not only was Hymer's argument poor competition policy analysis (competition policy experts would not automatically conclude that a firm had (antitrust) market power simply because it had valuable intangibles and intellectual property, but the proper question to ask is whether it has market power in a *relevant* (antitrust) market, not simply whether it has hard to imitate assets.

In a series of articles (Teece 1981a, b, 1985, 1986a, b) I built upon insights by two of my teachers, Ed Mansfield and Oliver Williamson, to identify particular failures in the market for know-how. I used this in turn to explain the horizontal and vertical expansion of the multinational enterprise. While it is true that others had identified internalization efficiencies as the basis of multinational enterprise and foreign direct investment (e.g. Buckley and Casson, 1976) my work explicitly focused on technology transfer issues. These issues remain compelling explanations for the international scope of the firm. Indeed, subsequent work on appropriability (Teece, 1986) provided additional generality to these explanations. When combined with Mansfield's work on spillovers and high social rates of return to innovation, this broader body of work strongly supports the thesis that the multinational firm can be an instrument of economic development, not a tool for the extraction of monopoly rents and the amplification of poverty. While Mansfield chose to stay away from some of these broader policy issues, it is rather transparent that his work is relevant to many of the great policy debates we are currently experiencing.

With respect to the focus of R&D in the multinational firm, Mansfield *et al.* (1979) were amongst the first to examine the reasons why firms 'outsourced' R&D (i.e. conducted it abroad). This work is now an important historical benchmark, as it shows that in the 1970s most foreign R&D was aimed at adapting technology to local market conditions. However, even back then some firms performed R&D abroad to access particular R&D resources not otherwise available. While this early work did not ask the theoretical/design question around what R&D should be done offshore, Mansfield's early interest in offshore R&D did stimulate me and one of my former students (Chesbrough) to design a framework to help answer those questions (Teece and Chesbrough, 1996). Indeed, much of my subsequent work has involved trying to stitch together Mansfieldian issues and ideas with those of his early contemporaries (Oliver Williamson from Penn and Nelson and Winter from Yale).[16] Indeed, I for one have taken Ed's admonition to be interdisciplinary very seriously, and have found ways to weave his ideas and findings into the broader tapestry of innovation studies. I am most grateful to have had such helpful early guidance from a great master.

8. Closing

Much progress has been done in recent years in the area of the economics of technology, but it still builds on the foundational work that Schumpeter and Mansfield and others did. Ed was undoubtedly the pioneer in the study of industrial research, and one of a few leading scholars in the economics of technological change. In 1996 Medoff reports that Mansfield received the 26th highest number of citations from 1971 to 1992 among non Nobel prize winning economists younger than 70. But in the economics of technological innovation, Grandstrand (1994) reports Mansfield was the most cited author in each of the 4 years he examined (also see Grandstrand, 2004). But this only confirms what his friends and students already knew: Ed was second to none in his field, and he chose a field of compelling significance to understanding the business enterprise, economic growth, and the future of Western Civilization.

Acknowledgment

I wish to thank Mie Augier for many helpful comments and suggestions on early drafts. Patricia Lonergan supplied helpful technical support.

Notes

1. Mansfield acknowledges Schumpeter as founding the field of the economics of technology (1995, p. ix).
2. But see for instance Nelson and Winter's (1977) early critique of neoclassical theory of innovation: 'to the extent that technical advance is important [in neoclassical theory], the set of ideas built into the formulation that individual firms are maximizing profits over a common .. choice set, and that the industry is in .. competitive equilibrium can be seen as serious structural misspecifications. It is exactly that some firms see alternatives that others do not, and that imitation is costly and takes time, that provides the incentive to try to innovate. It is a key structural characteristic ... of growth in a competitive market economy that there is a diversity of behavior (technologies used) by firms in the industry at any time. A chronic disequilibrium is what is driving the growth process. To assume .. equilibrium is to structurally misspecify the process'.
3. My doctoral work was referred to by Mansfield on several occasions; see for instance Mansfield (1975).
4. Ronald Coase admits to a similar benefit from his early field research in the U.S. in the 1930s (Coase, 1988).
5. The classical insights on the nature of tacit knowledge were provided by Hayek (1945) and Polyani (1966) and early applications to the study of technology include Mansfield (1975) and Teece (1981a).
6. Mansfield touched on some of the issues relating to imitation in an early paper 'Technical change and the Rate of Imitation' (1961).
7. Dosi's use of technological paradigms as a frame for understanding technological change can also accommodate the insights of dominating designs, technological regimes, etc. See Dosi (1982) for details.
8. In one of Ed's studies (Lee and Mansfield, 1996), it was established that the lack of intellectual property protection in certain host countries slowed technology transfer and direct foreign investment.
9. Contributions to the discussions of patent and patent protection include the early survey data from Mansfield *et al.*, 1981, Levin *et al.*, 1987. An extension and discussion of these studies can be found in Schankerman (1998). Moreover, Mansfield (1986) examined survey data of 100 manufacturing firms and found that—with the exceptions of the pharmaceutical and chemical industries—the firms found that most of their innovations would have been introduced even in the absence of patent protection.
10. Whether or not technology is exposed in this way is likely to depend in part on whether or not the technology enjoys intellectual property protection.
11. For Mansfield's most recent work on IP, see in particular Mansfield 1993, 1994.
12. A description of the results of an inquiry into appropriability conditions in manufacturing industries is found in Levin *et al.* (1987). Their data and discussion is consistent with the views discussed below.
13. As discussed below, Mansfield work on the private and social returns to innovation was pioneering (see in particular Mansfield 1977).
14. There have been very few studies of this kind. The most notable study was done by Mansfield (1968) where he

examined innovation in the petroleum industry. This study
was extended and updated by Teece (1977b).

15. In Teece (1976, 1977a) I showed that internal transfer
costs were generally less than the cost of transfer to unrelated
entities.

16. In addition, much of Mansfield's early ideas on R&D
originated while he was a consultant at the RAND Corporation—Winter and Nelson were also doing pioneering work on
R&D there.

References

Armour, H. and D. Teece, 1978, 'Organizational Structure
and Economic Performance: A Test of the Multidivisional
Hypothesis,' *The Bell Journal of Economics* 9 (2), 106–122.

Brynjolfsson, E. and S. Yang, 1999, *'The Intangible Costs and
Benefits of Computer Investments: Evidence From Financial
Markets,'* Working Paper, Sloan School, Massachusetts
Institute of Technology.

Buckley, P. and M. Casson, 1976, *The Future of the Multinational Enterprise*, London: MacMillan.

Coase, R.H., 1988, 'The Nature of the Firm: Origin, Meaning, Influence,' *Journal of Law, Economics, and Organization* 4 (1), 3–47.

Chan, S., J. Kesinger, and J. Martin, 1992, 'The Market
Rewards Promising R&D,' *Journal of Applied Corporate
Finance* 5, 59–62.

Chandler, A., 1968, *Strategy and Structure*, Cambridge: Harvard University Press.

Cole, A.H., 1968, 'The Entrepreneur, Introductory Remarks,'
American Economic Review 58 (2), 60–63.

Dosi, G., 1982, 'Technological Paradigms and Technological
Trajectories. A Suggested Interpretation of the Determinants and Directions of technical Change,' *Research Policy*
11, 147–162.

Evans, D., 2003, 'The Antitrust Economics of Multi Sided
Platform Markets,' *Yale Journal of Regulation* (forthcoming).

Grandstrand, O., 1994, 'Economics of Technology: An Introduction and Overview,' in Idem (ed.), *Economics of Technology*, Amsterdam: North-Holland.

Grandstrand, O., 2004, *Economics, Law, and Intellectual Property*, Boson: Kluwer.

Grant, R.M., 1996, 'Prospering in Dynamically Competitive
Environments: Organizational Capability as Knowledge
Integration,' *Organization Science* 7 (4), 375–387.

Hall, B., A. Jaffee, and M. Trajtenberg, 2000, *Market Value
and Patent Citations: A First Look*, Working Paper,
National Bureau of Economic Research.

Hand, J. and B. Lev, 2003, *Intangible Asset Values, Measures,
Risks*, Oxford: Oxford University Press.

Hayek, F.A., 1945, 'Economics and Knowledge,' in F.A.
Hayek, (ed.), *Individualism and Economic Order*, University
of Chicago Press.

Hymer, S., 1976, *International Operations of National Firms: A
Study of Direct Investment*, Cambridge, MA: MIT Press.

Lee, J.Y. and E. Mansfield, 1996, 'Intellectual Property Protection and US Direct Investment,' *Review of Economics
and Statistics* 78 (2), 181–186.

Kreps, D., 2004, 'Beliefs and Tastes: Confessions of an Economist,' in Augier and March (2004), *Models of a Man: Essays
in Memory of Herbert Simon*, Cambridge: MIT Press.

Levin, R., C. Klevorick, R. Nelson, and S.G. Winter, 1987,
'Appropriating the Returns from Industrial Research and
Development,' *Brookings Papers on Economic Activity* 3,
783–820.

Lippman, S. and R. Rumelt, 1982, 'Uncertain Imitability: An
Analysis of Interfirm Differences in Efficiency Under Competition,' *Bell Journal of Economics* 13, 418–438.

Machlup, F., 1967, 'Theories of the Firm: Marginalist, Behavioral, Managerial,' *American Economic Review* 57, 1–33.

Mansfield, E., 1961, 'Technical Change and the Rate of Imitation,' *Econometrica* 29 (40), 714–766.

Mansfield, E., 1968, *The Economics of Technological Change*,
New York: W.W. Norton & Company Inc.

Mansfield, E., 1975, 'International Technology Transfer:
Forms, Resource Requirements, and Policies,' *American
Economic Review* 65 (2), 372–376.

Mansfield, E., 1986, 'Patents and Innovation: An Empirical
Study,' *Management Science* 32, 173–181.

Mansfield, E., 1991, 'Social Returns from R&D: Findings,
Methods and Limitations,' *AAAS Science and Technology
Policy Yearbook* 24, 24–27.

Mansfield, E., 1993, 'Unauthorized use of Intellectual Prop-
erty: Effects on Investment, Technology Transfer, and
Innovation,' in M.B. Wallerstein *et al.* (eds.), *Global
Dimensions of Intellectual Property Rights in Science and
Technology*, Washington: National Academy Press.

Mansfield, E., 1994, *Intellectual Property Protection, Foreign
Direct Investment, and Technology Transfer*, IFC discussion papers, No. 19, Washington, D.C.: The World Bank.

Mansfield, E., 1995, 'Introduction,' in Idem (ed.), *Innovation,
Technology and the Economy: The Selected Essays of
Edwin Mansfield, Vol. 1*, Brookfield: Edward Elgar.

Mansfield, E., A. Romeo, M. Schwartz, D. Teece, S. Wagner,
and P. Brach, 1982, *Technology Transfer, Productivity, And
Economic Policy*, New York: W.W. Norton & Company.

Mansfield E., D. Teece and A. Romeo, 1979, 'Overseas
Research and Development by U.S.-Based Firms,' *Economica* 46 (May), 187–196.

Mansfield E., M. Schwartz and S. Wagner, 1981, 'Imitation
Costs and Patents: An Empirical Study,' *The Economic
Journal* 91, 907–918.

Mansfield, E., R. John, R. Anthony, W. Samuel, and B. George,
1977, 'Social and Private Rates of Return from Industrial
Innovations,' *Quarterly Journal of Economics* 91, 221–240.

Medoff, M., 1996, 'A Citation-Based Analysis of Economists
and Economics Programs,' *The American Economist* 40 (1),
46–49.

Morck, R. and B. Yeung, 2003, *Why Firms Diversify: Internalization v. Agency Behavior*.

Nelson, R. and S. Winter, 1977, 'In Search of a Useful Theory of Innovation,' *Research Policy* 6, 36–76.

Piekarz, R., 1983, 'R&D and Productivity Growth: Policy
Studies and Issues,' *American Economic Review* 73, 210–
214.

Polyani, M., 1966, *The Tacit Dimension*, New York: Doubleday.

Scherer, F., 1983, 'R&D and Declining Productivity Growth,' *American Economics Review* 73, 215–218.

Schankerman, M., 1998, 'How Valuable Is Patent Protection? Estimates by Technology Field', *Rand Journal of Economics* 29 (1), 77–107.

Shannon, C. and W. Weaver, 1949, *A Mathematical Theory of Communication*, Urbana: University of Illinois Press.

Szulanski, G., 1996, 'Exploring Internal Stickiness: Impediments to the Transfer of Best Practice Within the Firm,' *Strategic Management Journal* 17, 27–43.

Rochet, J. and J. Tirole, 2004, *Two Sided Markets: An Overview*, Mimeo, University of Toulouse.

Teece, D.J., 1976, *The Multinational Corporation and the Resource Cost of International Technology Transfer*, Cambridge, MA: Ballinger.

Teece, D.J., 1977a, 'Technology Transfer by Multinational Firms: The Resource Cost of Transferring Technological Know-how,' *The Economic Journal* 87, 242–261.

Teece, D.J., 1977b, 'Time-Cost Tradeoffs: Elasticity Estimates and Determinants for International Technology Transfer Projects,' *Management Science* 23 (8), 830–837.

Teece, D.J., 1980, 'The Diffusion of an Administrative Innovation,' *Management Science* 26 (5) (May), 464–470.

Teece, D.J., 1981a, 'The Market for Know-how and the Efficient International Transfer of Technology,' *The Annals of the Academy of Political and Social Science* 458, 81–196.

Teece, D.J., 1981b, The Multinational Enterprise: Market Failure and Market Power Considerations,' *Sloan Management Review* 22 (3), 3–17.

Teece, D.J., 1982, 'Towards an Economic Theory of the Multiproduct Firm,' *Journal of Economic Behavior and Organization* 3, 39–33.

Teece, D.J., 1985, 'Multinational Enterprise, Internal Governance, and Industrial Organization,' *American Economic Review* 75 (2), 233–238.

Teece, D.J., 1986, 'Profiting from Technological Innovation,' *Research Policy* 15 (6), 285–305.

Teece, D.J. and H. Chesbrough, 1996, 'Organizing for Innovation: When is Virtual Virtuous?,' *Harvard Business Review*.

Williamson, O.E., 1975, *Markets and Hierarchies: Analysis and Antitrust Implications*, New York: The Free Press.

COLLABORATIVE ARRANGEMENTS AND GLOBAL TECHNOLOGY STRATEGY:

SOME EVIDENCE FROM THE TELECOMMUNICATIONS EQUIPMENT INDUSTRY

Gary Pisano and David J. Teece

I. INTRODUCTION

The organization of the technological innovation process is changing worldwide, and particularly in the United States. These changes encompass both the way that research is organized and the way that new technology is commercialized. The traditional linear approach—R&D, prototyping, manufacturing startup, marketing and distribution all in-house— is giving way, particularly in some new industries, to less vertically integrated structures, usually involving collaboration with other industry

Research on Technological Innovation, Management and Policy
Volume 4, pages 227–256
Copyright © 1989 by JAI Press Inc.
All rights of reproduction in any form reserved.
ISBN: 0-89232-798-7
Reprinted with permission from Elsevier.

participants. Indeed, collaboration among unaffiliated enterprises for manufacturing and/or distribution has become the norm in some industries.

In this chapter we attempt to build a framework to explain this phenomenon. We hope this framework will assist in the design of appropriate technology strategies. In particular, we argue that technology strategy is no longer a matter of setting the R&D budget and selecting promising projects. Technology strategy also involves making key organizational decisions with respect to commercialization. These decisions relate in particular to whether such endeavors should be organized in-house or should involve the participation of unaffiliated firms, including potential rivals and competitors. They also involve decisions related to the governance of collaborative relationships. The framework presented in this paper suggests that different inter-firm governance structures will be appropriate for different types of collaborative activities. While there are many possible forms of inter-firm governance, in this paper we distinguish between relationships involving equity participation and those governed strictly by contracts. Section VI investigates the choice between equity and non-equity modes of governance in the context of technological collaborations in the telecommunications equipment industry.

Of course, interfirm collaborations are not new. They are common practice both domestically and internationally. What is new is the frequency with which collaborations of this kind are occurring in the development and commercialization of new products and processes. In order to give some precision to the discussion, we first provide a definition of collaboration as well as some examples.

We define collaborative agreements in the context of innovation as any interorganizational (firm, university, government lab, etc.) agreements, with or without equity, that involve the bilateral, multiparty, or unilateral contributions or exchange of assets or their services in a market. We are deeply concerned with such basic organizational issues as whether markets or hierarchies should be used to organize economic activity.

Collaboration under the definition just provided is not confined to the innovation process. Any joint venture, such as the famous ARAMCO and CALTEX joint ventures in the petroleum business, or COMALCO in aluminum, would qualify. Accordingly, we hereafter confine our analysis to collaborative arrangements that involve the development and/or commercialization of new products and processes. We have in mind the kind of collaboration witnessed between Lilly and Genentech for the development and commercialization of Humulin, between Merck and Chiron for Hepatitis B, between AT&T and Olivetti for the AT&T PC, and between McDonnell Douglas and Northrup for the F-18 jet fighter. All of these arrangements involve new products and processes. Human capital, rather than physical capital, is what is being shared.

II. THE ORGANIZATIONAL DIMENSIONS OF TECHNOLOGY STRATEGY

There are many elements of technology strategy. Firms must select projects, allocate R&D budgets, decide how much they are going to lay on those bets, and organize themselves in order to give those projects the best chance of generating positive commercial outcomes. The first two of these dimensions is captured on the vertical (y) axis in Figure 1. The third is represented in the other 2 axes (x and z). The more traditional model for firms has been vertical integration (shaded area in Figure 1), as illustrated by IBM's mainframe computer business. Increasingly, however, less integrated approaches are appearing. For example, Worlds of Wonder, Inc., a "producer" of high technology childrens' toys, contracts out for all of its manufacturing and some of its design.

The organizational question can thus be partitioned into two sets of choices. The first one relates to whether the established firm ought to rely on its own internal R&D capabilities or whether it should source technology externally.[1] The second relates to the organizational approach the firm should adopt for commercializing the technology. Should it attempt all of the relevant manufacturing and marketing in-house, or should it seek others with whom it can contract for these services? The firm may choose to perform all of the key functions in-house (and be what we call a "classical firm"), or it may choose to collaborate with other more qualified firms to ensure the product is presented to the market in the most attractive way (what we call a "network firm").[2]

In essence, organizational choices we have identified raise the question of whether the firm should use market modes (contracting/venturing with nonaffiliated firms), internal nonmarket modes, or mixed modes (contracting for some functions and performing others in-house). These organizational questions are not typically considered part of technology strategy. Technology strategy was once thought to consist of determining the level of R&D expenditures and the projects to which those resources ought to be allocated.

There are a number of factors that suggest that a much broader concept of technology strategy is now warranted:[3]

1. The frequency of technological discontinuities or technology paradigm shifts seems to have increased. When technological develop-

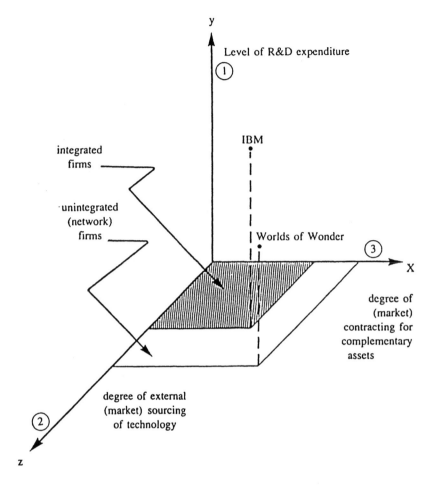

Figure 1. Organizational and Resource Dimensions of Technology Strategy

ment takes a new trajectory, the direction of technical development is no longer cumulative and self-generating. Development
requires repeated reference to the technical and commercial environment external to the firm. In short, the logic of previous
technical advance is broken; and the capabilities that the firm
possesses in-house may no longer suffice. Technological discontinuities have been a feature of technological advance since time

immemorial, but according to one source they are on the increase (Foster, 1986).

2. The costs of innovation have increased markedly, and the ability of a single firm to "go it alone," particularly with respect to large systems (e.g., the Boeing 767 or the Airbus A300), may have declined. In short, even setting aside matters of risk, the financial requirements may strain even giant enterprises.

3. The sources of innovation have become more diffused internationally; thus, the probability that any one firm, even if it is multinational, could command all the relevant expertise for a particular project is declining. Certainly, the technological dominance of American firms in several industries is being challenged.

4. The speed with which new technologies must be commercialized has increased to the point where few firms have the time to assemble all of the requisite capabilities in-house. In part, this is because of more rapid technological change. It is also because of rapid imitation. Accordingly, there are cases where collaboration with other firms that already have the requisite capabilities is appealing.

5. For large firms, the incentive properties of small firms—and, in particular, their ability to reward innovators handsomely in ways that large established firms find difficult to replicate—favor the pursuit of technical opportunities externally.

All of this suggests that simple-minded representations of innovation as ideally suited to the large-scale enterprise or to the small firm need to yield to a more eclectic view of innovation and its organizational and strategic requirements. In particular, we indicate that the key strategic/organizational issues for innovating firms to consider are the extent to which technology will be sourced internally, rather than externally, and the degree of involvement that other firms will be offered in the commercialization process.

III. FORCES DETERMINING TECHNOLOGY SOURCING STRATEGIES

Whether innovating firms ought to source technology internally or externally, we submit, depends on the interrelationships between three key sets of factors, each of which will be explored in turn:

1. The organizational location of the sources of invention/know-how
2. The ease of appropriability, i.e., whether the sponsoring firm is well positioned to capture the benefits from the research activity in question
3. The facility with which contracts for the purchase or sale of the technology in question can be written, executed, and enforced. (This can be referred to as the transaction cost.)

A. Sources of Know-how

Winter (1984) argues that innovation involves mixing public know-how, proprietary know-how external to the firm (imitation), and internal know-how. When innovation is driven primarily by internal know-how and capabilities, a firm's ability to exploit technical opportunities is constrained primarily by its accumulated stock of proprietary know-how, its organizational and learning skills, and its experience in the relevant activities. These assets take time to build and are a function of past activities in both research and production. Capabilities relevant to a particular technological paradigm over time become imbedded in its research routines (Nelson and Winter, 1982).

The skills, know-how, and experience necessary to innovate in one design paradigm, however, are usually quite different from those required in another. Thus, if a firm's established technological trajectory is particularly rich, or, if it is able to lead the shift in an industry from one design/technological regime to another, then that firm may be able to continue relying on internal capabilities to generate relevant know-how. However, shifts in technological regimes are often propelled by firms that do not have the deepest skills in the established paradigm. Thus, when the transistor replaced the vacuum tube in the mid-1950s, vacuum-tube manufacturers were not the pioneers. Indeed, Sylvania kept pouring money into increasingly sophisticated vacuum-tube designs until 1968! Rather, an entirely new set of producers emerged to develop and produce transistors (Malerba, 1985).

Hence, a shift in technological paradigms (a technological discontinuity) is likely to cause a shift in the locus of the most productive R&D efforts in a direction away from the incumbents. Incumbent firms will thus have to consider acquiring this technology. They may be able to do so through naked imitation; however, as we shall see, if the innovation in question is protected, the technology may need to be purchased externally.

Note that public institutions—universities and government laboratories—may be important sources of new technology, particularly in the early stages of an industry. Inasmuch as such establishments are unable or unwilling as a matter of policy to engage in commercialization activities, the requirement and the opportunity for collaboration with established firms are provided. In these circumstances, firms—both incumbents and new business ventures—are forced to seek technology externally.

B. Appropriability Issues

If new technology can be sourced externally or developed internally, then the choice of mode will likely depend upon appropriability and related transactions costs issues. If certain R&D resources allocated either externally or internally can be expected to produce equally beneficial outcomes, appropriability concerns are likely to favor internal procurement for at least two reasons. One is the cumulative nature of learning, and its particular location. The procuring firm, should it "contract out," is likely to deny itself important learning opportunities. If "one shot" improvements along a particular technological trajectory, as with research to meet a particular fixed regulatory standard, are all that is contemplated, then permitting the developer to benefit from learning may not present a problem. Generally, however, future advances are contemplated, and if these can profitably build upon earlier R&D activity, internalizing the activity will be necessary. Even though the developer may pass on the benefits of past learning acquired under previous R&D contracts with the procurer, there are circumstances under which this may not occur. In-house research guards against these contingencies. A second and related reason is that the unaffiliated developer of new products and processes is generally free to contract with other procurers. This can result in the leakage of technology, developed on one company's R&D dollar, to another. Internalization forces an exclusive contract, and avoids this spillover occuring through the R&D contracting process. It may still of course occur in other ways, as when R&D personnel switch employment.

The desirability of an external sourcing approach increases if the sources of relevant technology are external to the firm.[4] However, even if new technology emerges elsewhere, a firm's eagerness to engage in a commercial transaction to secure the technology depends on the viability and necessity of a contract for the technology in question. If the technology is of a kind for which intellectual-property law affords no protection and if copying is easy, then the acquiring firm need only imitate; and no commercial transaction results. If, on the other hand, the technology at issue is valuable and is protected by patents, trade secrets, and other legal structures, or is simply difficult to copy, then some kind of formal purchase contract and/or technology-transfer agreement will be called for.

While there are many exceptions, it is generally the case that very little know-how can be shielded effectively through patent and trade-secret protection alone. One major exception is chemical-based technologies, where patent protection, due to the nature of the technology, is intrinsically stronger. Xerography (Xerox) and instant photography (Polaroid) are other major exceptions. Patent protection is generally much weaker in machine and process equipment technologies because the nature of the technology makes it vulnerable to reverse engineering (see Levin et al., 1984).

If property rights are very strong, the innovator's reluctance to license is often overcome because the possibility of extracting an economic return comparable to that which could be obtained internally is increased. Conversely, when intellectual-property protection is weak, new technology, if it is developed at all, will be developed internally for internal use. According to Von Hippel (1982), the dominance of equipment users as innovators can be explained by this relative appropriability advantage. In short, strong patent protection allows the innovator to market its product or process innovation without exposing it to risks of imitation. In contrast, a tighter link, possibly even vertical integration, between sources and users of technology, is required when patent protection is weak. Integration, of course, enables trade-secret protection to shield the technology from would-be scrutinizers of the technology. The corollary is that users will have to come to terms with the sources of technology when they are external. If the appropriability regime is weak, they may simply be able to imitate. If it is strong, then imitation is less viable; and some kind of licensing arrangement may have to be sought. The viability of this depends, in turn, on transactions-cost considerations, which we now examine.

C. Transactions Costs

Transactions costs considerations lay behind the appropriability issues previously discussed. Transactions costs relate to the ease with which contracts for the purchase or sale of a commodity, in this case technology, can be written, executed, and enforced without leading to unexpected outcomes that impose large costs on one or both parties (Williamson, 1975, 1985; Teece, 1981). In the case of technology, license agreements are risky if one or both parties must make highly dedicated investments whose value depends on the other party's performing as anticipated.

The biggest transactional risks for the seller are associated with the buyer's using the technology in ways not anticipated by the contract, or which while anticipated cannot be easily prevented. These risks are usually ameliorated if the technology has good protection under relevant intellectual-property law. The biggest risks for the buyer stem from the fact that the technology may not perform at expected levels. The problem stems from the fundamental paradox of information: one often does not know what one has purchased until after the fact (Arrow, 1962). In short, a buyer must typically engage in a transaction in which he has incomplete information about the commodity being purchased (Teece, 1981).

Delivery is another problem. Technology must be transferred from seller to buyer for the transaction to be complete. This can be costly. Unless the technology is highly codified, transfer is likely to involve the transfer of technical personnel; and, depending on the complexities of the technology and the way in which the transfer is managed, the success of the transfer is uncertain (Teece, 1977). In short, the viability of a market relationship involving collaboration will be drawn in part by the transactions-cost conditions that will characterize the contract. It ought to be evident that high transactions costs will block an arrangement even when it would be warranted on other grounds. Such a condition is commonly referred to as "market failure." Market failures are nonevents. They cause deals to be avoided because it is not possible to formulate and/or enforce a mutually acceptable arrangement between buyer and seller. Figure 2 summarizes the implications for know-how procurement strategies that follow from the interactions among the loci of innovation, appropriability issues, and transactions costs.

IV. THE EXTERNAL PROCUREMENT OF KNOW-HOW

The external procurement of know-how is likely to be imperative for incumbent firms that, for one reason or another, find (1) that they are no longer capable of productively researching opportunities internally, and (2) that there are significant costs, particularly from having investment in traditional products stranded, associated with being closed out of the next

regime of appropriability

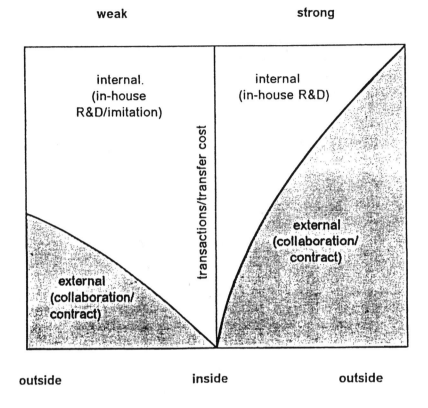

Figure 2. Know-how Procurement Strategy (Buyer's Perspective)

round of significant innovation. The former set of factors might be thought of as pro-active factors favoring external sourcing, while the second kind are reactive or defensive. Each is discussed in turn.

A. Pro-active Considerations

The external procurement of know-how by contract is likely to be the selected sourcing strategy when the centers of excellence in the relevant know-how are external to the firm, appropriability is tight, and transactional difficulties are manageable. The external sources may be suppliers, as in agriculture and housing, users, as in scientific instruments, or competitors, as in biotechnology, or not-for-profit organizations, such as universities and government laboratories.

The locus of innovation is most likely to lie external to incumbent firms when there is a technological discontinuity, or a paradigm shift as it might more meaningfully be called. Of course, what is external to one group of firms may be internal to another.

There are a number of modes by which technology lying external to the firm can be acquired. If it is easy to copy because it lacks intellectual-property protection and can be reverse-engineered at low cost, as with some microprocessors, then imitation is often a viable acquisition strategy. When the technology is legally protected, is hard to copy, and the innovator is willing to sell, then a number of possible contractual relationships are possible. They include licensing, contract R&D, R&D joint ventures, and bilateral collaborative arrangements.

Licensing is the most familiar of these approaches. A firm possessing valuable know-how that is protected can contract to let others use the technology in question. A license agreement will often be accompanied by a know-how agreement under which the owner of the intellectual property in question will contract to assist the buyer in developing a comprehensive understanding of the technology in question.

Contract R&D is also an important mode, though it is also fraught with hazards. When a buyer commissions R&D work to be performed under contract, it is usually in recognition of the fact that the provider of the R&D services is better positioned to generate a desirable output from R&D than is the buyer itself. Unless the technology to be developed can be specified with great precision, and the costs of the requisite development activities can be gauged with considerable accuracy, however, contracting to develop technology using fixed-price contracts is not easy as it is difficult to specify and cost-out the object of the development activity at issue. Modest technological endeavors can be arranged this way more satisfactorily than can ambitious ones (which can typically be organized externally only by cost plus contracts, but are exposed to obvious incentive hazards).

R&D joint ventures make sense as external procurement mechanisms when the other party can bring certain capabilities to the venture that the collaborating party does not possess. Other properties of joint ventures are that they reduce risk when project costs are high; and in the R&D area, they may reduce duplication without necessarily reducing variety.

An inherent flaw of capitalist-market economics is that they often cause patent races and other forms of socially wasteful R&D duplication. There may not be a better system for promoting innovation than capitalism, and gross inefficiencies associated with duplication can be reduced by joint ventures. Research consortia, such as the Microelectronics and Computer Corporation (MCC) formed by a group of computer companies, are an example.

Another collaborative mechanism involves bilateral exchanges of know-how and other assets, as with cross-licensing, patent-pooling, and, more recently, technology transfers, in return for some other nonpecuniary commercial favor, such as access to distribution facilities. These services are often difficult to obtain otherwise, particularly under simple purchase contracts; and the reciprocal nature of collaboration can bring a degree of incentive capability and stability to the arrangement that would not otherwise be available.

B. Reactive Considerations

The discussion so far has been focused primarily on how external sources of technology can be tapped and what the role of collaborators in this process is.

The strength of the imperative for incumbent firms—i.e., firms currently nicely positioned in the industry—to engage in such activity is more than just a function of the attractiveness of the technological opportunities that lie external to the firm. It may also reflect the fact that failure to shape the new technology may result in the stranding of investments supporting the existing technology. Often this is unavoidable, i.e., a new technology, requiring a new set of inputs and new processing equipment, once commercialized, will destroy the value of investments supporting the existing technology. Incumbents may sometimes be completely helpless before such competitive pressures; however, in some cases, new technologies can be fashioned to deliver superior performance while still placing a demand on the investment put in place to support the old technology. In these cases, affiliation with those developing and shaping new technology has obvious advantages.

C. Implications

The frequency of these various forms of collaboration appear to be increasing. It is not just a feature of new industries like biotechnology, where there are literally thousands of such agreements. It is also a feature of industries like telecommunication equipment and automobiles, and maturing industries like computers and semiconductors (see Mowery, 1988). So great has been the escalation of such activity that one is forced to ask very basic questions about the nature of the firms. Firms are becoming increasingly interconnected through long-term contractual relationships; as the external capabilities of others become increasingly critical to one's own success and as the opportunities for opportunism widen through dependence on fairly loose affiliation of one kind or another, the nature of the firm and the functions of management become transformed.

A number of more specific implications for organizational and business strategy also follow. With respect to incumbents, the analysis suggests that the emergence of technological discontinuities dictates that incumbents must shift gears, latching on to the relevant external sources of know-how, collaborating if necessary to do so. A variety of collaborative modes exist; their respective viability is a function of the degree of protection afforded the technology by intellectual-property protection, and the use of contractual instruments to access the technology in question. Failure to access the new technology may well lead to the demise of the firm. In some cases, this may be the inevitable consequence of a technological discontinuity; more often than not, however, the in-transfer of technology can protect, if not enhance, the competitive standing of incumbents.

Whether collaboration occurs, however, is not just a function of whether willing "buyers" exist. It is also a function of whether the party generating the new technology is willing to collaborate. Generally, there are a variety of factors that encourage them to do so. Besides the obvious infusion of cash that it frequently provides to the source of the innovation, collaboration with incumbents is likely to facilitate commercialization through providing access to complementary capacities in R&D, testing, manufacturing, and marketing.[5] It is to these considerations that we now turn.

V. ACCESSING COMPLEMENTARY ASSETS[6]

In almost all cases,[6] the successful commercialization of new technology requires that the know-how in question be utilized together with the services of other assets. Marketing, competitive manufacturing, and after-sales support are always needed to successfully commercialize a new product or process. These services are often obtained from complementary assets that are often specialized. For example, the commercialization of a new drug is likely to require the dissemination of information over a specialized distribution channel. In some cases, the complementary assets may be the other parts of a system. For instance, hypersonic aircraft may require different landing and servicing facilities.

As a new technology paradigm is developing, usually a number of competing designs are being worked on simultaneously. Before a dominant design emerges, there is little to be gained from firms deploying specialized assets, as scale economies are unavailable and price is not a principal competitive factor. As the leading design or designs begin to be selected by users, however, volumes increase; and opportunities for economies of scale and low cost production will induce firms to begin gearing up for mass production by acquiring specialized tooling and equipment, and possibly specialized distribution as well. Because these investments involve significant irreversibilities, and hence risks, producers must proceed with caution.

The degree of interdependence between the innovation and the complementary assets can, of course, vary tremendously. At one extreme, the complementary assets may be virtually generic, have many potential suppliers including incumbent firms, and be relatively unimportant when compared with the technological breakthrough represented by the innovation. At the other, successful commercialization of the innovation may depend critically on an asset that has only one possible supplier. Such assets might be labelled "bottleneck" assets.

Between these two extremes there is the possibility of "cospecialization"—where the innovation and the complementary assets depend on each other. An example of this would be containerized shipping, which requires specialized trucks and terminals that can work only in conjunction with each other.

A key commercialization decision the owners of the new technology have to make is what to do (build, buy, or rent) with respect to the complementary assets. Although there are a myriad of possible arrangements, two pure types stand out—namely, owning or renting. At one extreme, the innovator could integrate into (i.e., build or acquire) all of the necessary complementary assets. This is likely to be unnecessary as well as prohibitively expensive. It is well to recognize that the variety of assets and competences that need to be accessed is likely to be quite large even for only modestly complex technologies like personal computers.

To produce a personal computer, for instance, a company needs expertise in semiconductor technology, disk-drive technology, networking technology, keyboard technology, and several others. No company has kept pace in all of these areas by itself.

At the other extreme, the innovator could attempt to access these assets through collaborative contractual relationships (e.g., component supply contracts, fabrication contracts, distribution contracts, etc.). In many instances, contracts may suffice, although a contract does expose the innovator to various hazards and dependencies that it may well wish to avoid. An analysis of the properties of the two extreme forms ought to be instructive. A brief synopsis of mixed modes then follows. The perspective adopted is that of the new entrant, rather than that of the incumbent.

A. Contractual Modes

The advantages of collaborative agreements—whereby the innovator contracts with independent suppliers, manufacturers, or distributors—are fairly obvious. The innovator will not have to make the up-front capital expenditures needed to build or buy the assets in question. This reduces risks as well as cash requirements. Also, contractual relationships can bring added credibility to the innovator, especially if the innovator is relatively unknown while the contractual partner is established and viable. Indeed, arms-length contracting that embodies more than a simple buy-sell agreement is becoming so common that various terms (e.g., "strategic alliances," "strategic partnering") have been devised to describe it. Even large companies such as IBM are now engaging in it. For IBM, partners enable the company to "learn things [they] couldn't have learned without many years of trial and error."[7] IBM's arrangement with Microsoft to use the latter's MS-DOS operating system of software on the IBM PC facilitated the timely introduction of IBM's personal computer into the market. Had IBM developed its own operating system, it may have missed the market window.

It is most important to recognize, however, that strategic partnering is exposed to certain hazards, particularly for the innovator and particularly when the innovator is trying to use contracts to access special capabilities. For instance, it may be difficult to induce suppliers to make costly, irreversible commitments that depend for their success on the success of the innovation. To expect suppliers, manufacturers, and distributors to do so is to invite them to take risks along with the innovator. The problem that this poses for the innovator is similar to the problems associated with attracting venture capital. The innovator must persuade its prospective partner that the risk is a good one. The situation is open to opportunistic abuses on both sides. The innovator has incentives to overstate the value of the innovation, while the supplier has incentives to "run with the technology" should the innovation be a success.

In short, the current euphoria over "strategic partnering" may be partially misplaced. The advantages are being stressed (for example, McKenna, 1985) without a balanced presentation of transactional hazards. Briefly, (1) *there is the risk that the partner will not perform according to the innovator's perception* of what the contract requires; (2) *there is the added danger that the partner may imitate the innovator's technology* and attempt to compete with the innovator. Both problems stem from the transactions cost problems discussed earlier. The latter possibility is particularly acute if the provider of the complementary asset is uniquely situated with respect to the specialized assets in question and has the capacity to absorb and imitate the technology.

B. Integration Modes

Integration modes, which by definition involve equity participation, are distinguished from pure contractual modes in that they typically facilitate greater control and greater access to commercial information (Williamson, 1975; Teece, 1976). In the case of a wholly owned asset, this is, of course, rather extensive.

Owning, rather than renting, the requisite specialized assets has clear advantages when the complementary assets are in fixed supply over the relevant time period. It is critical, however, that ownership be obtained before the requirements of the innovation become publicly known; otherwise, the price of the assets in question is likely to be raised. The prospective seller, realizing the value of the asset to the innovator, may well be able to extract a portion, if not all, of the profits that the innovation can generate by charging a price that reflects the value of the asset to the innovator. Such "bottleneck" situations are not uncommon, particularly in distribution.

As a practical matter, however, an innovator may not have the time to acquire or build the complementary assets that ideally it would like to control. This is particularly true when imitation is so easy that timing becomes critical. Additionally, the innovator may simply not have the financial resources to proceed. Accordingly, innovators need to assess complementary, specialized assets as to their importance. If the assets are critical, ownership is warranted although if the firm is cash constrained, a minority position may well represent a sensible tradeoff. If the complementary asset in question is technology or other personnel-related assets, this calculation may need to be revised. This is because ownership of creative enterprises appears to be fraught with hazards as integration tends to destroy incentives and culture (Williamson, 1985).

Needless to say, when imitation is easy, strategic moves to build or buy complementary assets that are specialized must occur with due reference to the moves of competitors. There is no point in moving to build a specialized asset, for instance, if one's imitators can do it faster and cheaper. Figure 3 is a simplified view of how these factors ought to condition the integration decision for a firm that does not already own certain complementary assets needed to bring the new product or process to market successfully.

It is self-evident that if the innovator is already a large enterprise with many of the relevant complementary assets under its control, integration is not likely to be the issue that it might otherwise be because the innovating firm will already control many of the relevant specialized and co-specialized assets. In industries experiencing rapid technological change, however, it is unlikely that a single company has the full range of expertise needed to bring advanced products to market in a timely and cost-effective fashion. Hence, the integration issue is not just a small-firm issue.

C. Mixed Modes

The real world rarely provides extreme or pure cases. Decisions to integrate or license involve tradeoffs, compromises, and mixed approaches. It is not surprising, therefore, that the real world is characterized by mixed modes of organization, involving judicious blends of contracting and integration. Relationships can be engineered around contracts in ways that are functionally akin to integration; internalization can be so decentralized that it is akin to contracts. Still, comparative analysis of the extremes can provide important insights into mixed modes.

Between the extremes of pure contracts and internal organization lie a rich diversity of governance structures that mix elements of both. We view these as an attempt to judiciously combine the flexibility of arms-

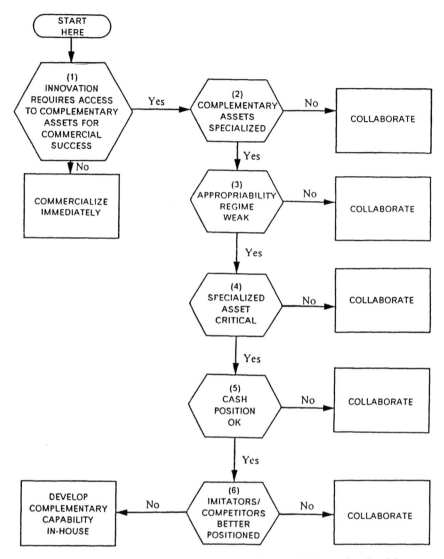

Figure 3.   Complementary Assets Integration v. Collaboration Decision

length contracts with the coordination and communication properties of internal organization. There are various mechanisms that can be used to build such intermediate structures. Two of these, equity joint ventures and direct equity participation, are examined below.

Equity Joint Ventures

An equity joint venture, the creation of a new entity jointly owned and operated by the collaborators, is the classic form of organizing collaborative activity. Indeed, most studies of jointly organized activities have focused almost exclusively on this legal form. Equity joint ventures have two governance properties that make them ideal for coordinating complex transactions involving specialized assets. First, they create an administrative hierarchy (quite similar to internal organization) for setting general operational and strategic policies as well as for settling disputes. This hierarchical structure dispenses with the need for collaborators to attempt the often impossible task of specifying a complete set of contractual provisions for conducting the collaboration. Instead, the collaborators need only agree on a broad set of governing rules that provide a framework for deciding on more specific conditions as more information becomes available. In addition, the governing body of the venture, usually composed of representatives of both companies, provides a channel for communicating pertinent information and for coordinating the collaborative roles of each partner.

The second advantage of equity joint ventures is that both parties hold a direct stake (through their equity position) in the success of the project. This feature aligns incentives and can lower the risk that one party will become opportunistic. Partners pay some share of the costs of any actions they take that hurt the viability of the venture. In addition, the formal ownership structure provides each party legal rights with respect to the technology of other strategic assets contributed to or developed by the venture. Parties can agree at the outset about the division of assets if the venture is terminated.

Joint ventures also entail certain costs that must be recognized. Generally, they take longer to negotiate and organize than other, less hierarchical forms of governance. Given these costs, they are usually appropriate only for longer-term projects that involve heavy capital or technological commitment by both parties.

Direct Equity Positions

An alternative to establishing a jointly owned company is for one partner to take a direct equity stake in the other. This is often used where a significant size differential exists between the collaborators, and it would be impossible for the smaller party to contribute enough equity into a jointly owned company. The direct-equity approach is similar to that of equity joint ventures, although generally providing for less joint control. First, the equity stake again helps to align incentives. It safeguards the smaller partner (or investee) by creating direct costs for the investor to act opportunistically. If the inventor takes any action that hurts the investee, it will bear some portion of the resulting costs through its equity stake. Usually, at the time the equity investment is made, the parties concurrently agree on a set of longer-run strategic and operational goals of the relationship. The contribution of equity helps to ensure that the investor will have an interest in ensuring that these strategic and operational goals are pursued in good faith.

Second, the direct-equity stake can provide some scope for hierarchical governance (as opposed to strictly contractual governance) if it allows the investor a seat on the other company's Board of Directors. The goal is generally not to achieve voting power. Instead, it is to gain a direct communication channel to the highest governing level of the other partner. This ensures that the top management of the partner stays interested in the business relationship. It can also help to ensure that critical problems and issues will be brought directly to the top management, rather than having to percolate up from the line managers in charge of the collaborative effort. The board position also helps information to circulate the other way, from the investee to the investor. Often, the corporate investor appoints one of its high-level executives to fill the board seat and thus provides the investee with a direct channel back to the corporate partner. Like the equity joint venture, direct equity relationships have advantages over non-equity, contractual forms of collaboration when the activities in question involve transaction-specific assets and uncertainty.

Sometimes mixed modes represent transitional phases. For instance, because of the convergence of computer and telecommunication technology, firms in each industry are discovering that they often lack the requisite technical capabilities in the other. Because the technological interdependence of the two requires collaboration among those that design different parts of the system, intense cross-boundary coordination and information flows are required. When separate enterprises are involved, agreement must be reached on complex protocol issues among parties that see their interests differently. Contractual difficulties can be anticipated because the selection of common technical protocols among the parties will often be followed by transaction-specific investments in hardware and software.

The use of contractual, equity, and internal forms of organization in the telecommunications-equipment industry are discussed in the following section.

VI. THE GOVERNANCE OF COLLABORATIVE RELATIONSHIPS IN THE WORLD'S TELECOMMUNICATIONS EQUIPMENT INDUSTRY

In this section, we apply the above framework to examine collaborative arrangements in the telecommunications equipment industry. We have chosen to study collaboration in telecommunications because fundamental changes in equipment technology and the structure of demand have altered the bundle of strategic assets necessary to compete. This situation has created a *market for strategic assets* among firms with distinctive technological and commercial competencies.

Consistent with the framework presented above, we can divide strategic assets in the telecommunications equipment industry into two broad categories: (1) upstream technical capabilities and know-how needed to develop complementary or critical input technologies; (2) downstream marketing and distribution needed to penetrate particular product, customer, or geographic markets. These strategic assets are traded through a rich variety of governance structures including arm's length contracts, equity joint ventures, and partial-equity linkages.

We focus our analysis on arrangements where firms collaborate in the development or exchange of technical know-how. These include cases where technology transfer or joint technological development form the sole functional basis for collaboration *and* cases where these technological functions are coupled to downstream functions (such as manufacturing and marketing) in a single collaborative relationship. There are several examples which also illustrate the varied motives behind such collaborations.

First, one motive for collaboration is legal. Firms with overlapping technologies may strike a licensing deal to avoid or settle patent litigation. These agreements, which are quite common in semiconductors (Malerba, 1985), generally involve cross-licensing and consist of little more than a grant of permission to use some proprietary technology.

A second motive, which goes beyond sheer legal considerations, is to tap the specialized technical expertise of another firm. In recent years, the functions of communications equipment have expanded rapidly. Traditionally, telecommunications equipment was designed for voice communications. Increasingly, telecommunications also encompasses the transmission of data, text, image, and video. This functional expansion has made it necessary for communications equipment to incorporate a far broader range of component and sub-system level technologies. As the range of technologies underlying telecommunications systems has expanded, it has become increasingly inefficient for telecommunications equipment firms to track all of the relevant technological frontiers through in-house R&D. Access to state-of-the-art technologies is often better served by collaborating with specialized producers of components (e.g., semiconductors) and sub-systems. As part of the functional expansion of telecommunications, equipment suppliers must ensure that these products are compatible with the various types of new terminal equipment (computers, facsimile devices, voice messaging devices, etc.) which have become part of telecommunications networks. To ensure equipment compatibility, firms license communications protocols and jointly develop complementary systems technologies. In all of the above cases, collaboration can stop at the technology stage or encompass downstream functions such as manufacturing and marketing.

We are interested in the organization and governance of these technology-based transactions. In particular, we are interested in the choice between purely contractual arrangements (which include both short- and long-term contracts) and what we call quasi-internal arrangements (equity joint ventures, direct investments, and organized consortium). The governance properties of equity joint ventures and direct equity relationships were discussed in Section V.A. Our general hypothesis is that these quasi-internal structures can more efficiently govern technical collaborations involving durable, transaction-specific investments and uncertainty. A test of this hypothesis is presented in the section below.

A. Source of Data

The source of data for our analysis is a database constructed by researchers at Futoro Organizzazione Risorse (F.O.R.) in Rome through an extensive review of the trade press.[8] A total of 974 collaborative arrangements were recorded over the period 1982–1985, 117 of which were in telecommunications equipment. Among the information recorded for each arrangement was the legal form, function (or motive), respective nationalities of the collaborators.

Construction of the Dependent Variable

To construct the categorical dependent variable, we used information on the legal form of each arrangement. These were classified as follows:

1. *Nonequity Agreements:* Agreements which do not include equity ties or the creation of new, jointly owned companies. Examples included contracts involving various activities and licensing agreements.
2. *Equity Agreements:* Agreements where one party acquires a minority equity interest in another for some industrial purpose (i.e., excluding purely financial investments).
3. *Joint Ventures:* Agreements in which a new legal entity is created and jointly owned by the partners.
4. *Consortia:* Joint ventures involving more than one partner.

These categories could be translated directly into our binary dependent variable classification scheme. The category "non-equity agreements" formed our "purely contractual governance" category while equity-agreements, joint ventures, and consortia were classified into our "quasi-internal" governance category.

Independent Variable

Constructing independent variables to reflect transaction specificity and uncertainty proved far more difficult. We had data neither on the levels of transaction-specific investments nor on the levels of uncertainty involved in the collaborative projects. We were therefore forced to use the functional purposes of the arrangements as a categorical indicator of both uncertainty and transaction-specificity. In the database, each arrangement was classified into one of the following nine functional purpose categories:

1. *Technology-transfer:* A unilateral assignment of licenses, which may also be accompanied by technical assistance.
2. *R&D Integration:* Cross-licensing, the provision of R&D services, and joint R&D for the development of new products.
3. *Supply Arrangements:* Agreements for the provision of goods, either short-term or long-term.

4. *Production Integration:* Joint production of intermediate or finished goods.
5. *Distribution/Marketing Integration:* Sales and marketing by one party for another or jointly by both parties.
6. *Integration of R&D and Production:* Combination of 2 and 4 above.
7. *Integration of R&D and Distribution/Marketing:* Combination of 2 and 5 above.
8. *Integration of Production and Distribution/Marketing:* Combination of 4 and 5 above.
9. *Integration of R&D, Production, and Distribution/Marketing:* Combination of 2, 4, and 5 above.

Our interest lies with those collaborations involving technology transfer or R&D integration as at least one functional motive. As discussed earlier, R&D collaboration and technology transfer may involve transactional difficulties. Such difficulties are likely to be compounded when collaboration couples technological activities with commercialization functions (production, distribution/marketing). Attempts to jointly create *and* utilize new technology require more communication and coordination between collaborators than when collaboration is limited to R&D. In addition to agreeing on technological goals and tactics, collaborators will also have to coordinate investments in production facilities and decisions on marketing/distribution. Governing the *link* between R&D and commercialization also imposes additional organizational burdens on collaboration. The hazards associated with transaction-specific capital are likely to be greater when partners must make investments in costly and durable downstream assets needed to utilize the know-how in question. For the above reasons, we expect collaborations that involve *both* technological activities and downstream functions to have a greater likelihood of being organized through quasi-internal governance structures than collaborations that only involve technological activities (i.e., technology transfer or R&D integration).

The raw data on function and form are summarized in Table 1. These data reflect the rich diversity of collaborative functions and forms through which collaboration takes place.

Methodology

To examine the hypothesis that technology collaborations that also involved downstream functions would be more likely to be organized

Table 1.   Frequency of Form and Function of Telecommunications
Cooperative Agreements

Function	Nonequity	Equity	Joint Venture	Consortium	Total
1. Technology Transfer	5	4	0	0	9
2. R&D Integration	23	2	1	1	27
3. Supply Arrangements	9	0	0	0	9
4. Production Integration	2	0	6	7	15
5. Distribution/Marketing Integration	26	1	8	0	35
6. R&D, Production Integration	2	0	5	0	7
7. R&D, Distribution/Marketing Integration	5	1	2	1	9
8. Production, Distribution/Marketing Integration	2	0	1	0	3
9. R&D, Production Distribution/Marketing Integration	1	0	2	0	3
Total	75	8	25	9	117

under quasi-internal arrangements than when they did not include down-stream activities, we conducted chi-square tests for homogeneity.[9] The null hypothesis in these tests is that a particular functional type of collaboration (e.g., R&D alone) will be organized under a particular governance form (e.g., quasi-internal) with roughly the same relative frequency with which another function is organized under the same form. For example, if in a sample of collaborative arrangements, quasi-internal governance forms represent 20% of arrangements, there would be a 20% probability that any given functional type of arrangement within that sample would have a quasi-internal governance form. Systematic deviations from the expected probability distribution should be explained by theory. The null hypothesis represents a view, contrary to our own, that there is no systematic relationship between the governance category and the functional category of collaborations. Before proceeding, the reader should be aware of the following caveats.

First, while we have been fortunate enough to have access to an extensive database of collaborative arrangements, it undoubtedly contains some biases based on the primary sources (i.e., the business press) from which it was gathered. The business press probably has a greater tendency to report collaborations struck between the major players in the marketplace. In addition, the press can cover only those arrangements that are not purposely kept secret by the collaborators. Generalizations based on our results should be limited to the relevant sampling frame (i.e., cases where an arrangement was publicly announced and where it involved a firm or project that was considered "newsworthy").

Second, we must stress another, more serious form of sample-selection bias inherent in this type of analysis. Our data includes only those cases where some form of collaboration actually took place: we do not (and cannot) observe those cases where it did not. In statistical terms, we have censored cases. The sample distribution is biased because it does not include those unobservable cases where firms did not choose internal organization over collaboration. This is particularly relevant to our analysis if a firm chose to organize a particular project internally due to the high transaction costs of collaboration. Unfortunately, the structure of our data does not permit us to apply any of the available statistical techniques to correct the problem.[10]

Finally, we must note that the information contained in each arrangement permits us to make judgments neither about the uncertainty nor about the transaction-specific investments involved in each. In lieu of such detailed information, we have relied on our knowledge about the nature of technology transfer, R&D, production, and distribution for telecommunications equipment. This approach obviously limits the degree to which we can make predictive statements about the relationship between form and function.

Despite these limitations, we think that our analysis is an important step forward in the study of collaborative organizations. It is one of the few attempts to analyze statistically the relationship between the form and function of collaborative arrangements within a transaction-costs framework (see also Pisano, 1988). The results are intended to stimulate further analysis along these lines.

Analysis and Results

Because our interest centers on technology-based collaborations, the relevant sample consists of those cases where R&D or technology-transfer represents *at least one function* (and perhaps the only function) in a collaborative arrangement. There are 55 arrangements that fit this criteria. Of these 55, 36 were cases where R&D integration or technology-transfer formed the sole functional basis of collaboration. For convenience, we will refer to this type of arrangement as "technology-only." The remaining 19 cases included collaborations that combined a technological function with either manufacturing, marketing, or both. We

Table 2

Function	Technology-only	Technology-plus	Total
Form:			
contract	28 (23.56)	8 (12.44)	36
quasi-internal	8 (12.44)	11 (6.56)	19
total	36	19	55
chi-square = 7.01*			

*results significant beyond .01 level

will refer to this category as "technology-plus." The technology-plus category was an aggregation of three types of functional cases found in the database: R&D plus manufacturing, R&D plus distribution, and R&D plus manufacturing and distribution.

Table 2 below shows the results of a contingency table analysis that compares the distribution of governance structures for technology-only and technology-plus arrangements. The expected frequencies for each cell are shown in parentheses.

The results allow us to reject the null hypothesi (at $p < .01$) that there is no systematic relationship between the functional category (technology-only vs. technology-plus) and the chosen governance structure (contract vs. quasi-internal). Comparing the actual frequencies with the expected frequencies in Table 2 also indicates that an independence model underpredicts the actual frequency with which technology-plus arrangements are organized under quasi-internal governance structures (11 actual cases versus 6.56 predicted cases). These results suggest that the actual frequency with which technology-plus arrangements are organized under quasi-internal governance structures can not be explained by purely random forces. This suggests that substantive differences between the two functional categories explain the relative difference in the frequency with which one type of governance structure is chosen over another.

One potential problem in our analysis is that the technology-plus category was formed by aggregating three different types of arrangements. This assumes that the three underlying functional types constitute a homogeneous population with respect to governance choices. We tested whether there was a basis for this assumption with chi-square tests for homogeneity. The results of these tests are provided below.

These results do not allow us to reject the null hypothesis that these

Table 3

Function	R&D/MFCT and R&D/MARKETING	R&D/MFCT/MKT	Total
Form:			
contract	7	1	8
quasi-internal	9	2	11
Total	16	3	19
chi-square = .11			

Function:	R&D/MFCT	R&D/MARKETING	Total
Form:			
contract	2	5	7
quasi-internal	5	4	9
Total	7	9	16
chi-square = 1.17			

functional categories are relatively homogeneous with respect to governance choices. The basis for aggregation appears to be sound.

VIII. CONCLUSIONS

In this paper a theory of the organization of R&D has been developed which we believe has normative implications for technology strategy. Technology strategy we argue involves not only an understanding of the commercial significance of technological development but also an understanding of how best to organize to take advantage of technological and commercial opportunities. Our data from the telecommunications equipment industry indicated that the exchange, development, or commercial exploitation of technology is a frequent motive for collaboration. However, the case of telecommunications equipment is not unique. Technological motives are a frequent motive for collaboration in industries such as biotechnology (Pisano, Shan, and Teece, 1988), semiconductors, robotics, and computers (see Mowery, 1988).

Our data analysis, while limited in many respects, suggested that the governance of collaborative arrangements is related to the function of collaboration. When collaboration is designed to couple technology and some downstream activity, there seems to be a tendency to go beyond pure contracts as a governing mechanism.

There are two major limits to our analysis which we hope that future research will address. First, our data did not allow us to examine internal vs. external choices. Secondly, data limitations prevented us from testing the normative aspects of our framework. Future empirical research should seek to link performance outcomes to governance choices (including internal organization) under a variety of conditions. These results will be of most interest to corporate managers whose responsibilities will increasingly involve choices about the appropriate organization to both exploit and acquire new technologies. Policymakers can also benefit from an understanding of how firms organize for innovation, and the properties of alternate structures.

ACKNOWLEDGMENT

We wish to thank Mel Horwitch and Mike Russo for helpful discussions on the subject matter of this paper. Research support from the NSF, grant # SRS-8410556, is gratefully appreciated.

NOTES

1. Needless to say, the corollary for the new technology-based business firm is whether it should license its technology to an established firm or attempt to commercialize it internally.
2. Horwitch (1988) refers to these as "post-modern" firms.
3. For a similar view, see Horwitch (1988, chapter 4).
4. This poses the issue in static terms. It may well happen that external sourcing strategies adopted in the past may deny the firm the ability to develop, at competitive cost, technologies relevant to today's market necessities.
5. If the source of the technology already owns the relevant assets, or has the capacity to build them, its motivation to collaborate will obviously be attenuated.
6. This section is based in part on Teece (1986, forthcoming).
7. Comments attributed to Peter Olson III, IBM's director of business development, in "The Strategy Behind IBM's Strategic Alliances," *Electronic Business*, October 1, 1985, p. 126.
8. We are deeply indebted to Enrico Ricotta for providing us with access to this data.
9. See Feinberg (1977) for a rigorous treatment of contingency table analysis.
10. For a discussion of the censored and truncated distributions and how to deal with them, see Maddala (1983), Chapter 6.

REFERENCES

Arrow, K., 1962. "Economic welfare and the allocation of resources for invention," in R. Nelson (ed.), *The Rate and Direction of Inventive Activity*. Princeton: Princeton University Press.

Feinberg, S., 1977. *The Analysis of Cross-Classified Categorical Data*. Cambridge: MIT Press.

Foster, R., 1986. "Timing Technological Transitions," in Mel Horwitch (Ed.), *Technology in the Modern Corporation*. NY: Pergamon Press.

Horwitch, M., 1988. *Post-Modern Management*. New York: Free Press.

Levin, R., A. Klevorick, R. Nelson, and S. Winter, 1984. "Survey Research on R&D, Appropriability, and Technological Opportunity." Unpublished manuscript, New Haven, CT: Yale University.

Maddala, G., 1983. *Limited-Dependent and Qualitative Variables in Econometrics*. Cambridge: Cambridge University Press.

Malerba, F., 1985. *The Semiconductor Business*. London: Frances Pinter.

McKenna, R., 1985. "Market Positioning in High Technology," *California Management Review*, 27, 3, (Spring).

Mowery, D. (ed.), 1988. *International Collaborative Ventures in U.S. Manufacturing*. Cambridge, MA: Ballinger Publishing Company.

Nelson, R., & S. Winter, 1982. *An Evolutionary Theory of Economic Change*. Cambridge, MA: Harvard University Press.

Pisano, G., 1988. *Innovation Through Markets, Hierarchies, and Joint Ventures: Technology Strategy and Collaborative Arrangements in the Biotechnology Industry*. Unpublished Ph.D. thesis, University of California, Berkeley, School of Business Administration.

Pisano, G., W. Shan, and D. Teece, 1988. "Joint Ventures and Collaboration in Biotechnology," in D. Mowery (ed.), *International Collaborative Ventures in U.S. Manufacturing*. Cambridge, MA: Ballinger Publishing Company.

Rothwell, R. & C. Freeman et al., 1974. "SAPPHO Updated-Project SAPPHO Phase II," *Research Policy* 3, pp. 258–291.

Teece, David J., 1977. "Technology Transfer by Multinational Firms: The Resource Cost of International Technology Transfer," *Economic Journal*, (June).

Teece, David J., 1981. "The Market For Knowhow and the Efficient International Transfer of Technology," *Annals of the Academy of Political and Social Science*. (November).

Teece, David J., 1986. "Profiting from Technological Innovation," *Research Policy* 15, No. 6, (December) pp. 285–305.

Teece, David J., forthcoming. "Market Entry Strategies for Innovators," *Journal of Strategic Management*.

Von Hippel, E., 1982. "Appropriability of Innovation Benefit as a Predictor of the Source of Innovation," *Research Policy*, 11:2, (April) pp. 95–115.

Williamson, Oliver E., 1975. *Markets and Hierarchies*. New York: Free Press.

Williamson, Oliver E., 1985. *The Economic Institutions of Capitalism*. New York: Free Press.

Winter, S., 1984. "Schumpeterian Competition in Alternative Technological Regimes," *Journal of Economic Behavior and Organization* 5, No.3–4, (September–December) pp. 287–320.

Firm Capabilities and Economic Development: Implications for Newly Industrializing Economies

David J. Teece

INTRODUCTION

The increase in the stock of useful knowledge and the extension of its application are the essence of modern economic growth. This much is understood. There is also recognition that the augmentation of the stock of useful knowledge as well as the extension of its application takes place primarily by business firms, admittedly pursuant to institutional structures and rules laid down by government.

Despite the centrality of the business firm to economic growth and economic development, development economics has given relatively short shrift to the firm as the agent of economic development. While firms are by no means neglected, the weight of the literature focuses on the role of macro-economic variables and the public sector in the development process. Capital availability, exchange rates, savings, and taxation issues are all well recognized and comprehensively studied, although their impact is still uncertain. The poor state of the development economics literature is possibly due to the relative neglect of the study of firms and the institutions that support firms.

In this chapter, recent work on the theory of the firm is discussed. In particular, recent work on competences and capabilities is discussed to see whether the enabling factors and the forces that assist economic development can be better illustrated. Over the last decade-and-a-half, a considerable amount of research and writing has been going on, principally at business schools, articu-

Reprinted with permission from *Technology, Learning, and Innovation: Experiences of Newly Industrializing Economies* (Cambridge University Press, 2000), edited by Linsu Kim and Richard R. Nelson, pp. 105–128.

lating a "dynamic capabilities" theory of firm performance and strategy.[1] To date, this body of writing has developed based on insights from the recent history of innovative firms in advanced industrial countries. While the institutional context is often rather different from what exists in newly industrialized countries, many of the basic processes of learning and advancement taking place inside the firm are applicable in other contexts as well. Indeed, a firm that is a new entrant into a market in the United States or other advanced industrial country experiences challenges not unlike those of the newcomer located in a newly industrialized country. While the local talent and the local knowledge base may be different, the processes of catching up and organizing for continuous innovation have important similarities. Thus, the purpose of this chapter is to describe certain concepts which some have found to be important to understanding the growth and development of firms in the developed countries, suggesting that the fundamental processes may in fact be more general, as some scholars believe to be the case (see, for instance Kim, 1993; Dodgson and Kim, 1997).

COMPETENCES AND CAPABILITIES

There are many dimensions of the business firm that must be understood if one is to develop distinctive competences/capabilities in business firms. In this chapter, I identify several classes of factors that will help determine a firm's strength. I am especially interested in developmental activities at the level of the firm. There is always a *static* aspect to firm performance, such as how to minimize cost for a given output level. But in the developmental context, *dynamic* issues are more important. The fundamental question then becomes, How does one profitably grow the business?

Such developmental activity has two major dimensions: (1) how to leverage existing assets into new and/or related business, and (2) how to learn, and how to combine and recombine assets to establish new businesses and address new markets. The challenge is to make sense of the rapidly changing context of global business and to find new ways of doing things. This typically involves

---

[1] This chapter draws in part on Teece, Pisano, and Shuen, 1997, "Dynamic Capabilities and Strategic Management," *Strategic Management Journal*, 18(7).

new business models and transformational activity inside the firm as well as with customers, suppliers, and competitors. Thus, where possible I try to distinguish between static and dynamic elements. I also endeavor to assess the particular role of business processes, market positions, and expansion paths in shaping economic development at the level of the firm.

Processes

Organizational processes have four roles: coordination/integration (a static concept); routinization; learning (a dynamic concept); and reconfiguration (also a dynamic concept). I discuss each in turn.

Coordination/Integration

While the price system supposedly coordinates the economy, managers effectuate cooperation/coordination/integration activity inside the firm (Barnard, 1938). How efficiently and effectively internal coordination or integration is achieved is very important (Aoki, 1990).[2] The same is true for external coordination.[3] Increasingly, competitive advantage requires the integration of external activities and technologies. The growing literature on strategic alliances, the virtual corporation, buyer-supplier relations, and technology collaboration evidences the importance of external integration and sourcing. External coordination is rather different from internal coordination, however, as one cannot appeal to hierarchy to effectuate action.

Routinization

Organizational performance is effectuated in large measure through standard ways of performing organizational tasks. Such

---

[2] Indeed, Ronald Coase, author of the pathbreaking 1937 article "The Nature of the Firm," which focused on the costs of organizational coordination inside that firm as compared to across the market, half a century later has identified as critical the understanding of "why the cost of organizing particular activities differs among firms" (Coase, 1988, p. 47). I argue that a firm's distinctive ability needs to be understood as a reflection of distinctive organizational or coordinative capabilities. This form of integration (i.e., inside business units) is different from the integration between business units; they could be viable on a stand-alone basis (external integration). For a useful taxonomy, see Iansiti and Clark (1994).

[3] Shuen (1994) examines the gains and hazards of the technology make-vs.-buy decision and supplier co-development.

procedures can be thought of as "routines." There is some field-based empirical research that provides support for the notion that the nature of business processes and routines inside the firm provide the source of differences in firms' competence in various domains. For example, Garvin's (1988) study of eighteen room air-conditioning plants reveals that quality performance was not related to either capital investment or the degree of automation of the facilities. Instead, quality performance was driven by special organizational routines. These include routines for gathering and processing information, for linking customer experiences with engineering design choices, and for coordinating factors and component suppliers.[4] The work of Clark and Fujimoto (1991) on project development in the automobile industry also illustrates the role played by coordinative routines. Their study reveals a significant degree of variation in how different firms coordinate the various activities required to bring a new model from concept to market. These differences in coordinative routines and capabilities seem to have a significant impact on such performance variables as development costs, development lead times, and quality.

Furthermore, Clark and Fujimoto tend to find significant firm-level differences in coordination routines, and these differences seemed to have persisted for a long time. This finding suggests that routines related to coordination are firm specific in nature. While these findings have been derived from firms in advanced countries, there is no reason to suppose that they are not applicable to firms in developing countries as well.

Also, the notion that competence/capability is embedded in distinct ways of coordinating and combining helps to explain how and why seemingly minor technological changes can have devastating impacts on incumbent firms' abilities to compete in a market. Henderson and Clark (1990), for example, have shown that incumbents in the photolithographic equipment industry were sequentially devastated by seemingly minor innovations. However, while seemingly minor, the innovations in question had major impacts on how systems had to be configured. Difficulties were experienced because systems-level or "architectural" innovations often require new routines to integrate and coordinate engineering tasks. These findings and others suggest that produc-

---

[4] Garvin (1994) provides a typology of organizational processes.

tive systems display high interdependency, and that it may not be possible to change one level without changing others. This appears to be true with respect to the "lean production" model (Womack and Roos, 1991) which has now transformed the manufacturing organization in the automobile industry.[5] Lean production requires distinctive shop floor practices and processes as well as distinctive higher-order managerial processes. Put differently, organizational processes often display high levels of coherence, and when they do, replication may be difficult because it requires systematic changes throughout the organization and also among interorganizational linkages, which might be very hard to effectuate. Thus, partial imitation or replication of a successful model may yield zero benefits.[6]

---

[5] Fujimoto (1994, pp. 18–20) describes key elements as they existed in the Japanese auto industry as follows: "The typical volume production system of effective Japanese auto makers of the 1980s (e.g., Toyota) consists of various intertwined elements that might lead to competitive advantages. Just-in-Time (JIT), Jidoka (automatic defect detection and machine stop), Total Quality Control (TQC), and continuous improvement (Kaizen) are often pointed out as its core subsystems. The elements of such a system include inventory reduction mechanisms by Kanban system; levelization of production volume and product mix (heijunka); reduction of muda (non-value adding activities), mura (uneven pace of production), and muri (excessive workload); production plans based on dealers' order volume (genyo seisan); reduction of die set-up time and lot size in stamping operation; mixed model assembly; piece-by-piece transfer of parts between machines (ikko-nagashi); flexible task assignment for volume changes and productivity improvement (shojinka); multitask job assignment along the process flow (takotei-mochi); U-shape machine layout that facilitates flexible and multiple task assignment; on-the-spot inspection by direct workers (tsukurikomi); fool-proof prevention of defects (poka-yoke); real-time feedback of production troubles (andon); assembly line stop cord; emphasis on cleanliness, order, and discipline on the shop floor (5-S); frequent revision of standard operating procedures by supervisors; quality control circles; standardized tools for quality improvement (e.g., 7 tools for QC; QC story); worker improvement in preventive maintenance (Total Productive Maintenance); low-cost automation for semi-automation with just-enough functions); reduction of process steps for saving of tools and dies, and so on. The human resource management factors that back up these elements include stable employment of core workers (with temporary workers in the periphery); long-term training of multiskilled (multitask) workers; wage system based in part on skill accumulation; internal promotion to shop floor supervisors; cooperative relationships with labor unions; inclusion of production supervisors in union members; generally egalitarian policies for corporate welfare, communication, and worker motivation. Parts procurement policies are also pointed out often as a source of the competitive advantage; relatively high ratio of parts outsourcing; multilayer hierarchy of supplier; long-term relations with suppliers; relatively small number of technologically capable suppliers at the first tier; subassembly functions of the first-tier parts makers; detail-engineering capability of the first-tier makers (design-in, back box parts); competition based on long-term capability of design and improvements rather than bidding; pressures for continuous reduction of parts price; elimination of incoming parts inspection; plan inspection and technical assistance by auto makers, and so on."

[6] For a theoretical argument along these lines, see Milgrom and Roberts (1990).

The notion that there is a certain rationality or coherence to processes and systems is not quite the same concept as corporate culture. Corporate culture refers to the values and beliefs that employees hold; culture can be a de facto governance system, as it mediates the behavior of individuals and economizes on more formal administrative methods. Rationality or coherence notions are more akin to the Nelson and Winter (1982) notion of organizational routines. However, the routines concept is a little too amorphous to properly capture the congruence among processes and between processes and incentives.

Consider a professional service organization like an accounting firm. If it is to have relatively high-powered incentives that reward individual performance, then it must build organizational processes that channel individual behavior; if it has weak or low-powered incentives, it must find symbolic ways to recognize the high performers, and it must use alternative methods to build effort and enthusiasm. What one may think of as styles of organization in fact contain necessary, not discretionary, elements to achieve performance.

Recognizing the congruences and complementarities among processes, and between processes and incentives, is critical to the understanding of organizational capabilities. In particular, they can help us explain why architectural and radical innovations are so often introduced into an industry by new entrants. The incumbents develop distinctive organizational processes that cannot support the new technology, despite certain overt similarities between the old and the new. The frequent failure of incumbents to introduce new technologies can thus be seen as a consequence of the mismatch that so often exists between the organizational processes needed to support the conventional product/service and the requirements of the new. Radical organizational reengineering will usually be required to support the new product, which may well do better embedded in a separate subsidiary where a new set of coherent organization processes can be fashioned.[7]

Learning
Learning is perhaps even more important than routinization. The two concepts are obviously linked. Learning is a process by which

---

[7] See Abernathy and Clark (1985).

repetition and experimentation enable tasks to be performed better and quicker and new production opportunities to be identified.[8] In the context of the firm, if not more generally, learning has several key characteristics. First, learning involves organizational as well as individual skills.[9] While individual skills are relevant, their value depends on their employment in particular organizational settings. Learning processes are intrinsically social and collective and occur not only through the imitation and emulation of individuals, as with teacher-student or master-apprentice, but also because of joint contributions to the understanding of complex problems.[10] Learning requires common codes of communication and coordinated search procedures. Second, the organizational knowledge generated by such activity resides in new patterns of activity, in "routines," or a new logic of organization. As indicated earlier, routines are patterns of interactions that represent successful solutions to particular problems. These patterns of interaction are resident in group behavior, though certain subroutines may be resident in individual behavior. Collaborations and partnerships can be vehicles for new organizational learning, helping firms to recognize dysfunctional routines and preventing strategic blind spots.

Reconfiguration and Transformation

In rapidly changing environments, there is obviously value in the ability to sense the need to reconfigure the firm's asset structure, and to accomplish the necessary internal and external transformation (Amit and Schoemaker, 1992; Langlois, 1994). This requires constant surveillance of markets and technologies, the willingness to adopt best practice, and the ability to see things differently and act accordingly. The capacity to see things differently, then reconfigure and transform, is itself a learned organizational skill. The more frequently practiced, the easier it is accomplished.

Change is costly and so firms must develop processes to minimize low payoff change. The ability to calibrate the requirements for change and to effectuate the necessary adjustments would appear to depend on the ability to scan the environment, to eval-

---

[8] For a useful review and contribution, see Levitt and March (1988).

[9] See Mahoney (1995).

[10] There is a large literature on learning, although only a small fraction of it deals with organizational learning. Relevant contributors include Levitt and March (1988), Levinthal and March (1981) and Nelson and Winter (1982).

uate markets and competitors, and to quickly accomplish recon-figuration and transformation ahead of competition. Firms that have honed these capabilities are sometimes referred to as high-flex firms.

Positions

The competitive posture of a firm is determined not only by its learning processes, the excellence of its operations, but also by the coherence of its internal and external processes and incentives, its asset and market positions, and the regulatory and policy envi-ronment in which it is embedded. By assets, I mean its difficult-to-trade knowledge assets and assets complementary to them, as well as its reputational and intangible assets. These help determine its market share and profitability at any time.

Technological Assets
While there is an emerging market for know-how (Teece, 1981), much technology does not enter it. This is either because the firm is unwilling to sell it[11] or because of difficulties in transacting in the market for know-how (Teece, 1980). A firm's technological assets may or may not be protected by the standard instruments of intellectual property law. Either way, the ownership, protection, and utilization of technological assets are clearly key differentia-tors among firms. The same applies to complementary assets.

Complementary Assets
Technological innovations require the use of certain related assets to produce and deliver new products and services. Prior commer-cialization activities require and enable firms to build such com-plementarities (Teece, 1986). Such capabilities and assets, while necessary for the firm's established activities, may have other uses as well. Such assets typically lie downstream. New products and processes either can enhance or destroy the value of such assets (Tushman, Newman, and Romanelli, 1986). Thus the development of computers enhanced the value of IBM's direct sales force in office products, while disk brakes rendered useless much of the auto industry's investment in drum brakes.

---

[11] Managers often evoke the "crown jewels" metaphor. That is, if the technology is released, the kingdom will be lost.

Financial Assets

In the short run, a firm's cash position and degree of leverage may have strategic implications. While there is nothing more fungible than cash, it cannot always be raised from external markets without the dissemination of considerable information to potential investors. Accordingly, what a firm can do in short order is often a function of its balance sheet. In the longer run, that ought not be so, as cash flow and the ability to raise capital will be more determinative.

Locational Assets

The legal, regulatory, and policy environment matters too. Uniqueness in certain businesses can stem from the institutional or "home base" environment. This may not be fully "tradable" or accessible to outsiders, since governments routinely favor domestic enterprise. More important, however, is whether the government makes credible commitments. Absent an environment for confident contracting, investment incentives will be inadequate.

Paths

Path Dependencies

The notion of path dependencies recognizes that "history matters." Bygones are rarely bygones, despite the predictions of rational actor theory. Thus a firm's previous investments and its repertoire of routines (its history) constrain its future behavior.[12] This follows because learning tends to be local. That is, opportunities for learning will lie in the neighborhood of what is already familiar, and thus will be transaction and production specific (Teece, 1988). This is because learning is often a process of trial, feedback, and evaluation. If too much is changing at once, the ability of firms to learn by conducting meaningful natural quasi-experiments is attenuated. Put differently, if many aspects of a firm's learning environment change simultaneously, the ability to ascertain cause-effect relationship is confounded because cognitive structures will not be formed, and rates of learning will diminish as a result.

---

[12] For further development, see Teece, Bercovitz, and de Figueiredo (1997).

The importance of path dependencies is amplified where conditions of increasing returns to adoption exist. This is a demand-side phenomenon, and it tends to make technologies and products embodying those technologies more attractive the more they are adopted. Attractiveness flows from the greater adoption of the product among users, which in turn enables them to become more developed and hence more useful. Increasing returns to adoption has many sources, including network externalities (Katz and Shapiro, 1985), the presence of complementary assets (Teece, 1986) and supporting infrastructure, learning by using, and scale economies in production and distribution. Competition between and among technologies is shaped by increasing returns. Early leads won by good luck or special circumstances can become amplified by increasing returns. This is not to suggest that first movers necessarily win. Because increasing returns have multiple sources, the prior positioning of firms can affect their capacity to exploit increasing returns. Thus, in Mitchell's (1989) study of medical diagnostic imaging, firms already controlling the relevant complementary assets could in theory start last and finish first.

In the presence of increasing returns, firms can compete passively, or they may compete strategically through technology-sponsoring activities.[13] The first type of competition is not unlike biological competition among species, although it can be sharpened by managerial activities that enhance the performance of products and processes. The reality is that companies with the best products will not always win, as chance events may cause "lock-in" on inferior technologies (Arthur, 1988) and may generate switching costs for consumers. However, while switching costs may favor the incumbent, in regimes of rapid technological change, switching costs can become quickly swamped by switching benefits. Put differently, new products employing different standards often appear suddenly in market environments experiencing rapid technological change.

[13] Because of huge uncertainties, it may be extremely difficult to determine viable strategies early on. Since the rules of the game and the identity of the players will be revealed only after the market has begun to evolve, the payoff is likely to lie with building and maintaining organizational capabilities that support flexibility. For example, Microsoft's recent about-face and vigorous pursuit of Internet business once the Netscape phenomenon became apparent is impressive, not so much because it perceived the need to change strategy, but because of its organizational capacity to effectuate a strategic shift.

Technological Opportunities

The concept of path dependencies is given forward meaning through the consideration of an industry's technological opportunities. It is well recognized that how far and how fast a particular area of industrial activity can proceed is in part due to the technological opportunities that lie before it. Such opportunities are usually a lagged function of the amount of forment and diversity in basic science, and the rapidity with which new scientific breakthroughs are being made.

However, technological opportunities may not be completely exogenous to industry. This is not only because some firms have the capacity to engage in or at least support fundamental research, but also because technological opportunities are often fed by innovative activity itself. Moreover, the recognition of such opportunities is affected by the organizational structures that link the institutions engaging in fundamental research (primarily the universities) to the business enterprise. Hence, the existence of technological opportunities can be quite firm specific.

Important for our purposes is the rate and direction in which relevant scientific frontiers are being advanced. Firms engaging in research and development (R&D) may find the path dead ahead closed off, though breakthroughs in related areas may be sufficiently close to be attractive. Likewise, if the path dead ahead is extremely attractive, there may be no incentive for firms to shift the allocation of resources away from traditional pursuits. The depth and width of technological opportunities in the neighborhood of a firm's prior research activities thus are likely to impact a firm's options with respect to both the amount and level of R&D activity that it can justify. In addition, a firm's past experience conditions the alternatives management is able to perceive. Thus, not only do firms in the same industry face "menus" with different costs associated with particular technological choices, but they also are looking at menus containing different choices.[14]

Assessment

The assessment of a firm's competitive advantage and strategic capability is presented here as a function of the firm's processes,

---

[14] This is a critical element in Nelson and Winter's (1982) view of firms and technical change.

positions, and paths.[15] What a firm can do and where it can go are thus heavily constrained by the topography of its processes, positions, and paths. I submit that if one can identify a firm's processes, positions, and paths and understand their interrelationships, one can at least predict the performance of the firm under various assumptions about changes in the external environment. One can also evaluate the richness of the menu of new opportunities from which the firm may select, and its likely performance in a changing environment.

The parameters I have identified for determining performance are quite different from those in the standard textbook theory of the firm, and in the competitive forces and strategic conflict approaches to the firm and to strategy.[16] Moreover, the agency theoretic view of the firm as a nexus of contracts would put no weight on processes, positions, and paths. While agency approaches to the firm may acknowledge that opportunism and shirking may limit what a firm can do, they do not recognize the opportunities and constraints imposed by processes, positions, and paths. Moreover, the firm is much more than the sum of its parts (or a team tied together by contracts).[17] Indeed, to some extent individuals can be moved in and out of organizations and, so long as the internal processes and structures remain in place, performance will not necessarily be impaired. A shift in the environment is a far more serious threat to the firm than is the loss of key individuals, as individuals can be replaced more readily than organizations can be transformed. Furthermore, the dynamic capabilities view of the firm would suggest that the behavior and performance of a particular firm may be quite hard to replicate, even if its coherence and rationality are observable. This matter and related issues involving replication and imitation are taken up in the section that follows.

---

[15] I also recognize that the processes, positions, and paths of customers also matter. See the earlier discussion on increasing returns, including customer learning and network externalities.

[16] In both, the firm is still largely a black box. Certainly, little or no attention is given to processes, positions, and paths.

[17] See Alchian and Demsetz (1972).

Replicability and Imitability of Organizational Processes and Positions

Thus far, I have argued that the competences and capabilities (and hence competitive advantage) of a firm rest fundamentally on processes, positions, and paths. However, competences can provide competitive advantage and generate superior profits only if they are based on a collection of routines, skills, and complementary assets that are difficult to imitate.[18] A particular set of routines can lose their value if they support a competence that no longer matters in the marketplace, or if they can be readily replicated or emulated by competitors. Imitation occurs when firms discover and simply copy another firm's organizational routines and procedures. Emulation occurs when firms discover alternative ways of achieving the same functionality. There is ample evidence that a given type of competence (e.g., quality) can be supported by different routines and combinations of skills. For example, the Garvin (1988) and Clark and Fujimoto (1991) studies both indicate that there is no one "formula" for achieving either high quality or high product development performance.

Replication
Replication involves transferring or redeploying competences from one concrete economic setting to another. Since productive knowledge is embodied, this cannot be accomplished by simply transmitting information. Only in those instances where all relevant knowledge is fully codified and understood can replication be collapsed into a simple problem of information transfer. Too often, the contextual dependence of original performance is poorly appreciated, so unless firms have replicated their systems of productive knowledge on many prior occasions, the acts of replication and transfer are often impossible absent the transfer of people, though this can be minimized if investments are made to convert tacit knowledge to codified knowledge. Often, however, this is simply not possible.

In short, organizational capabilities, and the routines upon

---

[18] I call such competences distinctive. See also Dierickx and Cook (1989) for a discussion of the characteristics of assets that made them a source of rents.

which they rest, are normally rather difficult to replicate.[19] This constrains the ability of firms to grow. Even understanding what all the relevant routines are that support a particular competence may not be transparent. Indeed, Lippman and Rumelt (1992) have argued that some sources of competitive advantage are so complex that the firm itself, let alone its competitors, does not understand them.[20] As Nelson and Winter (1982) and Teece (1982) have explained, many organizational routines are quite tacit in nature. Imitation can also be hindered by the fact that few routines are "stand-alone"; coherence may demand that a change in one set of routines in one part of the firm (e.g., production) requires changes in some other part (e.g., sales).

Some routines and competences seem to be attributable to local or regional forces that shape firms' capabilities at early stages in their lives. Porter (1990), for example, shows that differences in local product markets, local factor markets, and institutions play an important role in shaping competitive capabilities. Differences also exist within populations of firms from the same country. Various studies of the automobile industry, for example, show that not all Japanese automobile companies are top performers in terms of quality, productivity, or product development (see, for example, Clark and Fujimoto, 1991). The role of firm-specific history has been highlighted as a critical factor explaining such firm-level (as opposed to regional or national-level) differences (Nelson and Winter, 1982). Replication in a different context may thus be rather difficult.

At least two types of strategic value flow from replication. One is the ability to support geographic and product line expansion. To the extent that the capabilities in question are relevant to customer needs elsewhere, replication can confer value.[21] Another is that the ability to replicate also indicates that the firm has the foundations in place for learning and improvement. Considerable

---

[19] See Szulanski's (1993) discussion of the intrafirm transfer of best practice. He quotes a senior vice president of Xerox as saying "You can see a high performance factory or office, but it just doesn't spread. I don't know why." Szulanski also discusses the role of benchmarking in facilitating the transfer of best practice.

[20] If so, it is my belief that the firm's advantage is likely to fade, as luck does run out.

[21] Needless to say, there are many examples of firms replicating their capabilities inappropriately by applying extant routines to circumstances where they may not be applicable, such as Nestle's transfer of developed-country marketing methods for infant formula to the Third World (Hartley, 1989). A key strategic need is for firms to screen capabilities for their applicability to new environments.

empirical evidence supports the notion that the understanding of processes, both in production and in management, is the key to process improvement. In short, an organization cannot improve what it does not understand. Deep process understanding is often required to accomplish codification. Indeed, if knowledge is highly tacit, it indicates that underlying structures are not well understood, which limits learning because scientific and engineering principles cannot be as systematically applied.[22] Instead, learning is confined to proceeding through trial and error, and the leverage that might otherwise come from the application of scientific theory is denied.

Imitation

Imitation is simply replication performed by a competitor. If self-replication is difficult, imitation is likely to be even harder. In competitive markets, it is the ease of imitation that determines the sustainability of competitive advantage. Easy imitation implies the rapid dissipation of the innovator's superior profits.

Factors that make replication difficult also make imitation difficult. Thus, the more tacit the firm's productive knowledge, the harder it is to replicate by the firm itself or its competitors. When the tacit component is high, imitation may well be impossible, absent the hiring away of key individuals and the transfer of key organization processes.

However, another set of barriers impedes imitation of certain capabilities in advanced industrial countries. This is the system of intellectual property rights, such as patents, trade secrets, and trademarks, and even trade dress.[23] Intellectual property protection is of increasing importance in the United States, as the courts, since 1982, have adopted a more pro-patent posture. Similar trends are evident outside the United States. Besides the patent system, several other factors cause a difference between replication costs and imitation costs. The observability of the technology or the organization is one such important factor. Whereas vistas

---

[22] Different approaches to learning are required depending on the depth of knowledge. Where knowledge is less articulated and structured, trial and error and learning-by-doing are necessary, whereas in mature environments where the underlying engineering science is better understood, organizations can undertake more deductive approaches or what Pisano (1994) refers to as "learning-before-doing."

[23] Trade dress refers to the "look and feel" of a retail establishment – for example, the distinctive marketing and presentation style of The Nature Company.

into product technology can be obtained through strategies such as reverse engineering, this is not the case for process technology, as a firm need not expose its process technology to the outside in order to benefit from it.[24] Firms without product technology, on the other hand, confront the unfortunate circumstances that they must expose what they have in order to profit from the technology. Secrets are thus more protectable if there is no need to expose them in contexts where competitors can learn about them.

One should not, however, overestimate the importance of intellectual property protection; yet it presents a formidable imitation barrier in certain particular contexts. Intellectual property protection is not uniform across products, processes, and technologies, and is best thought of as "islands" in a sea of open competition. If one is not able to place the fruits of one's investment, ingenuity, or creativity on one or more of the islands, then one indeed is at sea.

I use the term *appropriability regimes* to describe the ease of imitation. Appropriability is a function both of the ease of replication and the efficacy of intellectual property rights as a barrier to imitation. Appropriability is strong when a technology is both inherently difficult to replicate and the intellectual property system provides legal barriers to imitate. When it is inherently easy to replicate, and intellectual property protection is either unavailable or ineffectual, then appropriability is weak. Intermediate conditions also exist.

IMPLICATIONS

When firms do not have cost advantages stemming from privileged positions in "input" or "factor" markets, they must compete through innovation. The development of proprietary and difficult-to-imitate technology thus becomes increasingly important to competitive advantage.

The knowledge assets of the firms consist of high-performance business processes/routines (organizational assets) and techno-

---

[24] An interesting but important exception to this can be found in second sourcing. In the microprocessor business, until the introduction of the 386 chip, Intel and most other merchant semiproducers were encouraged by larger customers like IBM to provide second sources – that is, to license and share their proprietary process technology with competitors like AMD and NEC. The microprocessor developers did so to assure customers that they had sufficient manufacturing capability to meet demand at all times.

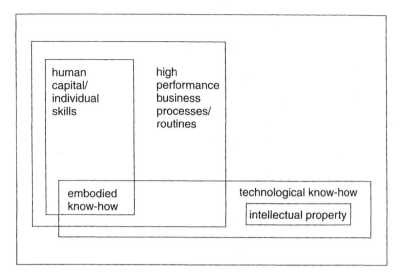

Figure 4.1. The firm's industrial knowledge assets.

logical know-how (Figure 4.1). The ability of the firm to combine and recombine, engineer and reengineer itself is critical to success. A simplified representation showing the centrality of such dynamic capabilities is contained in Figure 4.2. This shows that the firm's knowledge assets are of limited value, absent control of or access to the relevant complementary assets and complementary technologies. Hence, one must include the firm's complementary assets and its alliance structures as an integral part of the value creation capabilities of firms.[25]

The scarcity of firm-specific idiosyncratic assets and the complexity of integration and coordination processes constrains the growth of firms. Even simple replication of routines requires support from the firm's existing stocks of idiosyncratic human assets. Nor is it just managerial resources that are likely to be constraining (à la Edith Penrose); technical resources are also major constraints. Activities may be scalable in principle, but what can be accomplished in any one period is very much a function of what was in place in the prior period. The supporting infrastructure in the economy at large also matters, because this is likely to affect

[25] This is not to imply that all alliances add value, or that all assets inside the firm add value. For further discussion, see Chesbrough and Teece (1996).

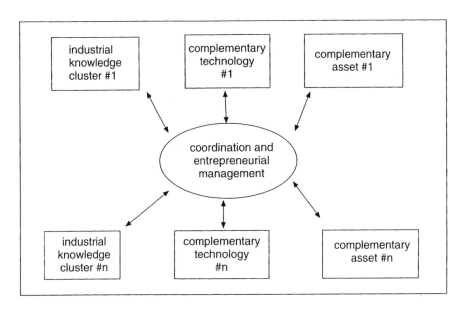

Figure 4.2. The business firm: Elements of dynamic capabilities.

the supply of appropriately educated and trained indigenous managerial and technological human resources. Indeed, the growth of firms is closely coupled to the availability in factor markets of trained personnel, indigenous or foreign.

The organization of this framework around processes, positions, and paths is hopefully instructive in some ways. The framework stresses the role of organization and management (processes) while suggesting that positioning can be undone (i.e., with original equipment manufacture, or OEM, contracts), and paths need not always disadvantage the latecomer inordinately. In laying out this framework, much has undoubtedly been overlooked. In particular, the framework is silent with respect to institutional context. However, if both product and intermediate markets are open, certain aspects of the institutional environment become a common factor and can lead to at least some similarity in firm growth and development in different country contexts. This possibility is employed in this chapter. Firm-level work on competency and capabilities in developed countries is put forward to assist the understanding of economic development in newly industrializing economies (NIEs).

RELEVANCE TO NIES

The experience of firms in NIEs, and the development process more generally, can be brought into sharper focus through the employment of the concepts outlined above. While the *positions* of firms in NIEs may not initially be advantageous, firms in NIEs can catch up by being better at *processes*, and by astutely selecting and following desirable *paths*. There are at least two structural features of advanced economies, particularly that of the United States, which facilitate catch-up by NIEs.

One is the presence of relatively open intermediate product markets. Thus firms in NIEs, although they may lack certain complementary assets needed for full scale success (i.e., distribution), can access these complementary assets through contractual relationships. In particular, the "OEM system" described by Michael Hobday (1997) and in Chapter 5 of this volume is simply a manifestation of how certain firms in NIEs have accessed complementary assets abroad and thereby shared to some degree in the benefits of innovation originating elsewhere.

The second feature is the relative openness of the international market for know-how. Firms in developed countries are willing to sell/license their know-how, often for modest fees relative to the original development costs. Coupled with (and encouraged by) the relative ease of imitation of product technology (facilitated by reverse engineering), the result is that technology developed elsewhere can in fact be readily accessed, if firms make the commitment to acquire it and establish the managerial processes to facilitate the absorption and integration of technical and industrial knowledge inside the firms.

Put differently, the disadvantages associated with poor market and asset positions can be readily overcome if there is the organizational commitment to do so, and the allocation of resources is made (relatively modest) to license-in technology. This leaves processes and paths as the differentiator. With respect to processes, many firms in advanced countries have demonstrated little in the way of special acumen in this area, enabling firms in NIEs to quickly draw even and possibly overtake them. With respect to paths, firms have some choice, but industry dynamics are likely to influence outcomes powerfully. The ability of firms in NIEs to cooperate on standards and strategies might well enable them to overcome the disadvantages of being the latecomer. In some instances, the latecomer may in fact have an advantage if new, more attractive evolutionary paths have been revealed.

Finally, the ability of firms to quickly configure and reconfigure is important to success in industries experiencing rapid change. The newcomer is less likely to be shackled by incumbency factors, such as the reluctance to cannibalize one's own products with new products. Innovation studies in developed countries reveal that the newcomers overturn the existing order with greater frequency than do other incumbents (Utterback, 1994). Looked at from the perspective of NIEs, firms located there will simply not be the incumbents in the global market. Rather, they are the challengers, bereft of the decision-making biases likely to burden firms with established market positions. Put differently, firms in NIEs have some of the same benefits as new entrants in developed countries, although their subsequent success might well lead to the same complacency.

CONCLUSION

In this chapter I have looked at basic properties of the firm with an eye toward the implications for economic development. I suggest that firms are the "engines" of economic development. Successful knowledge accumulation and the orchestration of complementary assets and technologies within a legal-political-financial and social system, enabling credible commitments and wealth accumulation, are at the heart of the process of economic development. To understand economic development, one must therefore understand the developmental processes inside firms. If firms are indeed the instruments of development, the study of economic development cannot take place separate from the study of the theory of the growth of the firm.

REFERENCES

Abernathy, W. J., and K. Clark. 1985. "Innovation: Mapping the Winds of Creative Destruction." *Research Policy*, 14, 3–22.

Alchian, A. A., and H. Demsetz. 1972. "Production, Information Costs, and Economic Organization." *American Economic Review*, 62, 777–795.

Amit, R., and P. Schoemaker. 1990. "Key Success Factors: Their Foundation and Application." University of British Columbia and University of Chicago. Working paper.

Aoki, M. 1990. "The Participatory Generation of Information Rents and the Theory of the Firm." In M. Aoki et al. (eds.), *The Firm as a Nexus of Treaties*. London: Sage.

Arthur, W. B. 1998. "Competing Technologies: An Overview." In G. Dosi et al. (eds.), *Technical Change and Economic Theory*. London: Pinter, 115–135.

Barnard, C. 1938. *The Functions of the Executive*. Cambridge, MA: Harvard University Press.

Barney, J. B., J. C. Spender, and T. Reve. 1994. *Crafoord Lectures*, Vol. 6. Bromley, U.K.: Chartwell-Bratt, and Lund, Sweden: Lund University Press.

Chesbrough, H. W., and D. J. Teece. 1996. "When Is Virtual Virtuous? Organizing for Innovation." *Harvard Business Review*, January–February, 65–73. Republished in J. S. Brown (ed.), *Seeing Things Differently: Insights on Innovation*, Cambridge, MA: Harvard Business School Press, 1997, 105–119.

Clark, K., and T. Fujimoto. 1991. *Product Development Per-formance: Strategy, Organization and Management in the World Auto Industries*. Cambridge, MA: Harvard Business School Press.

Coase, R. 1937. "The Nature of the Firm." *Economica*, 4, 386–405.

Coase, R. 1988. "Lecture on the Nature of the Firm, III." *Journal of Law, Economics and Organization*, 4, 33–47.

Dierickx, I., and K. Cook. 1989. "Asset Stock Accumulation and Sustainability of Competitive Advantage." *Management Science*, 35(12), 1504–1511.

Dodgson, M., and Y. S. Kim. 1997. "Learning to Innovate Korean Style: The Case of Samsung International." *Journal of Innovation Management*, 1(1), 53–71.

Domar, E. 1947. "Expansion and Employment." *American Economic Review*, March.

Freeman, J., and W. Boeker. 1984. "The Ecological Analysis of Business Strategy." In G. Carroll, and D. Vogel (eds.), *Strategy and Organization*. Boston, MA: Pitman, 64–77.

Fujimoto, T. 1994. "Reinterpreting the Resource-Capability View of the Firm: A Case of the Development-Production Systems of the Japanese Automakers." Faculty of Economics, University of Tokyo, draft working paper.

Garvin, D. 1988. *Managing Quality*. New York: Free Press.

Garvin, D. 1994. "The Processes of Organization and Management." Harvard Business School Working Paper #94–084.

Ghemawat; P. 1966. *Commitment: The Dynamics of Strategy*. New York: Free Press.

Harrod, R. F. 1939. "An Essay in Dynamic Theory." *Economic Journal*, March.

Hartley, R. F. 1989. *Marketing Mistakes*. New York: Wiley.

Hayes, R., and K. Clark. 1985. "Exploring the Sources of Productivity Differences at the Factory Level." In K. Clark, R. H. Hayes, and C. Lorenz (eds.), *The Uneasy Alliance: Managing the Productivity Technology Dilemma*. Boston, MA: Harvard Business School Press, 151–188.

Henderson, R. M., and K. B. Clark. 1990. "Architectural Innovation: The Reconfiguration of Existing Product Technologies and the Failure of Established Firms," *Administrative Science Quarterly*, 35, March, 9–30.

Henderson, R. M., and I. Cockburn. (eds.), "Measuring Core Competences." Massachusetts Institute of Technology working paper.

Hobday, M. 1997. *Innovation in East Asia: The Challenge to Japan*. United Kingdom: Edward Elgar.

Isansiti, M., and K. B. Clark. 1994. "Integration and Dynamic Capability: Evidence from Product Development in Automobiles and Mainframe Computers." *Industrial and Corporate Change*, 3(3), 557–605.

Kim, L. 1993. "National System of Industrial Innovation: Dynamics of Capability Building in Korea." In R. R. Nelson (ed.), *National Innovation Systems: A Comparative Analysis*. New York: Oxford University Press, Chap. 11.

Kuznets, S. 1966. *Modern Economic Growth: Rate, Structure and Spread*. New Haven, CT: Yale University Press.

Langlois, R. 1994. "Cognition and Capabilities: Opportunities Seized and Missed in the History of the Computer Industry." University of Connecticut, working paper presented at the conference on Technological Oversights and Foresights, Stern School of Business, New York University, March 11–12, 1994.

Levitt, B., and J. March. 1988. "Organizational Learning." *Annual Review of Sociology*, 14, 319–340.

Lewis, W. A. 1954. "Economic Development with Unlimited Supplies of Labor." The Manchester School, May.

Lippman, S. A., and R. P. Rumelt. 1992. "Demand Uncertainty and Investment in Industry-Specific Capital." *Industry and Corporate Change*, 1(1), 235–262.

Mahoney, J. 1995. "The Management of Resources and the Resources of Management." *Journal of Business Research*, 33(2), 91–101.

Meier, G. 1990. *International Economics*. New York: Oxford University Press.

Milgrom, P., and J. Roberts. 1990. "The Economics of Modern Manufacturing: Technology, Strategy, and Organization." *American Economic Review*, 80(3), 511–528.

Mitchell, W. 1989. "Whether and When? Probability and Timing of Incumbents' Entry into Emerging Industrial Subfields." *Administrative Science Quarterly*, 34, 208–230.

Nelson, R., and S. Winter. 1982. *An Evolutionary Theory of Economic Change*. Cambridge, MA: Harvard University Press.

North and Douglas. 1990. *Institutions, Institutional Change and Economic Performance*. New York: Cambridge University Press.

Pisano, G. 1994. "Knowledge Integration and the Locus for Learning: An Empirical Analysis of Process Development." *Strategic Management Journal*, 15, Winter Special Issue, 85–100.

Porter, M. E. 1990. *The Competitive Advantage of Nations*. New York: Free Press.

Rostow, W. W. 1956. "The Take-off into Self Sustained Growth." *Economic Journal*, March, 29–30.

Rostow, W. W. 1959. "The Stages of Economic Growth." *Economic History Review*, August, 1–17.

Shuen, A. 1994. "Technology Sourcing and Learning Strategies in the Semiconductor Industry" Unpublished Ph.D. dissertation, University of California, Berkeley.

Szulanski, G. 1993. "Intrafirm Transfer of Best Practice, Appropriate Capabilities, Organizational Barriers to Appropriation." Working paper, INSEAD.

Teece, D. J. 1980. "Economics of Scope and the Scope of an Enterprise." *Journal of Economic Behavior and Organization*, 1, 223–247.

Teece, D. J. 1981. "The Market for Know-How and the Efficient International Transfer of Technology." *The Annals of the Academy of Political and Social Science*, November 1981, 81–96.

Teece, D. J. 1982. "Towards an Economic Theory of the Multiproduct Firm." *Journal of Economic Behavior and Organization*, 3, 39–62.

Teece, D. J. 1986. "Profiting from Technological Innovation." *Research Policy*, 15(6), December, 285–305.

Teece, D. J. 1988. "Technological Change and the Nature of the Firm." In G. Dosi, et al. (eds.), *Technical Change and Economic Theory*. London: Pinter, 256–330.

Teece, D. J. 1993. "The Dynamics of Industrial Capitalism: Perspectives on Alfred Chandler's Scale and Scope (1990)." *Journal of Economic Literature*, 31, March, 199–225.

Teece, D. J., J. E. Bercovitz, and J. M. de Figueiredo. 1997. "Firm Capabilities and Managerial Decision-Making: A Theory of Innovation Biases." In R. Garud, P. Nayyar, and Z. Shapira (eds.), *Technological Innovation: Oversights and Foresights*. Cambridge: Cambridge University Press, 233–259.

Teece, D. J., G. Pisano, and A. Shuen. 1997. "Dynamic Capabilities and Strategic Management." *Strategic Management Journal*, 18(7), 509–533.

Tushman, M. L., W. H. Newman, and E. Romanelli. 1986. "Convergence and Upheaval: Managing the Unsteady Pace of Organizational Evolution." *California Management Review*, 29(1), Fall, 29–44.

Utterback, J. 1994. *Mastering the Dynamics of Innovation*. Boston, MA: Harvard Business School Press.

Williamson, O. E. 1996. *The Mechanisms of Governance*. New York: Oxford University Press.

Womack, J., D. Jones, and D. Roos. 1991. *The Machine that Changed the World*. New York: Harper-Perennial.

Reprinted from *Handbook of Organizational Learning and Knowledge* (pp. 89–117),
edited by Dierkes, M. *et al.*, 2001. By permission of Oxford University Press.

A Review and Assessment of Organizational Learning in Economic Theories

Christopher S. Boerner, Jeffrey T. Macher, and David J. Teece

One principal goal of economics is to help understand innovation and change. It is therefore surprising to many observers that mainstream economics has largely failed to develop a coherent approach to one of the primary means by which individuals innovate and change: learning. For the purposes of this chapter, learning is defined as the acquisition and use of existing knowledge and/or the creation of new knowledge with the purpose of improving economic performance. Strictly speaking, only individuals possess the ability to create knowledge. However, organizations provide a context within which individual learning takes place (Marshall 1965).

In particular, organizations have the capacity to support and channel individual knowledge creation in specific directions. Thus, organizational learning can be thought of as the capability of a firm to facilitate knowledge creation or acquisition, disseminate it throughout the organization, and embody it in products, services, and systems (Nonaka and Takeuchi 1995). So defined, organizational learning is a central concern of economics. Such learning enables firms to modify and develop new technologies, structures, and operating practices in the face of changing economic and business conditions. It enables the creation of intangible assets that are the basis of enduring competitive advantage (Burgelman 1990; Senge 1990; Teece 1998).

Despite the centrality of learning in fundamental economic issues, its treatment in the orthodox economics literature is sparse, and frequently a caricature. In spite of a substantial and growing body of economics literature that characterizes various aspects of learning, mainstream economics continues to ignore learning, not because it is unimportant but because embracing it tends to undermine perceived wisdom. It is admittedly difficult to define and differentiate a mainstream economics approach to learning. Indeed, organizational learning is given scant attention in standard graduate economics textbooks. With the exception of a brief discussion of learning curve models, neither the *New Palgrave Dictionary of Economics* (Eatwell, Milgate, and Newman 1987) nor the *Fortune Encyclopedia of Economics* (Henderson 1993) dealt with an economic perspective of learning. Indeed, the *International Encyclopedia of Business and Management* (Warner 1996) failed even to mention the subject (Albach and Jin 1998). Progress is nevertheless being made, for scholars in two subfields of economics have endeavored to grapple head-on with learning: the economics of innovation, and the theory of the firm.

In some sense, this slighting of organizational learning in economics is not surprising. As other chapters in this volume illustrate, inadequate theoretical appreciation of organizational learning is not unique to economics. The management science, history, and anthropology chapters, for example, highlight the difficulty that scholars in other disciplines have had in developing a coherent theoretical framework.

The neglect of learning in economics stems in part from the fact that economics is built upon a set of highly stylized assumptions about the behavior and decision-making processes of economic agents. In the environment based on these assumptions, agents are perfectly rational and able to respond optimally and instantaneously to changing conditions. The stylized nature of such an environment is summarized by Nelson and Winter (1982): 'Never is such a theoretical actor confused about a situation or distracted by petty concerns; never is he trapped in a systematically erroneous view of the problem; never is a plain old mistake made' (p. 8). Information asymmetries may exist in such models, but they come and go according to the model-builder's whim. Learning is generally not recognized; if it is, it is simply turned on and off in the model, with no attention being given to the mechanism itself. Within such theoretical confines, economists have been handicapped in developing useful models of organizational learning. The effort to develop an economic approach to organizational learning in the orthodox literature, therefore, has had to focus on moving away from this highly stylized setting.

In the next section of this chapter we explore a number of approaches that economists have employed to modify traditional assumptions and study issues related to learning. Although by no means exhaustive, the seven approaches examined are among the most prominent models of learning found in the orthodox literature. These approaches have also heavily influenced much of the subsequent work on learning found in other fields within economics. In the third and forth sections of the chapter we explore the treatment of organizational learning in two relatively influential fields in economics: the economics of innovation and the theory of the firm. These two streams of literature provide important new insights into individual learning processes and how individual learning is transformed into organizational learning. They also extend orthodoxy by examining not only how firms acquire and utilize existing knowledge but also how they create new knowledge. This extension is essential in progressing toward a more comprehensive and more dynamic framework for

understanding organizational learning than exists today.

Orthodox Models of Learning

In the overview of his graduate economics textbook, Kreps (1990) stated that microeconomic theory concerned 'the behavior of individual economic actors and the aggregation of their actions in different institutional frameworks' (p. 3). In this one sentence Kreps introduced four important economic concepts: actors, their behavior, the institutional framework, and equilibrium analysis. In most traditional microeconomic models there are two types of actors: consumers and firms. The behavior of these actors is portrayed as the selection from a specified set of options that maximizes some objective function. Consumers, for example, are typically assumed to maximize utility to the extent that budget constraints allow. Firms, on the other hand, maximize profits given production constraints. The maximizing choices that firms and consumers make are dependent upon the opportunities available in a given institutional setting. The institutional framework in economics describes the options that each actor faces and the outcomes that ensue from each action, given the behavior of all the other players. In most orthodox models, the institutional setting is an impersonal marketplace governed by prices. Finally, the actions that firms and consumers select, and the results that ensue, are predicted using various forms of equilibrium analysis. Generally speaking, equilibrium is a feedback system that aggregates individual actions into an overall outcome that, in turn, determines the constraints that individuals face and the outcomes they receive (Kreps 1990). Equilibrium in most economic models is a situation in which each individual agent is assumed to be doing as well as possible, given the actions taken by others and the institutional environment.

As the above description suggests, the assumptions that are typically associated with the core concepts in microeconomics depict a highly simplified world in which learning is generally absent. Economic actors have stable, well-defined preferences, rationally maximize utility, profits, or some other entity against those preferences, and operate in a completely transparent market in which prices reveal all relevant information. Behavioral adjustments are instantaneous, and changes in market conditions are known by all. Although these simplifying assumptions help derive important insights, they do not allow for meaningful analysis of learning. Indeed, economic agents in traditional neoclassical models have neither a need nor an incentive to learn.

In an effort to incorporate learning into traditional neoclassical models, economists since the early 1950s have attempted to modify the stylized setting depicted above. Much of the research on learning found in the mainstream literature can be seen as an effort to relax traditional assumptions about the behavior of economic actors, the institutional setting in which these actors operate, or the equilibrium conditions that are used to model outcomes. Though not exhaustive, Table 4.1 illustrates the primary modifications to basic assumptions that have been made so that learning dynamics can be recognized. These changes are now discussed in some detail.

Behavioral Modifications

Bounded Rationality

In traditional economic models it is assumed that decision-makers are rational. An agent is economically rational if decisions are based on (a) a known set of conceivable alternatives with corresponding outcomes, (b) an established rule or set of relations that produces a preference ordering of the alternatives, and (c) a maximization criterion (Alexis and Wilson 1967). Simon (1955) was one of the first economists to stress that the real world is such that these assumptions are not abstractions but gross distortions. Specifically, Simon formalized the idea that human cognitive limitations significantly affect the ability of economic agents to optimize. Rather than the hyperrationality as-

cribed to agents in traditional models, Simon (1957b) suggested the concept of bounded rationality, noting that 'the capacity of the human mind for formulating and solving complex problems is very small compared with the size of the problems whose solution is required for objectively rational behavior in the real world' (p. 198). Simon suggested that the 'key to the simplification of the choice process . . . is the replacement of the goal of *maximizing* with the goal of *satisficing*, of finding a course of action that is good enough. . . . [T]his substitution is an essential step in the application of the principle of bounded rationality' (Simon 1957b: 204–5).

Thus, for Simon, the complexity of real-life decision-making problems means that firms are simply unable to maximize over the entire set of conceivable options. Rather, firms employ simple decision-making rules and procedures to guide their actions. Due to the cognitive limits of individuals within firms, the decision-making rules that firms employ cannot be characterized as optimal in the sense that they reflect the results of global calculations (Nelson and Winter 1982). Rather, firms pick outcomes that are satisfactory, given certain targets and objectives. Simon (1955) suggested that this approach is analogous to the behavior of individuals selling a house. When selling a house, individuals typically have some reservation price and are willing to accept any offer that meets this price. (Unlike the concept of reservation prices in standard economic models, which are set where the expected gains from searching equal the costs, Simon's concept simply reflects a price with which people are satisfied.) This idea is similar to Alchian's (1950) assertion that firms are more likely to search for positive profits than for some universal optimum.

Simon's model of rationality has a number of useful properties with respect to organizational learning. First, the computational skills ascribed to managers are far less stringent than those ascribed to them in traditional models. Rather than computing the global optimum, managers must simply be able to compare outcomes to some predefined goal. Second,

Table 4.1. Modifications made in orthodoxy in order to accommodate learning

	Behavioral assumptions	Institutional environment	Equilibrium concept
Orthodoxy	• Hyperrationality • Certainty	• Frictionless adjustment	• Instantaneous adjustment
Modifications to orthodoxy	• Bounded rationality • Uncertainty	• Social learning • Path dependency	• Game-theoretic approaches • Bayesian updating • Learning-by-doing and learning curve models

economic agents need not be able to create a complete preference ordering of all conceivable alternatives. Instead, it is sufficient for managers to create partial orderings of relevant alternatives. Finally, because agents are assumed to be 'intendedly rational, but limitedly so' (Simon 1957a: xxiv; Simon's emphasis), they are free to update their preferences as additional information is revealed. Similarly, managers may acquire a better understanding of relationships between actions and outcomes the more exposure they have to a given set of decision-making problems.

These properties explicitly open the door for learning to enter economic analysis. Because agents are no longer assumed to have full cognizance of all the possible actions they may take and of the associated consequences, it is conceivable that learning takes place through trial and error or through the discovery of new or additional information. Models incorporating bounded rationality, many of which have implications for organizational learning, have been employed extensively in orthodox economics since Simon's early work (Conlisk 1996; Ellison and Fudenberg 1993; Heiner 1983; Winter 1971; for additional discussion of learning models based on bounded rationality, see Kreps 1990 and Conlisk 1996). Conlisk (1996), for example, applied bounded rationality to innovation. He noted that models employing complete rationality predict that many technological innovations should have occurred far earlier than they actually did. Bounded ration-

ality, according to Conlisk, is a major determinant of technological change. In Ellison and Fudenberg's (1993) model of learning by boundedly rational agents, decision-making is improved when agents incorporate into their decision-making processes the popularity of different actions. The authors modeled two learning situations, one in which the same technology is optimal for all players and one in which the optimal technologies differ. In both cases, players used rules of thumb that ignore historical information but may incorporate the popularity of the technology. Ellison and Fudenberg (1993) found that in some cases these simple heuristics can lead to efficient decisions in the long run.

Although learning models based on bounded rationality have been frequently employed in economics, two factors have hindered the development of a cumulative research tradition. First, bounded rationality models are far more complex mathematically than are models employing complete rationality (Alexis 1999). Second, although the concept of satisficing is appealing and has been employed extensively in other disciplines (e.g. psychology), it is one to which economists have had difficulty relating (Williamson 1996). Indeed, until recently the field of economics had few models in which satisficing is explicitly applied (Aumann 1985). These critiques notwithstanding, the concept of bounded rationality has been useful in exploring how economic agents learn in the face of cognitive limitations.

Uncertainty

A related way in which mainstream economists have modified traditional neoclassical assumptions in order to model organizational learning has been to explicitly include uncertainty. In economic theory it is frequently assumed that firms possess all the relevant information necessary to maximize profits. Alchian (1950), however, noted that firms operate in an uncertain world and typically lack the data and, in many cases, the skills to perform maximizing calculations. Whereas traditional models portray success as a function of firms' abilities to predict in these situations, Alchian argued that two types of learning may be operative. First, firms may engage in imitation. In particular, firms may choose, for lack of information or computational skills, to imitate other firms that appear to be doing well. Interestingly, this imitation may actually lead to unintended innovation. In attempting to copy the configuration or behavior of other successful players, firms may make mistakes and, as a result, end up with configurations that are even more successful (for an additional discussion of imitation learning, see Czarniawska, Ch. 5 in this volume). Second, Alchian suggested that trial-and-error learning may also be an important determinant of a firm's success in the face of uncertainty. He qualified this statement, however, noting that in order for trial-and-error learning to be effective it must be possible for economic agents to make inferences about the results of past trials. Alchian suggested that this possibly may not exist if the environment is changing rapidly. This discussion of imitation and trial and error suggests that learning may be partially influenced by chance. That is, economic actors may appear to be learning when in fact they are discovering decision-making rules that happen to be useful in a given situation.

Consumer learning in the context of uncertainty is also a central theme in Akerlof's (1970) examination of the market for 'lemons'. In this paper, Akerlof modeled how uncertainty about product quality can lead to market inefficiencies and, in the extreme case, to the elimination of markets altogether. Although the context for his paper was the market for used cars, he actually addressed the general problem of adverse selection. Adverse selection occurs when one party to a transaction has an informational advantage over another party. This lack of information leads to a condition in which only agents with unfavorable characteristics are willing to transact. In the case of used cars, adverse selection results in only the lowest quality cars (i.e. what Americans call 'lemons') being placed on the market.

The important point from the perspective of organizational learning is that, in the face of adverse selection, some type of learning or adaptation mechanism must be introduced if markets are to function properly. Four possible mechanisms for learning in this context are signaling, repeated interaction, advertising, and product branding. Each of these approaches allows the parties to a transaction to learn about the relevant quality characteristics of the products being exchanged.

Lastly, Stigler (1961) developed a model of uncertainty in which learning is a prominent feature of market transactions. In all markets, prices change. In response, buyers engage in a costly search for sellers offering the best deals. Likewise, sellers engage in a search for buyers. Searching in this context is costly for a number reasons. First, buyers may incur the costs of physically searching multiple stores for the best prices. Second, buyers may find it costly to determine what constitutes the best deal in a given context. Finally, buyers and sellers may incur costs associated with communicating with one another. Because of these costs, economic agents do not search indefinitely but rather until the additional cost of searching just equals the additional expected benefit associated with the search.

These models of uncertainty have two important implications for learning. First, they reinforce the previously made point that, in the face of cognitive limitations and uncertainty, economic agents may economize on learning by using simple heuristics and imitation. Rather than striving for complete information, economic agents select an optimal amount of learning such that costs and benefits are equated. Second, given cognitive limitations and positive search costs, various mechanisms arise to assist agents in learning relevant information. In the case of buyers searching for sellers offering the best deals, for instance, Stigler (1961) observed that advertising and specialized traders assist in reducing search costs.

Institutional Modifications

Social Learning

In the preceding discussion we noted that economic agents frequently use simple heuristics when faced with complex decision-making problems in order to compensate for cognitive limitations. One implication of this research is that agents acquire cues about appropriate behavior in a given instance by observing their institutional environment. A number of economists have therefore explored organizational learning by modifying the institutional framework within which economic agents operate so as to allow for learning. Recall that the institutional framework in economics describes the options faced by actors as well as the outcomes that ensue from each action, given the behavior of other players. In most real-world settings the behavior of other players has a direct impact on how a given economic agent perceives the environment in which he or she operates. Put simply, agents learn from one another. For instance, economic actors frequently accept certain ideas or approaches to solving problems simply because others do. Ellison and Fudenberg (1993) defined this form of learning as 'social learning'. Everyday examples of social learning abound: Individuals often decide where to shop, which restaurants to frequent, and even where to send their children to school according to the behavior and actions of others.

The concept of social learning has been studied extensively in economics, and recent explicit treatments include Bala and Goyal (1998), Banerjee (1992), Blonski (1999), Neeman and Orosel (1999), and Scharfstein and Stein (1990). Social learning is also an implicit feature in many other economic models. Keynes (1936), for example, though not referring to social learning directly, suggested that similar processes are operative in the behavior of investors in asset markets. Indeed, to the extent that social learning underpins the use of learning heuristics such as imitation, it is implicit in many of the models examined in this chapter and elsewhere in economics.

In an economic model of social learning developed by Banerjee (1992), economic agents rationally respond to the decisions of others because these decisions may reflect privately held information. One result of this model is herd behavior—everyone does what everyone else is doing even when their own private information suggests that they should do something different. As an example, consider the decision of a firm to enter a given market. In addition to the private information that each firm has about the long-term profitability of this market, the decision of other firms to enter may provide a signal of the market's value. If other firms enter that market, a potential entrant may become convinced that the market is in fact highly profitable. After a sufficient number of firms have entered the market, all potential entrants do the same regardless of their own private information (Albach and Jin 1998). Bikhchandani, Hirschleifer, and Welch (1998) referred to this learning process as an 'informational cascade' (p. 154), where it is optimal for an observer of preceding individuals to follow their behavior without regard to his or her own information. In the context of organizational learning, informational cascades may have dangerous consequences for firms. If a few investors have received wrong signals, all investors may end up worse off.

A major contribution of this literature has been the explicit recognition that the institutional environment in which economic actors operate not only provides a context for learning but also may facilitate learning. By observing the behavior of others, economic agents gain insight about the outcomes associated with certain actions and, thus, learn what action is best in a given situation. Although this interaction may or may not produce efficient outcomes, it is certainly important in understanding economic learning activities.

Path Dependency

The phenomenon of social learning suggests that the behavior of a given economic agent may depend upon learning that takes place among all agents. In a similar way, economists have recognized that learning processes may also depend upon the past behavior of economic agents (Arthur 1989, 1990; David 1986, 1990). That is, knowledge acquisition and creation may be path dependent. Arthur (1989), for example, developed a simple model that illustrates the evolutionary and path-dependent nature of technological improvement. The model consists of a large number of agents who have been divided equally into two groups, Type R and Type S. Each agent chooses between two types of technology, A and B. Type R agents are assumed to prefer technology A; Type S agents, technology B. The payoff to each agent from picking a given technology is equal to a payoff that is specific to that agent plus a returns parameter multiplied by the number of people using a given technology. This setup allowed Arthur to explore how the returns to technology (i.e. the change in the benefits of a technology given a change in its amount of use) influence the type of technology that is adopted. Three scenarios are considered in the model: increasing, constant, and decreasing returns. Arthur found that one can accurately predict the proportion of agents using each technology in the constant and decreasing returns cases but that there is no predictability in the case of increasing returns. Because there are increasing returns, the benefits from increased use of a given technology will eventually outweigh any individual preferences for other technologies. Thus, with increasing returns, it is likely that all agents will eventually prefer a single technology. Because timing is important, the technology that is ultimately chosen in the model is strongly influenced by the type of agent that moves first.

Arthur's model suggests that the development of technology may be subject to self-reinforcing cycles that, once initiated, may channel future development into a particular path. In this framework, even small, random events may have substantial downstream effects. Interestingly, the path of development that is followed need not be socially optimal *ex post*. David's (1990) account of the QWERTY typewriter keyboard provides a classic illustration of this phenomenon. In spite of what is presumed to be a superior *ex post* alternative, the QWERTY keyboard design became 'locked in'.[1] Other examples of technological lock-in are provided in Arthur (1990) and David (1990). The fundamental insight of this research is that initial conditions and chance events can dictate how economic agents acquire new knowledge. Put another way, 'history matters' in organizational learning (for a more extensive discussion of the impact of history on organizational learning and change, see Fear, Ch. 7 in this volume).

Equilibrium Modifications

Game Theory

A third approach used in economics to examine organizational learning is to change the equilibrium concept that is used to model outcomes in traditional models. An equilibrium concept can be thought of as a feedback system that aggregates individual actions into an overall outcome (Kreps 1990). Traditionally, this feedback system is assumed to be instantaneous, with players performing as well as they possibly can, given the behavior of others. The growing literature in economic game theory modifies this feedback concept to explicitly examine the ways in which players interact and learn about the benefits of certain actions from past performance and to gain an understanding of their opponents' strategies. Game theory has become one of the most popular means by which economists approach individual and organizational learning.

[1] Oliver Williamson (1996) provided an interesting critique of this literature, suggesting that many of the 'inefficiencies' highlighted in discussions of path dependency are irremediable. That is, no feasible alternative can be articulated and implemented.

An underlying theme in most of the game-theoretic literature is that history and the structure of the game enable players to learn about their environment and about the beliefs and strategies of their opponents, affording the players increased payoffs due to superior knowledge of the game (Alexis 1999). Although the game-theoretic literature on learning is extensive, two general approaches can be distinguished (Knight 1996; Milgrom and Roberts 1991). The first set of game-theoretic models deals with games that are played repeatedly and emphasizes specific rules according to which players form expectations about their opponents' current moves as a function of previous plays. The basic assumption is that a player's actions in period $t + 1$ can be perfectly predicted by actions in period t. This approach, frequently referred to as best-reply dynamics, has been used extensively in economics to study learning (Bernheim 1984; Moulin 1986) and is the basis for Cournot's (1960) analysis of duopoly. A variant of this approach, known as 'fictitious-play' logic, bases expectations of current play on the entire set of past plays of the game (Brown 1951; Milgrom and Roberts 1991). Players pick their strategies so as to maximize their returns, given the prediction that the probability distribution of opponents' play in round t will be the same as the empirical frequency distribution in the $t-1$ previous rounds. (Fictitious-play games are a game-theoretic variant of Bayesian learning, which is examined in the next section.)

A second set of learning models in game theory examines information about the payoffs in a game rather than about the past behavior of players. In models employing this approach (Aumann 1987; Bernheim 1984), actors use their knowledge of existing payoffs and their understanding of the rationality and information possessed by others to derive expectations about the behavior of their opponents (Knight 1996).

These two approaches to learning in game theory provide insights into how economic agents learn from the past or through an understanding of the structure of their environment and the behavior of others. Although they have

been used extensively in the literature, they are of limited utility. In many cases, for example, 'past-play' approaches place too much emphasis on recent events, ignoring important information from previous periods. Fictitious-play models, on the other hand, may overemphasize the distant past by weighting the first play equally with the last play, thereby ignoring the possibility that learning takes place in the interim (Milgrom and Roberts 1991). Finally, approaches that stress payoffs may ignore potentially useful information that one can gain by analyzing the relationship between payoffs and the types of players who seek those payoffs (Knight 1996). In an effort to overcome these limitations, Milgrom and Roberts (1991) developed a 'sophisticated' learning model that combines the knowledge that players have about the past with whatever information they have about their competitors' rationality, alternatives, and payoffs. Although relatively recent in its development, this approach reflects recognition that economic agents employ a variety of learning strategies and, as a result, may yield new insights into how individuals and organizations learn in different environments.

Bayesian Learning

In economics, as in most applied social sciences, deductive reasoning is used to solve problems. That is, economists typically derive hypotheses from practical experiences and test them against empirical observations (Albach and Jin 1998). As Popper (1959) noted, however, these tests can never definitively prove that a statement about the real world is true. The best that can be hoped for is that repeated tests will continue to decrease uncertainty and, in turn, increase confidence in the validity of a particular hypothesis. This updating process, known as Bayesian learning, is among the most widely utilized approaches to learning in economics. In traditional neoclassical models it is typically assumed that Bayesian updating is perfect and instantaneous. However, recent research combining psychology and economics is replete with reasons why perfect Bayesian updating may be implausible or simply too costly (Conlisk 1996; Rabin 1998; Tversky and Kahneman 1974, 1983). In these cases, more realistic and less costly forms of learning become important.

To understand Bayesian learning and its problems, it is useful to consider an example. Suppose an individual wants to know whether the demand for a given product next year will exceed demand this year. One approach is to survey customers and use the responses as a signal of next year's market demand. No matter how carefully survey techniques are implemented, one can never infer the true market demand from the results of the survey. However, it is possible to use the information gleaned from the survey to update prior beliefs about demand. Hence, a positive signal from the survey results would lead one to make an upward adjustment of expectations about demand. In other words, the new probability of increased demand exceeds the prior probability (Albach and Jin 1998). If one continues to receive positive signals through repeated surveying, the confidence that next year's demand will be higher than this year's will converge toward one. In the extreme, if an agent is able to observe the environment for a sufficiently long time, the agent will eventually acquire truth, at least in a probabilistic sense.

In traditional orthodox models it is frequently assumed that economic agents can observe and correctly interpret past signals over a sufficiently long period and thereby achieve probabilistic truth. However, Rabin (1998) and Kahneman and Tversky (1982) suggested that a variety of factors limit the ability of agents to engage in perfect updating. Economic agents, for example, tend to cling to previously held beliefs in spite of new signals, a phenomenon known as belief perseverance. Similarly, agents tend to look for signals that conform to strongly held prior beliefs (i.e. confirmatory biases). Finally, overconfidence in one's own judgment may inhibit perfect Bayesian updating. Once the reliability of signals or the ability of agents to correctly interpret received signals is questioned, it is no longer true that Bayesian learning will lead to probabilistic truth. In these cases, economic agents may employ quicker

and less costly forms of learning. March and Simon (1993), for instance, suggested that imitation may be a more effective form of learning in these contexts. Likewise, firms may employ simple heuristics to solve problems (Grether 1980) or utilize predefined procedures or solutions (Cohen, March, and Olsen 1972). Unlike traditional Bayesian approaches, these other forms of learning take into account that the feedback mechanisms used by economic agents in decision-making are imperfect and subject to biases.

Learning-by-doing and Learning Curve Models

In traditional neoclassical models it is typically assumed that feedback mechanisms work instantaneously. A substantial and growing body of research in economics, however, shows that the experience gained by individuals and organizations actually improves performance over time. There are two main variants of these so-called learning-by-doing models. The first branch focuses on learning by individuals. Economists have typically assumed that increases in individual productivity and skills result either from learning-by-doing on the job or from investments made in training. In the first case, productivity gains in human capital result from being able to increase the quality or speed of job performance as a result of previous exposure to a given set of tasks (Arrow 1962; Rosen 1972). Perhaps the most noted example of this form of learning is in Adam Smith's (1776/1976) example of a pin factory, in which repeated exposure to individual tasks in the pin-making process enabled workers to increase production substantially.

An alternative approach to individual learning is associated with Becker's (1964) training model of human capital accumulation. In this model, experience improves individual skills and productivity through a portion of experience that is invested in training. Unlike the pure learning-by-doing approach, in which individuals learn through current productive activities, the investment in training model is based on the assumption that workers dedicate a portion of their workday to training and thereby trade off current production for increases in future productive performance. For instance, when a firm sends an individual to a training program to learn how to use a new machine, the firm is giving up a portion of that worker's current productive capacity for expected increases in future capacity. (For a useful effort to combine this training focus with the learning-by-doing approach to human capital, see Killingsworth 1982, who developed a model in which human capital accumulation occurs through both training and learning-by-doing.) In both Becker's human capital model and models of individual learning-by-doing, organizations are assumed to reap the benefits of productivity gains resulting from individual learning. However, the mechanisms by which individual learning is transformed into organizational learning are rarely clearly specified.

The second major approach focuses on learning in organizations. Learning-by-doing in firms may take place through individuals gaining knowledge through experience, improved capital usage, firm knowledge gained through experience with a given technology, capital design improvement, and improved coordination (Arrow 1962). Thus, an important distinction between this approach and the individual learning models described above is that firm learning can increase productivity in multiple factors, whereas individual learning is focused solely on human capital. Gruber (1992) provided a classic example of learning-by-doing at the organizational level in his examination of semiconductor firms. Gruber found that the process of semiconductor chip manufacturing is so sensitive to production processes that many of the chips produced in early stages are unusable. Yields in later stages increase considerably, primarily because of gained experience. As firms become increasingly proficient at specific tasks, they are said to move along their 'learning curve', which depicts the relationship between a firm's cumulative experience and productivity. Hatch and Mowery (1998) also examined semiconductor manufacturing and the relationship between process innovation

and learning-by-doing. Yield improvements are shown empirically to be the product of deliberate activities by the semiconductor manufacturer, rather than the incidental by-product of production volume. Interestingly, some of the knowledge gained through learning-by-doing during new process development is specific to the production environment where the process is developed and is effectively lost when the new process is transferred to the manufacturing environment. Likewise, Teece (1977) found that strong learning exists in the process of technology transfer. The first effort to transfer manufacturing technology abroad is typically fraught with hazards and cost overruns, whereas subsequent efforts occasion much lower costs. Typically, economists assume that as cumulative output increases the production costs per unit decrease because of experience efficiencies. Average costs will decrease with increases in production until the firm eventually reaches a point when no additional gains to learning can be realized.

Learning curve models have been explored in many firms in both the manufacturing and service sectors. Some of the first applications were in aircraft production (Alchian 1963; Asher 1956; Wright 1936). Wright (1936), for example, noticed that labor, material, and overhead requirements declined with increased aircraft production, and he estimated that production input requirements decreased by 20 per cent for every doubling of cumulative past production. Similarly, Alchian's (1963) examination of twenty-two different types of World War II military aircraft revealed that learning rates varied significantly across plane types. Learning curve effects have also been found in a variety of industries, including shipping (Rapping 1965), power plants (Joskow and Rose 1985; Zimmerman 1982), machine tools (Hirsch 1952, 1956), and electronics (Adler and Clark 1987; for other applications of learning curve models, see Argote and Epple 1990 and Dutton and Thomas 1984).

One recent application of learning curve models is Benkard's (1999) analysis of commercial aircraft production. Utilizing a unique data set covering the entire production of the

Lockheed L-1011 Tri-Star, Benkard found support for the traditional learning curve hypothesis about declining average costs of production. Interestingly, Benkard also found considerable support for organizational forgetting, or the hypothesis that the firm's production experience depreciates over time, as well as for incomplete spillovers of production expertise from one generation of aircraft production to another. Specifically, labor costs per plane decreased as expected during the first portion of the L-1011's production, but then took a striking upturn during later production periods. Benkard suggested that this rise could be explained by the depreciation in Lockheed's human capital due to turnover, relatively low aircraft production rates, and the introduction of a new 500-series aircraft, which had a fundamentally different design than previous models. Benkard argued that the skills needed to produce previous models were not entirely relevant to the production of the 500-series aircraft and that the firm consequently experienced both a setback in learning and increased production costs for the whole program. These results add another level of complexity to traditional learning models and have important implications for many areas of industrial organization. Notably, this research suggests that learning may be a stochastic process. That is, during task completion, learning takes place in some instances but not in others. This characteristic of learning suggests a need to better understand what properties of the firm and of production are most important in determining when learning and forgetting occur (for additional discussion of the implications that learning curve models have for industrial organization, see Cabral and Riordan 1994).

Summary

As the above subsections illustrate, a substantial and growing body of literature in mainstream economics explores various aspects of individual and organizational learning. By modifying traditional neoclassical assumptions, mainstream economists have made at least three major contributions to the understanding of organizational learning. First, by relaxing traditional behavioral assumptions, economists have somewhat clarified the picture of how cognitive limitations and environmental uncertainty affect how economic agents update their prior beliefs. Second, utilizing various game-theoretic and non-game-theoretic techniques, economists have considerably sharpened their awareness of how strategic interaction and history affect learning processes. Lastly, over the past half-century economists have explored the productivity effects of one important form of learning, learning-by-doing.

These contributions notwithstanding, the orthodox literature's treatment of learning is far from adequate. First, the portrayal of learning is still highly stylized. For the most part, learning is presented as a relatively simple, automatic, and low-cost process. In the case of learning-by-doing, for example, organizational learning is essentially a free good: a joint output of productive activity. Second, mainstream economists frequently ignore the various sources of organizational learning and ways in which internal firm processes and capabilities interact and affect learning. Finally, and perhaps most important, many of the portrayals of learning in the mainstream economics literature are fundamentally static, detailing how firms acquire and utilize existing knowledge. Much of the strategic value of learning, however, comes not from utilizing existing knowledge but from creating *new* knowledge.

Learning and Innovation

Although critical aspects of learning have been largely neglected in mainstream economics, the process by which organizations create knowledge is of central importance in a large and growing stream of research examining the economics of innovation. Broadly speaking, innovation concerns the processes by which firms acquire and put into practice new product and process technologies (Nelson and

Rosenberg 1993). Since the early work of Schumpeter (1942) and Hayek (1945), economists interested in innovation have attempted to define the nature and character of these processes. A central theme of the innovation literature is that the means by which firms develop new product and process technologies are not random; rather, technological innovation is structured and orderly and typically occurs within fairly well-defined frameworks (Dosi 1982; Dosi and Orsenigo 1988; Pavitt 1987; Zuscovitch 1986). In an effort to improve understanding of these identifiable and well-defined structures, innovation scholars have placed considerable emphasis on organizational learning processes (Metcalfe 1995). The insights provided by these scholars build upon and, in important ways, extend the treatment of learning found in the mainstream literature.

An important insight coming out of the innovation literature pertains to the complex nature of technology. Developing a new product or process is a highly uncertain venture, entailing the interaction of a host of frequently complex technological and market factors (Kline and Rosenberg 1986). Successful development involves bringing together knowledge from a variety of sources and effectively meeting performance criteria that differ along multiple dimensions (Patel and Pavitt 1998). Complexity means that knowledge, which can be easily codified, is rarely a sufficient guide to practice. As Patel and Pavitt (1998) noted, 'theoretical laws and models, often developed "under laboratory conditions," or assuming "other things being equal," are unable to predict the operating performance of complex technological artifacts' (p. 11). Rather, firms frequently rely on knowledge that is difficult, if not impossible, to articulate and codify (Polanyi 1967; Winter 1987). This tacit knowledge is acquired through experience and on-the-job training in multiple learning activities, including design, production engineering, testing, and development. Frequently, this knowledge is embodied in an organization's system of coordinating and managing tasks, that is in its organizational routines (Nelson and Winter 1982).

The tacit component of technological knowledge makes its transfer between organizations difficult. As a result, a portion of an organization's technological knowledge is often highly specific to that firm or research entity. This fact explains why imitation costs (the costs of copying an existing process or product design) are frequently on par with the costs of innovation (the costs of developing a new product or process design). Mansfield, Schwarz, and Wagner (1981), for example, showed that imitation costs are on average as much as 70 per cent of innovation costs. As with innovation, success in imitation requires the ability to control many variables with complex interactions (Patel and Pavitt 1998). These interactions can rarely be reduced to simple, codifiable algorithms, so trial and error and operating experience are required. The specificity of technological knowledge also explains why the diffusion of new technology frequently depends on the mobility of engineers and scientists (Teece 1977). Because tacit knowledge is often embodied in human capital, transferring that knowledge may depend critically on the movement of experienced personnel.

The explicit recognition of the complexity of technology has enabled scholars to derive a number of insights about organizational learning and, ultimately, the nature of technological innovation. At least three main implications for organizational learning can be distinguished in this literature (Malerba 1992; Metcalfe 1995). First, various types of learning processes can be identified, each of which is associated with different activities that take place within the firm. Second, learning involves the interaction of internal and external sources of knowledge. Third, learning is cumulative and supports localized and primarily incremental innovation. Each of these insights is explored in the remainder of this section.

Types of Learning Processes

Among the most important contributions of the innovation literature to the study of organizational learning has been the explicit recognition that learning within firms occurs in many different varieties. Technological innovation has usefully been described as consisting of several different categories of learning, each of which is relevant in varying degrees during the different activities associated with the innovation process (Rosenberg 1982). Four categories of learning processes within the firm are frequently highlighted in this literature. As noted above, much of the attention given to organizational learning in economics has focused on learning-by-doing, a category of learning that is most closely associated with manufacturing activities (Malerba 1992; Rosenberg 1982). During this stage, learning primarily involves the acquisition of increasing skills in production in order to reduce input factor costs per unit of output. However, the traditional view of learning-by-doing is but one category of learning that affects only one part of a spectrum of activities related to technological innovation.

A second category of learning, scientific learning, is most frequently associated with basic research but is also operative in other stages of the innovation process. Scientific learning entails acquiring knowledge about the fundamental laws of science and nature. As the stock of scientific knowledge increases, the cost of undertaking science-based invention decreases (Rosenberg 1974). Nelson and Winter (1982) argued that the importance of science in the learning process is that it narrows the set of research options and directs attention to approaches that appear to hold the most promise of success. Evenson and Kislev (1976) enriched this view, suggesting that another role of science in the learning process is that it may enlarge the pool of approaches to solving a particular technological problem. As the number of candidate approaches increases, the likelihood of success and the expected payoff increase, albeit at the cost of broadening the search (Cohen 1998). Cohen and Klepper (1992) offered a related argument according to which a strong base of scientific knowledge, rather than simply increasing the number of approaches to achieving a given objective, actually increases the number of technological

objectives that a firm may pursue. In each of these views, scientific learning plays an essential role in the processes of technological change. It provides not only many of the tools that are useful in the search for new products and processes but also a powerful heuristic that guides this search process (Cohen 1998).

A third form of learning identified in the innovation literature is learning-by-searching. Whereas basic research is most closely, though not exclusively, associated with research activities, learning-by-searching entails searching out and discovering the optimal design of a new product or process (Rosenberg 1982). This form of learning is most closely associated with development activities and has a strong commercial dimension. For example, firms may engage in a search to discover the specific product characteristics that are desired in the marketplace and then seek to incorporate them into their designs. Firms may also attempt to innovate by scanning the technology sets of rival firms (Metcalfe 1995). A number of authors have examined the various search routines that firms employ in the context of innovation (Dosi 1988a; Nelson and Winter 1982; Winter 1986). All these scholars found that firms are unlikely to survey the entire stock of knowledge before making their technological choices. Because technological knowledge is often highly tacit and specific to a given firm, innovation decisions are frequently made with reference to a firm's current technological capability. Thus, firms will seek to improve and diversify their technology by searching in those zones that best exploit and enhance their existing technological base (Dosi 1988a). The use of relatively narrow search routines is one explanation of why technological innovation tends to be cumulative.

As Rosenberg (1982) noted, the three forms of learning identified thus far relate to generating knowledge that is either incorporated into the designs of new products and processes or used to improve the production process associated with new products. A final type of learning frequently discussed by innovation scholars occurs only after new products are used. Learning-by-using is the process by which the performance and maintenance characteristics of a new product are determined through feedback from consumers who have extensive experience with the product (Rosenberg 1982). This form of learning is particularly important in determining the optimal characteristics of new, highly complex technologies. Rosenberg (1982) stated:

For in an economy with complex new technologies, there are essential aspects of learning that are a function not of the experience involved in producing the product but of its utilization by the final user. . . . For a range of products involving complex, interdependent components or materials, . . . the outcome of the interaction of these parts cannot be precisely predicted. In this sense, we are dealing with performance characteristics that scientific knowledge or techniques cannot predict very accurately. The performance of these products, therefore, is highly uncertain. (p. 122)

Learning-by-using generates two different types of knowledge that assist in alleviating this uncertainty. First, the feedback from users deepens understanding of the relationship between a product's design and its performance. This information can subsequently be used to make necessary product design modifications. For instance, user feedback about the failure under stress of jet engine turbine blades in the Boeing 747 during the late 1960s led to aircraft design modifications (Rosenberg 1982). Second, learning-by-using may result in product-related knowledge that leads to new performance or operating practices. In this case, the information revealed by utilization never actually becomes embodied in the product's design. Rather, learning-by-using leads to new practices that lengthen the product's life or reduce its operating costs. In the airline industry, for example, early operating experience generated data about how various flight conditions affect airplane fuel consumption and overall performance. Although such information might not get incorporated into aircraft designs, it would likely be used to modify training and operating procedures (Rosenberg 1982).

This discussion of the various categories of learning suggests that what is typically referred to as research and development (R&D) is a multifaceted learning process. In conducting R&D, firms employ different types of learning methods. Although each of these types of learning is closely associated with a particular set of innovative activities their utility is by no means limited to these activities. Rather, firms employ these various approaches to learning during multiple stages of innovation. For example, scientific learning is not confined to basic research activities, but rather takes place at all points along the chain of innovation (Kline and Rosenberg 1986). Kline and Rosenberg (1986) noted that complex feedback loops between innovative activities frequently allow knowledge acquired during one stage of innovation to be incorporated into other activities. Moreover, distinctions within these four categories of learning can be sharpened. For instance, innovation scholars point out that a firm's specific types of scientific learning differ across the various stages of innovation. During initial analytic design activities, for example, pure, long-range scientific learning is frequently important, whereas during development activities the emphasis is on applied learning (Kline and Rosenberg 1986). Thus, in explicitly recognizing that organizations employ various categories of learning, innovation scholars not only have created a useful taxonomy but also have facilitated the examination of many subtle aspects of organizational learning.

Sources of Knowledge

In addition to the recognition that firms employ many different types of learning processes, a second important insight of the innovation literature is that learning is linked to different sources of knowledge that may be either internal or external to the firm (Malerba 1992). As noted above, a portion of a firm's existing knowledge base is highly tacit and, thus, idiosyncratic to a given organization or research unit. Other knowledge, however, can be articulated and even codified in journals, manuals, and precise algorithms (Dosi 1982). This knowledge can be easily transferred between organizations and may actually exist in the public domain. Even knowledge that is privately held or that is highly tacit frequently spills over organizational boundaries through, for instance, the movement of experienced personnel. These spillovers of technological knowledge, experience, and skills are essentially externalities that flow between adjacent users and producers of innovation (Geroski 1998). As a result of these externalities, interdependencies and synergies between sectors, firms, and even business units or production stages within a given firm are created (Dosi 1988a). The level of learning achieved in a given organization depends not only on its own research efforts but also on the entire pool of knowledge that is available to it and on its ability to take advantage of these spillovers (Griliches 1998). Understanding the dynamics of internal and external spillovers, therefore, is critical to developing a comprehensive view of organizational learning.

The importance of knowledge spillovers to learning at various organizational levels has been examined extensively in the innovation literature. Westney and Sakakibara (1986), Mansfield (1988), Odagiri and Goto (1993), and Rosenberg and Steinmueller (1988) noted the importance of spillovers at the national level. Odagiri and Goto, for example, observed that the ability of firms to absorb Western economic and technological knowledge rapidly has been critical to Japanese industrial growth since the mid-nineteenth century. Similarly, industry-level spillovers have been documented in a number of sectors, notably the aluminum and computer industries (Bresnahan 1986; Brock 1975; Peck 1962). At the organizational level, learning from spillovers may take the form of drawing on knowledge generated by various external sources, such as rival firms, universities, and government research organizations (Griliches 1991). Arora and Gambardella (1990), Jaffe (1989), and Mansfield (1991) each noted that firm-level innovation is strongly influenced by spillovers of knowledge from university research (for economic models of these externalities, see Griliches 1979 and Romer 1990). Alternatively, March and Simon (1958: 34–47) observed that organizations may learn

by imitating and borrowing from their rivals. Rosenberg and Steinmueller (1988), for instance, argued that the economic success of Japanese firms is due in part to their ability to imitate the successful practices of U.S. firms. Research on the sources of innovation supports the observation that imitation is an important means of technological diffusion and change (Cohen and Levinthal 1990). Finally, knowledge spillovers are important at the intraorganizational level. Considerable research suggests that a firm's innovative performance is strongly influenced by knowledge generated outside the firm's formal R&D unit (Mansfield 1968; Patel and Pavitt 1998).

Taken together, the research discussed thus far in this section suggests that an organization's innovative performance is strongly influenced by a variety of internal and external sources of knowledge. Table 4.2 highlights the various sources of learning. The specific factors that affect the ability of organizations to assimilate and absorb knowledge from these internal and external sources are examined by Cohen and Levinthal (1990). These authors argued that the ability of an organization to recognize the value of new information, assimilate it, and apply it to commercial ends (i.e. a firm's absorptive capacity) is a function of the firm's level of prior related knowledge. Drawing on cognitive research that indicates that learning is cumulative, Cohen and Levinthal suggested that organizations are better able to absorb external knowledge when it is closely related to the organization's existing stock of knowledge than when it is not. Thus, firms that invest in R&D are not only generating new knowledge but also enhancing their ability to learn in the future. This twofold effect suggests that an organization's innovative performance is partially path-dependent, for failure to invest adequately in an area of technological expertise may foreclose the future development of capabilities in that area (Cohen and Levinthal 1990).

Similarly, an organization's current learning processes may limit its ability to recognize and respond to external changes. Henderson and Clark (1990), for example, argued that, in an

Table 4.2. Categories of learning in the innovation literature

Type of learning	Locus	Innovative focus
Learning-by-doing	Internal to the firm	Production activities
Learning-by-searching	Primarily internal to the firm	Commercial focus mainly R&D-related
Scientific learning	Internal and external to the firm	Absorption of new scientific and technological knowledge
Learning-by-using	Internal to the firm	Use of products and inputs
Spillover learning	External to the firm	Absorbing external knowledge and imitating the practices of rivals

Note: For a discussion of these basic learning types, see Malerba 1992.

environment in which a given technology's design is stable, an organization will tend to focus its learning efforts on a specific product architecture. That is, engineers within the organization will concentrate on learning about the product's components and the way these components relate to one another. Eventually, this knowledge becomes embedded in the practices and procedures of the organization, a useful property as long as the product's fundamental design is stable. When this product's architecture changes, however, two problems arise. First, established organizations may be slow to respond to these technological changes. Because the organization's active learning is focused on the old technological architecture, the organization may fail to recognize the importance of technological changes immediately. Second, once an organization has recognized the nature of an architectural innovation, it may be unable to respond effectively. Because knowledge of the old product architecture is embedded in the organization, responding to the new innovation entails fundamentally switching from one mode of learning to another. This switch is complicated by the fact that the organization must build new architectural knowledge in a context in which some of its old architectural knowledge may be relevant. Thus, a firm's existing learning processes may fundamentally handicap it in the

face of certain types of technological changes. This same theme is also featured in work by Anderson and Tushman (1990) and Christensen and Rosenbloom (1995).

Incremental and Cumulative Learning

The discussion of the previous two subsections suggests that organizational learning is often an incremental and cumulative process. Dosi (1982, 1988*a*) made this point explicitly, arguing that technological innovation frequently evolves in certain path-dependent ways, contoured and channeled by what can be thought of as technological paradigms. A technological paradigm contextually defines a firm's opportunities for innovation and the basic procedures that are available to exploit these opportunities. The crucial point is that paradigms are fundamentally shaped by an organization's prior technological performance. As noted above, both the search routines that a firm employs in developing new products and processes and the ability of that firm to absorb external knowledge are largely determined by the organization's current stock of technology. In such a circumstance, organizational learning tends to be incremental (Dosi 1988*a*; Malerba 1992). The technological problems and opportunities that an organization perceives frequently relate to its current activities. Thus, a considerable portion of a firm's innovative activities consists of modifications and improvements to existing products and processes. In many instances, incremental innovations result not from any deliberate research activities but rather from improvements discovered during a product's manufacturing process or through a feedback from users (Dosi 1988a). Because firms differ in their stock of knowledge and in the learning processes they employ, the trajectories of incremental technological change also differ (Malerba 1992). Therefore, one would expect that new product and process developments for a particular organization lie in the technological neighborhood of previous successes (Nelson and Winter 1982; Teece 1996; for an additional discussion of the importance of technological paradigms in learning processes, see Dierkes, Marz, and Teele, Ch. 12 in this volume).

This last point also suggests that technology development, particularly within a given paradigm, proceeds *cumulatively* along the path defined by that paradigm. According to Dosi (1988a), '[w]hat the firm can hope to do technologically in the future is heavily constrained by what it has been capable of doing in the past. Once the cumulative and firm specific nature of technology is recognized, its development over time ceases to be random, but is constrained to zones closely related technologically to existing activities' (p. 225). To the extent that innovative learning is local and specific to a given technology paradigm but is shared by other firms operating on that technology, one is likely to see the sort of industry lock-in and path dependence discussed in David (1975, 1985) and Arthur (1989, 1990). Alternatively, to the extent that learning is local and cumulative at the level of individual organizations, firm-specific lock-in and path dependence are likely to be operative. In this case, an organization's technical capabilities are likely to be 'close in' to previous technological accomplishments (Teece 1996: 195). For instance, specific technological skills in one field (e.g. pharmaceuticals) may be applicable to closely related fields (e.g. pesticides) but are not likely to be useful in distant areas (e.g. airplanes) (Teece 1988).

Summary

In some sense, all technological innovation entails organizational learning. Thus, any attempt to summarize the contribution of the innovation literature to organizational learning in a few pages is bound to be inadequate. Nevertheless, in this section we identified three main contributions of this kind. The first two insights—that there exist different categories of learning involving internal and external sources of knowledge—are summarized in Table 4.2. This table, along with the above discussion, suggests that learning is not the free good it is portrayed as being in much of the economics literature but rather that learning is a costly and multifaceted process (Malerba 1992). Moreover, this discussion dispels the notion that learning takes place in a vacuum. Instead, various internal and external sources are instrumental in the accumulation of a firm's stock of knowledge. It is this existing pool of knowledge capital and the specific learning processes employed by a firm that generate unique trajectories of incremental and cumulative technological innovation, the third major insight of this literature. Taken together, these three insights present a more realistic and comprehensive picture of organizational learning processes. In the next section we examine how contributions from the innovation literature are influencing emerging work on the economic theory of the firm.

Organizational Learning and the Theory of the Firm

Much of the work reported in the innovation literature suggests that, to the extent that learning is localized in individual firms, one is likely to observe that firms with specific technological competencies follow unique trajectories of innovation. Any useful treatment of economic learning, therefore, must address a key question: How do firms organize so as to develop and exploit their specialized competencies for knowledge creation in the best way? For this purpose, we turn to emerging economic theories of the firm. The literature in economics exploring the theory of the firm and the economics of organization emerged during the late 1930s but did not receive focused theoretical and empirical attention until the late 1970s. One main thrust of this literature is that the principal objective of economic organization is to adapt to changing circumstances (Barnard 1938; Hayek 1945; Williamson 1996). Given the importance of adaptation in learning processes (Huber 1991; Levitt and March 1988), much of this literature can therefore be seen as fundamentally addressing how organizations learn. (Various literature reviews of organizational learning note that the terms 'adaptation' and 'learning' are frequently used interchangeably; see Nonaka and Takeuchi 1995: 54.) Indeed, work coming out of this branch of economics has been central in developing a coherent and dynamic approach to organizational learning.

Antecedents

Learning and learning processes have long been central components in the understanding of the economics of organization. The early Austrian economist Frederich von Hayek (1945) was among the first to draw attention to the role of the market form of organization in facilitating learning among economic agents. According to Hayek, the process of a market reaching its equilibrium is fundamentally a learning process. In reaching this conclusion, Hayek made a distinction between two types of economic knowledge: knowledge of general rules and principles (i.e. scientific knowledge) and knowledge of particular circumstances of time and location. Whereas the former type of knowledge is mainly of interest to theorists, it is the latter type that is most relevant in determining economic outcomes. The main problem of economic organization in Hayek's view, is coordinating the use of this dispersed, context-specific knowledge in the face of changing circumstances that continually redefine the relative importance of the knowledge possessed by any given individual. According to Hayek,

> The peculiar character of the problem of a rational economic order is determined precisely by the fact that the knowledge of the circumstances of which we must make use never exists in concentrated or integrated form but solely as dispersed bits of incomplete and frequently contradictory knowledge which all the separate individuals possess. The economic problem of society is thus not merely a problem of how to allocate 'given' resources[,] . . . it is a problem of the utilization of knowledge not given to anyone in its totality. (pp. 519–20)

It is the price mechanism, Hayek (1945) argued, that provides the solution to this core economic problem. Although its workings may not be fully understood by market participants, the price system serves as a communication network that allows agents to share relevant economic information. It is through this fundamentally spontaneous process that economic learning occurs.

Whereas Hayek (1945) concentrated on the role of the market in facilitating economic learning, Ronald Coase (1937) emphasized the limits of market learning. Coase was the first to observe that what is unique about firms and markets is that they are alternative means for organizing the same transactions. Whether economic activity is organized in one mode or another in a given instance hinges largely on the costs of managing the transaction inside the firm as compared with the costs of mediating it through the market. For Coase, the central transaction cost associated with the market mode of organization is that of learning what the relevant prices are. These costs of learning are largely eliminated when transactions are internalized inside the firm. Thus, from Coase's perspective, firms arise in part because of difficulties of learning in markets. Unlike Hayek (1945), who extolled the virtues of markets in this respect, Coase (1964) recognized that all forms of organization (including markets) are flawed and that the central problem of organizations is determining which arrangements work best in practice. Researchers interested in learning and innovation, therefore, are encouraged to examine which organizational arrangement is most conducive to knowledge creation and exploitation in a given instance.

Transaction-cost Economics

Though first suggested by Coase (1937), this comparative institutional approach has been most fully developed in the work of Oliver Williamson (1975, 1985, 1996) and scholars working in transaction-cost economics (e.g. Joskow 1987; Klein, Crawford, and Alchian 1978; Masten 1996; Masten, Meehan, and Snyder 1991; Williamson 1985, 1996; for more thorough review of the empirical work in transaction-cost economics, see Shelanski and Klein 1995). Consistent with Coase, transaction-cost economists maintain that economizing on transaction costs is mainly responsible for the choice of one form of organization over another. The theory's main prediction is that transactions, which differ in their attributes, are aligned with governance structures, which differ in their costs and competencies, in a discriminating and mainly transaction-cost-economizing fashion (Williamson 1996). The primary ways in which transactions differ, it is argued, are frequency, uncertainty, and the degree to which the assets involved can be redeployed for alternative uses or to alternative users without loss of productive value (i.e. asset specificity). Though all three characteristics are important, many of the strongest refutable implications are associated with asset specificity (Williamson 1985). Where assets are largely nonredeployable, contracting parties become locked into the transaction. This condition of bilateral dependency creates the potential that one or both parties will behave in ways that do not maximize joint profits when contractual conditions change in ways not fully accounted for in the original agreement. As a consequence, economic agents will be inclined to devise governance structures that better align the parties' incentives and limit the scope of *ex post* opportunistic behavior (Williamson 1996). As asset specificity and other contractual hazards increase, added (i.e. more hierarchical) modes of governance will be required to safeguard the transaction.

Although transaction-cost economics has been remiss in addressing organizational learning directly (Williamson 1999), its insights have been used extensively to improve understanding of how innovative activities should be organized. Teece (1988) and Dosi (1988b), for instance, observed that market transactions involving innovative activities generally exhibit the following characteristics: (a) incomplete specifications of contracts due to uncertainty about the outcomes of innovative activities, (b) high monitoring costs, (c) a lack of adequate protection for proprietary knowledge (i.e. appropriability problems), (d) weak incentives to least-cost performance, and (e) bilateral dependencies among research suppliers. Given these inherent hazards, the authors suggested that innovative activities are rather likely to occur in more formal organizations (e.g. R&D laboratories in vertically integrated firms, government and university labs) than in markets involving individual innovators. Performing R&D activities in formal organizations has a number of potential benefits. Williamson (1985), for example, noted that, in integrated firms, the flow of information between R&D laboratories and the people in the firm who implement new technologies is superior to that in markets. Kogut and Zander (1996) similarly suggested that firms facilitate the sharing and transfer of knowledge. In addition, there may be important appropriability benefits to hierarchical modes of governance. Dosi (1988b), for instance, observed that formal organizations limit cross-organization information leaks. Liebeskind (1996) likewise suggested that firms have particular institutional capabilities that enable them to protect knowledge from expropriation better than markets do. Teece (1996) pointed out that if the innovation at issue is a process technology, the vertically integrated firm may be able to use the technology in-house and take profits not by selling the technology but by selling the products that embody or use the process. Because contracting in these cases is entirely internal, specialized assets are better protected than in markets and recontracting hazards are attenuated.

The above discussion does not imply that innovative activities *never* occur outside a formal integrated setting. Indeed, one often observes market and hybrid transfers of innovations through, for example, licensing and joint ventures (Dosi 1988*b*; Teece 1989, 1992; Teece, Pisano, and Shuen 1997). However, these alternative modes are not all-or-nothing substitutes for in-house research. In fact, the work of Cohen and Levinthal (1990) cited in the third section of this chapter suggests that firms must possess considerable capabilities in order to absorb many of the innovations that are obtained through market mechanisms. Thus, this literature suggests that industrial research will *primarily* occur in integrated research organizations. This prediction is largely substantiated by studies documenting the growth of R&D activities in American industry over the last century (Mowery 1980; Rosenberg 1985; Teece and Armour 1977).

Resource-based and Evolutionary Theories of the Firm

In addition and, in many respects, complementary to the transaction-cost economics perspective discussed above, a growing number of theories of learning and knowledge creation in firms emphasize organization-level factors. Penrose (1959) was a pioneer in these approaches, arguing that the firm is fundamentally a repository of knowledge and that learning is central to the firm's growth. According to Penrose, the firm is 'both an administrative organization and a collection of productive resources, both human and material' (p. 31). The services rendered by these resources are the primary inputs into a firm's production processes and are firm-specific in the sense that they are a function of the knowledge and experience that the firm has acquired over time. When services that are currently going unused are applied to new lines of business, these services also function as a growth engine for the firm. In Penrose's view, a firm possesses idle resources primarily because of learning that enables the organization to utilize its re-

sources better and more efficiently than it has previously. By implication, then even firms that maintain a constant level of capital may nevertheless be able to grow as services are freed up for new uses as a result of organizational learning. Thus, Penrose's analysis suggests that a firm's resources and learning processes have an important impact on strategic performance and growth.

This basic idea underpins much of the research by scholars working on the resource-based theory of the firm (Dierickx and Cool 1989; Prahalad and Hamel 1990; Stalk, Evans, and Shulman 1992). In the resource-based approach it is argued that unique and difficult-to-imitate resources are the primary source of sustainable competitive advantage for firms. These resources enable firms to have markedly lower costs or offer high-quality products and performance than their competitors. Because of the inability of firms to quickly develop new competencies internally or to acquire often highly tacit skills and knowledge externally, resource endowments can differentiate performance and provide for competitive advantage. At least in the short run, therefore, firms with superior competencies will tend to be more profitable than their competitors. Although much of this literature focuses on the importance of existing firm-specific resources and does not directly address learning in organizations, this perspective does invite consideration of managerial strategies for developing *new* resources. In fact, because controlling difficult-to-imitate resources is a crucial source of economic profits, the management of knowledge and learning are critical strategic issues (Shuen 1994; Wernerfelt 1984). These issues are examined below.

The importance of knowledge and learning in firms was also addressed extensively in Nelson and Winter's work on the evolutionary nature of the firm (Nelson and Winter 1982; Winter 1988). Consistent with Penrose (1959) and Hayek (1945), Nelson and Winter (1982) suggested that business firms are essentially repositories for a range of highly specific productive knowledge. This knowledge, these authors argued, can be thought of as residing in an organization's standard operating procedures, or routines. Much like the genes of biological evolutionary theory, routines are patterns of interactions that represent successful solutions to particular problems. These patterns of interaction are fundamentally social in nature and are thus most often resident at the group level, though certain subroutines may be operative in individual behavior. An important aspect is that organizational routines shape how firms comprehend and address both familiar and unfamiliar situations. Organizational routines are therefore central to organizational learning. Although the character of routines varies within and across organizations, one unifying feature is that the knowledge embodied in them is typically highly tacit (Nelson and Winter 1982; Winter 1988). This characteristic implies that routines can rarely be fully codified or articulated. As a result, the routines themselves and the ability of managers to call upon them as needed are crucial aspects of an organization's learning capabilities.

Teece, Rumelt, Dosi, and Winter (1994) distinguished two main types of routines. Static routines are those that enable firms to replicate previously performed functions. Although these routines are constantly being updated and thus are not truly static, they nevertheless reflect responses to relatively familiar situations. The learning curve economies discussed in the second section of this chapter frequently reflect the presence of static routines. In contrast, dynamic routines are directed at new learning and the development of novel products and processes. The search routines that firms employ in innovative activities, for example, typically rely on dynamic routines. These routines assist firms in deciding where, how, and how long to search for innovations (Teece *et al.* 1994).

The above discussion suggests that routines have at least two important qualities with respect to learning. First, by storing previously successful responses to familiar and repetitious problems, routines enable organizations to improve the performance of everyday tasks. Second, by patterning useful approaches to innovation, routines facilitate experimenta-

tion and the identification of new production opportunities. In short, routines embody the common codes of communication and coordination that are essential to all aspects of organizational learning. Moreover, because the knowledge embodied in routines is typically highly tacit, copying routines from one context to another is often difficult. In this respect, routines contribute to a firm's distinctive learning capabilities and are largely responsible for the regular and predictable behavioral patterns that differentiate firms from one another (Winter 1988; for an additional discussion of routines, see Kieser, Beck, and Tainio, Ch. 27 in this volume).

Dynamic Capabilities and the Knowledge-creating Organization

Nelson and Winter's work on dynamic routines began to explore the internal processes by which firms learn and develop new, strategically relevant competencies. Research examining the dynamic nature of firm capabilities has further developed these issues. First fully elaborated in the work of Teece and Pisano (1994), the dynamic capabilities approach traces its intellectual origins to early work by Joseph Schumpeter (1951), who argued that the emergence of new products and processes results from new combinations of knowledge. In a similar vein, it is argued in the dynamic capabilities approach that competitive success arises from the continuous development and reconfiguration of firm-specific assets (Teece and Pisano 1994; Teece, Pisano, and Shuen 1997). Whereas Penrose and resource-based scholars recognize the competitive importance of firm-specific capabilities, researchers of the dynamic capabilities approach attempt to outline specifically how organizations develop and renew internal competencies. Thus, the latter approach is concerned with a subset of a firm's overall capabilities, namely, those that allow firms to create new knowledge and to disseminate it throughout the organization. Stated differently, proponents of the dynamic capabilities approach attempt to isolate those internal factors that facilitate organizational learning.

Teece and Pisano (1994) highlighted the importance of three main factors: the firm's managerial and organizational processes, its strategic position, and the paths that are available to the firm. Managerial and organizational processes refer essentially to how things get done in firms (Teece and Pisano 1994). Central in this regard is how well management organizes, coordinates, and integrates various internal firm processes. A number of empirical studies, for example, suggest that the organization and coherence of production processes can lead to important differences in competencies across firms (Clark and Fujimoto 1991; Garvin 1988). Likewise, a firm's learning routines are a critical dimension of its managerial and organizational processes. The strategic position of a firm pertains to its current endowment of technology and intellectual property as well as its customer base and upstream relations with suppliers (Teece and Pisano 1994). Particularly important in this respect are difficult-to-replicate assets and those complementary assets that are required to produce and deliver new products and services (Teece 1986). Finally, the paths that are available to a firm are the strategic alternatives that it faces. As noted in the work of Dosi (1988a), Arthur (1989), and David (1985, 1986), the path a firm can take is largely constrained by its current position. Path dependencies and established technological trajectories shape the productive and technological opportunities faced by firms and the attractiveness of these opportunities.

Economists who focus on dynamic capabilities suggest that these three factors shape the ability of an organization to learn, adapt, change, and renew itself over time. Central to the dynamic capabilities approach is the idea that, in the face of a changing business environment, competitive success depends on the ability of firms to reconfigure internal and external organizational skills and resources appropriately. This sentiment is echoed in Kogut and Zander (1992), who argued that organizational learning is a function of a firm's 'combinative capabilities' to generate new applications from existing knowledge. Underlying Kogut and Zander's claim is the idea that a firm's capabilities cannot be separated from how it is currently organized. The main advantage of learning through recombinations is that it enables firms to take advantage of existing relational structures. Other similar approaches to firm-learning can be found in Dierickx and Cool (1989), Prahalad and Hamel (1990), and Stalk, Evans, and Shulman (1992). The chief contribution of these dynamic views is that they explore not only how firms acquire and utilize existing knowledge but also how they generate and benefit from new knowledge.

This image of a knowledge-creating organization—as opposed to simply a knowledge-using organization—is further refined and extended in recent work by Nonaka (1991, 1994) and Nonaka and Takeuchi (1995). Because other chapters in this volume examine this work directly, it is redundant to summarize it here. However, research by Nonaka complements the work examined in this chapter in that he has attempted to provide a comprehensive and dynamic theory of firm-learning. Particularly useful in this regard is Nonaka and Takeuchi's (1995) discussion of the specific organizational factors that facilitate the 'knowledge spiral' (p. 70) through which learning occurs. These insights help clarify how it is that individual learning is transformed into group knowledge and, ultimately, into new *organizational* knowledge. Nonaka and Takeuchi noted that this knowledge, once embodied at the organizational level, can then be made available to affiliated organizations, such as subsidiaries, customers, suppliers, or even competitors. The specific mechanisms by which these interorganizational transfers of knowledge occur have become the subject of considerable interest among economists. Recent work by Mowery, Oxley, and Silverman (1996, 1998), for example, suggested that interorganizational collaboration provides a means by which firm-specific knowledge can be exchanged between organizations. Likewise, Hamel (1991) and Kogut (1988) observed the use of joint ventures as a means of transferring knowledge between firms (see also Merkens, Geppert, and Antal, Ch. 10 in this volume).

Interorganizational learning in a global perspective is also explored in Part VI of this volume.

Summary

In this section we have reviewed the contributions that various economic theories of the firm have made to organizational learning. Building on much of the economics and innovation research reviewed in the previous sections, this literature has been instrumental in the progress toward a comprehensive and dynamic understanding of organizational learning processes. In particular, three contributions are evident. First, the economic theory of the firm developed in the early work of Hayek and Coase and extended by Williamson stressed the central role of economic organization in facilitating adaptation and articulated the fundamental distinctions between various modes of organization. These authors' insights highlighted the limitations and possibilities for learning associated with different forms of economic organization. Second, subsequent work by resource-based scholars and those working on the evolutionary theory of the firm have emphasized the crucial dimensions along which individual firms vary in their ability to acquire and exploit knowledge. The importance of organizational routines and firm-specific assets and capabilities have generally been cited as driving this heterogeneity. Lastly, in their recent work on the dynamic aspects of firm strategy scholars have begun to recognize the organizational processes and mechanisms that firms employ not only to acquire and utilize existing knowledge but also to create new knowledge. The distinction between a knowledge-using company and a knowledge-creating company has been articulated. This final contribution has been central in the development of a dynamic theory of organizational learning.

Conclusion

In this chapter we have explored the contribution of economics to the study of organizational learning. We hope it is apparent that learning is by no means a novel concept in economics. Few, if any, modern economists would question the paramount importance of learning and learning processes to a firm's competitive performance. Moreover, many of the field's most noted forefathers, including Schumpeter, Coase, Hayek, and Marshall, made important early contributions to the study of learning. However, as we noted above, the ability of economists to develop a comprehensive, realistic, and dynamic theory of organizational learning has been substantially limited by the highly stylized assumptions that ground much research in mainstream economics. Indeed, many of the contributions to learning that have been made in economics result from modifications to a number of these restrictive assumptions. The contributions of the mainstream literature notwithstanding, we note that many of the most valuable insights into organizational learning come from two main branches within economics. Researchers studying the economics of innovation have highlighted the various types of learning that organizations employ and have noted that organizations take advantage of various internal and external sources of learning. This literature also points to the incremental and cumulative nature of learning and innovation. Economists working on the theory of the firm have utilized these insights into the nature and sources of learning in order to explore how internal firm processes affect the ability of economic organizations to develop and exploit new and existing forms of knowledge. What emerge from economics, therefore, though not a complete portrait of organizational learning, are useful vignettes of various critical aspects of learning processes. Considerable work remains to be done in piecing these snapshots together in order to provide a comprehensive and unified theory of how organizations learn.

References

Adler, P. and Clark, K. (1987). *Behind the Learning Curve: A Sketch of the Learning Process*. Boston: Harvard Business School, Harvard University.

Akerlof, G. A. (1970). 'The Market for "Lemons": Quality Uncertainty and the Market Mechanism'. *Quarterly Journal of Economics*, 84: 488–500.

Albach, H. and Jin, J. (1998). 'Learning in the Market', in H. Albach, M. Dierkes, A. Berthoin Antal, and K. Vaillant (eds.), *Organisationslernen—institutionelle und kulturelle Dimensionen. WZB Jahrbuch 1998*. Berlin: edition sigma, 355–72.

Alchian, A. (1950). 'Uncertainty, Evolution, and Economic Theory.' *Journal of Political Economy*, 58: 211–21.

—— (1963). 'Reliability of Progress Curves in Airframe Production'. *Econometrica*, 31: 679–93.

Alexis, M. (1999). 'The Treatment of Organizational Learning in Economics', in M. Dierkes, M. Alexis, A. Berthoin Antal, B. L. T. Hedberg, P. Pawlowsky, J. Stopford, and L. S. Tsui-Auch (eds.), *The Annotated Bibliography of Organizational Learning*. Berlin: edition sigma, 143–292.

—— and Wilson, C. (1967). *Organizational Decision Making*. Englewood Cliffs, NJ: Prentice Hall.

Anderson, P. and Tushman, M. L. (1990). 'Technological Discontinuities and Dominant Designs: A Cyclical Model of Technological Change'. *Administrative Science Quarterly*, 35: 604–33.

Argote, L. and Epple, D. (1990). 'Learning Curves in Manufacturing'. *Science*, 247: 920–4.

Arora, A. and Gambardella, A. (1990). 'Complementarity and External Linkages: The Strategies of the Large Firms in Biotechnology'. *Journal of Industrial Economics*, 38: 361–80.

Arrow, K. J. (1962). 'The Economic Implications of Learning by Doing'. *Review of Economic Studies*, 29: 155–73.

Arthur, W. B. (1989). 'Competing Technologies, Increasing Returns, and Lock-in by Historical Events'. *Economic Journal*, 99/394: 116–31.

—— (1990). 'Positive Feedbacks in the Economy'. *Scientific American*, 262/2: 92–9.

Asher, H. (1956). *Cost–quantity Relationships in the Airframe Industry*. Santa Monica, Calif.: Rand.

Aumann, R. (1985). 'What Is Game Theory Trying to Accomplish?' in K. J. Arrow (ed.), *Frontiers of Economics*. Oxford: Basil Blackwell, 28–78.

—— (1987). 'Correlated Equilibrium as an Expression of Bayesian Rationality'. *Econometrica*, 55: 1–18.

Bala, V. and Goyal, S. (1998). 'Learning from Neighbours'. *Review of Economic Studies*, 65: 595–621.

Banerjee, A. V. (1992). 'A Simple Model of Herd Behavior'. *Quarterly Journal of Economics*, 107: 797–817.

Barnard, C. I. (1938). *The Functions of the Executive*. Cambridge, Mass.: Harvard University Press.

Becker, G. S. (1964). *Human Capital: A Theoretical and Empirical Analysis, with Special Reference to Education*. New York: Columbia University Press.

Benkard, L. C. (1999). *Learning and Forgetting: The Dynamics of Aircraft Production*. Palo Alto, Calif.: Graduate School of Business, Stanford University.

Bernheim, B. D. (1984). 'Rationalizable Strategic Behavior'. *Econometrica*, 52: 1007–28.

Bikhchandani, S., Hirschleifer, D., and Welch, I. (1998). 'Learning from the Behavior of Others: Conformity, Fads, and Informational Cascades'. *Journal of Economic Perspectives*, 12/3: 151–70.

Blonski, M. (1999). 'Social Learning with Case-based Decisions'. *Journal of Economic Behavior and Organization*, 38: 59–77.

Bresnahan, T. (1986). 'Measuring the Spillovers from Technical Advance: Mainframe Computers in Financial Services'. *American Economic Review*, 76: 742–55.

Brock, G. W. (1975). *The U.S. Computer Industry*. Cambridge, Mass.: Ballinger.

Brown, G. W. (1951). 'Iterative Solution of Games by Fictitious Play', in T. C. Koopmans (ed.), *Activity Analysis of Production and Allocation: Proceedings of a Conference*. New York: Wiley, 374–80.

Burgelman, R. A. (1990). 'Strategy-making and Organizational Ecology: A Conceptual Framework', in J. V. Singh (ed.), *Organizational Evolution: New Directions*. Newbury Park, Calif.: Sage, 164–81.

Cabral, L. M. B. and Riordan, M. H. (1994). 'The Learning Curve, Market Dominance, and Predatory Pricing'. *Econometrica*, 62: 1115–40.

Christensen, C. M. and Rosenbloom, R. S. (1995). 'Explaining the Attacker's Advantage: Technological Paradigms, Organizational Dynamics, and the Value Network'. *Research Policy*, 24: 233–57.

Clark, K. B. and Fujimoto, T. (1991). *Product Development Performance: Strategy, Organization, and Management in the World Auto Industry*. Boston: Harvard Business School Press.

Coase, R. H. (1937). 'The Nature of the Firm'. *Econometrica*, 4: 386–405.

—— (1964). 'The Regulated Industries: Discussion'. *American Economic Review*, 54: 194–7.

Cohen, M. D., March, J. G., and Olsen, J. P. (1972). 'A Garbage Can Model of Organizational Choice'. *Administrative Science Quarterly*, 17: 1–25.

Cohen, W. M. (1998). 'Empirical Studies of Innovative Activity', in P. Stoneman (ed.), *Handbook of the Economics of Innovation and Technological Change*. Oxford: Blackwell, 182–264.

—— and Klepper, S. (1992). 'The Tradeoff between Firm Size and Diversity in the Pursuit of Technological Progress'. *Small Business Economics*, 4: 1–14.

—— and Levinthal, D. A. (1990). 'Absorptive Capacity: A New Perspective on Learning and Innovation'. *Administrative Science Quarterly*, 35: 128–52.

Conlisk, J. (1996). 'Why Bounded Rationality'. *Journal of Economic Literature*, 34: 669–700.

Cournot, A. (1960). *Researches into the Mathematical Principles of the Theory of Wealth*. London: Hafner.

David, P. A. (1975). *Technical Choice, Innovation and Economic Growth*. London: Cambridge University Press.

—— (1985). 'Clio and the Economics of QWERTY'. *American Economic Review*, 75: 332–7.

—— (1986). 'Technology Diffusion, Public Policy, and Industrial Competitiveness', in R. Landau and N. Rosenberg (eds.), *The Positive Sum Strategy: Harnessing Technology for Economic Growth*. Washington, DC: National Academy Press, 373–91.

—— (1990). 'The Dynamo and the Computer: An Historical Perspective on the Modern Productivity Paradox'. *American Economic Review*, 80: 355–61.

Dierickx, I. and Cool, K. (1989). 'Asset Stock Accumulation and Sustainability of Competitive Advantage'. *Management Science*, 35: 1504–14.

Dosi, G. (1982). 'Technological Paradigms and Technological Trajectories: A Suggested Interpretation of the Determinants and Directives of Technological Change'. *Research Policy*, 11: 147–62.

—— (1988a). 'The Nature of the Innovative Process', in G. Dosi, C. Freeman, R. Nelson, G. Silverberg, and L. Soete (eds.), *Technical Change and Economic Theory*. New York: Pinter, 221–38.

—— (1988b). 'Sources, Procedures, and Microeconomic Effects of Innovation'. *Journal of Economic Literature*, 26: 1120–71.

—— and Orsenigo, L. (1988). 'Coordination and Transformation: An Overview of Structures, Behaviors, and Change in Evolutionary Environments', in G. Dosi, C. Freeman, R. Nelson, G. Silverberg, and L. Soete (eds.), *Technical Change and Economic Theory*. New York: Pinter, 13–37.

Dutton, J. and Thomas, J. (1984). 'Treating Progress Functions as a Managerial Opportunity'. *Academy of Management Review*, 36: 235–47.

Eatwell, J., Milgate, M., and Newman, P. (eds.) (1987). *The New Palgrave Dictionary of Economics*. London: Norton.

Ellison, G. and Fudenberg, D. (1993). 'Rules of Thumb for Social Learning'. *Journal of Political Economy*, 101: 612–43.

Evenson, R. E. and Kislev, Y. (1976). 'A Stochastic Model of Applied Research'. *Journal of Political Economy*, 84: 265–81.

Garvin, D. A. (1988). *Managing Quality*. New York: Free Press.

Geroski, P. (1998). 'Markets for Technology: Knowledge, Innovation and Appropriability', in P. Stoneman (ed.), *Handbook of the Economics of Innovation and Technological Change*. Oxford: Blackwell, 90–131.

Grether, D. M. (1980). 'Bayes' Rule as a Descriptive Model: The Representativeness Heuristic'. *Quarterly Journal of Economics*, 95: 537–57.

Griliches, Z. (1979). 'An Exploration of a Production Function Approach to the Estimation of the Returns to R&D'. *Bell Journal of Economics*, 10: 92–116.

——(1991). *The Search for R&D Spillovers*. Cambridge, Mass.: National Bureau of Economic Research.

——(1998). 'R&D and Productivity: Econometric Results and Measurement Issues', in P. Stoneman (ed.), *Handbook of the Economics of Innovation and Technological Change*. Oxford: Blackwell, 52–89.

Gruber, H. (1992). 'The Learning Curve in the Production of Semiconductor Memory Chips'. *Applied Economics*, 24: 885–94.

Hamel, G. (1991). 'Competition for Competence and Inter-partner Learning within International Strategic Alliances'. *Strategic Management Journal*, 12 (Summer special issue): 83–103.

Hatch, N. W. and Mowery, D.C. (1998). 'Process Innovation and Learning by Doing in Semiconductor Manufacturing'. *Management Science*, 44: 1461–77.

Hayek, F. A. v. (1945). 'The Use of Knowledge in Society'. *American Economic Review*, 35: 519–30.

Heiner, R. A. (1983). 'The Origin of Predictable Behavior'. *American Economic Review*, 73: 560–95.

Henderson, D. (ed.) (1993). *The Fortune Encyclopedia of Economics*. New York: Warner.

Henderson, R. M. and Clark, K. (1990). 'Architectural Innovation: The Reconfiguration of Existing Product Technologies and the Failure of Established Firms'. *Administrative Science Quarterly*, 35: 9–30.

Hirsch, W. Z. (1952). 'Manufacturing Progress Functions'. *Review of Economics and Statistics*, 34: 143–55.

——(1956). 'Firm Progress Ratios'. *Econometrica*, 24: 136–43.

Huber, G. P. (1991). 'Organizational Learning: The Contributing Processes and the Literatures'. *Organization Science*, 2: 88–115.

Jaffe, A. (1989). 'Characterizing the "Technological Position" of Firms, with Application to Quantifying Technological Opportunity and Research Spillovers'. *Research Policy*, 18: 87–97.

Joskow, P. L. (1987). 'Contract Duration and Relation Specific Investments: Empirical Evidence from Coal Markets'. *American Economic Review*, 17: 168–85.

——and Rose, N. L. (1985). 'The Effects of Technological Change, Experience, and Environmental Regulation on the Construction Cost of Coal-burning Generating Units'. *Rand Journal of Economics*, 16: 1–27.

Kahneman, D. and Tversky, A. (1982). 'On the Study of Statistical Intuitions'. *Cognition*, 11: 123–41.

Keynes, J. M. (1936). *The General Theory of Employment, Interest and Money*. London: Macmillan.

Killingsworth, M. R. (1982). '"Learning by Doing" and "Investment in Training": A Synthesis of Two Rival Models of the Life Cycle'. *Review of Economic Studies*, 49: 263–71.

Klein, B., Crawford, R. G., and Alchian, A. A. (1978). 'Vertical Integration, Appropriable Rents, and the Competitive Contracting Process'. *Journal of Law and Economics*, 21: 297–326.

Kline, S. J. and Rosenberg, N. (1986). 'An Overview of Innovation', in R. Landau and N. Rosenberg (eds.), *The Positive Sum Strategy: Harnessing Technology for Economic Growth*. Washington, DC: National Academy Press, 275–305.

Knight, J. (1996). *Institutions and Social Conflict*. Cambridge: Cambridge University Press.

Kogut, B. (1988). 'Joint Ventures: Theoretical and Empirical Perspectives'. *Strategic Management Journal*, 9: 319–32.

——and Zander, U. (1992). 'Knowledge of the Firm, Combinative Capabilities, and the Replication of Technology'. *Organization Science*, 3: 383–97.

————(1996). 'What Firms Do? Coordination, Identity, and Learning'. *Organization Science*, 7: 502–18.

Kreps, D. M. (1990). *A Course in Microeconomic Theory*. Princeton: Princeton University Press.

Levitt, B. and March, J. G. (1988). 'Organizational Learning'. *Annual Review of Sociology*, 14: 319–40.

Liebeskind, J. P. (1996). 'Knowledge, Strategy, and the Theory of the Firm'. *Strategic Management Journal*, 17: 93–107.

Malerba, F. (1992). 'Learning by Firms and Incremental Change'. *Economic Journal*, 102: 845–59.

Mansfield, E. (1968). *Industrial Research and Technological Innovation*. New York: W. W. Norton.

——(1988). 'The Speed and Cost of Industrial Innovation in Japan and the United States'. *Management Science*, 34: 1157–68.

——(1991). 'Academic Research and Industrial Innovation'. *Research Policy*, 20: 1–12.

——Schwarz, M., and Wagner, S. (1981). 'Imitation Costs and Patents: An Empirical Study'. *Economic Journal*, 91: 907–18.

March, J. G. and Simon, H. A. (1958). *Organizations*. New York: John Wiley.

—— ——(1993). *Organizations* (2nd edn). Cambridge, Mass.: Blackwell.

Marshall, A. (1965). *Principles of Economics*. London: Macmillan.

Masten, S. E. (ed.) (1996). *Case Studies in Contracting and Organization*. New York: Oxford University Press.

——Meehan, J., and Snyder, E. (1991). 'The Costs of Organization'. *Journal of Law, Economics, and Organization*, 7: 1–22.

Metcalfe, S. (1995). 'The Economic Foundations of Technology Policy: Equilibrium and Evolutionary Perspectives', in P. Stoneman (ed.), *Handbook of the Economics of Innovation and Technological Change*. Oxford: Blackwell, 409–512.

Milgrom, P. and Roberts, J. (1991). 'Adaptive and Sophisticated Learning in Normal Form Games'. *Games and Economic Behavior* 3: 82–100.

Moulin, H. (1986). *Game Theory for the Social Sciences*. New York: New York University Press.

Mowery, D. C. (1980). *The Organization of Industrial Research in Great Britain, 1900–1950*. Economics. Palo Alto, Calif.: Stanford University, 351–74.

——Oxley, J. E., and Silverman, B. S. (1996). 'Strategic Alliances and Interfirm Knowledge Transfer'. *Strategic Management Journal*, 17 (Winter special issue): 77–91.

—— —— ——(1998). 'Technological Overlap and Interfirm Cooperation: Implications for the Resource Based View of the Firm'. *Research Policy*, 27: 507–23.

Neeman, Z. and Orosel, G. O. (1999). 'Herding and the Winner's Curse in Markets with Sequential Bids'. *Journal of Economic Theory*, 85: 91–121.

Nelson, R. R. and Rosenberg, N. (1993). 'Technological Innovation and National Systems', in R. R. Nelson (ed.), *National Innovation Systems: A Comparative Analysis*. New York: Oxford University Press, 3–21.

——and Winter, S. G. (1982). *An Evolutionary Theory of Economic Change*. Cambridge, Mass.: Belknap Press.

Nonaka, I. (1991). 'The Knowledge-creating Company'. *Harvard Business Review*, 69/6: 96–104.

——(1994). 'A Dynamic Theory of Organizational Knowledge Creation'. *Organization Science*, 5: 14–37.

——and Takeuchi, H. (1995). *The Knowledge-creating Company: How Japanese Companies Create the Dynamics of Innovation*. New York: Oxford University Press.

Odagiri, H. and Goto, A. (1993). 'The Japanese System of Innovation: Past, Present, and Future', in R. R. Nelson (ed.), *National Innovation Systems: A Comparative Analysis*. New York: Oxford University Press, 76–114.

Patel, P. and Pavitt, K. (1998). 'Patterns of Technological Activity: Their Measurement and Interpretation', in P. Stoneman (ed.), *Handbook of the Economics of Innovation and Technical Change*. Oxford: Basil Blackwell, 14–51.

Pavitt, K. (1987). 'The Objectives of Technology Policy'. *Science and Public Policy*, 14: 182–8.

Peck, M. J. (1962). 'Inventions in the Postwar American Aluminum Industry', in R. R. Nelson (ed.), *The Rate and Direction of Inventive Activity*. Princeton: Princeton University Press, 279–98.

Penrose, E. T. (1959). *The Theory of the Growth of the Firm*. Oxford: Basil Blackwell.

Polanyi, M. (1967). *The Tacit Dimension*. Garden City, NY: Doubleday.

Popper, K. (1959). *The Logic of Scientific Discovery*. London: Hutchinson.

Prahalad, C. K. and Hamel, G. (1990). 'The Core Competence of the Corporation'. *Harvard Business Review*, 68/3: 79–91.

Rabin, M. (1998). 'Psychology and Economics'. *Journal of Economic Literature*, 36: 11–46.

Rapping, L. (1965). 'Learning and World War II Production Functions'. *Review of Economics and Statistics*, 47: 81–6.

Romer, P. M. (1990). 'Endogenous Technological Change'. *Journal of Political Economy*, 98: 71–102.

Rosen, S. (1972). 'Learning by Experience as Joint Production'. *Quarterly Journal of Economics*, 86: 366–82.

Rosenberg, N. (1974). 'Science, Innovation, and Economic Growth'. *Economic Journal*, 84: 90–108.

——(1982). *Inside the Black Box*. Cambridge: Cambridge University Press.

——(1985). 'The Commercial Exploitation of Science by American Industry', in K. B. Clark, R. H. Hayes, and C. Lorenz (eds.), *The Uneasy Alliance: Managing the Productivity–Technology Dilemma*. Cambridge, Mass.: Harvard Business School Press, 19–51.

—— and Steinmueller, W. E. (1988). 'Why Are Americans Such Poor Imitators'. *American Economic Review*, 78: 229–34.

Scharfstein, D. and Stein, J. (1990). 'Herd Behavior and Investment'. *American Economic Review*, 80: 465–79.

Schumpeter, J. A. (1942). *Capitalism, Socialism and Democracy*. London: Allen and Unwin.

——(1951). *The Theory of Economic Development*. Cambridge, Mass.: Harvard University Press.

Senge, P. M. (1990). *The Fifth Discipline: The Art and Practice of the Learning Organization*. New York: Doubleday.

Shelanski, H. A. and Klein, P. G. (1995). 'Empirical Research in Transaction Cost Economics'. *Journal of Law, Economics, and Organization*, 11: 335–61.

Shuen, A. (1994). *Technology Sourcing and Learning Strategies in the Semiconductor Industry*. Doctoral dissertation, Walter A. Haas School of Business, University of California at Berkeley.

Simon, H. A. (1955). 'A Behavioral Model of Rational Choice'. *Quarterly Journal of Economics*, 69: 99–118.

——(1957a). *Administrative Behavior: A Study of Decision-making Processes in Administrative Organization*. New York: Macmillan.

——(1957b). *Models of Man: Social and Rational; Mathematical Essays on Rational Human Behavior in a Social Setting*. New York: Wiley.

Smith, A. (1976). *The Wealth of Nations*. Chicago: University of Chicago Press. (Original work published 1776)

Stalk, G., Evans, P., and Shulman, L. E. (1992). 'Competing on Capabilities: The New Rules of Corporate Strategy'. *Harvard Business Review*, 70/2: 57–69.

Stigler, G. J. (1961). 'The Economics of Information'. *Journal of Political Economy*, 69: 213–25.

Teece, D. J. (1977). 'Technology Transfer by Multinational Firms: The Resource Cost of Transferring Technological Know-how'. *Economic Journal*, 87: 242–61.

——(1986). 'Profiting from Technological Innovation: Implications for Integration, Collaboration, Licensing and Public Policy'. *Research Policy*, 15: 285–305.

——(1988). 'Technological Change and the Nature of the Firm', in G. Dosi, C. Freeman, R. R. Nelson, G. Silverberg, and L. Soete (eds.), *Technical Change and Economic Theory*. New York: Pinter, 256–81.

——(1989). 'Inter-organizational Requirements of the Innovation Process'. *Managerial and Decision Economics*, 10 (Spring special issue): 35–42.

——(1992). 'Competition, Cooperation, and Innovation: Organizational Arrangements for Regimes of Rapid Technological Progress'. *Journal of Economic Behavior and Organization*, 18: 1–25.

——(1996). 'Firm Organization, Industrial Structure, and Technological Innovation'. *Journal of Economic Behavior and Organization*, 31: 193–224.

——(1998). 'Capturing Value from Knowledge Assets: The New Economy, Markets for Know-how, and Intangible Assets'. *California Management Review*, 40/3: 55–79.

—— and Armour, H. O. (1977). 'Innovation and Divestiture in the U.S. Oil Industry', in D. J. Teece (ed.), *R&D in Energy Implications of Petroleum Industry Coorganization*. Palo Alto, Calif.: Institute for Energy Studies, Stanford University, 7–93.

—— and Pisano, G. (1994). 'The Dynamic Capabilities of Firms: An Introduction'. *Industrial and Corporate Change*, 3: 537–56.

—— —— and Shuen, A. (1997). 'Dynamic Capabilities and Strategic Management'. *Strategic Management Journal*, 18: 509–33.

—— Rumelt, R., Dosi, G., and Winter, S. (1994). 'Understanding Corporate Coherence: Theory and Evidence'. *Journal of Economic Behavior and Organization*, 23: 1–30.

Tversky, A. and Kahneman, D. (1974). 'Judgment under Uncertainty: Heuristics and Biases'. *Science*, 185: 1124–31.

—— —— (1983). 'Extensional versus Intuitive Reasoning: The Conjunction Fallacy in Probabilistic Judgment'. *Psychological Review*, 90: 293–315.

Warner, M. (ed.) (1996). *International Encyclopedia of Business and Management*. New York: Routledge.

Wernerfelt, B. (1984). 'A Resource-based View of the Firm'. *Strategic Management Journal*, 5: 171–80.

Westney, D. E. and Sakakibara, K. (1986). 'The Role of Japan-based R&D in Global Technology Strategy', in M. Hurowitch (ed.), *Technology in the Modern Corporation*. London: Pergamon, 217–32.

Williamson, O. E. (1975). *Markets and Hierarchies: Analysis and Antitrust Implications*. New York: Free Press.

—— (1985). *The Economic Institutions of Capitalism: Firms, Markets, Relational Contracting*. New York: Free Press.

—— (1996). *The Mechanisms of Governance*. New York: Oxford University Press.

—— (1999). *Strategy Research: Governance and Competence Perspectives*. Berkeley: Business and Public Policy.

Winter, S. G. (1971). 'Satisficing, Selection, and the Innovation Remnant'. *Quarterly Journal of Economics*, 85: 237–61.

—— (1986). 'Schumpeterian Competition in Alternative Technological Regimes', in R. Day and G. Elliasson (eds.), *The Dynamics of Market Economies*. Amsterdam: North Holland, 199–232.

—— (1987). 'Knowledge and Competence as Strategic Assets', in D. J. Teece (ed.), *The Competitive Challenge: Strategies for Industrial Innovation and Renewal*. Cambridge, Mass.: Ballinger, 159–84.

—— (1988). 'On Coase, Competence, and the Corporation'. *Journal of Law, Economics, and Organization*, 4: 163–80.

Wright, T. P. (1936). 'Factors Affecting the Cost of Airplanes'. *Journal of the Aeronautical Sciences*, 3: 122–8.

Zimmerman, M. B. (1982). 'Learning Effects and the Commercialization of New Energy Technologies: The Case of Nuclear Power'. *Bell Journal of Economics*, 13: 297–310.

Zuscovitch, E. (1986). 'The Economic Dynamics of Technologies Development'. *Research Policy*, 15: 175–86.

Research Directions for Knowledge Management

Ikujiro Nonaka and David J. Teece

The Need for Transdisciplinary Enquiry

The emerging interest in knowledge management requires, and will probably receive, considerable attention and be a focus of scholarly enquiry. As research advances, it ought to be especially sensitive to preserving and building on the already significant literature concerning the management of technology, entrepreneurship, innovation and business strategy. Indeed, there is a real danger that knowledge management will become discredited if it proceeds in ignorance of this large body of existing literature, as it would thereby create unnecessary intellectual clutter and confusion. Properly understood, the knowledge management umbrella can be a convenient rubric for integrating important work in accounting, economics, entrepreneurship, organizational behaviour, philosophy, marketing, sociology and strategy. Each of these fields provides important insights into one aspect or another of knowledge management, whereas standing alone none provides an integrating framework. What is required is transdisciplinary research that goes beyond mere interdisciplinary activity.

Some Research Issues

While there are many potentially valid research issues that be could identified, there are several topics that are particularly salient and warrant special attention. These are the following.

The assembling of evidence to test the proposition that firm-level competitive advantage in open economies flows from difficult-to-replicate knowledge assets

This proposition, advanced by the editors, is one that may not be uniformly accepted. The empirical evidence needs to be further developed.

There clearly is some seemingly contradictory evidence, but perhaps this tends to prove the rule. For example, regulations (such as state and federal telecom regulations in the US) create rent-seeking opportunities that arise

Reprinted with permission from *Managing Industrial Knowledge: Creation, Transfer and Utilization* (SAGE Publications, 2001), edited by Ikujiro Nonaka and David Teece, pp. 330–335.

from the ability to out-lawyer or out-influence one's rivals in the courts and political arenas. Witness the success of MCI in entering the long-distance phone markets in the United States in the 1970s or the political alliance against Microsoft that has leaned on the US Department of Justice to cripple Microsoft. Such instances illustrate that government regulations, which frequently serve to limit competition, create incentives for firms to expend resources to influence regulation in ways that favour particular competitors over others.

As another example, trade barriers are still ubiquitous in many countries, and there are domestic policies that shield competitors (such as government restrictions) on entry into particular markets. Accordingly, there are more than a few nooks and crannies where rents still flow from old-fashioned restrictions on trade (the protected French automobile industry and US dairy industry, for example). Domestic competitors may compete away some of these rents unless there are further restrictions on entry or if there are scale effects that favour incumbents.

However, surveys of industries exposed to global competition (and not shielded by governmentally imposed controls) will demonstrate that superior profits stem from intangible assets, such as know-how, customer relationships, brands and superior business processes. One indicator of the new regime is how the sources of wealth creation have changed over time. John D. Rockefeller, Andrew Carnegie, Henry Ford and other capitalists in the late nineteenth and early twentieth centuries, gained wealth in ways rather different from Bill Gates (Microsoft), Richard Branson (Virgin), Lawrence Ellison (Oracle), Michael Dell (Dell Computers) and Gordon Moore (Intel). An analysis of industrial and business wealth creation today might be rather suggestive of the role of intangible assets and dynamic capabilities.

The task is quite challenging methodologically. To analyse these issues quantitatively, one would need to establish measures for intangible assets as well as dynamic capabilities (the entrepreneurial way in which such assets are deployed). However, as an interim step, qualitative historical comparisons can be made. More quantitative approaches are also possible, such as using histories of matched pairs of leading firms analysed with non-parametric statistics, where the 'treatment' is investment in intangibles or some other such proxies for intangible assets (see Teece, 1981). Other approaches that are initial steps in this direction include Hirschey and Weygandt (1985), who demonstrated that Tobins Q ratios are cross-sectionally correlated with R&D intensity.

Making greater efforts to quantify the value of intangible assets

Balance sheets prepared under Generally Accepted Accounting Practices endeavour to represent the firm's tangible assets, but completely omit intangibles – with the exception of goodwill. As a consequence, balance sheets are, at best, a poor guide to the value of an enterprise: at worst, they can be almost useless and quite misleading.

There have been various efforts to create adjusted balance sheets by capitalizing the value of income streams earned by certain intangibles, most notably technological know-how, brands and customer relationships (see Lev and Songiannis, 1995). This is a very useful beginning and is suggestive of further work that can be done.

The value of some types of intellectual property can be observed when certain rights of use are sold (licensed) or exchanged (cross-licensed) in arm's-length transactions. Patent, trade secret and copyright licences are not infrequently granted. Royalty rates are sometimes reported publicly, and vary considerably by sector and the strength of the intellectual property rights involved. The orders of magnitude – into double digits as a percentage of sales for very valuable patents and patent portfolios – suggest that intellectual property can have great value. Brands, likewise, can have great value.

Understand generic inputs, idiosyncratic inputs and profitability

The information/knowledge/competences dimensions of inputs (especially intangibles) used to create products remains almost completely unexplored in economics and strategy. There is some recognition that information economics does not conform too much to standard economic theory (see Arrow, 1962). Indeed, the economics of knowledge and competence (which is distinct from the economics of information) is even more primitive.

As with information, the development of knowledge and competence involves certain important costs, but it is different in that the marginal cost of subsequent use is by no means zero. As with ordinary (generic) inputs, knowledge assets and other intangibles are required in production on a repetitive/continuous basis. Another difference is that the costs of transfer are generally high and, as noted, such assets are difficult to trade.

Also, because these 'inputs' cannot be purchased on the market, the growth of the firm is limited in the short run by the 'stock' of such intangibles and competences possessed by the firm. In the longer run, investment in training can soften these restraints.

Further research is clearly needed on imitation and replication. Relevant research now exists in the form of the study of the replication of quality processes and best practices (see Szukanski, 1993, and Cole, 1995). Because of the tacit elements of knowledge, replication can only be accomplished internally; imitation from the outside is difficult. Thus, value flows from a profitable business model undergirded by intangible assets and supported by business processes with a high tacit component.

It is obviously desirable to test such a theory. However, if it is possible to identify circumstances where these factors are at play, then investment opportunities abound. Put differently, any researcher who can work this out can also make money on Wall Street, assuming such characteristics are not already fully understood by investors. Accordingly, the internal credibility of any published statistical analysis is questionable. Nevertheless, empirical work along these lines would be of great interest and ought to be strongly encouraged. An important starting point will be coming up with acceptable operational indices of superior financial performance. Market-based approaches (such as Tobins Q) are likely to be preferable.

Explore the importance of entrepreneurial versus administrative capabilities

In today's world of converging technology and markets, rapid innovation can transform markets overnight. Administrative systems that effect organizational control, while necessary, no longer provide the underpinnings of value creation. Control of internal cash flow is, likewise, of marginal value. If not astutely crafted, administrative systems can stifle initiative and weaken performance-based incentives. Moreover, they no longer suffice for value creation because the relevant organizational skills are so ubiquitous.

Accordingly, performance differentials should open up between firms that excel at the entrepreneurial, while nevertheless possessing administrative skills. Firms that are more entrepreneurial are likely to rely on more high-powered incentives, are likely to be more decentralized and have open and transparent governance. Such firms are likely to favour investment in innovative activities, but not necessarily by establishing centralized R&D facilities. A changing kaleidoscope of alliances and joint ventures is also likely to characterize firms that elevate the entrepreneurial over the administrative. Characteristics of such 'high flex' Silicon Valley-type organizations are identified elsewhere (Teece, 1996), suggesting obvious possibilities for empirical research.

Reflections on the Berkeley Initiative

Throughout this book and in the Berkeley Forum, it has been clearly demonstrated that researchers and practitioners from diversified fields have been involved in developing knowledge-based theories and practices. In the era of the knowledge society, nothing much can be explained without the concept of knowledge. While management researchers initiated the present wave of research, scholars and practitioners from other fields – such as psychology, linguistics, cognitive science, philosophy, anthropology, city and regional planning, sociology and economics – are now joining the fray.

As these fields branched out from philosophy, the interrelationships among them have been vague and messy. The knowledge paradigm can encourage researchers to escape from out of this jungle.

Looking back over the past three years of the Berkeley Forum, we note that the first year's Forum was mainly populated by strategy and management researchers. In the second year, quite a few renowned economists and psychologists joined. In the third year, additional researchers from anthropology, city and regional planning, as well as sociology joined. While research in management may have stimulated initial breakthroughs, insights and methodologies from other well-established fields are now driving much of the enquiry. The challenge now is whether or not we can unify them into a new paradigm of social science that would help us understand a wide variety of human activities in the emerging knowledge economy.

There are quite a few hurdles standing in the way of a new paradigm. In these closing remarks, we will briefly discuss three important requirements for future success.

First, as noted earlier, we need to conduct transdisciplinary research – that is, integrate different disciplinary approaches. Insightful enquiry into the nature of knowledge often requires flexible combinations of different disciplines. Transdisciplinary research is, however, not just interdisciplinary (merely combining two or more different approaches) – it goes further, integrating existing approaches and creating a new view of human behaviour. These approaches include cognition, group activities, and corporate management. For example, knowledge-based theories of the firm and organization may be constructed by integrating the theories concerning firm boundaries, cognition and action, language, knowledge creation and leadership.

Second, we need to further expand the unit of analysis for knowledge-based theories and practices. In particular, it should range from individual to group, firm to industry and region to nation. Currently, while some areas are well researched, others are not. An even harder challenge is to coherently connect research with different units of analysis. Although each unit is expected to provide important insights, all must be integrated in order to provide the entire picture of the new paradigm.

Third, we need to deepen our understanding of different types of 'group' epistemology, which is a shared discipline of knowledge creation within a group. While, traditionally, philosophers have been working on individual epistemology, knowledge-based theorists from management fields have introduced the concept of corporate epistemology. The concept has helped us understand the diversification of different management styles among successful firms. This 'group' can be an organization, community, region, city or nation, as well as a corporation. As traditional social science fields such as psychology, sociology, anthropology and economics have been working on these units, insights from such fields would be helpful in enhancing our understanding of different levels of 'group' epistemology.

They should be fully integrated if our understanding of the knowledge-creation processes is to be comprehensive.

We hope that interested researchers and practitioners are all heading towards the establishment of a new paradigm. We are especially optimistic that more philosophers will find this initiative interesting and regard it as an opportunity. We believe that building a philosophical foundation is the key to the development of a unified theory.

The journey may be long, but the torch has been well and truly lit. We believe that a new paradigm will be a major driving force, enabling a better understanding of the business firm in our Internet-enabled knowledge-based economy.

References

Arrow, K. (1962) 'Economic welfare and the allocation of resources for invention', in R. Nelson (ed.), *The Rate and Direction of Inventive Activity*. Princeton, NJ: Princeton University Press.

Cole, R. (1995) *The Death and Life of the American Quality Movement*. New York: Oxford University Press.

Hirschey, M., and Weygandt, J. (1985) 'Amortization policy for advertising and research and development expenditures', *Journal of Accounting Research*, 23: 326–35.

Lev, B., and Sougiannis, T. (1995) 'The capitalization, amortization, value relevance of R&D', unpublished working paper.

Szulanski, G. (1993) 'Intrafirm transfer of best practice, appropriate capabilities, organizational barriers to appropriation', working paper, INSEAD.

Teece, D. (1981) 'Internal organization and economic performance: an empirical analysis of the profitability of principal firms', *Journal of Industrial Economics*, 30 (2): 173–99.

Teece, D. (1996) 'Firm organization, industrial structure, and technological innovation', *Journal of Economic Behavior and Organization*, 31: 193–224.

Part III

MARKET ENTRY AND LICENSING
STRATEGIES FOR INNOVATIVE FIRMS

Capturing Value from Technological Innovation: Integration, Strategic Partnering, and Licensing Decisions

DAVID J. TEECE

School of Business Administration
University of California
Berkeley, California 94720

The competitive potential embedded in new technology is not always captured by the innovator. Follower firms, customers, and suppliers are often the principal beneficiaries. When innovating firms lose to followers or imitators, the reason is often the failure of the innovator to build or access competitive capacity in activities, such as manufacturing, which are complementary to the innovation. This paper analyzes the make-or-buy decision with respect to these capacities in different competitive environments, including that of rapid technological change and easy imitation. Often it is pointless for firms to invest in R&D unless they are also willing to invest in the development of certain complementary capacities, at home or abroad.

It is commonly recognized that firms responsible for technological breakthroughs and for technological enhancement of existing products and processes are often unable to commercialize the product so that the product concept ultimately fails. Myriads of would-be innovators have discovered that technical success is necessary but not sufficient for establishing economic utility and commercial acceptance. A less commonly recognized but equally important phenomenon is the firm that is first to commercialize a new product concept but fails to extract economic value from the innovation, even though it is of great value to consumers

MARKETING — NEW PRODUCTS
PLANNING — CORPORATE

INTERFACES **18**: 3 May-June 1988 (pp. 46-61)

Reprinted by permission. Copyright © 1988, the Institute for Operations Research and the Management Sciences, 7240 Parkway Drive, Suite 310, Hanover, MD 21076, USA.

and is the source of economic rents (profits) to competitors. The phenomenon unquestionably exists and has obvious significance for the dynamic efficiency of the economy as well as for the distribution of income, domestically and internationally. In the international context, it has important ramifications for economic relations, for commercial policy, and for corporate strategy.

I offer a framework that may shed light on the factors that determine who wins from innovation: the firm that is first to market or those that follow. The follower firms may or may not be imitators. The framework seems useful for explaining the share of the profits from innovation accruing to the innovator compared to the followers (Figure 1), and for explaining a variety of interfirm activities such as joint ventures, coproduction agreements, cross

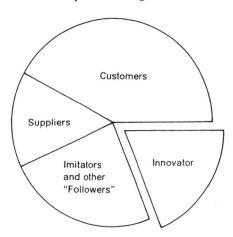

Figure 1: The benefits from innovation, sometimes referred to as economic rents, are divided among innovator, imitators, suppliers, and customers. A normative framework developed in this paper can guide innovating firms to capture a large portion of the rents in environments where imitation is easy.

distribution arrangements, and technological licensing.

The Phenomenon

The EMI Scanner is a classic case of a losing innovation [Martin 1984]. By the early '70s, the UK firm, Electrical Musical Industries (EMI) Ltd., was producing a variety of products including phonographic records, movies, and advanced electronics. EMI had developed high resolution TVs in the '30s, pioneered airborne radar during World War II, and developed the UK's first all solid-state computers in 1952.

In the late '60s Godfrey Houndsfield, an EMI senior research engineer, engaged in research on pattern recognition, which resulted in his displaying a scan of a pig's brain. Subsequent clinical work established that computerized axial tomography (CAT) was viable for generating cross-sectional "views" of the human body; this was the greatest advance in radiology since the discovery of X-rays in 1895.

The US was the major market for the product. However, EMI was UK based and lacked a marketing capability or presence in medical electronics in the United States. Because the scanner was a complex product, it required an organization that had service and training capacity as well as marketing ability. EMI's competitors, such as Siemens and GE, had these assets.

A market for CAT scanners rapidly emerged after EMI displayed advanced prototypes in Chicago in November 1972. By 1975, EMI had an order backlog of £55 million. Expectations of £100 million a year in scanner sales by EMI were projected by investors, and stock analysts began to think of EMI as shaping up for a success of the magnitude of Xerox's in the previous decade.

By the mid-'70s imitators had emerged, most notably GE with faster scanners tailored more closely to the needs of the medical profession and supported in the field by experienced marketing and service personnel. Simultaneously, health care regulations in the United States imposed a requirement that hospitals obtain certificates of need before purchasing high priced items like scanners. EMI was forced to sell its scanner business and in April of 1980 announced a sale to GE. At that time EMI indicated that it had lost £26 million on the business. Meanwhile, GE's operations were believed to be quite profitable. Subsequently, GE and Johnson & Johnson each paid EMI $100 million in damages for patent infringement.

Other examples of losing innovators are RC Cola, Bowmar, Xerox, and de Havilland. RC Cola, a small beverage company, was the first to introduce cola in a can and the first to introduce diet cola. Both Coca Cola and Pepsi followed almost immediately, depriving RC of any significant advantage from its innovation. Bowmar, which introduced the pocket calculator, was not able to withstand competition from Texas Instruments, Hewlett Packard, and others and went out of business. Xerox failed to succeed with its entry into the office computer business, even though Apple succeeded with the MacIntosh, which contained many of Xerox's key product ideas, such as the mouse and icons. The de Havilland Comet saga has some of the same features. The Comet I

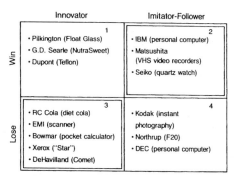

Figure 2: There is lore, but little analytics, to explain when and why innovators lose out to imitators and followers. Xerox, for instance, has been first to commercialize key computer technologies developed in its Parc facility; however, in several instances it has failed to recover its investment, while competitors, such as Apple, have done fabulously well with derivative technology.

jet was introduced into the commercial airline business two years or so before Boeing introduced the 707, but through an unfortunate series of events, de Havilland failed to capitalize on its substantial early advantage.

Capturing the Rent Stream from Innovation: Basic Building Blocks

In order to develop a coherent framework within which to explain the distribution of outcomes illustrated in Figure 2, three fundamental building blocks must first be described: the appropriability regime, complementary assets, and the dominant design paradigm.

Regimes of Appropriability

The term *regime of appropriability* refers to aspects of the commercial environment, excluding firm and market structure, that govern an innovator's ability to capture the rents associated with innovation. The most important dimensions of such a regime are the nature of the technology and the efficacy of legal mechanisms of protection such as patents, copyrights, and trade secrets.

It has long been known that patents do not work in practice as they do in theory. Rarely, if ever, do patents confer perfect appropriability, although they do afford considerable protection on new chemical products and on some mechanical inventions. Many patents can be "invented around" at modest costs. They are especially ineffective at protecting process innovations. Often patents provide little protection because the legal requirements for upholding their validity or for proving their infringement are high.

In some industries, particularly where the innovation is embedded in processes, trade secrets are a viable alternative to patents. Trade secret protection is possible, however, only if a firm can put its product before the public and still keep the underlying technology secret. Usually only chemical formulas and industrial-commercial processes (for example, cosmetics and recipes) can be protected as trade secrets after the products are "out."

The degree to which knowledge is tacit or codified also affects the ease with which it can be imitated. Codified knowledge is easy to transmit and receive and is more exposed to industrial espionage and the like. Tacit knowledge by definition is difficult to articulate, and so its transfer is difficult unless those with the know-how can demonstrate it to others [Teece 1981].

Empirical research by Levin, Klevorick, Nelson, and Winter [1984] demonstrates that patents and trade secrets often do not afford significant protection. Their results show considerable collinearity among certain mechanisms of appropriability. They conclude that "at the expense of some oversimplification, the data suggest that the mechanism of appropriation may reduce to two dimensions: one associated with the use of patents, the other with lead time and learning-curve advantages. For process innovations, secrecy is closely connected with exploiting lead time and learning advantages. For product innovation, sales and service efforts

Who wins from innovation?

are part of the package" [p. 18]. These findings are tentative and must be interpreted with care. They do, however, indicate that methods of appropriability vary markedly across industries and probably within industries as well.

The property rights environment within which a firm operates can thus be classified according to the nature of the technology and the efficacy of the legal system to assign and protect intellectual property. While a gross simplification, a dichotomy can be drawn between products for which the appropriability regime is "tight" (technology is relatively easy to protect) and those for which it is "weak" (technology is almost impossible to protect). An example of the former is the formula for Coca Cola syrup; an example of the latter is the Simplex algorithm in linear programming.

The Dominant Design Paradigm

Thomas Kuhn's seminal work [1970] describes the history and social psychology of science on the basis of the notion of a paradigm. The concept of a paradigm as applied to scientific development is broader than that of a theory. In fact, a paradigm is a Gestalt that embodies a set of scientific assumptions and beliefs about certain classes of phenomenon. Kuhn suggests that there are two stages in the evolutionary development of a given branch of a science: the preparadigmatic stage, when there is no single generally accepted conceptual treatment of the phenomenon in a field of study, and the paradigmatic stage, which begins when a body of theory appears to have passed the canons of scientific acceptability. The emergence of a dominant paradigm signals scientific maturity, and the acceptance of agreed upon standards by which what Kuhn calls "normal" scientific research can proceed. These standards remain in force unless or until the paradigm is overturned. Revolutionary science is what overturns normal science, as when the Copernicus theories of astronomy overturned Ptolemy's in the 17th century.

Abernathy and Utterback [1978] and Dosi [1982] have provided a treatment of the technological evolution of an industry which appears to parallel Kuhnian notions of scientific evolution. In the early stages of industry development, product designs are fluid, manufacturing processes are loosely and adaptively organized, and generalized capital is used in production. Competition among firms manifests itself in competition among designs, which are markedly different from each other. This might be called the preparadigmatic stage of an industry.

At some point after considerable trial and error in the marketplace, one design

or a narrow class of designs begins to emerge as the more promising. Such a design must be able to meet a whole set of user needs in a relatively complete fashion. The Model T Ford, the IBM 360, and the Douglas DC-3 are examples of dominant designs in the automobile, computer, and aircraft industries.

Once a dominant design emerges, competition shifts to price and away from design. Competitive success then shifts to a

---

Expectations of £100 million a year in scanner sales by EMI were projected.

---

whole new set of variables. Scale and learning become much more important, and specialized capital is deployed as competing firms seek to lower unit costs by exploiting economies of scale and learning. Reduced uncertainty over product design provides an opportunity to amortize specialized long-lived investments.

Innovation is not necessarily halted once the dominant design emerges; as Clarke [1985] points out, it can occur lower down in the design hierarchy. For instance, a "V" cylinder configuration emerged in automobile engine blocks during the 1930s with the emergence of the Ford V-8 engine. Niches were quickly found for it. Moreover, once the product design stabilizes, there is likely to be a surge of process innovation as producers attempt to lower production costs for the new product (Figure 3).

The Abernathy-Utterback framework does not characterize all industries. It

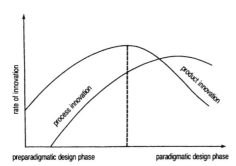

Figure 3: When new technologies are commercialized, process innovation often follows product innovation. As the rate of product innovation slows, designs in the marketplace tend to become more standardized, providing the opportunity for large-scale production and the deployment of specialized assets. The nature of competition and the requirements for marketplace success shift dramatically as the market evolves from its early preparadigmatic phase (with competition based on features and product performance) to its post paradigmatic phase (with competition based more on price).

seems more suited to mass markets where consumer tastes are relatively homogeneous. It appears less characteristic of small niche markets where the absence of scale and learning economies attaches much less of a penalty to multiple designs. In these instances, generalized equipment will be employed in production.

The existence of a dominant design watershed is of great significance to the distribution of rents between innovator and follower. The innovator may have been responsible for the fundamental scientific breakthroughs as well as the basic design of the new product. However, if imitation is relatively easy, imitators may enter the fray, modifying the product in important ways, yet relying on the fundamental designs pioneered by the innovator. When the game of musical chairs

stops, and a dominant design emerges, the innovator might well end up at a disadvantage. Hence, when imitation is possible, and when it occurs coupled with design modification before a dominant design emerges, a follower's modified product has a good chance of being anointed as the industry standard.

Complementary Assets

Let the unit of analysis be innovation. An innovation consists of certain technical knowledge about how to do things better. Assume that the know-how in question is partly codified and partly tacit. In order for such know-how to generate a rent stream, it must be sold or used in the market.

In almost all cases, the successful commercialization of an innovation requires that the know-how in question be utilized in conjunction with such services as marketing, competitive manufacturing, and after-sales support. These services are often obtained from complementary assets that are specialized. For example, the commercialization of a new drug is likely to require the dissemination of information over a specialized information channel. In some cases, as when the innovation is systemic, the complementary assets may be other parts of a system. For instance, computer hardware typically requires the development of specialized software, both for the operating system and for applications. Even when an innovation is autonomous, the services of certain complementary assets will be needed for successful commercialization (Figure 4).

Whether the assets required for least cost production and distribution are specialized to the innovation turns out to be

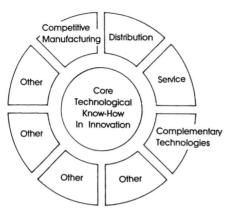

Figure 4: **In order to innovate, firms need complementary assets and technologies to support the commercialization of some core technology. These assets typically include manufacturing, distribution, and sales and service. They may already reside in-house. If not, they are conceivably available through merger, acquisition, or contract. The key consideration is the terms upon which they are available to the innovator.**

important in the development presented below. Complementary assets can be generic, specialized, or cospecialized.

Generic assets are general purpose assets that do not need to be tailored to the innovation. Specialized assets are those on which the innovation depends, tailored to that innovation. Cospecialized assets are those for which there is a bilateral dependence. For instance, specialized repair facilities are needed to support Mazda's rotary engine. These assets are cospecialized because of the mutual dependence of the innovation and the repair facility. Container shipping required a similar deployment of cospecialized assets in specially designed ships and terminals. However, the dependence of trucking on containerized shipping was less than that of containerized shipping on trucking:

trucks can convert from containers to flat beds at low cost. An example of a generic asset would be the manufacturing facilities needed to make running shoes. Generalized equipment can be used except for the mold for the sole.

Implications for Profitability

These three concepts can now be related in a way that will shed light on the imitation process and the distribution of rents between innovator and follower. In those few instances where the innovator has ironclad patent or copyright protection, or where trade secrets effectively deny imitators access to the product, the innovator is almost assured of capturing the lion's share of available profits for some period of time. Even if the innovator does not have the desirable complementary assets, ironclad protection of intellectual property will afford it time to obtain them. If these assets are generic, a contractual relationship may suffice; the innovator may simply license its technology. Specialized R&D firms are viable in such an environment. Universal Oil Products, an R&D firm developing refining processes for the petroleum industry, was such an innovator. If, however, the needed complementary assets are specialized or cospecialized, contractual relationships are exposed to hazards, because one or both parties will have to commit capital to certain irreversible investments, which will be valueless if the relationship between innovator and licensee breaks down. Accordingly, the innovator may want to integrate by owning the specialized and cospecialized assets. Fortunately, the factors which make for difficult imitation will enable the innovator to build or acquire those complementary assets without competing with innovators for their control.

Competition from imitators is thus muted in tight appropriability regimes, which sometimes characterizes the petrochemical industry. In this industry, the protection offered by patents is fairly easily enforced. A factor that helps the licensor is that most petrochemical processes

---

RC Cola was the first to introduce cola in a can and the first to introduce diet cola.

---

are designed around a specific variety of catalysts that can be kept proprietary. An agreement not to analyze the catalyst can be extracted from licensees, affording extra protection. Even if such requirements are violated by licensees, the innovator is still well positioned: the most important properties of a catalyst are related to its physical structure, and the process for generating this structure cannot be deduced from structural analysis alone. Every reaction technology a company acquires is thus accompanied by an ongoing dependence on the innovating company for the catalyst appropriate to the plant design. Failure to comply with the licensing contract can result in a cutoff in the supply of the catalyst and possibly in facility closure.

Similarly, if an innovator comes to market in the preparadigmatic phase with a sound product concept but the wrong design, a tight appropriability regime will afford it the time needed to get the

design right. The best initial design concepts often turn out to be hopelessly wrong, but if the innovator possesses an impenetrable thicket of patents, or simply has technology that is difficult to copy, then the market may well afford the innovator the time necessary to find the right design.

However, tight appropriability is the exception rather than the rule. Most innovators must formulate and implement complex business strategies to keep imitators at bay. The nature of the strategic challenge will vary according to whether the industry is in the paradigmatic or preparadigmatic phase.

In the preparadigmatic phase, the innovator, with little or no intellectual property protection available for its technology, must be careful to let the basic design float until the design seems likely to become the industry standard. In some industries this may be difficult as little opportunity exists for product modification. In microelectronics, for example, designs become locked in when the circuitry is chosen. Product modification is limited to debugging and software changes. An innovator must begin the design process anew if the product does not fit the market well. To some extent, new designs are dictated by the need to meet certain compatibility standards so that the new hardware can interface with existing applications software. In one sense, therefore, design for the microprocessor industry today is relatively straightforward: deliver greater power and speed while meeting the industry standards of the existing software base. However, from time to time windows of opportunity allow the introduction of entirely new families of microprocessors that will define a new industry and software standard. Then basic design parameters are less defined and can float until market acceptance is apparent.

The early history of the automobile industry — an industry characterized by a weak appropriability regime — exemplifies the importance of selecting the right design in the preparadigmatic stages. None of the early steam cars survived when the closed-body, internal combustion engine automobile emerged as the dominant design. The steam car, nevertheless, had virtues, such as reliability, that the internal combustion engine autos of that time did not.

The British fiasco with the Comet I is also instructive. De Havilland had picked an early design with significant flaws. By racing on to production, the innovator suffered an irreversible loss of reputation that seemed to prevent it from converting to what subsequently became the dominant design.

In general, innovators in weak appropriability regimes need to be intimately connected with the market so that designs are based on user needs. When multiple parallel and sequential prototyping is feasible, it has clear advantages. Usually, it is too costly. Development costs for a large commercial aircraft can exceed one billion dollars; variations on one theme are all that is possible.

Hence, the probability that the first firm to commercialize a new product design will enter the paradigmatic phase with the dominant design is problematic. The probabilities will be higher the lower the cost of prototyping and the more tightly coupled the firm is to the market. The firm's relationship to the market is a function of organizational design and can be influenced by managerial choices. The cost of prototyping is embedded in the technology and cannot be greatly influenced by managerial decisions. Hence, in industries with large developmental and prototyping costs — where choices are irreversible and where innovation of the product concept is easy — the innovator would be unlikely to emerge as a winner at the end of the preparadigmatic stage if the appropriability regime is weak.

In the preparadigmatic phase, complementary assets do not loom large. Rivalry is focused on trying to identify the design that will dominate the industry. Production volumes are low, and little can be gained from deploying specialized assets since scale economies are unavailable and price is not a principle competitive factor. However, as the leading design or designs are revealed by the market, volumes increase and firms gear up for mass production by acquiring specialized tooling and equipment, and possibly specialized distribution as well. Since these investments are irreversible, they are likely to proceed with caution. Islands of asset specificity will thus begin to form in a sea of generalized assets.

However, as the terms of competition begin to change and prices become increasingly unimportant, complementary assets become critical. Since the core technology is easy to imitate, commercial success depends on the terms under which the required complementary assets can be accessed.

At this point, specialized and cospecialized assets become critically important. Generalized assets, almost by definition, are always available in an industry, and even if they are not, they do not involve significant irreversibilities. Even if there is insufficient capacity, additional capacity can be put in place with little risk. Specialized assets, on the other hand, involve significant irreversibilities and cannot be easily accessed by contract. Recontracting hazards abound when dedicated assets that do not have alternative uses are supported entirely by contractual arrangement [Williamson 1975, 1981, 1985, Teece 1980, 1982, 1985]. Owners of cospecialized assets, such as distribution channels or specialized manufacturing capacity, are clearly advantageously positioned relative to an innovator. Indeed, when they hold an airtight monopoly over specialized assets, and the innovator is in a regime of weak appropriability, they could command all of the rents to the innovation. Even without a monopoly, specialized assets are often not as easy to replicate as the technology. For instance, the technology in cardiac pacemakers was easy to imitate; competitive success was determined by who controlled the specialized marketing. A similar situation exists in the US for personal computers:

> There are a huge number of computer manufacturers, companies that make peripherals (e.g., printers, hard disk drives, floppy disk drives), and software companies. They are all trying to get marketing distributors because they cannot afford to call on all of the US companies directly. They need to go through retail distribution channels, such as Businessland, in order to reach the marketplace. The problem today, however, is that many of these companies are not able to get shelf space and thus are having a very difficult time marketing

their products. The point of distribution is where the profit and the power are in the marketplace today [Norman 1986, p. 438].

Channel Selection Issues

Access to complementary assets is critical if the innovator is to avoid handing over the lion's share of the profits to imitators or to the owners of specialized and cospecialized complementary assets. What controls should the imitator establish over these critical assets?

Many channels can be employed. At one extreme, the innovator could integrate into all of the necessary complementary assets, an option that is probably

---

Patents do not work in practice as they do in theory.

---

unnecessary and prohibitively expensive. The assets and competencies needed may be numerous, even for quite simple technologies. To produce a personal computer, for instance, a company needs expertise in semiconductor technology, display technology, disk-drive technology, networking technology, keyboard technology, and several others. No company, not even IBM, has kept pace in all of these areas by itself.

At the other extreme, from handling all technologies internally the innovator could attempt to access these assets through contractual relationships (for example, component supply contracts, fabrication contracts, and distribution contracts). In many instances, contracts may suffice, although they expose the innovator to various hazards and dependencies that it may want to avoid. In between these two extremes are a myriad of intermediate forms and channels. I will analyze the properties of two extremes and also describe a mixture.

Contractual Modes

The advantages of a contractual solution — whereby the innovator contracts with independent suppliers, manufacturers or distributors — are obvious. The innovator will not have to make the capital expenditures needed to build or buy the assets. This reduces risks as well as cash requirements. Also, contractual relationships can bring added credibility to the innovator, especially if the innovator is unknown and the contractual partner is established and viable. Indeed, arms-length contracting which embodies more than a simple buy-sell agreement is becoming so common and is so multifaceted that the term strategic partnering has been devised to describe it. Even large companies such as IBM are now engaging in it. For IBM, partnering buys access to new technologies enabling the company to learn things they couldn't have learned without many years of trial and error. IBM's arrangement to use Microsoft's MS-DOS operating system software on the IBM PC facilitated the timely introduction of IBM's personal computer into the market. Had IBM developed its own operating system, it would probably have missed the market window.

Smaller, less integrated companies are often eager to sign on with established companies because of the name recognition and reputation spillovers. For instance, Cipher Data Products contracted with IBM to develop a low-priced version of IBM's 3480 0.5 inch streaming cartridge drive, which is likely to become the industry standard. Cipher management recognizes that one of the biggest advantages to dealing with IBM is that, once you've created a product that meets the high quality standards necessary to sell into the IBM world, you can sell into any arena. Similarly, IBM's contract with Microsoft meant instant credibility to Microsoft [McKenna 1985, p. 94].

It is important to recognize that strategic partnering, which is currently very fashionable, exposes the innovator to certain hazards, particularly when the innovator is trying to use contracts to access special capabilities. First, it may be difficult to induce suppliers to make costly irreversible commitments which depend for their success on the success of the innovation. To expect suppliers, manufacturers, and distributors to do so is to expect them to take risks along with the innovator. For the innovator, this poses problems similar to those associated with attracting venture capital. The innovator must persuade its prospective partner that the risk is a good one. The situation is open to opportunistic abuses on both sides. The innovator has incentives to overstate the value of the innovation, while the supplier has incentives to "run with the technology" should the innovation be a success.

Instances of both parties making irreversible capital commitments nevertheless exist. Apple's Laserwriter — a high resolution laser printer which produces near typeset quality text graphics — is a case in point. Apple persuaded Canon to participate in the development of the Laserwriter; Canon provided subsystems from its copiers, but only after Apple contracted to pay for a certain number of copier engines and cases. In short, Apple accepted a good deal of the financial risk in order to induce Canon to assist in the development and production of the Laserwriter. The arrangement appears to have been prudent, yet there were clearly hazards for both sides. It is difficult to write, execute, and enforce complex development contracts, particularly when the design of the new product is still floating, which it often is, even after commercialization. Apple was exposed to the risk that its co-innovator Canon would fail to deliver, and Canon was exposed to the risk that the Apple design and marketing effort would not succeed. Still, Apple's alternatives may have been rather limited, in that it did not have the technology to go it alone.

The current euphoria over strategic partnering may be partially misplaced. Its advantages are being stressed (for example, by McKenna [1985]) without a balanced presentation of costs and risks. These have been described by Williamson [1975, 1985]. Briefly, there is the risk that the partner will not perform according to the innovator's perception of what the contract requires; there is the added danger that the partner may imitate the innovator's technology and attempt to compete with the innovator. The danger is particularly acute if the provider of the complementary asset is uniquely situated with respect to that asset and also can absorb and imitate the technology. Contractual or partnering strategies are unambiguously preferred, however, where the complementary assets are generic and in competitive supply. Because alternatives exist, failure of the partner to perform according to the contract is not particularly damaging on the innovator.

Integration Modes

An alternative organizational arrangement is for the firm to provide the necessary complementary assets internally. This in-house approach facilitates greater control, but it is costly in terms of managerial and financial resources.

There are clear advantages to integration when assets are in fixed supply over the relevant time period. To avoid a speculative price run-up, the assets in question must be acquired by the innovator before their connection with the innovation is public knowledge. If the value of the complementary asset to the innovator leaks out, the owner of a critical complementarity could extract a portion of the rent stream that the innovation was expected to generate. Such bottleneck situations are not uncommon, particularly in distribution.

However, an innovator may not have the time or the money to acquire or build the complementary assets it would like to control. Particularly when imitation is easy, timing becomes critical. Innovators, therefore, need to rank complementary assets as to their importance. If the complementary assets are critical, ownership is warranted, although if the firm is cash constrained, a minority equity position may well be a sensible trade-off. If the complementary asset in question is technology, this calculus needs to be revised in terms of the desired equity position. This is because ownership of complementary enterprises appears to be fraught

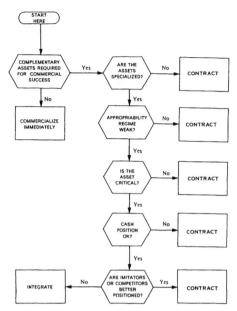

Figure 5: When making R&D and commercialization decisions, managers must identify, preferably ahead of time, the complementary assets the innovation will need for successful commercialization. Contractual alternatives will make strategic sense if the complementary assets are not specialized, or if the innovators' position regarding its intellectual property is ironclad, or for assets which are not critical, or for assets in which the innovator does not have or cannot obtain the necessary financial resources, or for assets in which imitators are in any case already irrevocably better positioned. Otherwise, the integration (in-house) alternative ought to be preferred.

with hazards, as integration tends to destroy incentives and cultures, particularly when a deep hierarchy is involved.

When imitation is easy, building or buying specialized complementary assets must be considered in light of the moves of competitors. Building loses its point if one's imitators can do it faster. Figure 5 summarizes the factors to be considered in deciding between contracting and

building or buying (mixed modes and intermediate solutions are ignored in order to simplify the analysis.)

If the innovator is a large enterprise that controls many of the relevant complementary assets, integration is not likely to be the issue it might be for a smaller company. However, in industries experiencing rapid technological change, no single company is likely to have the full range of expertise needed to bring advanced products to market in a timely and cost-effective fashion. In such industries, integration is an issue for large as well as small firms.

Mixed Modes

Organizational reality rarely affords the possibility of choice among pure forms of economic organization. Integration and contract are, accordingly, rarely seen without some accommodation to each other. The reality of business is that mixed modes — involving the blending of elements of integration and contract — are rather common. Still, in examining such intermediate forms, it is instructive to bear in mind the simple economics of pure forms.

Sometimes mixed modes represent transitional phases. For instance, because computer and telecommunication technologies are converging, firms in each industry are discovering that they need the technical capabilities of the other. This interdependence requires the collaboration of those who design different parts of the system; intense cross-boundary coordination and information flows must be supported. When separate companies collaborate, the parties must often agree on complex protocol issues. Contractual difficulties can be anticipated since the selection of common technical protocols among the parties will often be followed by investments in specialized hardware and software. There is little doubt that this was a key part of IBM's motivation in purchasing 15 percent of PBX manufacturer Rolm in 1983 and expanding that position to 100 percent in 1984. IBM's stake in Intel, which began with a 12 percent purchase in 1982, is most probably not a transitional phase leading to 100 percent purchase, because both companies realized that the two corporate cultures are not very compatible.

An example of how profoundly changing technology can affect the boundaries of the firm — and the identity of the firm at the nexus of contracts needed to develop and manufacture complex products — can be found in the jet fighter business. Avionics now constitutes about one third of the cost of a fighter, up from about 15 percent a decade ago (Figure 6). Avionics is expected to be even more important in the future, both in terms of cost and in terms of performance. Given

the fairly widespread diffusion of airframe and propulsion technology, the superiority of fighters today and in the future will depend primarily upon the sophistication and capability of the aircraft's electronics. Indeed, in the future, computer manufacturers like AT&T and IBM may become prime contractors for advanced weapons systems, including fighters. In a related way, VHSIC technology is regarded as a key factor in reestablishing what the US sees as a necessary degree of operational supremacy for its forces against the numerical superiority of the Soviet Union and the Warsaw Pact. It will be an essential ingredient of new aircraft programs such as the USAF's ATF advanced tactical fighter, the US Navy's VFMX air superiority fighter, and the US Army's LHX light battlefield helicopter, not to mention extensive upgrading of current equipment such as the F-15 and F-16 fighters and AH-64 helicopter [*Jane's All the World's Aircraft* 1983-84, p. 24].

Of particular relevance here is the USAF's advanced tactical fighter (ATF). While it is still too early to discuss

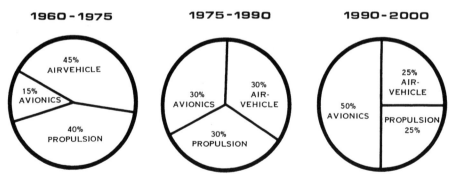

Figure 6: The trend in fighter plane subsystem costs has been away from air vehicle and propulsion and toward avionics, and this trend is likely to continue. An implication is that companies in the electronics industry, like IBM and AT&T, may be prime contractors for future generations of aircraft.

electronics definitively, according to *Jane's* [1983-84, p. 26], a number of technological areas can be identified that will be required in the ATF, including the integration of flight and propulsion control systems, fly-by-wire, and integration of cockpit displays, probably with a voice command system to enhance the HOTAS (hands on throttle and stick). Advanced heads-up display and VHSIC technology will also be critical.

In order to compete in the advanced fighter market in the future, prime contractors will have to be on the leading edge with respect to avionics technology. A manufacturer that fails to develop or acquire such technology must expect to be shut out of a growing portion of the market.

Airframe companies without considerable in-house electronics capability will probably not be able to contract with electronics companies for the requisite subsystems. Because avionics is becoming the core technology that dictates other elements of design, it will not be enough for airframe companies to contract with both avionics and propulsion companies. Indeed, the leading fighter manufacturers — such as General Dynamics and McDonnell Douglas — have developed in-house avionics capabilities. Were these companies to fail to build a substantial in-house capability, it might be impossible, in the future, for them to design competitive fighter planes using avionics subcontractors.

The reason is that complex trade-offs often exist between avionics and air-vehicle design — trade-offs that are much more complex and dynamic than between

air vehicle and propulsion. Moreover, much of the avionics of a fighter plane is specific to that aircraft. In the absence of in-house avionics capabilities, jet fighter manufacturers would be unable, without extremely close collaboration with avionics' subcontractors, to formulate and implement new fighter plane concepts. Moreover, the kind of collaboration required would require deep dependence of a kind very likely to lead to contractual vulnerabilities.

Conclusion

Clearly, the boundaries of an innovating firm are an important strategic variable, particularly when intellectual property protection is weak, as with microelectronics. The control of complementary assets, particularly when they are specialized or cospecialized, helps establish who wins and who loses from innovation. Imitators can do better than innovators if they are better positioned on cost and quality with respect to critical complementary assets, such as manufacturing.

There are important implications for corporate strategy. Except in unusual circumstances, innovating firms must emphasize the development of cost-competitive capabilities in the activities downstream from R&D if they are to profit from investment in R&D. Being first to market is no longer a guarantee of commercial success, particularly if to achieve early market entry the innovating firm engages in risky contracts with manufacturers, distributors, and developers of complementary technologies.

For public policy, a related set of implications follow. Government policy which equates policies to assist innovation with policies to assist R&D is increasingly wide of the mark. Except in special circumstances, national prowess in research and development is neither necessary nor sufficient to ensure that the innovator (rather than followers) captures the greater share of the profits available from innovation. Public policy towards science and technology must recognize how important the technological infrastructure (particularly education at all levels and manufacturing) is to the ability of domestically-based firms to build the requisite competitive capacities needed to capture value from innovation.

Acknowledgments

I thank Raphael Amit, Harvey Brooks, Therese Flaherty, Richard Gilbert, Heather Haveman, Mel Horwitch, Gary Pisano, Richard Rumelt, Raymond Vernon, and Sidney Winter for helpful discussions relating to the subject matter of this paper. A related treatment of the issues in this paper was published in *Research Policy* 1986, Vol. 15, No. 6.

References

Abernathy, W. J. and Utterback, J. M. 1978, "Patterns of industrial innovation," *Technology Review*, Vol. 80, No. 7 (January/July), pp. 40–47.

Clarke, Kim B. 1985, "The interaction of design hierarchies and market concepts in technological evolution," *Research Policy*, Vol. 14, No. 5 (October), pp. 235–251.

Dosi, G. 1982, "Technological paradigms and technological trajectories," *Research Policy*, Vol. 11, No. 3 (June), pp. 147–162.

Jane's All the World's Aircraft 1983-84, McGraw-Hill, New York.

Kuhn, T. 1970, *The Structure of Scientific Revolutions*, University of Chicago Press, Chicago, Illinois.

Levin, R.; Klevorick, A.; Nelson, N.; and Winter, S. 1984, "Survey research on R&D appropriability and technological opportunity,"
unpublished manuscript, Yale University.

Martin, Michael 1984, *Managing Technological Innovation and Enterpreneurship*, Reston Publishing Company, Reston, Virginia.

McKenna, R. 1985, "Market positioning in high technology," *California Management Review*, Vol. 27, No. 3 (Spring), pp. 82–108.

Norman, D. A. 1986, "Impact of entrepreneurship and innovations on the distribution of personal computers," in *The Positive Sum Strategy*, eds: R. Landau and N. Rosenberg, National Academy Press, Washington, DC, pp. 437–439.

Teece, D. J. 1980, "Economics of scope and the scope of the enterprise," *Journal of Economic Behavior and Organization*, Vol. 1, No. 3, pp. 223–247.

Teece, D. J. 1981, "The market for know-how and the efficient international transfer of technology," *Annals of the American Academy of Political and Social Science*, Vol. 458 (November), pp. 81–96.

Teece, D. J. 1982, "Towards an economic theory of the multiproduct firm," *Journal of Economic Behavior and Organization*, Vol. 3, No. 1, pp. 39–63.

Teece, D. J. 1985, "Multinational enterprise, internal governance, and industrial organization," *American Economic Review*, Vol. 75, No. 2 (May), pp. 233–238.

Williamson, O. E. 1975, *Markets and Hierarchies*, The Free Press, New York.

Williamson, O. E. 1981, "The modern corporation: Origins, evolution, attributes," *Journal of Economic Literature*, Vol. 19, No. 4 (December), pp. 1537–1568.

Williamson, O. E. 1985, *The Economic Institutions of Capitalism*, The Free Press, New York.

Managing Intellectual Capital:

LICENSING AND CROSS-LICENSING IN SEMICONDUCTORS AND ELECTRONICS

Peter C. Grindley
David J. Teece

One of the most significant emerging business developments in the last decade has been the proactive management of intellectual capital by innovating firms. While firms have for decades actively managed their physical and financial assets, until quite recently intellectual property (IP) management was a backwater. Top management paid little attention and legal counsel did not participate in major managerial decisions. This is changing. High-technology firms now often have "IP" managers as well as "IT" managers.[1] In some firms considerations of intellectual capital management have expanded from the mere licensing of residual technology to become a central element in technology strategy. This development is spurred by the increasing protection afforded IP worldwide and by the greater importance of technological know-how to competitive advantage. These developments herald a new era for management.

Patents and trade secrets have become a key element of competition in high-technology industries. In electronics and semiconductors, firms continually make large investments in R&D in their attempts to stay at the frontier and to utilize technological developments external to the firm. Fierce competition has put a premium on innovation and on defending IP from unlicensed imitators. As IP owners have taken a more active stance regarding their patent portfolios, industry participants increasingly find it necessary to engage in licensing and cross-licensing.[2] Moreover, and relatedly, royalty rates have risen. The effect has been positive for firms with strong portfolios, who are now able to capture considerable benefit from their patent estates. Firms that are high net users of others' patents have a choice. They must increasingly pay royalties, or they must develop their own portfolios so as to bring something to the table in cross-licensing negotiations.

The new environment affords new challenges. If a firm is to compete with advanced products and processes, it is likely to utilize not only its own technology, but also the patents of others. In many advanced products, the range of technology is too great for a single firm to develop its entire needs internally. In cumulative technology fields such as electronics and semiconductors, one innovation builds on another. There are inevitably overlapping developments and mutually blocking patents. It is likely that firms will need to cross-license patents from others to ensure that they have freedom to manufacture without infringement. Thus in many industries today, firms can generate value from their innovation not only by embedding it in new products and processes, but also through engaging in licensing and cross-licensing.

In electronics and semiconductors, cross-licensing is generally more complex than the exchange of individual patent rights. The size of the patent portfolios of some firms is often too great for it to be feasible to identify individual infringements. Companies may own thousands of patents, used in literally tens of thousands of products, and may add hundreds more each year. With this degree of overlap of technology, companies protect themselves against mutual infringement by cross-licensing portfolios of all current and future patents in a field-of-use, without making specific reference to individual patents. It is simply too cumbersome and costly to license only the specific patents you need for specific products. The portfolio approach reduces transactions costs and allows licensees freedom to design and manufacture without infringement.[3]

An important dimension of field-of-use cross-licensing is the calculation of balancing royalty payments, according to the relative value of the patent portfolios of each party. This calculation is made prospectively, based on a sample of each firm's leading patents. Weight is given to the quality and market coverage of the patents. Desirable portfolios have excellent patents covering technology widely used in the industry. A quality portfolio is a powerful lever in negotiating access to required technology and may lead to significant royalty earnings or, at a minimum, to reduced payments to others. Obviously, a firm which is a large net user of other firms' patents, without contributing comparable IP in exchange, is likely to have to pay significant royalties.

Many managers now understand the use of licensing and cross-licensing as part of business strategy as well as the importance of a valuable patent portfolio. The key to successful cross-licensing is a portfolio of quality patents that covers large areas of the partner's product markets. Significantly, for the balancing process, the firm should not necessarily emulate the portfolio of its cross-licensing partner. Rather it should concentrate R&D in those areas in which it does best and has the most comparative advantage to develop patents that its partners need. This will give maximum leverage in negotiating access and balancing royalties. This might be in product design, software, or manufacturing processes, wherever the firm's R&D is most effective and its IP most widely used. In this sense, cross-licensing has a double positive effect on innovation. It allows firms greater means of earning a return on innovation (to help fund further

R&D), while allowing firms to concentrate their innovation and patenting activities according to their comparative advantage. In this way, firms can develop complementary rather than duplicative technology, thereby benefiting the public interest.

The unprecedented rates of technological development in the electronics industries have been made possible by a combination of the ability to capture value from innovation and the freedom to design and manufacture. Cross-licensing has been crucial. A key lesson for managers is to be aware of the value of developing a strong, high-quality IP portfolio and the effect this can have on licensing and cross-licensing strategies. This protects the firm's innovations and may significantly reduce royalty payments and fund further R&D.

The Licensing Legacy

Background—The Formation of RCA

Cross-licensing is not a new phenomenon in electronics; it goes back almost to the beginning of the industry. Cross-licensing is typical of industries involved in "cumulative systems technologies," where one innovation builds on another and products may draw on several related technologies. Multiple firms develop patented innovations in the same technological fields, and the "state of the art" of the technology tends to be covered by a large number of different patents held by different firms. Because of the potential for mutually blocking patents, firms typically cross-license all patents in a field-of-use to ensure adequate access to technology. The strongest examples of cumulative systems technologies are in electronics, including computers and semiconductors, where extensive cross-licensing ensures "design freedom" or "freedom-to-manufacture."[4] Note that this is a different situation than in some other industries not characterized by cumulative systems technologies, such as chemicals and pharmaceuticals, where cross-licensing, or, rather, reciprocal licensing, is typically aimed at exchanging technology rather than avoiding patent interference.[5]

An important instance of field-of-use cross-licensing is the development of radio in the first quarter of this century.[6] It epitomizes the complexities surrounding intellectual property arrangements that may be encountered with cumulative systems technologies. Also, many of the cross-licensing ideas used later by the electronics industry were pioneered during the early days of radio.

The commercialization of radio required a number of basic inventions. The scientific basis for wireless was developed by university scientists such as Maxwell, Hertz, and Lodge in the 19th century. Their discoveries were first applied to practical communication with the development of wireless telegraphy by Marconi in Britain in 1896. The first speech transmissions were made in the U.S. by Fessenden in 1900, using a high-frequency alternator. Further basic innovations were made over the next two decades.[7]

Many of these inventions were initially developed by individuals working independently of each other. Indeed, many carry the name of the inventor, such as the Poulsen arc, the Fleming valve, and the de Forest triode.[8] As the potential for radio became apparent, and the need for large-scale R&D and investment grew, large corporations entered the field. The pace of development accelerated and the number of patents multiplied. The companies involved included Marconi, General Electric (GE), Westinghouse, AT&T, Telefunken, and others. In addition to their considerable R&D effort, these corporations also acquired key patents where appropriate.[9] There was considerable competition, and with research teams in different companies working in parallel, patent interferences were common.[10] By 1918, it was apparent that several technologies were needed to manufacture radio systems, and each of these technologies itself involved multiple patents from different firms. In the words of Armstrong, one of the pioneers of radio, "It was absolutely impossible to manufacture any kind of workable apparatus without using practically all of the inventions which were then known."[11]

The result was deadlock. A number of firms had important patent positions and could block each other's access to key components. They refused to cross-license each other. It was a "Mexican standoff," with each firm holding up the development of the industry.[12] The situation arose in large part as a result of the way radio had developed. Key patent portfolios had been developed by different individuals and corporations, who were often adamant about refusing to cross-license competitors. Also, in a new industry in which large scale interference was a novel problem, there was no well developed means of coordinating cross-licensing agreements between these groups.

The situation was resolved in the U.S. only when, under prompting by the U.S. Navy, the various pioneers formed the Radio Corporation of America (RCA) in 1919.[13] This broke a key source of the deadlock. RCA acquired the U.S. rights to the Marconi patents, and cross-licensed the U.S. rights for other major patent portfolios.[14] The major U.S. patent holders became shareholders in RCA. In this way, RCA acquired the U.S. rights to all the constituent radio patents under one roof—amounting to over 2,000 patents.[15] It established RCA as the technical leader in radio, but also enabled the other cross-licensees to continue their own development of the technology for use in other fields or as suppliers to RCA. The RCA cross-licensing agreements became a model for the future.[16]

The case shows that because of the reluctance of the parties to cross-license, technological progress and the further commercialization of radio was halted. In this case, the debacle was resolved only by the formation of RCA, a rather radical organizational solution. However, it became clear from the experience that the same ends—namely design freedom—may be achieved more simply, without such fundamental reorganization, by cross-licensing alone. This helped set the stage for further development of cross-licensing in electronics.

AT&T's Cross-Licensing Practices

The need to achieve design freedom was soon experienced in other fields of electronics and resulted in patent cross-licensing agreements. One of the most influential firms in shaping the industry practices was AT&T, whose licensing and cross-licensing policy, especially from the 1940s until its breakup in 1984, has been crucial to the development of similar practices in U.S. electronics and semiconductor industries.

Over its long history, AT&T's licensing policy has had three phases, reflecting changes in its overall business strategy. First, from AT&T's establishment in 1885 until its first antitrust-related commitment in 1913, it used its IP rights in a forthright fashion to establish itself in the service market.[17] In the second phase, from 1914 until 1984, AT&T became a regulated monopoly. Its policy (as a matter of law under the 1956 antitrust consent decree) was to openly license its IP to everyone for minimal fees. Reasons of technology access similar to those in radio led to patent cross-license agreements between the major producers of telephone equipment, starting in the 1920s. This developed into a more widespread policy. It was during this period that the transistor was invented at Bell Labs. This and other breakthroughs laid the foundation for the semiconductor industry and shaped the development of the telecommunications, computer, and electronics industries. In the current phase, dating from divestiture in 1984, AT&T is no longer bound by the consent decree, and its IP licensing can be aligned with its proprietary needs.[18]

The 1956 antitrust consent decree required AT&T to openly license all patents controlled by the Bell System to any applicant at "reasonable royalties," provided that the licensee also grant licenses at reasonable royalties in return. AT&T was also required to provide technical information with the licenses on payment of reasonable fees; licensees had the right to sublicense the technology to their associates.[19] The impact of AT&T's liberal licensing on the industry was considerable, especially when considered in parallel with that at IBM.[20]

To a large extent, the licensing terms in AT&T's 1956 decree simply codified what was already AT&T policy. As an enterprise under rate-of-return regulation, it had little reason to maximize royalty income from its IP. Instead, it used its technology and IP to promote new services and reduce costs. It procured a tremendous amount of equipment and materials on the open market and apparently figured that its service customers would be better off if its technologies were widely diffused amongst its actual and potential suppliers, as this would lower prices and increase the performance of procured components.[21] It was the first company we are aware of to have "design freedom" as a core component of its patent strategy. It did not see licensing income as a source of funds for R&D, as Bell Labs research was largely funded by the "license contract fee," assessed on the annual revenues of the Bell operating companies. This very stable source of research funding supported a constant stream of basic innovations.[22] Using its own portfolio as leverage, AT&T was able to obtain the (reciprocal) rights it needed to continue to innovate, unimpeded by the IP of others. It successfully accomplished this limited objective.

An interesting aspect of AT&T's IP strategy was that technologies (though not R&D programs) were often selected for patent protection based on their potential interest to other firms generating technology of interest to AT&T. Since the legal requirement for open licensing specifically did not extinguish all of AT&T's intellectual property rights, the company was able to gain access to the external technology that it needed, while contributing enormously to innovation in telecommunications, computers, and electronics worldwide.[23]

The terms of AT&T's licenses set a pattern that is still commonplace in the electronics industries. The "capture model" was defined in the consent decree.[24] Under this arrangement, the licensee is granted the right to use existing patents and any obtained for inventions made during a fixed capture period of no more than five years, followed by a survivorship period until the expiration of these patents and with subsequent agreement renewals. The open licensing regimes this led to were persistent, since with the long survivorship period on many of the basic patents, there was limited scope to introduce more stringent conditions for new patents.

AT&T's licensing policy had the effect of making its tremendously large IP portfolio available to the industry worldwide for next to nothing. This portfolio included fundamental patents such as the transistor, basic semiconductor technology, and the laser, and included many other basic patents in telecommunications, computing, optoelectronics, and superconductivity. Shaped under antitrust policy reflecting the needs and beliefs of an era in which U.S. firms did not have to worry much about foreign competition, such a liberal policy appears quite anachronistic today. However, there is no doubt that it provided a tremendous contribution to world welfare. It remains as one of the most unheralded contributions to economic development—possibly far exceeding the Marshall Plan in terms of the wealth generation capability it established abroad and in the United States.

The traditional cross-licensing policy of AT&T was greatly extended following the invention of the transistor. Widespread "field-of-use" licenses in the semiconductor industry is a legacy, as the industry was founded on the basic semiconductor technology developed by AT&T. In the early days of semiconductor technology, AT&T controlled most of the key patents in the field. It soon realized that, given the importance of semiconductor technology, other electronics companies were developing their own technologies and could eventually invent around the AT&T patents. Cross-licensing ensured that AT&T would have reciprocal access to this technology and be able to develop its own technology without risking patent interference.[25]

AT&T's liberal licensing allowed the semiconductor industry to grow rapidly, and members of the industry did not care much about individual patents. The culture of the industry still reflects this, with a tradition of spin-outs and new ventures, open communications and frequent job changes.[26] The continued speed of technological progress in the industry and the difficulty of monitoring technological use are reasons why there is still a need for the transactional simplicity associated with "lump-sum" or bundled licensing.[27] With individual product life cycles short compared with the long patent lives, any new innovation is likely to infringe several existing patents. Licensing thus typically involves clusters of patents.

Not surprisingly, AT&T now uses its IP more strategically. No longer bound by the consent decree, and with R&D funding no longer guaranteed by the telephone subscribers, its IP policy is necessarily linked more closely to individual business opportunities. This is especially true of trade secret licensing, which is often a key component of international joint ventures, involving omnibus IP agreements combining patents, trademarks, and know-how.

Cross-Licensing in the Computer Industry—IBM

A second major influence on licensing practice across the electronics industry has been IBM. It has long been heavily involved in licensing and cross-licensing its technology, both as a means of accessing external technology and to earn revenues. In many ways, it has been in a similar position to AT&T in that it has been a wellspring of new technology but was also subject to a consent decree in 1956 that had certain compulsory licensing terms. Under the IBM consent decree, IBM was required to grant non-exclusive, non-transferable, worldwide licenses for any or all of its patents at reasonable royalties (royalty free for existing tabulating card/machinery patents) to any applicant—provided the applicant also offered to cross-license its patents to IBM on similar terms. The provision covered all existing patents at the time of the decree (i.e., as of 1956) plus any that were filed during the next five years. The rights lasted for the full term of the patents.[28]

IBM's cross-licensing activity continues today. IBM states that it is "exploiting our technology in the industry through agreements with companies like Hitachi, Toshiba, Canon, and Cyrix." Patent and technology licensing agreements earned $640 million in cash for IBM in 1994.[29] IBM is one of the world's leading innovators, with more U.S. patents granted in each of the three years from 1993 to 1995 than any other company (see Table 1).

The central importance IBM attaches to its patent portfolio in providing an arsenal of patents for use in cross-licensing and negotiating access to outside technology has been borne out in public statements by the company.[30] For IBM, the main object of its licensing policy has been "design freedom," to ensure "the right to manufacture and market products." To be able to manufacture products, IBM needs rights to technology owned by others:

> Market driven quality demands that we shorten our cycle times. This means we have to speed up the process of innovation. And that means there is less time to invent everything we need. We can't do everything ourselves. IBM needs to have access to the inventions of others.[31]

P. C. Grindley & D. J. Teece

TABLE 1. Top Ten U.S. Patent Recipients (1990-1995)

Company	US Patents Received					
	1990	**1991**	**1992**	**1993**	**1994**	**1995**
IBM	608	684	851	1,088	1,305	1,383
Canon	868	831	1,115	1,039	1,100	1,088
Motorola	396	614	662	731	839	1,012
NEC	448	441	462	602	901	1,005
Mitsubishi	862	964	977	944	998	971
Toshiba	891	1,031	1,036	1,064	985	970
Hitachi	902	962	973	949	1,002	909
Matsushita	351	467	616	722	782	852
Eastman Kodak	720	863	778	1008	890	772
General Electric	785	818	943	942	973	757

Source: IFI/Plenum Data Corp., USPTO

It acquires these rights "primarily by trading access to its own patents, a process called 'cross-licensing'."[32] IBM has often had the reputation of being a "fast follower" in some areas of technology, and it has used the power of its patent portfolio to negotiate the access needed. The company notes that:

> You get value from patents in two ways: through fees, and through licensing negotiations that give IBM access to other patents. Access is far more valuable to IBM than the fees it receives from its 9,000 active [U.S.] patents. There is no direct calculation of this value, but it is many times larger than the fee income, perhaps an order of magnitude larger.[33]

The effect of the consent decree for IBM, as for AT&T, was in large part to formalize policies that were already partly in effect. While IBM already used cross-licensing for design freedom where appropriate, the consent decree expanded the scope and in a sense prodded IBM into treating licensing and cross-licensing as a central aspect of its business.

Impact of Consent Decrees on Industry Development

The combined cross-licensing of basic technology by the technologically leading firms—AT&T, IBM, and others—had a profound influence on the development of the post-war electronics industry. The effect of the 1956 AT&T and IBM consent decrees was to make a huge range of basic semiconductor and telecommunications technology widely available for next to nothing to domestic and foreign firms. Even so, for AT&T and its existing cross-licensing partners, the AT&T 1956 consent decree merely formalized what was already established corporate policy. This was exchanged for rights to related technology where this was available; otherwise it was offered at low royalty payments. The availability of the basic technology formed the basis for the rapid growth of the semiconductor industry. Given the common technological base, firms relied on the rapid development and introduction of new products to succeed.

Yet the very prevalence of AT&T, IBM, and others in licensing at low royalties also created a mind set in the industry that became accustomed to artificially low royalties. This contributed to some initial agitation, if not outrage, in some quarters when in the 1980s some intellectual property owners such as Texas Instruments began to seek market returns on their IP.[34]

Licensing Practice at a Semiconductor Company— Texas Instruments[35]

Licensing Objectives

In the semiconductor industry, IP licensing is an integral and essential element of competition, and a corollary of innovation. As noted above, the industry was launched with the invention of the transistor by Bell Laboratories in 1947. First commercial transistor production took place in 1952. By 1995, worldwide sales of the industry were over $150 billion. Like other parts of the electronics industry, the semiconductor industry is characterized by wide use of cross-licensing. The main purpose of cross-licensing is to ensure "freedom-to-operate" or "design freedom" in an industry where there are likely to be large numbers of overlapping patents. Given rapid technological development and many industry participants, the probability is high that any new product or process will overlap technology developed by other firms pursuing parallel paths. Also, the technology often overlaps that developed in related industries, such as computers and telecommunications.

The licensing procedures and royalty rate determination process at Texas Instruments (TI) illustrates the ways in which cross-licensing agreements are used in practice. TI has two main licensing objectives. The first and primary objective is to ensure freedom to operate in broad areas of technology supporting given product markets, without running the risk of patent infringement litigation by other firms with similar technology. Agreements cover groups of patents within designated "fields-of-use," including existing and new patents developed within the fixed term of the agreement. The second objective is to obtain value from the firm's IP, in the form of its patent portfolio, by generating royalty income. The purpose and result of royalty payments received under cross-licensing agreements is "competitive re-balancing," which equalizes the net cost and profit advantage for imitators who otherwise might free-ride on technology TI developed.

Buying "freedom-to-operate" is vital in the semiconductor industry, with its rapid innovation, short product life cycles, and ubiquity of patents. In a typical technological field, there may be as many as a half dozen other firms with patents that an innovator could potentially infringe while implementing its independent research strategy. In semiconductor devices and manufacture, there are huge numbers of patents to consider, with many more generated each year, as seen in Table 2. Bear in mind that a particular product can utilize technology from several other technology fields, such as computers, software, materials, communications, and general systems, each with large patent establishments.

At the start of an R&D program, possible infringements cannot be easily predicted, as firms are quite ignorant of the R&D and product development plans of competitors. Yet a firm investing in R&D and product development needs to be confident that patents developed through independent R&D efforts by others will not hinder commercialization of its technology. Consider that a wafer production facility now costs $1 billion.[36] The facility may have a five-year life or longer, and it is not known in advance what products will be developed for manufacture during that time. R&D is similarly becoming more expensive. Companies need to be able to develop new products to fill the wafer fabrication facilities without being concerned that startup may be blocked by patents owned by competitors and other companies inside and outside the industry.

TABLE 2. U.S. Patents Granted in Semiconductor Devices and Manufacture (1969-1994)

Company*	Patents granted (1969-94)	Patents granted (1994)
IBM	3,435	220
Toshiba	2,492	245
Texas Instruments	2,366	231
AT&T	2,342	110
Hitachi	2,218	170
Motorola	1,882	210
Mitsubishi	1,691	275
RCA	1,601	0
Siemens	1,518	46
U.S. Philips	1,482	61
General Electric	1,446	48
NEC	1,360	261
Fujitsu	1,335	125

* Companies with over 1,000 semiconductor patents granted (1969-94).
Source: USPTO, 1995

One approach for a developer to deal with the IP rights of others would be simply to identify all infringements as they arise, and negotiate separate licenses for each. However, the transactions costs of such an approach would be inordinate.[37] Moreover, it would expose the potential licensee to large risks.

A typical cross-license includes all patents that licensees may own in a given field-of-use, giving each firm the freedom to infringe the other's existing and future patents for a given period, typically five years. Such licenses are typically non-exclusive and rarely include any trade-secret or know-how transfer or sublicensing rights.[38]

In a cross-license, technology is not usually transferred, as the parties each are capable of using the technology in question without assistance. Firms will usually gain access to the relevant technology either by developing it themselves, or by other means such as reverse engineering, hiring consultants, other technical agreements, or technical publications.[39] In either case, the cross-license primarily confers the right to use the patented technology without being sued for infringement. This avoids monitoring costs and adjusts royalty payments to reflect overall contributions to the stock of IP currently in use.[40]

In the semiconductor industry, licensing agreements sometimes go further, and may include transfer of trade secrets and know-how. However, trade secret licenses are quite different, typically involve technology transfer, and often accompany a joint venture or strategic alliance. Technology transfer involves significant costs and managerial effort, and often "creates competitors', as it frequently transfers to the licensee important technological capabilities otherwise inaccessible.[41]

Types of Cross-Licenses

There are two main models for cross-licensing agreements in the semiconductor industry: "capture" and "fixed period." In the "capture" model the licensee has rights to use, in a given field-of-use, all patents within a technological field which exist or are applied for during the license period, usually five years, and, importantly, retains "survivorship" rights to use the patents until they expire, up to 20 years later. The agreement does not generally list individual patents, but some patents of particular strategic importance to the licensor may be excluded. In the "fixed period" model the licensee has similar rights to use patents existing or applied for during the license period, but with no survivorship rights once the license period has expired. This requires full renegotiation of the cross-license for succeeding periods.

TI has been a leader in the use of fixed period licensing, which is becoming more widely used. The capture model became widespread through the industry following its use by AT&T and IBM. It gives broad rights to patents for a long period. The fixed period model allows more flexible commercialization of patent portfolios, since licensing terms can be periodically adjusted to account for changes in competitive conditions and the value of the technology. This increases strategic flexibility and allows the parties more freedom to negotiate royalty terms so that they more closely mirror the value of the patents. It is a logical evolution of licensing practices reflecting the difficulties and changes in the market for know-how.

"Proud List" Royalty Valuation Process

Balancing payments are negotiated as part of the agreement, to account for the relative value of the IP contributed by two firms. Each firm's contribution is evaluated by estimating the value of a firm's patent portfolio to its licensing partner, with the net royalty payment to the one with the greater contribution. Where both firms contribute similar portfolio values, the net payment will be small or zero. Where one firm has developed little technology and the other a great deal, the payments may be significant. Occasionally, cross-licenses are royalty-free because contributions are either very close or difficult to assess. However, even in royalty-free agreements it should not be assumed that a detailed patent balancing process has not taken place. Also, the cross-license may be included as part of a larger joint venture.

Royalty balancing is performed according to a "proud list" procedure. In this procedure, each firm identifies a sample list of its most valuable patents and this is used as a representative proxy group for estimating the value of the entire portfolio. There is a great deal of preparation before the negotiations. Having identified a potential cross-licensing candidate, TI first performs extensive reverse engineering of the other's products to assess the extent of any infringement—called "reading" the patents on the infringer's products—and identifies product market sizes involved. This may take a year of effort.[42] As part of this effort, it generates the proud list of about 50 of its major patents which it believes are being infringed, and which apply over a large product base of the other firm. The other firm also prepares a proud list of its own strongest patents.

In the negotiations, each of the sample patents is evaluated by both sides according to its quality and coverage. Quality measures include: the legal validity and enforceability of the patent; the technological significance of this feature to the product compared with other (non-infringing) ways of achieving the same end; and the similarity between the infringing features and the patent. These determine quality weighting factors for each patent so that a legally strong patent, which is hard to invent-around and is close to the infringing feature, has a high relative weight. The coverage is the size of the infringer's product market using the patent. Each patent is assigned a nominal royalty rate, which is then multiplied by its quality weighting factor and the annual sales of the affected product base to arrive at a dollar amount. Certain patents of particular strategic significance to the technology are assigned a flat rate as a group and do not go through the weighting process.

The dollar amounts are summed for all the listed patents and expressed as a royalty rate percentage of the licensee's total sales. Typically, the values of each side's estimated royalty payments are netted out to give a single royalty rate paid by the firm with the less valuable portfolio.[43] This royalty rate applies to the licensee's sales for the term of the license. When the license expires the same procedure will be used to reevaluate the relative portfolio values for the next five years.[44]

Strategic Considerations

TI's procedures provide a formal mechanism for determining royalty rates based on best estimates of the economic and technological contribution of the patent portfolios of the two firms. These procedures have been applied to a wide variety of relative IP contributions, both where these are roughly in balance and where not. Even so, there are often other considerations to include in final negotiations of a licensing agreement. Much depends on the individual needs of the parties, their negotiating strength, and the broader strategic considerations of each firm. Individual rates and the overall rates also tend to recognize overall competitive effects of the royalty payments, as well as "what the market will bear."[45]

There is obviously an upper limit on royalties, since royalties that are too high will cripple the competitive capacities of the licensee, causing royalty payments to decline. If a potential problem in this respect exists, it is usually not with an individual agreement, which is likely to be set at reasonable royalty rates. Rather, problems may arise when a licensee is subject to claims from several licensors and the cumulative royalty payments become onerous. This can create serious problems in negotiating agreements with would-be licensees. There does not seem to be an easy solution to this problem, given that agreements are negotiated individually.[46]

Royalty rates may also be affected by longer-term strategic considerations. For one thing, both parties are likely to need to renew the agreement in future, and an aggressive royalty rate now may make negotiations more difficult later, when the balance of IP may have shifted in a different direction. The firms may have, or expect to have, overlapping interests in other market areas, which will also condition negotiations. Licenses often may also be part of a cooperative venture of some kind. Patents can often be traded for know-how, or used as an entry ticket to a joint development arrangement. For example, rather than seek royalties, TI has had technology development agreements with Hitachi. It also has several manufacturing joint ventures around the world.

Strategic considerations may also affect the usual licensing process where the technology is intended to become part of an industry standard. Industry standards bodies sometimes require that patent holders agree to license their patents with low or zero royalty fees, often on a non-discriminatory basis. Similarly, when trying to establish a *de facto* market standard, a firm may charge low royalty rates.[47] The aim is to ensure the wide adoption of the technology as an industry-wide standard. Value from the technology may then be earned through product sales in an expanded market. The "reasonable rate" royalty involved is likely to be low, though need not be zero.[48]

Impact of TI's Licensing Strategy

TI has led industry moves to take a more active stance on licensing and cross-licensing. The impact of its licensing strategy on its capability to compete and innovate is of particular interest. TI instituted its current licensing strategy in 1985. Cumulative royalty earnings of over $1.8 billion had been achieved during the period from 1986 to 1993. Among other effects, this enabled TI to maintain a high level of R&D spending during 1989-91, when the semiconductor market was in a downturn, as shown in Figure 1. However, moving to a more active licensing strategy and the aggressive assertion of its IP rights was a major step for the company—and the industry—and involved considerable risk.[49] TI's strategy was enhanced by the stronger U.S. treatment of IP after 1982.

FIGURE 1. Texas Instruments: Royalty Earnings, Net Income and R&D

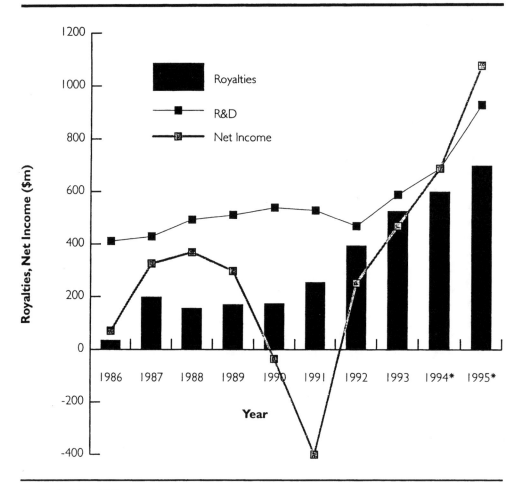

*Royalties for 1994 and 1995 estimated
Source: Annual Reports

  TI's IP portfolio has been valuable in negotiating R&D cooperation. For example, TI has had a series of ventures with Hitachi for the joint technological development of DRAM memory chips. TI's ability to supply technology, supported by its IP rights, was a crucial component in making these agreements.[50] TI's changed IP strategy has allowed it to implement new product market strategies to expand its manufacturing capacity by means of joint ventures, based partly on the negotiating value of its IP portfolio, and expanding its development of high value added components. It has been a partner in a number of international manufacturing joint ventures to set up production facilities for memory

TABLE 3. Top 10 Merchant Semiconductor Firms: 1980-1995

	1980			1990			1995		
	Company	$m	%	Company	$m	%	Company	$m	%
1	Texas Inst.	1,580	12.2	NEC	4,952	8.6	Intel	13,830	8.9
2	Motorola	1,110	8.5	Toshiba	4,905	8.5	NEC	11,360	7.3
3	Philips	935	7.2	Hitachi	3,927	6.8.	Toshiba	10,190	6.6
4	NEC	787	6.1	Intel	3,135	5.5	Hitachi	9,420	6.1
5	National	747	5.7	Fujitsu	3,019	5.3	Motorola	9,170	5.9
6	Toshiba	629	4.8	Motorola	3,692	6.4	Samsung	8,340	5.4
7	Hitachi	622	4.8	Texas Inst.	2,574	4.5	Texas Inst.	8,000	5.2
8	Intel	575	4.4	Mitsubishi	2,476	4.3	Fujitsu	5,510	3.6
9	Fairchild	566	4.4	Matsushita	1,945	3.4	Mitsubishi	5,150	3.3
10	Siemens	413	3.2	Philips	1,932	3.4	Philips	4,040	2.6
	Others	5036	38.7	Others	24,943	43.4	Others	69,990	45.2
	Total	**13,000**	**100.0**	**Total**	**57,500**	**100.0**	**Total**	**155,000**	**100.0**

Source: Dataquest

chip production.[51] TI and Hitachi also entered a joint venture in 1996 to manufacture DRAMs in Texas.

These changes have had a major impact on TI's performance, helping the company to grow and to increase its world market share since the mid 1980s. This helped reverse a relative decline in its position beginning in the mid-1970s due to inroads made in world markets by foreign producers, as seen in Table 3.

IP Management and Cross-Licensing in an Electronics Company—Hewlett-Packard[52]

Innovation Strategy

Many aspects of licensing elsewhere in electronics are similar to those described for semiconductors. The electronics industry shares many of the basic features of the semiconductor industry: rapid technological innovation, short product life cycles, and significant patenting. The computer, telecommunications, electronics, and semiconductor industries also use many of the same technologies and have been influenced by the practices of AT&T and other major corporations. Field-of-use cross-licensing is used widely.

However, a difference between many electronics firms outside of semiconductors is the breadth of technologies that are practiced. In addition to semiconductor technology, product development may involve integrating many aspects of computing, telecommunications, software, systems design, mechanical engineering, ergonomics and so forth. There are also likely to be complex manufacturing and marketing requirements. Thus, IP strategies in such firms are likely to involve broader considerations.

Hewlett-Packard (HP) produces many different types of products, from laser printers and computers to hand-held calculators and electronic instruments. HP is currently organized into Computer Products, Systems, Measurement Systems, and Test and Measurement organizations.

To maintain its high rate of innovation, a high priority for HP in its IP strategy is maintaining "design freedom." It has two principal objectives: ensuring that its own technology is not blocked by competitors' patents; and ensuring that it has access to outside technology. HP's products include complex systems that typically involve several different technologies, some of which may be developed by other firms and other industries. HP alone can not develop the complete range of technologies used in its products. To obtain access to needed technologies, Hewlett-Packard needs patents to trade in cross-licensing agreements. The company has a huge portfolio of patents and know-how in leading-edge technologies, developed as part of its extensive R&D programs. This IP portfolio is the basis for protecting HP's own products; it is also invaluable as leverage to ensure access to outside technology.

Licensing Objectives

One type of HP cross-licensing takes place as "program licensing," which is aimed at acquiring access to specific technologies. The company identifies firms with technologies of interest. There may be several different technologies at a given firm so the strategic overlaps must be considered in assessing each licensing opportunity.

HP's licensing activities are not focused primarily on cash income. With a wide range of products, the company's interests in one area are likely to overlap with those in other areas. It may encounter licensing partners in several different markets in a variety of circumstances—a competitor in one field may be a supplier or customer in another. HP does not want negotiations in one product group to interfere with those in another. This leads to a long-term bias towards meaningful cross-licensing agreements and a soft approach to royalties. HP recognizes that it is likely to deal with the same partners repeatedly and therefore normally does not require high royalty rates that could be used as a precedent against it in the future.

There are some exceptions in that some strategic patents are only licensed at high royalty rates, or more likely are not licensed at all. In products where HP has a strong leadership position (e.g. printers), it is unlikely to license out its core IP rights. HP's IP policy in this area is aimed, as it must be, at the aggressive protection of a key source of competitive advantage. The company would normally consider licensing such IP rights only as part of a specific strategic alliance and would normally exclude such technology from cross-licensing agreements.

The form of the cross-license agreements is quite standard, with a limited capture period, usually with survivorship rights. The objective is to estimate the relative value of the infringements that are likely to take place over a five-year period. Other inputs to the licensing decision include the expected R&D spending in the field by each firm, the number of patents held by each party in the particular field, and determination of the value to the infringer of a limited number of pertinent patents. Each side to the agreement may select a limited number of patents which it has determined are being infringed by the other party's products. This may be as few as six to twelve patents each. The imputed royalty fee for these patents over the next five years becomes one of the inputs to the negotiation. In general, this balancing process is not unlike that which exists in the semiconductor industry.

Royalties are often paid as a lump sum. Agreements almost never include sublicensing rights, since the company could lose control of its own technology if sublicensing were permitted. Exclusive licensing is also rare, partly because of potential antitrust concerns, but also because the historical practice of non-exclusive cross-licensing leaves fewer innovations that could be treated as exclusive.

Even after a patent cross-license agreement is concluded, HP policy is not to over-use the technology of the other party to the agreement. This is again related to a long-term view of licensing. The agreement will probably need to be renewed in the future and the more of the other party's technology HP uses, the greater the leverage the other party would have the next time around. Also, patents are lagging indicators of research, so that to be at the forefront of technology each party will need to have developed its own application of the technology well before the patents are issued. One purpose of the agreement is to be able to use the technology in the development of new products without worrying about "accidental infringement."

Licensing is only secondarily seen as a source of royalty earnings. Royalty earnings are significant but not material, given the overall size of HP's operations. However, there are some cases where licensing for revenue is pursued. One is where the company has world-class technology and is approached by others seeking a license. If the technology is not of strategic importance to HP, the company may license it out for profit. Another is the "rifle shot" license, where a single patent may be licensed, if it has specific value to a licensee. Licensing terms in either case are usually very simple, amounting to an agreement to allow use of the innovation for a royalty payment or lump sum without being subject to an infringement claim.

IP Management

Given the importance of IP to Hewlett-Packard, a formal IP strategy has been developed for managing its large and diverse IP portfolio. Since products combine many technologies, IP may need to be even more closely integrated with business strategy than at a single product corporation. HP has a series of

FIGURE 2. Intellectual Property and Patenting Decision Process at HP

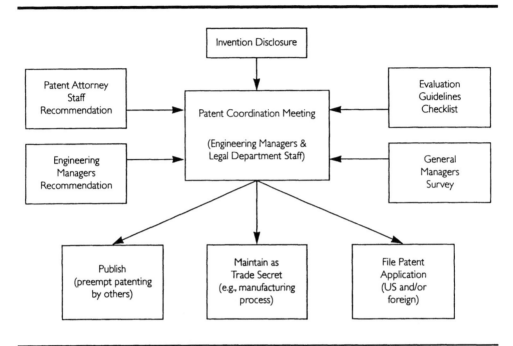

procedures for identifying technological areas to stress for patent protection and for making individual decisions about the best method of protecting innovations. Obtaining and maintaining patent protection is costly, and hence only selected innovations are patented. This process starts with "templates" to guide what IP should be protected. The templates are updated each year to protect technologies that will be strategically important to the company in the future. These templates are developed by a process that rates and prioritizes products and technologies and reviews patent needs throughout the world. This does not go as far as targeting R&D programs at innovations that will be useful in negotiating cross-licenses; rather it aims to make maximum use of innovations by creating patent portfolios that will be strategically valuable. This supports rather than directs corporate strategy.

The IP protection decision process for individual innovations is shown in Figure 2. When a product or process innovation is developed, a determination is made whether to patent it, to keep it as a trade secret, or, if it not believed worthwhile to patent, to publish it. The inputs to this decision take place in an internal committee process, with inputs from engineering management and the legal (IP) department. Innovations that are likely to be of strategic value are either patented immediately or, if they are not yet completed or proven, are reviewed again at a later time. If the innovation is valuable but its use by an imitator would be undetectable (such as for some process innovations), then the innovation may be kept as a trade secret. Marginal ideas are published immediately to preempt patenting by a competitor who might later block their use by HP. "Vanity publishers" for publicly disclosing the results of research exist for this purpose.[53]

Managing Intellectual Capital in the Electronics Industry

Contrasting IP Management Objectives

The case studies indicate several similarities in the way firms in the electronics industry use licensing and cross-licensing to ensure design freedom as well as some level of licensing earnings. They also illustrate how differences in management objectives are reflected in cross-licensing strategies.

RCA represents a rather complex organizational response to the problem of design freedom, in which a single company acquired exclusive cross-licensed rights to all the patents needed for radio manufacture. It then licensed out these rights to other manufacturers. Partly as a result, RCA was able to dominate the radio market for many years.

AT&T, as a regulated monopoly before 1984, was primarily interested in the dissemination of technology to as many producers as possible, to develop technologies that would be useful in its telecommunications services—as purchased components or in its own systems development. It was barred from competing in product markets, so it cross-licensed on liberal terms with the aim of stimulating development and obtaining access to new technology.

A primary concern of IBM in cross-licensing has been design freedom. As one of the world's leading innovators it has been very active in using its IP for competitive advantage, both in products and to obtain the widest possible access to other technology. IBM's interests have spanned a wide range of computer related markets and it has needed broad access to many different technologies. It also obtains significant income from its licenses.

TI's interests have generally been more specific to the semiconductor industry, although it also has interests in other areas of electronics. Its concerns have been to obtain freedom-to-operate given the dense patent concentration in semiconductors, and to obtain cash from cross-licensing its IP, to help fund R&D and to equalize any advantage it would otherwise be allowing competitors using its IP.

Finally, HP is in a somewhat similar position to IBM in having a broad range of interests in different markets and being especially interested in design freedom for products spanning many technologies. HP's breadth of interests—in which a competitor in one field may be a customer, supplier, or venture partner in another—moderates its approach to seeking high royalties. IP is central to its business, needed to support its rapid product innovation and to trade for technology access. It has well developed procedures for developing and protecting IP across its diverse fields.

Changing IP Modes in the Semiconductor Industry

The strengthening of IP rights and increased licensing and cross-licensing have extended the ability of the innovator to earn a reward from R&D. In addition to providing better IP protection for new products, there are greater opportunities for earning value via access to technology, joint ventures, technology exchanges, and R&D collaboration. Royalty earnings have become more significant. Much of this is a recent development and there are many questions as to how much strategic emphasis firms should place on licensing and cross-licensing compared with manufacturing, and on the importance of licensing revenue earning compared with freedom-to-operate.

It may help put these questions in context by reviewing the changing modes of competition in semiconductors, where firms have gradually needed to place increased stress on innovation, IP protection, and licensing and cross-licensing as a basis for product competition. There have been major changes in the way firms have obtained value from innovation as the industry has developed. The weak IP regime in effect during the first two or three decades of the industry was not a barrier to R&D and investment, and the liberal licensing practices used by AT&T and others accelerated the initial diffusion of the technology. This nurtured the early growth of a new industry. However, firms could not operate successfully in today's technological and competitive environment with the strategies and policies in place in the 1950s and 1960s. Competition to stay at the forefront of innovation is sharper and R&D and investment take place on a much bigger scale. AT&T no longer has a franchise monopoly, the market power of other industry participants is at best a phantom, and the industry is global.

Initial Growth Phase

From 1950 until the late 1970s, semiconductor and electronics firms used technology to open up new markets. Semiconductor technology was new and developing rapidly, and was too big and too important to be developed and commercialized adequately within one organization. There were benefits from having multiple sources of innovation. This was epitomized by AT&T's policy. As a major consumer of semiconductors, it wished to spread the use of the technology as widely as possible. Elements of this reasoning applied to other firms, who benefited from the rapid expansion of technology and markets. And, given the weak protection of IP afforded by the courts at this time, patents were not seen as a major factor in building competitive advantage.[54]

At that time, firms relied primarily on time-to-market advantages to keep ahead. The basic semiconductor patents were already widely licensed, so any individual patent had limited power.[55] Product life cycles were short and often firms would simply not bother to patent inventions, believing that there was no point in patenting products and processes that would soon be obsolete. The fragmented structure of the new "merchant" semiconductor industry (which had grown up around spin-offs from Bell Labs and others), the rapidity of innovation, and the high level of competition reflected the fact that not much attention was paid to protecting IP.[56] The predominant strategy for capturing value from technology involved "riding the experience curve"—reducing prices rapidly as unit costs fell with the hope of earning enough to fund the next round of development.[57]

Second sourcing, licensed or not, was often required by many of the large customers to ensure continuous and competitive supplies. There was significant cross-licensing (often associated with second sourcing), but it rarely involved significant royalty payments.[58] Customers like the Department of Defense (DOD) had sufficient clout to force small suppliers like Intel to second source. During this period, licenses were mainly used to get some residual value from an innovation when it could not be recovered via the product market because of investment restrictions or trade restrictions. An example is the difficulty U.S. firms had selling products in Japan. Faced with effective trade protection, most U.S. firms' only recourse was to license technology to Japanese firms.[59]

At this time, TI was one of the first firms to make strategic use of its IP. It established a production plant in Japan in 1968, one of the very few foreign firms to do so. It achieved these rights from MITI by using the power of its patent portfolio.[60] This heralded a new role for IP in global commerce and firm competitiveness.

Increased Global Competition

The competitive environment began to change during the 1970s. The complexity of the technology and the scale of investment in R&D and capacity were rising, increasing the business risk of each new development. Moreover, as requirements for specialized investment increased, the business risk associated with a patent holder's ability to obtain an injunction (in the case of inadvertent or intentional infringement) increased.

Managers were at first distracted by the increasing size of the total market when new mass markets opened up in the 1970s for consumer electronics (including calculators, watches, and later personal computers) and computer memories. By the early 1980s, new competitors from Japan (and later Korea) had entered the world markets and were challenging the U.S. firms, using technology largely developed in the United States. Changes were most dramatic in the manufacture of "commodity" DRAM memory chips, in which U.S. manufacturers' share of the world market fell from 75% in 1980 to 17% in 1986, while over the same period Japanese memory share rose from 25% to 79%.[61] U.S. firms could no longer rely on success in the product market alone to obtain returns from innovation.

The new entrants to the industry depended on access to existing technology and often sought to cross-license it. Yet nominal or royalty-free cross-licenses, which had been common in the industry prior to the 1980s, came to be seen as unfair when the entrants from outside the industry offered to pay the nominal cross-license fees, but with no balancing portfolios of patents to offer. Royalty fees also reflect payment for access to technology accumulated in prior years, often at great expense. TI and others realized that more detailed evaluation of relative contributions to cross-licenses were required.

Innovation Leadership

The situation today is that, with numerous qualified competitors, competitive advantage requires more emphasis on strong IP rights. Stronger IP protection calls for dual strategies for capturing value from technology—the simultaneous use of product manufacturing using the IP in question together with IP licensing. Market developments have put more emphasis on chip design, developed close to the customer, and on being able to protect this and leading-edge process technology from imitation by fully able competitors. The increase in cooperative R&D and manufacturing joint ventures, often underpinned by IP rights, represent a market response to increased costs and the risks of development.

A regime shift occurred when many of the once small semiconductor firms such as Intel could no longer be forced into second sourcing their products. The demise of contractually required second sourcing suddenly made the value of IP more significant. The successful blunting of buyers' demand for second sourcing made IP more important—so much so that many companies, such as Intel, now have designated IP managers.

Many in the semiconductor industry have been opposed to stronger assertion of IP rights, having grown accustomed to a relatively open exchange of ideas and personnel. Not surprisingly, advocates of this view include start-ups, who claim that if they pay the full price of technology, it would limit their ability to compete. This may be true, but it is also trite. We observe that supporters of open ideas often become more protective once they have invested heavily in R&D. Most significantly, there has been a change in the global competitive reality. What may have been a useful model in the early days of the industry (in which it may be argued that all firms in a local market benefit from mutual exchange of ideas), becomes a different equation when firms are global.[62]

Lessons for Innovation Management

To an extent, management today has little choice but to adopt a more active IP and licensing stance. IP rights have been strengthened and, not surprisingly, firms have become more strategic about commercializing IP. Cross-licensing enables firms to protect their IP while at the same time obtaining freedom to manufacture. The new IP and licensing circumstances have increased incentives to build IP portfolios and to innovate. In these new circumstances, there are some key lessons for innovation management.

Using IP to Support Core Business

Despite, or because of, the growing importance of licensing and cross-licensing, IP strategy should still be designed primarily to support technological developments and strategies surrounding the firm's core business. The global marketplace still rewards firms primarily for developing and commercializing products and processes as such, not for developing IP. Accordingly, few firms target technologies primarily for their value in earning royalties or for trading IP rights in future cross-licensing agreements.

Furthermore, for long-term success, firms typically need to be closely involved with the markets in which they operate and to develop core capabilities (in manufacture and design) closely linked to the products and processes. Maintaining a stream of valuable innovations requires extensive, up-to-date information about market demand and technological possibilities, especially in industries where technology is changing rapidly. Although this depends on the nature of the product, it usually also calls for close functional links between design, production, and marketing. These needs are typically best served by active participation in the product market.[63]

The alternative—becoming a pure "licensing company" not directly involved in the product market and increasingly remote from the manufacture and design of the product itself—can be a risky strategy. Such a strategy, on its own, not only risks the erosion of the dynamic capabilities of the firm to continue innovating, it also is likely to be less financially rewarding than developing and commercializing products.[64]

Importance of Developing a Valuable Patent Portfolio

Developing a valuable patent portfolio is an increasingly important part of strategy. In the electronics industry, patents are valuable because they provide protection from imitation for new proprietary products and services; they provide bargaining chips in negotiating access to other firms' technology (to avoid patent blocking and ensure freedom-to-operate); and patents may be an additional source of earnings or of reduced royalty fees the firm might otherwise have to pay.

The value of a portfolio is greatest when it has a high proportion of high-quality patents that cover significant product markets. These patents affect each of the reasons for holding a portfolio, but are seen most directly in the effect on cross-licensing. Patents have greatest cross-licensing value when they give the firm maximum leverage to obtain a favorable cross-license. This means that the patents should be legally and technically strong and should cover key aspects of the licensee's product base.

Concentrate R&D Where the Firm Is Strongest

In developing its patent portfolio, the firm can concentrate its R&D in those areas where it has the greatest competitive advantage in developing valuable innovations, provided these are also areas needed by other firms. It need not focus on those technological areas where its cross-licensee is strongest in an attempt to duplicate or avoid the licensee's patents—a hopeless task with complex cumulative technology, such as electronics, where infringement is almost inevitable.[65] This might be in the same fields that it wishes to cross-license from its partners, or it might be in a more specialized area. For cross-licensing with a multidivisional corporation with interests in several markets, it might be in a different business area or field-of-use than the one from which it wishes to access technology. As argued above, a firm is most likely to create valuable IP where it is actively involved in the market, i.e., its core business. Provided this is also a commercially important field to cross-licensing partners, the firm can concentrate on developing and protecting IP in this field, rather than seeking another.

Licensing and cross-licensing enable firms to capture value from technology so long as they contribute to the common pool of industry knowledge. Innovators who are contributors have every incentive to avoid duplicative R&D investments, since a contribution to an industry's useful stock of proprietary knowledge is recognized no matter what the precise domain of applicability. Firms are advised to focus on innovating where they can best make a contribution to the development of quality patents they and other firms are likely to need. Cross-licensing thus enables firms to play to their technological strengths.

Although the number of patents a firm holds is important, of even greater importance is their quality. A single key patent is often worth more than a portfolio of questionable ones when it comes to assessing the ability of a patent owner to stop an infringer. The most effective way to acquire a portfolio of valuable patents is likely to be through in-house R&D. Occasionally, firms can purchase a portfolio of patents with which to establish cross-licensing relationships; but quality patents often are not available in this fashion.

In summary, the reality of the global marketplace today indicates that firms should proactively develop IP portfolios with an eye towards value in the market for know-how. A corollary is that to create a valuable patent portfolio for cross-licensing, it matters little where R&D is aimed, so long as it creates quality patents in a field that one's competitors need to license.

Policy Issues

Intellectual property is more critical than ever to competitive advantage and, as a result, is being given increasing attention by strategists and policy makers. IP protection has been strengthened and firms are more actively defending and exploiting their IP. Coincident with the increased importance of patents is the increased importance of licensing and cross-licensing. Cross-licensing has become a significant dimension of competition. Absent the ability to offer an equivalent IP portfolio, licensees must incur considerable costs. This in and of itself is a spur to innovation.

Cross-licensing outcomes do not, however, tilt towards the large firm at the expense of the small. Rather, they favor firms with significant IP regardless of size. In a particular market niche where patents from two firms overlap, a small firm may have as many patents as a large firm, and as much bargaining power as the large firm. It may have sufficient IP leverage to block a larger competitor by pursuing a claim in court (or credibly threatening to do so). Indeed, in the evaluation process, a small innovator with a strong patent may be the net gainer, if the patent applies to a high-volume product of a large corporation.[66] Some competitors may possess "equal patents but unequal products." Nor need the licensing process disadvantage a new entrant firm. If a new entrant has significant relevant technology, it can in principle be a beneficiary of the cross-licensing regime.

Those investing in R&D need to ensure that they earn an adequate return, and royalties from licensing are an increasingly significant part. A company that develops technology will be at a competitive disadvantage in the market if its competitors are free to use its technology without incurring any expenses. Licensing fees on patented technology help ensure that the innovator earns an adequate return, which helps support future R&D. Cross-licensing helps balance the costs for developers and imitators. Thus, products manufactured by imitators who have not performed R&D do not have a competitive advantage merely by virtue of engaging in "copycat" imitation. If both parties to a licensing agreement have contributed similarly to a product field-of-use—in terms of the number, quality, product base coverage, and commercial significance of the patents included in the agreement—then the net royalty payments will be small, or possibly zero. In short, royalty payments help level the playing field, thereby ensuring competition on the merits.

The result is that IP now often has great value, both as a lever to obtain design freedom and as a vehicle to assist innovators in capturing value from innovation. This is of considerable consequence to firms without much IP—they must expect to pay—and also for firms with significant IP portfolios. IP and other knowledge assets are the core assets of many high-technology companies.

However, and perhaps because IP rights have become more valuable, infringers do not always step forward and offer to pay royalties. Accordingly, patent owners must often be proactive in obtaining royalty payments. Litigation or the threat of it may sometimes be necessary to enforce one's rights. Unfortunately, at least in the U.S., litigation is often slow and costly, and antitrust and patent misuse defenses are often raised, sometimes frivolously. The archaic state of the law on patent misuse may further handicap the chances of efficient and socially desirable outcomes.[67] Moreover, antitrust attorneys are often ready to argue that a package license is a tying arrangement with anticompetitive effects, and/or that cross-licensing is a front for collusion. However, the truth of the matter is that such arguments are out of step with the new competitive order.

Such arrangements are pro-innovation and pro-competitive. There would appear to be a significant knowledge gap in some circles with respect to the nature, purposes, and effects of cross-licensing. For instance, the field-of-use cross-licensing of patents in widespread use today is quite different from the traditional practice of licensing and cross-licensing involving individual patents. In the electronics industries, it is simply too cumbersome and transactionally costly to license specific patents for specific products, and so licensing commonly proceeds on a portfolio basis. Yet patent misuse and patent antitrust arguments often assume a world where infringement is easy to detect and costless to enforce. This is rarely the case in the electronics industry today.

At the most elementary level, licensing and cross-licensing involve merely the sale or exchange of property rights. Indeed, it often involves precisely that and no more. However, such arrangements ensure that firms have freedom-to-operate in developing and using innovations, without risking infringement claims from holders of patents in the same field of technology. In industries experiencing rapid technological innovation, patents, even when developed independently, will inevitably overlap technological domains worked by other firms. Cross-licensing agreements provide firms active in R&D with protection against inadvertent infringement and the rights to use the licensee's patents. Cross-licensing arrangements provide a mechanism for recognizing contributions through the establishment of balancing royalty payments. Royalty flows thus recognize the relative contributions to the product technology of the parties, thereby providing a mechanism for net takers to compensate net contributors. The arrangements thereby provide some limited protection against "free riders" who wish to use an industry's stock of proprietary knowledge without contributing. Balancing royalty payments are part of most cross-licenses, even when the main purpose is freedom-to-operate. "Pure" royalty free cross-licenses are rare for some companies and nowadays tend only to apply where the patent portfolios of both firms are large and the overall technological balance is both hard to assess and roughly equal.

Conclusion

Licensing is no longer a marginal activity in semiconductors and electronics. Whereas the management of patents and other forms of IP have always been of great importance in some industries like chemicals and pharmaceuticals, the ascendancy of IP in electronics is relatively recent. This is not just because the industry is new, but because regulatory and judicial distortions which impaired the value of IP have now been substantially rectified. The U.S. Department of Justice (DOJ) and the Courts forced AT&T, and to a lesser extent IBM, to license their technologies way below market value.[68] Not surprisingly, the electronics industry worldwide grew up with a distorted view of the value of intellectual property. This was reinforced by second sourcing requirements imposed by the DOD and other large buyers of integrated circuits that could, and did, insist on licensing for second sourcing purposes at low or zero royalties. Moreover, AT&T itself, being a significant purchaser of telecommunications and electronic equipment, and with protected service markets, had private incentives to diffuse technology rather than use it to build competitive advantage.

This confluence of very special factors has ended. The AT&T consent decree is gone, and AT&T must now be far more proprietary with its technology. The IBM patent provisions ended in 1961. Intel, TI, and other integrated circuit producers are no longer forced to second source. Moreover, the courts are more inclined to enforce IP rights than ever before. In these respects, hopefully the DOJ/FTC 1995 Antitrust Guidelines for the Licensing of IP, which include statements regarding the potential efficiency benefits of licensing and cross-licensing, are an important step in the right direction and reflect more modern thinking about IP.[69] However, these guidelines are non-binding in litigation, though one would of course hope that the courts would take them into account.

The old regime—whereby the antitrust authorities pressed major IP owners to give up whatever rights they held, where the courts were reluctant to enforce IP rights and were eager to see IP as a barrier to competition rather than as an instrument of it—has faded away. Meanwhile, the ability of the buyers of electronic componentry to bargain for and achieve second source arrangements (which indirectly lowered the value of IP by causing owners to create their own competition) has declined. As a result of these developments, a new order has emerged in which IP rights are valuable. Firms must either invest in R&D and develop patentable technology, or pay to license the patent portfolios of others. The free ride appears to be coming to an end, and IP management is now critical to the success of new entrants and incumbents alike.

Notes

1. By "IT," we refer of course to information technology.
2. In cross-licensing, two or more firms license their IP to each other.
3. Cross-licensing is not the same as a patent pool, in which member firms contribute patents to a common pool and each member accesses them on the same conditions. In cross-licensing, firms agree one-on-one to license their IP to each other and retain control over their proprietary technology, which is used for competitive advantage via product manufacturing and further licensing.
4. Other examples of "cumulative systems" include aircraft and automobiles. In aircraft, problems of blocking patents, stemming from different approaches by pioneers such as the Wright Brothers and Curtiss, were only resolved during World War II when automatic cross-licensing was introduced. In automobiles, the Association of Licensed Automobile Manufacturers (although formed to exploit the Selden patent) developed means for automatic cross-licensing of patents early this century. In both cases, the lack of cross-licensing probably held up industry development. R. Merges and R. Nelson, "On the Complex Economics of Patent Scope," *Columbia Law Review*, 90 (1990): 839-916.
5. In chemicals and pharmaceuticals, although patenting is extensive, individual technology development paths are less likely to overlap, and cross-licensing may be used to ensure broad product lines. For licensing strategy in the chemicals industry, see P. Grindley and J. Nickerson, "Licensing and Business Strategy in the

Chemicals Industry," in R. Parr and P. Sullivan, eds., *Technology Licensing Strategies* (New York, NY, NY: Wiley, 1996), pp. 97-120.

6. The early history of radio is described in: G. Archer, *History of Radio to 1926* (New York, NY: American Historical Society, 1938); W. Maclaurin, *Invention and Innovation in the Radio Industry* (New York, NY: Macmillan, 1949); J. Jewkes, D. Sawers, and R. Stillerman, *The Sources of Innovation* (New York, NY: Norton, 1969), pp. 286-288; G. Douglas, *The Early Days of Radio Broadcasting* (Jefferson, NC: McFarland, 1987); Merges and Nelson, op. cit., pp. 891-896.

7. These included the high-frequency alternator, high-frequency transmission arc, magnetic amplifier, selective tuning, crystal detector, heterodyne signal detection, diode valve, triode valve, high vacuum tube, and directional aerials.

8. Not all early inventors were independent. Alexanderson—who improved the Fessenden alternator, invented a magnetic amplifier, electronic amplifier, and multiple tuned antenna, and co-invented the "Alexanderson-Beverage static eliminator"—was a General Electric employee.

9. AT&T acquired the de Forest triode and feedback patents in 1913-1914 for $90,000, and his remaining feedback patents in 1917 for $250,000; Westinghouse cross-licensed the Fessenden heterodyne interests in 1920, and acquired the Armstrong super heterodyne patents in 1920 for $335,000. Archer, op. cit., p. 135; Maclaurin, op. cit., p. 106.

10. The fact that GE and AT&T alone were each devoting major research attention to the vacuum tube led to no less than twenty important patent interferences in this area. Maclaurin, op. cit., p. 97.

11. Federal Trade Commission, *The Radio Industry* (Washington DC: FTC, 1923); Maclaurin, op. cit., p. 99.

12. To cite one important example, Marconi and de Forest both had critical valve patents. Marconi's diode patent was held to dominate de Forest's triode patent. Both technologies were vital to radio, yet the interests refused to cross-license. [Archer, op. cit., pp. 113-114; Douglas, op. cit., p. 12.] The application of the triode (audion) to feedback amplification was also the subject of a long-running patent priority dispute between de Forest and Armstrong (finally resolved in de Forest's favor by the Supreme Court in 1934). Its use in transmission oscillation was the subject of four-way patent interference between Langmuir, Meissner, Armstrong, and de Forest. [Maclaurin, op. cit., p. 77.] These problems held up the use of the triode—a crucial component of signal transmission, detection, and amplification, which has been called "the heart and soul of radio" [Douglas, op. cit., p. 8], and "so outstanding in its consequences it almost ranks with the greatest inventions of all time" [Nobel Prize physicist Rabi, quoted in Maclaurin, op. cit., p. 70].

13. A main concern of the U.S. Navy was that international wireless communications were dominated by the British firm Marconi, and the patent impasse helped perpetuate this. It favored the establishment of an "All American" company in international communications. RCA was formed by GE in 1919, and simultaneously acquired the American Marconi Corp. Major shareholders included GE, AT&T (1920) and Westinghouse (1921). Archer, op. cit., pp. 176-189; Maclaurin, op. cit., p. 105.

14. As part of its role in the formation of RCA, the U.S. Navy also initiated cross-licensing to resolve the patent situation in radio manufacture. It wished to have clear rights to use the radio equipment it purchased, without risking litigation due to the complex patent ownership—noting in 1919 that "there was not a single company among those making radio sets for the Navy which possessed basic patents sufficient to enable them to supply, without infringement, . . . a complete transmitter or receiver." A formal letter suggesting "some agreement between the

several holders of permanent patents whereby the market can be freely supplied with [vacuum] tubes," sent from the Navy to GE and AT&T in January 1920, may be seen as an initiating point for cross-licensing in the industry. Archer, op. cit., pp. 180-186; Maclaurin, op. cit., pp. 99-110.

15. RCA concluded cross-license agreements with firms including GE, Westinghouse, AT&T, United Fruit Company, Wireless Specialty Apparatus Company, Marconi (Britain), CCTF (France), and Telefunken (Germany). Archer, op. cit., p. 195; Maclaurin, op. cit., p. 107.

16. A distinction was that the RCA cross-licenses typically granted (reciprocal) exclusive rights to use the patents in given territories or markets, compared with the non-exclusive cross-licenses that became the norm later. The cross-license with GE (and later Westinghouse) included provisions for the supply of components to RCA. The RCA cross-licenses were for very long terms—many for 25 years, from 1919 to 1945. They covered current and future patents. Other radio manufacturers took licenses with RCA, starting in the late 1920s. Some of RCA's cross-licensing policies were later questioned on antitrust grounds, and modified following a consent decree in 1932. Archer, op. cit., pp. 381-387; Maclaurin, op. cit., pp. 107-109, 132-152.

17. Historical perspective on competition in the telecommunications industry is given in: M. Irwin, "The Telephone Industry," in W. Adams, ed., *The Structure of American Industry*, 5th ed. (New York, NY: Macmillan, 1977), pp. 312-333; G. Brock, *The Telecommunications Industry: The Dynamics of Market Structure* (Cambridge, MA: Harvard University Press, 1981); Office of Technology Assessment, *Information Technology Research and Development: Critical Trends and Issues* (New York, NY: Pergamon Press, 1985); R. Noll and B. Owen, "The Anticompetitive Uses of Regulation: United States *v.* AT&T," in J. Kwoka and L. White, eds., *The Antitrust Revolution* (New York, NY: Macmillan, 1989); G. Rosston and D. Teece, "Competition and "Local" Communications: Innovation, Entry, and Integration," *Industrial and Corporate Change*, 4/4 (1995).

18. OTA, op. cit.; M. Noll, "Bell System R&D Activities: The Impact of Divestiture," *Telecommunications Policy*, 11 (1987): 161-178; R. Harris, "Divestiture and Regulatory Policies," *Telecommunications Policy*, 14 (1990): 105-124.

19. The two substantive provisions of the 1956 consent decree were that (a) it confined AT&T to providing regulated telecommunications services, and its manufacturing subsidiary Western Electric to making equipment for those services (effectively prohibiting it from selling semiconductors in the commercial market), and (b) all patents controlled by the Bell System should be licensed to others on request. Licenses for the 8,600 patents included in existing cross-licensing agreements were royalty free to new applicants, and licenses to all other existing or future patents were to be issued at a non-discriminatory "reasonable royalty" (determined by the court if necessary). AT&T was also to provide technical information along with the patent licenses for reasonable fees. Licenses were unrestricted, other than being non-transferable. [*USA v. Western Electric Co. Inc. and AT&T*, Civil Action, 17-49, Final Judgment, January 24, 1956; Brock, op. cit., pp. 166, 191-194; R. Levin, "The Semiconductor Industry," in R. Nelson, ed., *Government and Technical Progress* (New York, NY: Pergamon, 1982), pp. 9-101.] In fact, AT&T went beyond the Consent Decree in its efforts to diffuse transistor technology, including symposia and direct efforts to spread know-how. [Levin, op. cit., pp. 76-77.]

20. See section later in this article on "Lessons for Innovation Management."

21. "We realized that if [the transistor] was as big as we thought, we couldn't keep it to ourselves and we couldn't make all the technical contributions. It was to our interest to spread it around." AT&T executive, quoted in Levin, op. cit., p. 77, after

J. Tilton, *International Diffusion of Technology: The Case of Semiconductors* (Washington, D.C.: The Brookings Institution, 1971).

22. By 1983, Bell Labs had received 20,000 patents. This may be compared to about 10,000 currently at IBM and 6,000 at Texas Instruments.

23. W. Kefauver, "Intellectual Property Rights and Competitive Strategy: An International Telecommunications Firm," in M. Wallerstein, M. E. Mogee, and R. Schoen, eds., *Global Dimensions of Intellectual Property Rights in Science and Technology* (Washington, D.C.: National Academy Press, 1993), pp. 236-240.

24. For the capture model, see section below on "Policy Issues." The survivorship period could be as much as 17 years from the grant date (possibly several years after filing), under U.S. patent rules prior to 1995, or 20 years from the filing date, after 1995.

25. In the U.S., during 1953-1968, 5,128 semiconductor patents were awarded. Bell Laboratories was granted 16% of these; the next five firms were RCA, General Electric, Westinghouse, IBM, and Texas Instruments. Tilton, op. cit.

26. E. von Hippel, "Cooperation Between Rivals: Informal Know-How Trading," *Research Policy*, 16 (1987): 416-424; A. Saxenian, "Regional Networks and the Resurgence of Silicon Valley," *California Management Review*, 33/1 (Fall 1990): 89-112.

27. There are also transactions costs reasons for using bundled licensing, as noted previously.

28. If the parties could not agree on a reasonable royalty rate, the court could impose one. Patent rights could be very long lived, since, at that time, patent life was 17 years from the grant date, which might be some years after the filing date. The patent licensing provisions ended in 1961. The decree also included other provisions related to the sale of IBM products and services. USA v. International Business Machines Corporation, CCH 1956 Trade Cases para. 68, 245, SDNY 1956.

29. This increased from $345 million in 1993 [IBM Annual Report, 1994]. IBM initiated a more active approach to licensing in 1988, when it increased the royalty rates sought on its patents from 1% of sales revenue on products using IBM patents to a range of 1% to 5%. Computerworld, April 11, 1988, p. 105.

30. R. Smith, "Management of a Corporate Intellectual Property Law Department," *AIPLA Bulletin* (April/June 1989), pp. 817-823; C. Boyer, "The Power of the Patent Portfolio," *Think*, 5 (1990): 10-11.

31. Gary Markovits, IBM patent process manager, in Boyer, op. cit., p. 10.

32. Jim McGrody, IBM VP and director of research, in Boyer, op. cit.

33. Roger Smith, IBM assistant general counsel, in Boyer op. cit. In all, IBM has about 11,000 active inventions, with about 35,000 active patents around the world. Smith, op. cit.

34. Many firms in the U.S. semiconductor industry were reported to be "dismayed" and "outraged" over the higher royalties and more active IP strategies of TI and others. [S. Weber, "The Chip Industry is Up in Arms Over TI's Pursuit of Intellectual Property Rights at the ITC," *Electronics* (February 1991), p. 51.] For example, T. J. Rodgers, CEO of Cypress Semiconductor described the practice of increased litigation over patent rights as a "venture capital investment." [*Upside* (December 1990).] Others have questioned whether the strengthening of patent rights might be hindering innovation, by enabling IP holders to demand "crippling royalties from young companies." Several small Silicon Valley semiconductor firms, including Cypress Semiconductor, LSI Logic, and VLSI Technology, formed a consortium to defend themselves against patent suits. [B. Glass, "Patently Unfair: The System Created to Protect the Individual Inventor May be Hindering Innovation," *InfoWorld*, October 29, 1990, p. 56.] Although some Japanese manufacturers reportedly described royalty demands as "possibly exorbitant," the Japanese

response has generally been to increase their own patenting effort. [*Computergram*, September 14, 1990; Weber, op. cit.] Similar objections to increased patent strength and licensing activity have also been evident in resistance to the growing use of patents for computer software, which it has been claimed may restrict innovation by small enterprises. [B. Kahin, "The Software Patent Crisis," *Technology Review* (April 1990), pp. 53-58.] However, here too, many software firms who at first resisted the trend have now accepted the need to build their own patent portfolios. [M. Walsh, "Bowing to Reality, Software Maker Begins Building a Patent Portfolio," *The Recorder*, August 17, 1995, p. 1.]

35. This section is based in part on discussions with Texas Instruments executives. However, the views expressed here are those of the authors and should not be seen as necessarily reflecting those of Texas Instruments.

36. The costs of manufacturing facilities have risen dramatically. A new wafer fabrication plant cost $10-20 million in 1975 (4-kilobit DRAM), $300-400 million in 1990 (16-megabit DRAM) and over $1 billion in 1991 (256-megabit DRAM). SEMATECH, *Annual Report, 1991*; "Foreign Alliances Which Make Sense," *Electronic Business*, September 3, 1990, p. 68.

37. Without field-of-use cross-licenses, a typical semiconductor firm might need to reverse engineer an average of two or three competitors' products a day, as each is introduced over the course of a five-year license, to ascertain whether these are infringing its patents. It must do the same for its own products. This would be prohibitively expensive. Tracking sales by each of hundreds of affected products, on a patent by patent basis, to ascertain royalties, would be virtually impossible.

38. In some cases, where there are only a few very specific overlaps between two firms' technology needs, firms may choose to license single patents. Although an option, it is rarely convenient compared with field-of-use cross-licensing when there are substantial technology overlaps.

39. R. Levin, A. Klevorick, R. Nelson, and S. Winter, "Appropriating the Returns to Industrial R&D," *Brookings Papers on Economic Activity*, 3 (1987): 783-820. Of course, even reading the patent is a helpful guide to someone knowledgeable in the field.

40. The most powerful threat to enforce a patent is an injunction to close down the infringer's production line. This could be ruinous for a manufacturing corporation, especially in fast developing markets such as electronics and semiconductors. The threat of damages may also be important, but as these are often based on projected royalties (and hence may be little worse than freely negotiated licensing terms) they are less potent, unless multiplied by the court.

41. For the economics of technology transfer see D. Teece, "The Market for Know-How and the Efficient International Transfer of Technology," *Annals of the American Academy of Political and Social Science*, 458 (1981): 81-96.

42. Reverse engineering a semiconductor product is not a simple matter, involving as it does decapping and microscopic examination at the submicron level. Although the process is by now largely automated, it can take 400-500 man-hours per device.

43. For cross-licenses with firms outside the semiconductor industry, such as the personal computer industry, the process used is simpler. In this case, there may be few patents to balance against the proffered patents. Licensing follows precedents long established in the computer industry, primarily under the leadership of IBM, as the holder of many of the patents used in the industry. The negotiations are similar, but the weighting process is not involved. Royalty rates are influenced by industry norms.

44. In some cases licensees may only wish to license a few selected patents, rather than all patents in a field-of-use. For this reason licenses are generally also offered

for individual or specific patents, as well as for all patents in a given field. However, there are significant transactions savings to both sides from a field-of-use license, and the cost per patent is likely to be higher when only a few patents are licensed.

45. For general considerations affecting royalty rates, see M. Lee, "Determining Reasonable Royalty," *Les Nouvelles*, 27 (1992): 124-128; R. Parr, *Intellectual Property Infringement Damages: A Litigation Support Handbook* (New York, NY: Wiley, 1993).

46. To an extent this may be a transitional problem. As licensing becomes more widespread, individual licenses are more likely to be negotiated in the knowledge that other licenses, potential or actual, must be taken into account.

47. For strategies to establish standards see R. Hartman and D. Teece, "Product Emulation Strategies in the Presence of Reputation Effects and Network Externalities," *Economics of Innovation and New Technology*, 1 (1990): 157-182; L. Gabel, *Competitive Strategies and Product Standards* (London: McGraw-Hill, 1991); P. Grindley, *Standards, Strategy, and Policy: Cases and Stories* (Oxford: Oxford University Press, 1995).

48. However liberal the licensing terms, the patent holder should not inadvertently assign away IP rights beyond those specifically needed to operate the standard, and may need to condition rights over its IP to uses related to the standard. The innovator might otherwise be deterred from participating in standards setting. There is a balance to be drawn between committing to an open standard and limiting that commitment to what is needed for the standard and to keep access open in future.

49. Risks include the likelihood that the validity of the patents would be challenged in court, that firms—and nations—would retaliate, and that the corporate image with customers would suffer. Patent assertion against customers and partners is an especially sensitive area.

50. R&D agreements with Hitachi have ranged from a 4-megabit DRAM know-how exchange in 1988 to a 256-megabit DRAM co-development agreement in 1994. According to Yasutsugu Takeda of Hitachi, "You can't create [a successful cooperative venture] just because you sign up a lot of companies that are barely committed and don't have anything to bring." The Hitachi-TI collaboration on 256-megabit memory chips has been successful because it is a "meeting of equals" [*Business Week*, June 27, 1994, p. 79]. Complementary capabilities are generally considered important factors in selecting international collaborative venture partners. D. Mowery, "International Collaborative Ventures and the Commercialization of New Technologies," in N. Rosenberg, R. Landau, and D. Mowery, *Technology and the Wealth of Nations* (Stanford, CA: Stanford University Press, 1992), pp. 345-380.

51. TI entered joint ventures during 1989-1990 to build manufacturing plants with total investments over $1 billion: with the Italian government; Acer (Taiwan); Kobe Steel (Japan); and the Singapore government, HP, and Canon (Singapore).

52. This section is based in part on discussions with Hewlett-Packard executives. However, the views expressed here are those of the authors, and should not be seen as necessarily reflecting those of Hewlett-Packard.

53. Examples include *Research Disclosure* and other publications. Such journals charge fees to authors, yet often have large circulations for reference libraries and research laboratories.

54. Surveys of executives in a range of industries taken in the early 1980s typically rated methods such as lead time and superior sales and service effort as the most effective means of protecting innovations, rather than patent protection, which was considered relatively ineffective. Levin et al., op. cit.

55. The original transistor process patents were held by AT&T, so that all transistor manufacturers needed to cross-license their own patents at least with AT&T.

Similarly, the key patents for the integrated circuit (IC) technology were held by two firms, TI and Fairchild, ensuring that these too were widely licensed. With the critical patents widely available, the cumulative nature of innovation guaranteed broad cross-licensing. Levin, op. cit., pp. 79-82.

56. The first commercial producers of transistors in the 1950s, using AT&T licenses, included Shockley Labs, Fairchild, Motorola and TI. These gave rise to a wave of spin-off companies in the 1960s, such as National Semiconductor, Intel, AMD, Signetics and AMI, which in turn gave rise to subsequent waves of new companies, such as, Cypress Semiconductor, Cyrix, LSI Logic, Chips and Technologies, Brooktree Semiconductor, and others.

57. At TI this approach was formalized in the Objectives, Strategies, and Tactics (OST) product development management process, including "design to cost" methods formalizing experience curve pricing procedures. *Business Week*, September 18, 1978; B. Uttal, "TI Regroups," *Fortune*, August 9, 1982, p. 40; M. Martin, *Managing Technological Innovation and Entrepreneurship* (Reston, VA: Reston, 1984).; R. Burgelman and M. Maidique, *Strategic Management of Technology and Innovation* (Homewood, IL: Irwin, 1988).

58. Tilton, op. cit.; M. Borrus, J. Millstein, and J. Zysman, *International Competition in Advanced Industrial Sectors: Trade and Development in the Semiconductor Industry* (Washington, D.C.: U.S. Department of Commerce, 1982).

59. Borrus et al., op. cit.

60. The same is broadly true of IBM's entry into Japan.

61. Dataquest figures, quoted in United Nations Organization (UNO), *The Competitive Status of the U.S. Electronics Sector* (New York, NY: United Nations Organization, 1990). For comments on the U.S. recovery since the late 1980s, see W. Spencer and P. Grindley, "SEMATECH After Five Years: High-Technology Consortia and U.S. Competitiveness," *California Management Review*, 35/4 (Summer 1993): 9-32; P. Grindley, D. Mowery, and B. Silverman, "SEMATECH and Collaborative Research: Lessons in the Design of High-Technology Consortia," *Journal of Policy Analysis and Management*, 13 (1994): 723-758.

62. For contrasting views on the responses of Silicon Valley to international competition, see R. Florida and M. Kenney, "Why Silicon Valley and Route 128 Can't Save Us," *California Management Review*, 33/1 (Fall 1990): 66-88; Saxenian, op. cit.

63. Hazards for innovation when a firm is remote from business transactions, and hence from the technological frontier, are outlined in J. de Figueiredo and D. Teece, "Strategic Hazards and Safeguards in Competitor Supply," *Industrial and Corporate Change*, vol. 5.2 (1996). The similar vulnerability of the "virtual corporation," which contracts out development and manufacturing, is discussed in H. Chesbrough and D. Teece, "When Is Virtual Virtuous: Organizing for Innovation," *Harvard Business Review* (January/February 1996), pp. 65-73.

64. For the nature of dynamic capabilities of firms and their relationship to innovation, see D. Teece and G. Pisano, "The Dynamic Capabilities of Firms: An Introduction," *Industrial and Corporate Change*, 3.3 (1994): 537-556; D. Teece, G. Pisano, and A. Shuen, "Dynamic Capabilities and Strategic Management," *Strategic Management Journal* (forthcoming in 1997). For the role of complementary assets in commercializing innovation, see D. Teece, "Profiting from Technological Innovation," *Research Policy*, 15 (1986): 285-305.

65. Indeed, in some cases the firm might conceivably do better if it has strengths in an area where the licensee is relatively weak, since it will have greatest difficulty avoiding their patents in those areas, whereas where it is strongest it may have more ability to invent around the patents.

66. An example is Brooktree Corporation, a small semiconductor design company in San Diego, which concluded a favorable cross-licensing agreement with TI in 1993.
67. See E. Sherry and D. Teece, "The Patent Misuse Doctrine: An Economic Reassessment," in *Antitrust Fundamentals*, ABA Section of Antitrust Law, Chicago (forthcoming).
68. IP rights to the transistor were given away to U.S. and foreign firms for very small amounts. Levin, op. cit.
69. DOJ/FTC, *Antitrust Guidelines for the Licensing of IP*, April 6, 1995 (Washington, DC: U.S. Department of Justice and the Federal Trade Commission, 1995).

Patents, Licensing, and Entrepreneurship: Effectuating Innovation in Multi-invention Contexts

DEEPAK SOMAYA AND DAVID J. TEECE

1. Introduction

In recent years, patents have become more significant as mechanisms to capture value from innovation. Simultaneously, the innovation context has become more complicated, not only because many patents are implicated in "multi-invention" or "systemic" innovation, but also because there is great dispersal in the ownership of patents. Accordingly, many new products require the use of patents owned by several different entities. This creates both challenges and opportunities for entrepreneurs. Sometimes these challenges are easily worked through; on other occasions it requires "new combinations" not just of patents, but of tangible assets, components, and technologies in order to enable innovations to proceed to market. This paper maps opportunities and challenges, identifies possible solutions, and discusses how (entrepreneurial) firms have responded to these opportunities and challenges.

2. Intellectual Property and Entrepreneurship

The patent system grants the inventor/patent owner time-bound exclusive rights to practice the technology that is covered by the patent. In exchange for this right, the inventor recognizes that the invention will be disclosed when the patent is published. Absent the patent system, inventions could be more readily imitated. It is frequently argued that patents are needed to help provide incentives not only for invention, but also for the commercial application of inventions (Kitch 1977). Small inventors and entrepreneurs are among the most enthusiastic supporters of the patent system. Their support stems in part from the perception that the system provides safeguards for the inventor, who might otherwise be subject to use of the invention without compensation. This is corroborated by a survey in the U.S. semiconductor

Reprinted with permission from *Entrepreneurship, Innovation, and the Growth Mechanism of the Free-Enterprise Economies* (Princeton University Press, 2007), edited by Eytan Sheshinski, Robert J. Strom, and William J. Baumol, pp. 185–212.

industry (Hall and Ziedonis 2001), where small start-up firms were found to be champions of patents, who recognize that patents can assist them in acquiring investment funds from venture capitalists. And, it is in sharp contrast to the perception of some commentators that patents may be harmful to small firms and the entrepreneurship process.

In industries where innovation requires the combination of a very large number of inventions to create new products and services, what we term here the multi-invention or systemic innovation[1] context, additional opportunities and constraints arise from patenting. In these situations, patents may provide leverage to the entrepreneur or individual inventor, while at the same time requiring new entrants and incumbents alike to navigate patent thickets where the relevant patents required for a particular innovation have distributed ownership; that is, the patents needed to design and manufacture a product may be held by several unrelated entities. These environments may require the exercise of entrepreneurial skills as well as the establishment of potentially quite different organizational arrangements (modes) to enable an innovation to proceed to market.

According to Schumpeter (1934), the entrepreneur drives economic growth. The function of the entrepreneur is to innovate, to "carry out new combinations." In Schumpeter's treatment, the entrepreneur is not the inventor. Rather, the entrepreneur exploits the invention to effectuate innovation in the marketplace. Nor is the entrepreneur a risk bearer, as that function is performed by the capitalist (the venture capitalists in today's vernacular). The Schumpeterian entrepreneur has an organizing and decision-making role. Typically that role is exercised under considerable uncertainty, and usually with quite limited information.

An important function for the entrepreneur is to assemble assets and exploit complementarities among them. By exploring and exploiting co-specialization, rent streams can be generated (Teece 1986, 2003a). Competitive advantage is obtained when tangible and intangible assets are assembled that yield joint returns that are more than the sum of the parts (Lippman and Rumelt 2003).

Although possibly amplified in the context of untested patents,[2] the condition whereby factor/asset owners and entrepreneurs have different beliefs about the value of different factor/asset combinations is not uncommon in the economy. It is the role of the entrepreneur to perceive value that no one else can; or even if others perceive it, the entrepreneur is able to organize resources to achieve ends that other (nonentrepreneurial) individuals (or managers) are unable or unwilling to achieve. Entrepreneurial opportunities inherently depend upon asymmetries of information, belief, and individual and organizational capability.[3] As Baumol (1993) has explained, entrepreneurship is certainly not an optimization process by which people make mechanical calculations in response to a given set of alternatives imposed upon them. Clearly, entrepreneurship is a scarce resource. History is replete with examples where inventors and incumbents alike did not initially see commercial opportunities resulting from the invention of new technologies (Rosenberg 1994).

The particular opportunities and challenges afforded by multi-invention (systemic) innovation require particular entrepreneurial responses. These can be of two kinds. First, entrepreneurs must understand and address the challenges and opportunities of combining inventions from a variety of disparate sources in a multi-invention or systemic context. Organizational barriers and transaction costs can be a significant hurdle in unlocking the value hidden in a new invention or combination of inventions. Moreover, patents owned by others may appear to block the road ahead and amplify organizational challenges. Second, entrepreneurs must evaluate how best to appropriate value from the unique combinations that they create. There is no benefit to engaging in entrepreneurial efforts if another enterprise can simply appropriate all the returns. Entrepreneurs must therefore pay attention to how they will appropriate returns while at the same time creating the factor/asset combinations necessary to effectuate innovation.

In this essay we explain that workable solutions usually exist to both these challenges. A variety of organizational arrangements can help manage the challenges of combining inventions in multi-invention settings. Some solutions require action in technology and component markets, and some require actions in the market for corporate control (i.e., mergers). In other instances, the lowering of transaction costs in patent licenses may require certain bargaining and negotiating skills. Further, in each instance, there are implications for the role of patents in helping to appropriate returns for the entrepreneur. In other words, the organizational responses used to effectuate innovation in a multi-invention or systemic context need to be supported by an appropriate patent strategy. To our knowledge, the literature has not explored these issues in any systematic way, and certainly not with attention to entrepreneurial solutions that are in our view central to the issues at hand.

3. The Multi-invention (Systemic Innovation) Context

In many high-tech sectors of the economy, multi-invention contexts are the norm; that is, very large numbers of inventions are combined to develop end products and services. In semiconductors, increasing miniaturization has made it feasible to manufacture large and complex electronics systems on a single chip (so-called systems-on-a-chip, or SOCs). This creates the need for large numbers of patented inventions to be combined in any single product (Teece 1998; Linden and Somaya 2003). In biotechnology, increasingly large portfolios of inventions in genomics, research tools, and other areas need to be assembled to bring new medical solutions to fruition. Similarly, hundreds or thousands of patentable software inventions may be combined in contemporary software programs, and this trend is intensifying with the increasing size and complexity of software products.

Innovation in these industries comes from multiple sources—from within large firms, from start-ups and specialized players, from firms outside the industry, and even from universities and other research establishments— creating phenomenal entrepreneurial opportunities to combine knowledge in innovative ways and create valuable new products. But these multiple sources of invention also imply a tangled web of patent rights, which must be navigated for commercial success. A central challenge for entrepreneurs in such multi-invention contexts is to determine how the production of end products from large numbers of potential inventions can be most effectively organized, and what role the entrepreneurial firm will play in this organizational structure.

Broadly, one can think of two types of organizational arrangements or modes (or business "models") by which inventions may be combined— integrated modes and nonintegrated modes. Integrated modes arise when firms innovate by using their own internal technologies and resources, without relying on external access. Nonintegrated modes can broadly be separated into licensing and component modes, where access to external technologies is obtained in abstract and product-embodied forms, respectively. Of course, these distinctions are somewhat stylized. In any given multi-invention context, entrepreneurs may choose to develop some technologies internally in an integrated fashion, and use market (nonintegrated) arrangements to access others. Furthermore, actual organizational arrangements (or business model choices) may exhibit hybrid integrated and nonintegrated characteristics—for example, interfirm alliances—or hybrid licensing and component characteristics—for example, transfer of highly flexible components (like a programmable chip) or highly codified product designs (which would enable component manufacture, but not transfer any know-how).

Which organizational mode should be chosen by the (entrepreneurial) firm for effectuating innovation depends on the associated organizational costs and benefits in each mode. Generally, integrated modes are considered to be advantageous for overcoming transaction costs of various kinds, whereas nonintegrated modes are considered advantageous in terms of incentives and access to best-of-class inventions or components.

When transaction costs in know-how, licensing, or component markets are low, it makes sense for entrepreneurs to innovate by transacting for complementary assets and inventions through these markets. Otherwise, the costs of developing the required technologies and capabilities in-house and the added cost of internal bureaucracy produce a significant drag on commercialization. However, when these transaction costs are high, it makes sense to seek more integrated solutions, either through internal development or through the market for corporate control (mergers and acquisitions).

The study of transaction costs has become a significant research enterprise (Williamson 1985, 1996; Shelanski and Klein 1995), to which we surely cannot do justice in the limited space available. However, we draw attention to some types of transaction costs that are particularly relevant in technology-related transactions. First, there are barriers that arise due to the *technological interconnectedness* (Linden and Somaya 2003) or *the systemic nature* (Teece 1996) of innovation in some multiproduct contexts. In essence, the difficulty of partitioning the problem domain in these contexts makes it very costly to transact because of the various technologies that must work together as a whole. Another source of transaction costs is the potential *leakage of know-how* through transactions in technology markets (Arrow 1971; Teece 1982). When (entrepreneurial) firms either buy or sell technologies and components, they may end up disclosing elements of inventions to their partners, which (despite the existence of nondisclosure agreements) subsequently undermines their own ability to appropriate returns. In addition, there are often disagreements between firms over the contribution to value that is created by each of their technologies when used together in a particular product. These *value allocation* problems can lead to significant delays in negotiating contractual arrangements, and are particularly exacerbated by the idiosyncratic nature of each invention (Merges and Nelson 1994; Somaya 2005), and by the fact that there may be uncertainty over patent validity and infringement.

The transaction cost issues surrounding valuation and know-how leakage tend to be somewhat greater with "know-how" and intellectual property markets compared to "product" or "component" markets. Components are tangible products with measurable performance characteristics. Components are often easier to value against competing alternatives; also, it is likely to be more difficult for the technologies embedded in a component to inadvertently leak out. In addition, component markets also have lower *monitoring and metering* costs than licensing markets because each use of the technology is limited to a single well-defined physical artifact. With know-how and intellectual property, it is often difficult to ascertain how, where, and how often a technology is being used by the licensee and whether patents are valid. Both questions can lead to uncertainties and disputes about value and royalty payments.

Ultimately, entrepreneurs must evaluate the potential costs and benefits arising from each organizational mode, and choose that which has the best performance characteristics. In other words, careful attention must be paid to the business model and the organizational challenges of innovation if entrepreneurship is to succeed in multi-invention contexts. In the case of Kentron, discussed below, the firm encountered high transaction costs in licensing and had to quickly modify its strategy to a component-focused one. Each organizational strategy in turn must be complemented by a suitable patent strategy so as to ensure that the firm is also able to appropriate returns from its innovation.

4. Understanding Patent Strategy

One can think of patent strategy as occurring in three related domains of activity—patenting, licensing, and enforcement. "Patenting" refers to the gamut of actions whereby patent rights are obtained, renewed, maintained, and protected, including through the purchase of others' patents in the secondary market. "Licensing" involves the provision of exclusive and nonexclusive rights to use the patent. Distinctions can be made between the instances in which patent rights are licensed along with know-how transfer, and those in which only patent rights are licensed. "Enforcement" entails the use or threatened use of litigation to persuade infringers to desist or pay royalties. Since no one would take a naked patent license absent fear of a court sanctions at some level, patent licensing (as distinct from pure know-how licensing) always takes place in the shadow of court-enforced sanctions against infringement.

Patent strategy ought to be formulated in the broader context of the business strategies required for establishing and maintaining competitive advantage at the enterprise level. While there are no doubt specific issues that arise in each domain of patent strategy—patenting, licensing, or enforcement—some important commonalities cut across all of them. Three generic patent strategies are presented below—namely, proprietary use, defensive use, and royalty generation.

4.1. Proprietary Use (No Licensing)

Patents and other forms of intellectual property have long been recognized as tools that can in some cases protect technologies from imitation by rivals. Put differently, patents are "isolating mechanisms" (Rumelt 1984) that can help protect "rent" streams. Indeed, in the popular literature, the role of patents in enabling firms to "stake out and defend a proprietary market advantage" has been characterized as "their most powerful benefit" (Rivette and Kline 2000, 4). The central insight here is that the ownership of IP conveys the right to *exclude* others from the use of patented invention. In most circumstances, of course, this does not convey the ability to exclude competitors from a market. Such power is only conveyed with very fundamental patents, which cannot be worked around for one reason or another. Even then, the period of exclusion is of course limited by the length of time the patent has to run. In the real world, situations where patents confer market power are quite rare. Furthermore, the use of patents to protect fundamental new areas of technology has been acknowledged as one of the critical functions of the patent system, without which firms might be reluctant to make additional investments to commercialize their inventions (Kitch 1977; Mazzoleni and Nelson 1998).

If a business enterprise has a fundamental interest in a particular opportunity, and seeks to control the technology, there are implications for how the enterprise will need to conduct its patent-related activities (Somaya 2003). One implication is that the firm would most likely need to invent follow on technologies and also patent these. Another implication, naturally, is that such patents will generally not be licensed. It is of course the patent owner's choice not to license. As discussed in Teece (1986), the strategy of eschewing licensing is likely to be preferred only if the enterprise's patent portfolio is strong, the enterprise does not need access to anyone else's patent, and the enterprise is well positioned in the complementary assets required to successfully commercialize the innovation. Furthermore, to sustain a proprietary strategy with respect to select patents, infringement of these patents by others would need to be prosecuted aggressively.

4.2. "Design Freedom" (Defensive) Patent Strategies

Defensive strategies relate to the actions of business enterprises to protect themselves against the use of patents by their rivals in the marketplace. In fast-paced high-technology industries, enterprises often desire the freedom to design, innovate, and manufacture without being too constrained by the patent rights, present and future, of other firms. In part, this desire for design and operating freedom may be motivated by irreversible investments that they have made or expect to make, including investments in highly capital intensive manufacturing facilities, as in the case of the semiconductor industry. These investments, and the firm's commercial interests in general, can potentially be put at risk by others' patents, including those that had not issued at the time investment or commercialization decisions are made. As a result, these patents pose a significant threat to the firm—entire lines of business may be put at risk and significant royalties may have to be paid to license necessary patents. These may reflect the firms' much higher ex post willingness to pay (Sherry and Teece 2003). Needless to say, these issues are more common in multi-invention contexts, where the likelihood of infringing one or more patents among hundreds or thousands is quite high.

In some cases, the enterprise's own patents can be used as bargaining chips. Attempts by rivals to assert their own patents can be countered with threats to enforce the firm's own patents against them. This situation of "mutual holdup" can facilitate the negotiation of reasonable terms between the parties, and the effective removal of patent barriers (Grindley and Teece 1997; Somaya 2003). Research in the semiconductor industry has demonstrated that firms often engage in reciprocal cross-licensing as part of their patent strategy. Such firms accumulate large portfolios of patents in part because they are desirous of achieving design and operating freedom (Hall and Ziedonis 2001). It is important to bear in mind, however, that defensive patenting may not be effective under all circumstances, especially because it assumes that the threat of reciprocal patent enforcement is effective. When this is not the case (for example, with individual inventors or universities who have few commercial interests that can be held up), this defensive strategy may not work and a license may need to be taken. This may be comparatively costly in many multi-invention contexts, particularly if the invention is important and good alternatives do not exist.

4.3. Royalty Generation Strategies

Licensing on an exclusive or nonexclusive basis is the other obvious strategy for capturing value from a patent. The licensing of technologies is a much-studied phenomenon in the management and economics literature (Teece 1986, 2000, 2003b; Arora 1995). Much of the literature has tended to assume that patents and know-how are always bundled together; however, patent-only licensing has grown considerably in recent years. Firms like IBM and Texas Instruments have earned very substantial licensing revenues from licensing patent rights (an average of $580 million a year over 1999–2001 for IBM alone).[4] While some know-how transfer may accompany patent-licensing deals, TI's and IBM's primary focus is the granting of rights to use patents to companies that are already using (i.e., infringing) the technology in question. When patents are strong and provide utility to an entire industry, they are natural candidates for licensing in this manner. If the incumbent firms are already infringing the patent(s) and have invested substantially in using patented technologies, they may have few practical alternatives to licensing the patent(s). Royalty generation in this manner is supported by the business enterprise's efforts to identify potential licensees, its negotiating and bargaining skills, and the implicit threat of sanctions obtained from a court (or the International Trade Commission if imported goods implicate the patent).

With respect to enforcement of property rights, there are significant differences between intangible and tangible goods. When the input is a tangible good, it is impossible for the manufacturer of the final product to produce it unless the physical input is delivered. Stolen goods are not acceptable. However, when the use of patented technology already known to the user is the input,[5] production can commence and sale of the final product can be completed without "delivery" of the IP rights. This is because the manufacturer can simply go ahead and infringe the patent. The only barrier is the prospect of a court-ordered injunction and the court's determination that damages should be paid. Therefore, legal enforcement of property rights (patents) plays a critical role with respect to intangible property, when compared with tangible property, for the collection of monies for the use of the input.

5. Entrepreneurship and Patent Strategy in Multi-invention Contexts

What, then, are the implications for entrepreneurship emerging from our understanding of multi-invention (or systemic) contexts and patent strategy? Interest in the role of patents in multi-invention settings goes at least as far back as Kitch (1977), who contended that patent rights should facilitate coordination between owners of related inventions. Subsequent research has focused considerable attention on a particular type of multi-invention context, namely sequential innovation (Merges and Nelson 1990, 1994; Scotchmer 1991, 1996; Chang 1995; Green and Scotchmer 1995). These studies have primarily addressed the desirable scope of patents, implicitly taking entrepreneurship as given (at what we think is a low level). More recent work has focused on the transactional challenges posed by patents in multi-invention contexts, leading—according to the authors—to the potential underutilization of innovative resources, a so-called "tragedy of the anticommons" (Heller and Eisenberg 1998). These transaction costs may arise from *diffuse ownership* and associated *royalty stacking* problems in patent licensing (Teece 2000, 208–9; Somaya 2005), or from *valuation disputes* that are due at least in part to the *fuzzy boundaries* of patents (Teece 2000, 149–50; Somaya 2005).

However, in our view, Eisenberg and Heller may have exaggerated the problems associated with the so-called "anticommons." They provide no compelling evidence of the scope of the "problem." It is well known that patents can also facilitate transactions in technology, for example by facilitating transactions in know-how without the fear of misappropriation (Teece 1982; Arora 1995; Oxley 1999). Ultimately, transaction costs, both in general and those induced (or remedied) by patent rights, speak to the need for entrepreneurship in multi-invention settings. Entrepreneurs play an important role in figuring out the right organizational arrangements (or business model) for innovation. In addition, entrepreneurs and managers must choose appropriate patent strategies to support their innovative efforts. These strategies are likely to depend in large part on the precise organizational arrangements chosen for commercialization. We assess the implications for both integrated and nonintegrated modes below, using mini case studies drawn from past multi-invention contexts.

5.1. Integrated Modes

Entrepreneurs and managers should choose an integrated mode to innovate when the transaction costs in licensing and component markets for complementary technologies are relatively high. Given this choice, the main challenge for the entrepreneur becomes how to assemble all the required assets and technologies within a single firm. Given the nature of innovation in multi-invention contexts, it would be highly unlikely that a single firm has invented and patented all the technologies necessary to commercialize the end product, and will continue to do so in the future. Integrated approaches therefore employ different ways of obtaining both the technologies and the patents rights needed for commercialization.

One alternative is to develop all the technologies needed in-house, but rely on patent licensing to obtain access to the patent rights *owned* by other enterprises. Access to patents could be obtained in a number of ways, including patent pools, cross-licenses, and other patent-sharing arrangements. Since this form of integrated innovation implicitly acknowledges the existence of patents that may be infringed by the enterprise, defensive patent strategies are especially important for ensuring freedom to design and innovate. In industries like semiconductors, electronics, and computers, these defensive strategies are often pursued through the building up of large patent portfolios, and the proactive development of cross-licensing relationships.

Beyond the firm's defensive needs, however, patents may also be used in this context to generate licensing revenues. Later entrants and noninnovators in such a market may have weaker patent portfolios, reflecting their limited contribution to technological advances in the industry. Firms with a more robust history of innovation and patenting need not license their own patents to these firms on a purely reciprocal basis. In other words, offsetting royalty payments can be negotiated to reflect the asymmetry among the patent portfolios. The case of AT&T, IBM, and Texas Instruments in electronics and semiconductors provides a graphic illustration of the entrepreneurial creation of patent exchange mechanisms to deal with defensive concerns, and the use of strong patent portfolios to generate royalty income.

CROSS-LICENSING IN ELECTRONICS AND SEMICONDUCTORS

In the electronics and semiconductor industries, the multi-invention context is frequently the norm. In many advanced products, the range of technology is simply too great for a single firm to develop its entire needs internally. The "state of the art" of the technology tends to be covered by a large number of different patents held by different firms. Companies may produce hundreds of products, which use literally thousands of patents, and many hundreds more may be added each year. One innovation builds on another. Overlapping developments and mutually blocking patents are inevitable. To solve these problems, the business practice of cross-licensing has emerged. Enterprises cross-license patents from others to ensure that they themselves have the freedom to innovate and manufacture without inadvertent infringement. Cross-licenses typically cover portfolios of all current and future patents in a field of use, without making specific reference to individual patents. It is simply too cumbersome and costly to license only specific patents needed for specific products. The portfolio approach reduces transactions costs and allows licensees freedom to design and manufacture without triggering infringement, inadvertent or otherwise.

Cross-licensing has developed in a quite sophisticated fashion (Grindley and Teece 1997).[6] An important feature is the calculation of balancing royalty payments, according to the relative value of the patent portfolios of each party. This calculation is made prospectively, based on a sample of each firm's leading patents. Weight is given to the quality and market coverage of the patents. The key to successful cross-licensing is a portfolio of quality patents that covers large portions of the licensing partner's product markets. A quality portfolio is a powerful lever in negotiating access to required technology and may lead to significant royalty generation or, at a minimum, to reduced payments to others. Obviously, a firm that is a large net user of other firms' patents, without contributing comparable IP in exchange, is likely to have to pay significant royalties. Significantly, for the balancing process, the firm should concentrate its patenting in those areas where it does best and has a comparative advantage to develop patents that its cross-licensing partners need. In this way, firms can develop complementary rather than duplicative technology, thereby also benefiting the public interest.

In patent cross-licenses, technology is not usually transferred, as the parties are often capable of using the technology in question without assistance. Rather, these licenses confer the right to use the intellectual property without being sued for infringement. The licensing agreements sometimes include transfer of trade secrets and know-how. However, these licenses are quite different, as they involve technology transfer, and may accompany a joint venture or strategic alliance.

AT&T'S CROSS-LICENSING PRACTICES

Cross-licensing is not a new phenomenon in electronics; it goes back almost to the beginning of the industry.[7] One of the most influential firms was AT&T, whose licensing and cross-licensing practices, especially from the 1940s until its breakup in 1984, were the initial templates for the development of similar programs by other firms. Over its long history, AT&T's licensing policy has had three phases, reflecting changes in its overall business strategy. First, from AT&T's establishment in 1885 until its first antitrust-related commitment in 1913, it used IP rights in a forthright exclusive fashion to establish itself in the service market.[8] In the second phase, from 1914 until 1984, AT&T was a regulated monopoly. The need for access to patents led to cross-license agreements between the major producers of telephone equipment, starting in the 1920s, which soon developed into a more widespread policy. In the last phase, dating from divestitures in 1984, AT&T was no longer bound by the consent decree, and its IP licensing has been increasingly aligned with its commercial needs (OTA 1985; Noll 1987, 161–78; Harris 1990, 105–24).

AT&T's policy was to openly license its IP to everyone for minimal fees. The 1956 consent decree required AT&T to license all patents at "reasonable royalties," provided that the licensee also grants licenses at reasonable royalties in return. AT&T was also required to provide technical information in exchange for the payment of reasonable fees, and licensees had the right to sublicense the technology to their associates.[9] The impact of AT&T's liberal licensing on the industry was considerable, especially when considered in parallel with that at IBM.

To a large extent, the licensing terms in AT&T's 1956 decree simply codified what was already AT&T policy. As an enterprise under rate-of-return regulation, it had little reason to maximize royalty income from its IP. It perhaps figured that its service customers would be better off if its technologies were widely diffused among suppliers, as this would lower the prices and increase the performance of procured components

(Levin 1982, 77). It appears to be the first company to have had "design freedom" as a core component of its patent strategy. However, it did not see licensing income as a source of funds for R&D, as Bell Laboratories' research was largely funded by the "license contract fee," assessed on the annual revenues of the Bell operating companies. By 1983, Bell Laboratories had received 20,000 patents, as compared to about 10,000 held by IBM in 1995 and 6,000 by Texas Instruments. AT&T's portfolio was fundamental, and included patents such as the transistor, basic semiconductor technology, and the laser, and indeed many other basic patents in telecommunications, computing, optoelectronics, and superconductivity.

Using its own portfolio as leverage, AT&T was able to obtain the (reciprocal) rights it needed to continue to innovate, unimpeded by the IP of others. An interesting aspect of AT&T's IP strategy was that technologies (though not R&D programs) were often selected for patent protection based on their potential value to other firms generating technology of interest to AT&T. Since the legal pressures by the regulators for open licensing did not extinguish all of AT&T's intellectual property rights, the company was able to gain access to the external technology that it needed (Kefauver 1993).

The terms of AT&T's licenses set a pattern that is still commonplace in the electronics industry through the "capture model," which was defined in the 1956 consent decree. Under this arrangement, the licensee is granted the right to use existing patents plus any obtained for inventions made during a fixed future capture period of no more than five years, followed by a survivorship period until the expiration of the patents. The licensing regimes this led to were persistent, since the long survivorship period on many of the basic patents provided only limited scope to introduce more stringent conditions for new patents.

The traditional cross-licensing policy of AT&T was greatly extended following the invention of the transistor in 1947. Widespread "field-of-use" licensing in the semiconductor industry is one of AT&T's legacies, as the industry was founded on the basic semiconductor technologies developed by the company. AT&T soon realized that other electronics companies were developing their own semiconductor technologies and obtaining patents, which led to its policy of cross-licensing by field of use.[10] These cross-licenses ensured that the company had reciprocal access to patents and was able to develop its own technology without risking patent infringement.

Not surprisingly, AT&T/Lucent Technologies has subsequently used its IP more strategically. No longer bound by the consent decree, with R&D facilities mainly in Lucent Technologies (which has legacy connections back to AT&T's manufacturing arm known as Western Electric), its IP policy has necessarily been linked more closely to particular business opportunities.

IBM'S CROSS-LICENSING PRACTICES

A second major influence on licensing practice across the electronics industry has been IBM. The company has long been involved in licensing and cross-licensing its technology, both as a means of accessing external technology and to gain profit (generate royalties). In many ways, it has been in a similar position to AT&T in that it has been a wellspring of new technology, and was subject to a 1956 consent decree that contained certain compulsory licensing terms. Under the consent decree, IBM was required to grant nonexclusive, nontransferable, worldwide licenses for all of its patents at reasonable royalties (royalty free for existing tabulating card/machinery patents)—provided the applicant also offered to cross-license its patents to IBM on similar terms.[11]

The importance IBM attaches to its patents for use in cross-licensing and negotiating access to outside technology is reflected in its public statements (Smith 1989, 817–23; Boyer 1990). The main object of its licensing policy has been "design freedom," and to ensure "the right to manufacture and market products" by obtaining rights to use technologies and patents owned by others. IBM acquires these rights primarily by trading access to its own patents, that is, through cross-licensing.[12] IBM has often had the reputation of being a "fast follower" in some areas of technology, and it has used the power of its patent portfolio to negotiate access. The company has noted that "You get value from patents in two ways; through fees, and through licensing negotiations that give IBM access to other patents. Access is far more valuable to IBM than the fees it receives from its 9,000 active (U.S.) patents. There is no direct calculation of this value, but it is many times larger than the fee income, perhaps an order of magnitude larger."[13]

IBM's cross-licensing activity continues today. But, the company has complemented this essentially defensive policy with a strategy to generate royalty income from its licenses. IBM initiated this more active approach to licensing in 1988, when it increased the royalty rates sought on its patents from 1 percent of sales revenue (on products using IBM patents) to a range of 1–5 percent.[14] The company has also adopted a proactive strategy for identifying potential patent infringement and negotiating royalty-yielding licenses with them. Cash revenues earned from IBM's patent and technology licensing agreements increased from $345 million in 1993 to $640 million in 1994, and were well over $1 billion per year by the end of the decade.[15] It is important to bear in mind that these revenues carry low incremental costs, and accrue in large measure to the company's bottom line. In terms of their profit impact, these licensing operations are equivalent to a multi-billion-dollar business for IBM. IBM is one of the world's leading innovators, with more U.S. patents granted to it than any other company in every year since 1993. The company's licensing strategy has enabled IBM to appropriate some of the returns to its inventions by essentially charging users for access to these technologies.

LICENSING PRACTICES AT TEXAS INSTRUMENTS

Like other parts of the electronics industry, the semiconductor industry is characterized by widespread use of cross-licensing.[16] The licensing procedures at Texas Instruments (TI) illustrate the ways in which cross-licensing is used in the modern electronics industry. TI has two main licensing objectives. The first and primary objective is to ensure freedom to operate in broad areas of technology, without running the risk of patent infringement litigation by other firms in given product markets. Thus the first strategic goal is fundamentally a defensive one. The second objective is to obtain value from the firm's IP, in the form of its patent portfolio, by generating royalty income. The purpose and result of royalty generation through cross-licensing agreements is "competitive re-balancing," which offsets the advantage for imitators who might otherwise free-ride on technology TI developed.

Establishing "freedom to operate" is vital in the semiconductor industry, with its rapid innovation, short product life cycles, and ubiquity of patents. At the start of an R&D program, possible patent infringements cannot be easily predicted, as firms are quite ignorant of the R&D and patenting plans of competitors. Yet when it invests in R&D and product development, TI needs to be confident that patents developed by others through independent R&D efforts will not hinder commercialization of its technology. This need is heightened by the significant investments TI makes in capital-intensive semiconductor manufacturing facilities. TI has responded to this challenge by building a robust portfolio of semiconductor patents, which it essentially uses to defend against other's patents and to negotiate preemptive cross-licenses. It has also divested from DRAM (**dynamic random access memory**) fabrication in part to minimize its potential infringement of others' patents, and to enhance the royalty generation capacities of its IP strategy.

There are two main models for cross-licensing agreements in the semiconductor industry: "capture" and "fixed period." In the "capture" model discussed earlier, the licensee retains "survivorship" rights to use the patents until they expire, sometimes up to 20 years later. In the "fixed period" model the licensee has similar rights to use patents existing or applied for during the license period, but with no survivorship rights once the license period has expired. Full renegotiation of the cross-license is required for succeeding periods. Texas Instruments (TI) has been a leader in the use of fixed period licensing, which has gained in popularity in the industry. The fixed period model allows more flexible commercialization of patent portfolios, since licensing terms can be periodically adjusted to account for changes over time. For example, it mitigates the possibility of being locked into a cross-license even though the licensing partner has stopped contributing new inventions to the focal field of use. Thus, fixed period licensing allows TI to carefully calibrate the "openness" of its cross-licensing policy to avoid potential abuse by noninventors. Like IBM, TI has also been successful in generating royalties for access to its pioneering patents through its licensing efforts and enforcement actions. In the latter half of the 1980s, when the company was facing stiff competition in the DRAM market, licensing royalties sometimes exceeded the net profits of the company. Absent these revenues, TI would not have been profitable.

Licensing arrangements, including the cross-licensing of patents, may not always be easy to achieve in multi-invention contexts. Reliance on such licensing assumes a willingness to license on the part of others, an assumption that will be strongly challenged if some patent owners have somewhat different strategic goals or a different appreciation of the value of their own technology. In these cases, entrepreneurs can sometimes overcome the barriers in the licensing market by using the markets for corporate control to acquire technologies and patents. Firms like Cisco Systems have championed this approach, typically acquiring smaller innovative firms with technologies (and patents) that the company needs. Similarly, in the agricultural biotechnology industry, a number of firms have consolidated to bring together germplasm, genomic, and plant variety patents relating to specific crops.

From the perspective of a small entrepreneurial firm, setting oneself up as an acquisition target would be an appropriate strategy when organizational costs dictate an integrated mode, but there are also significant barriers to developing complementary technologies in-house and to obtaining access to the necessary patents. A strong set of blocking patents, which has the potential for generating patent exclusivity for the merged firm, while simultaneously dissuading potential merger partners from a go-it-alone strategy, would increase the attractiveness of the entrepreneurial firm in the market for corporate control. Even among larger firms, entrepreneurial opportunities exist to agglomerate businesses across firms so as to pool technologies and patents, and overcome transaction costs in patent licensing. For example, in 1998, when a long-running patent dispute between Digital and Intel (relating to Digital's Alpha processor patents) had reached a stalemate, Intel was able to break the impasse by simply buying out Digital's semiconductor business. Perhaps one of the earliest examples of entrepreneurship to consolidate inventions into a single firm, in this case spurred by a major customer (the U.S. Navy), was the creation of RCA for the development of radio in the first quarter of the twentieth century.[17]

THE FORMATION OF RCA

Early developments in wireless radio epitomize the complexities surrounding intellectual property arrangements that may be encountered with systems innovation (or multi-invention) technologies. The commercialization of radio required a number of basic inventions. The scientific basis for wireless was developed by university scientists such as Maxwell, Hertz, and Lodge in the nineteenth century. Their discoveries were first applied to practical communication with the development of wireless telegraphy by Marconi in Britain in 1896. The first speech transmissions were made in the United States by Fessenden in 1900, using a high-frequency alternator. Further basic innovations were made over the next two decades.[18]

Many of these inventions were initially developed by individuals working independently of each other. Indeed, many carry the name of the inventor, such as Poulsen arc, the Fleming valve, and the de Forest triode.[19] As the potential for radio became apparent, and the need for large-scale R&D and investment grew, large corporations entered the field. The pace of development accelerated, and the number of patents multiplied. The companies involved included Marconi, General Electric (GE), Westinghouse, AT&T, Telefunken, and others. In addition to their considerable R&D effort, these corporations also acquired key patents (Archer 1938, 135; Maclaurin 1949, 106).[20] There was considerable competition, and with research teams in different companies working in parallel, patent interferences were common (Maclaurin 1949, 97).[21] By 1918, it was apparent that several technologies were needed to manufacture radio systems, and each of these technologies itself involved multiple patents from different firms. In the words of Armstrong, one of the pioneers of radio, "It was absolutely impossible to manufacture any kind of workable apparatus without using practically all of the inventions that were then known" (Federal Trade Commission 1923; Maclaurin 1949, 99).

The result was deadlock. A number of firms had important patent positions and could block each other's access to key components. They refused to cross-license. This held up the development of the industry (Archer 1938, 113–14; Douglas 1987, 8, 12; Maclaurin 1949, 77).[22] The situation arose in large part as a result of the way radio had developed.

Key patent portfolios had been developed by different individuals and corporations, who were often adamant about refusing to cross-license competitors. In addition, in a new industry in which large-scale patent overlaps were a novel problem, there was no well-developed means of coordinating licensing agreements between these groups.

The situation was resolved in the United States only when, under prompting by the U.S. Navy, the various pioneers formed the Radio Corporation of America (RCA) in 1919 (Archer 1938, 176–89; Maclaurin 1949, 105).[23] This broke a key source of the deadlock. RCA acquired the U.S. rights to the Marconi patents, and the other major U.S. patent holders became shareholders in RCA.[24] In this way, RCA acquired the U.S. rights to all the constituent radio patents under one roof—amounting to over 2,000 patents (Archer 1938, 195; Maclaurin 1949, 107).[25] It established RCA as the technical leader in radio, but also granted cross-licenses to the other firms to continue their own development of the technology for use in other fields or as suppliers to RCA.[26]

The RCA example highlights the perils to the economy when patent owners pursue exclusivity too vigorously in multi-invention contexts. Without the willingness to allow others access to one's own patents, there is virtually no prospect for reciprocal access. Because of the high transactions costs reflected in this reluctance to cross-license, technological progress and the further commercialization of radio was halted. In this case, the debacle was resolved only by the formation of RCA. However, it is now clear that the same ends—namely design freedom—may often be achieved more simply, without such fundamental reorganization, by cross-licensing alone. The wireless patent-licensing deadlock and the formation of RCA helped set the stage for further development of cross-licensing in electronics.

5.2. Nonintegrated Modes

Nonintegrated modes use licensing and component markets to supply intellectual property bundled-in with their technologies or component products. In this way, specialized firms can avoid the need to develop all the complementary technologies in-house. The use of such nonintegrated modes or "business models" usually occurs when the transaction costs in the associated (licensing or component) market are not especially high. One fundamental challenge for entrepreneurs is to recognize opportunities for commercializing inventions in this fashion, instead of resorting to integrated commercialization by default.

It is important to understand that when technologies are licensed or components are sold, there is definite risk that knowledge may leak out and the transaction partner may learn too much about the firm's technology. Attempts to barricade the company's know-how may fail because successful commercialization may require joint problem solving and the exchange of technical information. This is a very serious problem because uniqueness of the company's technology is often the primary business proposition of enterprises employing nonintegrated modes of innovation. Patents can play a vital role by limiting misappropriation of the firm's technology, and facilitating transactions between the entrepreneurial firm and its business partners. Naturally, enterprises relying on patent protection to sustain a licensing or component-product business model would take a more proprietary view in their IP strategy. We illustrate the type of entrepreneurship entailed in nonintegrated modes by reviewing two case studies, which highlight the differences in strategy not only between integrated and nonintegrated modes, but also among nonintegrated modes.

SYSTEM ON A CHIP (SOC) AND ARM, LTD.

In semiconductors, relentless miniaturization has made it possible to put entire electronic systems on a single semiconductor chip (Teece 1998; Linden and Somaya 2003). Market demand for the advantages in size, power consumption, and production cost that such systems-on-a-chip (SOCs) promise has also been growing rapidly. Previously, it was common for semiconductor technologies to be transferred between firms through the sale of various component integrated circuits (ICs), where the technology itself was transferred in "embodied" form. However, when entire electronic systems needed to be put on a single chip or IC, it became practically impossible to conduct transactions in technology by conducting transactions in components.

One solution to this problem in the component market was pioneered by new "chip-less" firms, who went about creating a licensing market for design modules that other firms can license and integrate into their own system-on-a-chip designs. ARM, Ltd., based in Cambridge in the United Kingdom, is one of the leading firms that adopted this approach. ARM's RISC (reduced instruction set computer) processor designs are used in literally tens of millions of cell phones and handheld devices sold around the world. ARM is a **spin-off** from the Power-PC consortium assembled by Apple Computer, IBM, and Motorola to design and manufacture microprocessors. The company resisted the temptation to be acquired by a large semiconductor firm, or to expand the scope of its own technological domain. Instead, it specialized in developing processor designs, which it then sought to license to other firms. As the SOC revolution took root, ARM's licensing-based strategy turned out be extremely successful.

ARM appears to have taken patent protection of its technologies very seriously and accumulated a portfolio of over 80 patents by 2000. When picoTurbo, a rival firm based in Milpitas, California, came up with a product that could essentially run any software written for ARM's processor, the company immediately filed suit.[27] PicoTurbo's technology threatened the exclusive position that ARM had built up in many ways. First and foremost, it threatened to invade the installed base of complementary ARM-related software and software programmers, and thus in effect invent around ARM's technology. Given the importance of an exclusive position for ARM's commercial success, it is no surprise that the company enforced its patents so aggressively. Eventually, the suit was settled with ARM simply acquiring picoTurbo with all its product designs and IP assets.

Dolby, which licenses its noise reduction designs for high-fidelity sound systems, and Rambus from the semiconductor industry are other prominent examples of firms that have pursued a licensing mode to commercialize their inventions. In both these cases, well-developed patent strategies are important to the viability of the licensing option, and indeed their business model more generally.

COMPONENTIZATION AT KENTRON TECHNOLOGIES

Sometimes licensing and component sales are transparent alternatives, in the sense that after pursing one strategy, the entrepreneur changes gears and adopts another. Kentron Technologies, a semiconductor firm, developed a technology to (effectively) double the bandwidth of DRAM modules by interleaving signals from two slower "single data rate" DRAMs, rather than using the patented "double data rate" technology developed by Rambus.[28] Kentron originally offered to license its technology for a 5 percent royalty, but did not get any takers. Kentron subsequently changed its patent strategy to offer "royalty free" licenses if DRAM users would buy special switches from Kentron that enable the interleaving to occur.[29]

Put differently, Kentron took the payment for the use of its technology and patents in the form of a premium price for the switches. Robert Goodman, Kentron's CEO, indicated that (1) the price of the special switch was set at a level that yielded Kentron the same revenue as a 5 percent royalty would have yielded, (2) users resisted taking a license from Kentron.[30] However, they were willing to pay Kentron for the use of its technology. Quite simply, the users may have perceived the transaction costs in the licensing market to be too high for Kentron's technology. The value of the technology may have seemed uncertain absent a physical component that could be evaluated, and potential licensees may have discounted its importance. There may have also been concerns about how well this technology would work with their own DRAM designs, in other words, about *technological interconnectedness*. Firms may also have wanted to avoid the monitoring and compliance costs associated with a license (tracking infringing sales, and calculating and paying royalties), and preferred to have the price of Kentron's technology built into the price of the physical switches instead. Because Kentron had a strong patent position built up around its pioneering technology, DRAM manufacturers could not simply appropriate its technology for internal use, nor could they effectively invent around Kentron's patent position.

The ARM and Kentron examples show how licensing a technology or selling components in which the technology is embedded are alternative strategies for commercialization. One of the functions of the entrepreneur is to recognize which organizational approach is most appropriate for generating value from an innovative idea, and to implement this organizational strategy. A second important function of the entrepreneur is to ensure that the firm captures value from its innovation, and does not simply dissipate it to other firms. In part, this implies designing the appropriate patent strategies for a given organizational mode.

6. Conclusion

In this chapter, we have described some of the challenges presented to entrepreneurs by multi-invention contexts, and analyzed implications for entrepreneurship and patent strategy in these contexts. Our analysis provides two main insights. First, to maximize chances of success, entrepreneurs must assess the relative organizational costs and benefits of different organizational modes or business "models," and commercialize inventions by using the most effective mode in a given multi-invention context. Second, patent strategies must be chosen to complement the choice of business model.

Entrepreneurship is critical for effectuating new combinations of assets, resources, and technologies in multi-invention contexts. Often incumbent firms face significant inertia to change their existing modes of behavior and organization. In many cases, they are unable to perceive the potential value that can be generated by developing a new invention or combining existing inventions in a new way. However, entrepreneurship is also likely to fail if the business models adopted are too cumbersome or flawed. In addition, it is not enough to unlock the potential value hidden in multi-invention or systemic contexts. It is equally important to devise strategies that appropriate some of this value to compensate for the entrepreneur's efforts. Appropriate patent strategy can play a useful role in capturing this value.

In response to transactional problems in multi-invention contexts, the instinctive public policy remedy sought by some is often a weakening of patent rights. While this solution may address certain transaction cost problems, it also means a weakening of incentives for innovation and the reinforcement of integrated modes of innovation and production. Licensing and component modes, on the other hand, benefit from patents because of stronger incentives, and in some cases, because of lower transaction costs. Evaluation of these alternative organizational forms and business models is essential in any attempt to address concerns about patents in multi-invention contexts. Often, astute management and entrepreneurial efforts are sufficient to allow technology and component markets to work effectively. Thus entrepreneurship and patent rights may have a symbiotic relationship that can be undermined by policy responses that do not account for all possible organizational arrangements through which innovation can take place.

Notes

1. For a discussion of systemic innovation, see Teece 2000.

2. By untested, we mean that the validity of the patent has not yet been tested in court.

3. The treatment of entrepreneurship here is sympathetic to the work of Hayek (1945), Casson (1982), Kirzner (1973), as well as Schumpeter himself.

4. IBM 2001 annual report.

5. This could be due to the user reading the patent, or it could be due to the user's independent invention of the patent, or hearing about it from some source.

6. Cross-licensing is not the same as "patent pooling," in which member firms contribute patents to a common pool and each member accesses them on the same terms and conditions. In cross-licensing, firms agree one-on-one to license their IP to each other and retain control over their proprietary technology, which is used for competitive advantage via product manufacturing and further licensing.

7. Note that the situation is different in other industries not characterized by cumulative systems technologies, such as chemicals and pharmaceuticals, where cross-licensing or, rather, reciprocal licensing, is typically aimed at exchanging technology rather than avoiding patent conflicts. In chemicals and pharmaceuticals, although patenting is extensive, individual technology development paths are less likely to overlap, and cross-licensing may be used to ensure broad product lines. For licensing strategy in the chemicals industry, see Grindley and Nickerson 1996, 97–120.

8. Historical perspective on competition in the telecommunications industry is given in Irwin 1977, 312–33; Brock 1981; OTA 1985; Noll and Owen 1989; and Rosston and Teece 1997.

9. The two substantive provisions of the 1956 consent decree were that (*a*) it confined AT&T to providing regulated telecommunications services, and its manufacturing subsidiary Western Electric to making equipment for those services (effectively prohibiting it from selling semiconductors in the commercial market), and (*b*) all patents controlled by the Bell System should be licensed to others on request. Licenses for the 8,600 patents included in existing cross-licensing agreements were royalty-free to new applicants, and licenses to all other existing or future patents were to be issued at a nondiscriminatory "reasonable royalty" (determined by the court if necessary). AT&T was also to provide technical information along with the patent licenses for reasonable fees. Licenses were unrestricted, other than being nontransferable (*USA v. Western Electric Co. Inc., and AT&T*, Civil Action, 17–49, Final Judgment, January 24, 1956; Brock 1981, 166, 191–94; Levin 1982, 9–101).

10. "We realized that if [the transistor] was as big as we thought, we couldn't keep it to ourselves and we couldn't make all the technical contributions. It was to our interest to spread it around" (AT&T executive, quoted in Levin 1982, 77, after Tilton 1971). The strategy appears to have been prescient. In the United States, during 1953–68, 5,128 semiconductor patents were awarded. Bell Laboratories was granted only 16 percent of these; the next five firms were RCA, General Electric, Westinghouse, IBM, and Texas Instruments, all AT&T cross-licensees (Tilton 1971).

11. The provision covered all existing patents at the time of the decree (i.e., as of 1956) plus any that were filed during the next five years. The rights lasted for the full term of the patents. If the parties could not agree on a reasonable royalty rate, the court could impose one. Patent rights could be very long lived, since, at that time, patent life was 17 years from the grant date, which might be some years after the filing date. The patent-licensing provisions ended in 1961. The decree also included other provisions related to the sale of IBM products and services (*USA v. International Business Machines Corporation*, CCH 1956 Trade Cases par. 68, 245, SDNY 1956).

12. Jim McGrody, IBM VP and director of research, in Boyer 1990, 10–11.

13. Roger Smith, IBM assistant general counsel, in Boyer 1990.

14. *Computerworld*, April 11, 1988, 105.

15. IBM Annual Report, 1993, 1994, 2000, 2001.

16. This section is based in part on discussion with Texas Instruments executives. However, the views expressed here are those of the authors, and should not be seen as reflecting those of Texas Instruments.

17. The early history of radio is described in Archer 1938; Jewkes, Sawers, and Stillerman 1969; Douglas 1987; and Merges and Nelson 1990, 891–96.

18. These included the high-frequency alternator, high-frequency transmission arc, magnetic amplifier, selective tuning, crystal detector, heterodyne signal detection, diode valve, triode valve, high vacuum tube, and directional aerials.

19. Not all early inventors were independent. E.F.W. Alexanderson—who improved the Fessenden alternator, invented a magnetic amplifier, electronic amplifier, and multiple tuned antenna, and co-invented the "Alexanderson-Beverage static eliminator"—was a General Electric employee.

20. AT&T acquired the de Forest triode and feedback patents in 1913–14 for $90,000, and his remaining feedback patents in 1917 for $250,000; Westinghouse cross-licensed the Fessenden heterodyne interests in 1920, and acquired the Armstrong super heterodyne patents in 1920 for $335,000 (Archer 1938, 135; Maclaurin 1949, 106).

21. The fact that GE and AT&T alone were each devoting major research attention to the vacuum tube led to no less than 20 important patent interferences in this area (Maclaurin 1949, 97).

22. To cite one important example, Marconi and de Forest both had critical valuable patents. Marconi's diode patent was held to dominate de Forest's triode patent. Both technologies were vital to radio, yet the interests refused to cross-license (Archer 1938, 113–14; Douglas 1987, 12). The application of the triode (audion) to feedback amplification was also the subject of a long-running patent priority dispute between de Forest and Armstrong (finally resolved in de Forest's favor by the Supreme Court in 1934). Its use in transmission oscillation was the subject of four-way patent interference between Langmuir, Meissner, Armstrong, and de Forest (Maclaurin 1949, 77). These problems held up the use of the triode—a crucial component of signal transmission. Detection and amplification, which has been called "the heart and soul of radio" (Douglas 1987, 8) and "so outstanding in its consequences it almost ranks with the greatest inventions of all time" (Nobel Prize physicist Rabi, quoted in Maclaurin 1949, 70).

23. RCA was formed by GE in 1919, and simultaneously acquired the American Marconi Corporation. Major shareholders included GE, AT&T (1920), and Westinghouse (1920) (Archer 1938, 176–89; Maclaurin 1949, 105). A major concern of the U.S. Navy was that international wireless communications were dominated by the British firm Marconi, and the patent impasse helped perpetuate this. The Navy favored the establishment of an "All American" company in international communications. A similar concern on the eve of U.S. entry into World War I prompted the U.S. government (the secretaries of war and the navy) to also intervene in the case of aircraft patents, and create a patent pooling arrangement in January 1917 (Bittlingmayer 1988).

24. As part of its role in the formation of RCA, the U.S. Navy also initiated cross-licensing to resolve the patent situation in radio manufacture. It wished to have clear rights to use the radio equipment it purchased, without risking litigation due to complex patent ownership—noting in 1919 that "there was not a single company among those making radio sets for the Navy which possessed basic patents sufficient to enable them to supply, without infringement, . . . a complete transmitter or receiver." A formal letter suggesting "some agreement between the several holders of permanent patents whereby the market can be freely supplied with [vacuum] tubes," sent from the navy to GE and AT&T in January 1920, may be seen as an initiating point for cross-licensing in the industry (Archer 1938, 180–86; Maclaurin 1949, 99–110).

25. RCA concluded cross-license agreements with firms including GE, Westinghouse, AT&T, United Fruit Company, Wireless Specialty Apparatus Company, Marconi (Britain), CCTF (France), and Telefunken (Germany) (Archer 1938, 195; Maclaurin 1949, 107).

26. A distinction was that the RCA cross-licenses typically granted (reciprocal) exclusive rights to use the patents in given territories or markets; compared with the nonexclusive cross-licenses that became the norm later. The cross-license with GE (and later Westinghouse) included provisions for the supply of components to RCA. The RCA cross-licenses were for very long terms—many for 25 years, from 1919 to 1945. They covered current and future patents. Other radio manufacturers took licenses with RCA, starting in the late 1920s. Some of RCA's cross-licensing policies were later questioned on antitrust grounds, and modified following a consent decree in 1932 (Archer 1938, 381–87; and Maclaurin 1949, 107–9, 132–52).

27. See online: http://www.reed-electronics.com/electronicnews/article/ CA186719.html (accessed October 27, 2005).

28. One of the authors (Teece) is familiar with the Kentron example from his work as an expert in *In the Matter of Rambus, Inc.*, FTC Docket No. 9302. In this paper, we are relying only on the public testimony given by Mr. Robert Goodman, Kentron's CEO, and not on any information that is subject to the protective order in that case. See *In the Matter of Rambus, Inc.*, June 19, 2003, 6020–29, 6041, 6078–87.

29. As a news story indicates: "Kentron makes the special QBM module switches, which is [sic] used in its modules and those of licensees. Bob Goodman, Kentron's CEO, said the firm licenses its QBM technology on a royalty-free basis, and derives revenues from the sale of its QBM switches." See http://siliconstrategies.com/article/printableArticle.jhtmlarticle4ID=10806590 (accessed September 16, 2003).

30. At the public hearing *In the Matter of Rambus, Inc.*, FTC Docket No. 9302.

References

Archer, G. 1938. *History of Radio to 1926*. New York: American Historical Society.

Arora, A. 1995. "Licensing Tacit Knowledge: Intellectual Property Rights and the Market for Know-How." *Economics of Innovation and New Technology* 4: 41–59.

Arrow, K. J. 1971. *Essays in the Theory of Risk-Bearing*. Chicago: Markham.

Baumol, W. 1993. "Formal Entrepreneurship Theory in Economics: Existence and Bounds." *Journal of Business Venturing* 8: 197–210.

Bittlingmayer, G. 1988. "Property Rights, Progress, and the Aircraft Patent Agreement." *Journal of Law and Economics* 31 (1): 227–48.

Boyer, C. 1990. "The Power of the Patent Portfolio." *Think* 5: 10–11.

Brock, G. 1981. *The Telecommunications Industry: The Dynamics of Market Structure*. Cambridge: Harvard University Press.

Casson, M. 1982. *The Entrepreneur*. Totawa, N.J.: Barnes and Noble.

Chang, H. F. 1995. "Patent Scope, Antitrust Policy, and Cumulative Innovation." *Rand Journal of Economics* 26 (1): 34–57.

Douglas, G. 1987. *The Early Days of Radio Broadcasting*. Jefferson, N.C.: McFarland.

Federal Trade Commission. 1923. *The Radio Industry*. Washington, D.C.: Government Printing Office.

Green, J. R., and S. Scotchmer. 1995. "On the Division of Profit in Sequential Innovation." *Rand Journal of Economics* 26 (1): 20–33.

Grindley, P. C., and J. Nickerson. 1996. "Strategic Objectives Supported by Licensing." In *Technology Licensing: Corporate Strategies for Maximizing Value*, ed. R. L. Parr and P. H. Sullivan. New York: John Wiley and Sons.

Grindley, P. C., and D. J. Teece. 1997. "Managing Intellectual Capital: Licensing and Cross-Licensing in Semiconductors and Electronics." *California Management Review* 39 (2): 8–41.

Hall, B. H., and R. M. Ziedonis. 2001. "The Patent Paradox Revisited: An Empirical Study of Patenting in the Semiconductor Industry, 1979–1995." *Rand Journal of Economics* 32 (1): 101–28.

Harris, R. 1990. "Divestiture and Regulatory Policies." *Telecommunications Policy* 14: 105–24.

Hayek, F. A. 1945. "The Use of Knowledge in Society." *American Economic Review* 35 (4): 519–30.

Heller, M. A., and R. S. Eisenberg. 1998. "Can Patents Deter Innovation? The Anticommons in Biomedical Research." *Science* 280 (5364): 698–701.

Irwin, M. 1977. "The Telephone Industry." In *The Structure of American Industry*, ed. W. Adams. 5th ed. New York: Macmillan.

Jewkes, J., D. Sawers, and R. Stillerman. 1969. *The Sources of Innovation*. New York: Norton.

Kefauver, W. 1993. "Intellectual Property Rights and Competitive Strategy: An International Telecommunications Firm." In *Global Dimensions of Intellectual Property Rights in Science and Technology*, ed. M. Wallerstein, M. E. Mogee, and R. Schoen. Washington, D.C.: National Academy Press.

Kitch, E. W. 1977. "The Nature and Function of the Patent System." *Journal of Law and Economics* 20: 265–90.

Kirzner, I. 1973. *Competition and Entrepreneurship*. Chicago: University of Chicago Press.

Levin, R. 1982. "The Semiconductor Industry." In *Government and Technical Progress*, ed. R. Nelson. New York: Pergamon.

Linden, G., and D. Somaya. 2003. "System-on-a-Chip Integration in the Semiconductor Industry: Industry Structure and Firm Strategies." *Industrial and Corporate Change* 12 (3): 545–76.

Lippman, S. A., and R. P. Rumelt. 2003. "A Bargaining Perspective on Resource Advantage." *Strategic Management Journal* 24: 1069–86.

Maclaurin, W. 1949. *Invention and Innovation in the Radio Industry*. New York: Macmillan.

Mazzoleni, R., and R. R. Nelson. 1998. "The Benefits and Costs of Strong Patent Protection: A Contribution to the Current Debate." *Research Policy* 27 (3): 273–84.

Merges, R. P., and R. R. Nelson. 1990. "On the Complex Economics of Patent Scope." *Columbia Law Journal* 90 (4): 839–916.

———. 1994. "On Limiting or Encouraging Rivalry in Technical Progress: The Effect of Patent Scope Decisions." *Journal of Economic Behavior and Organization* 25 (1): 1–24.

Office of Technology Assessment (OTA). 1985. *Information Technology Research and Development: Critical Trends and Issues.* New York: Pergamon.

Oxley, J. E. 1999. "Institutional Environment and the Mechanisms of Governance: The Impact of Intellectual Property Protection on the Structure of Interfirm Alliances." *Journal of Economic Behavior and Organization* 38 (3): 283–309.

Noll, M. 1987. "Bell System R&D Activities: The Impact of Divestiture." *Telecommunications Policy* 11: 161–78.

Noll, R., and B. Owen. 1989. "The Anticompetitive Uses of Regulation: United States v. AT&T." In *The Antitrust Revolution*, ed. J. Kwoka and L. White. New York: Macmillan.

Rivette, K. G., and D. Kline. 2000. "Discovering New Value in Intellectual Property." *Harvard Business Review*, January–February, 2–12.

Rosenberg, N. 1994. *Exploring the Black Box.* Cambridge: Cambridge University Press.

Rosston, G. L., and D. J. Teece. 1997. "Competition and 'Local' Communications: Innovation, Entry, and Integration." In *Globalism and Localism in Telecommunications*, ed. E. M. Noam and A. J. Wolfson. North Holland: Elsevier.

Rumelt, R. P. 1984. "Towards a Strategic Theory of the Firm." In *Competitive Strategic Management*, ed. R. B. Lamb. Englewood Cliffs, N.J.: Prentice-Hall.

Schumpeter, J. 1934. *Capitalism, Socialism, and Democracy.* New York: Harper and Row.

Scotchmer, S. 1991. "Standing on the Shoulders of Giants: Cumulative Research and the Patent Law." *Journal of Economic Perspectives* 3: 29–41.

———. 1996. "Protecting Early Innovators: Should Second-Generation Products be Patentable?" *Rand Journal of Economics* 27 (2): 322–31.

Shelanski, H., and P. G. Klein. 1995. "Empirical Research in Transaction Cost Economics: A Review and Assessment." *Journal of Law, Economics, and Organization* 11 (2): 335–61.

Sherry, E., and D. J. Teece. 2003. "Standards Setting and Antitrust." *Minnesota Law Review* 87 (6): 1913–94.

Smith, R. 1989. "Management of a Corporate Intellectual Property Law Department." *AIPLA Bulletin*, April–June, 817–23.

Somaya, D. 2003. "Strategic Determinants of Decisions Not to Settle Patent Litigation." *Strategic Management Journal* 24: 17–38.

———. 2005. "Combining Inventions in Multi-invention Products: Patents, Organizational Alternatives, and Public Policy." Working paper, University of Maryland.

Teece, D. J. 1982. "Towards an Economic Theory of the Multiproduct Firm." *Journal of Economic Behavior and Organization* 3 (March): 39–64.

———. 1986. "Profiting from Technological Innovation: Implications for Integration, Collaboration, Licensing, and Public Policy." *Research Policy* 15 (6): 285–305.

———. 1996. "Firm Organization, Industrial Structure, and Technological Innovation." *Journal of Economic Behavior and Organization* 31 (2): 193–224.

———. 1998. "Capturing Value from Knowledge Assets: The New Economy, Markets for Know-how, and Intangible Assets." *California Management Review* 40 (3): 55–79.

————. 2000. *Managing Intellectual Capital.* New York: Oxford University Press.

————. 2003a. "Explicating Dynamic Capabilities: Asset Selection, Cospecialization, and Entrepreneurship in Strategic Management Theory." Working paper.

————. 2003b. *Essays in Technology Management and Policy.* Hackensack, N.J.: World Scientific Publishing.

Tilton, J. 1971. *International Diffusion of Technology: The Case of Semiconductors.* Washington, D.C.: Brookings Institution.

Williamson, O. E. 1985. *The Economic Institutions of Capitalism.* New York: Free Press.

————. 1996. *Mechanisms of Governance.* New York: Free Press.